Praise for *Battling Healthcare Burnout*

"'You cannot give what you do not have.' Clinicians who suffer burnout in their work cannot offer patients, families, and communities the help they need. In this book, Dr. Mayer offers powerful, evidence-based frameworks for understanding, preventing, managing, and reversing burnout. His counsel is invaluable, and the benefits to healers and patients alike can be enormous."
—**Donald M. Berwick, MD, President Emeritus and Senior Fellow, Institute for Healthcare Improvement**

"Burnout has been a major challenge in healthcare for decades, and Dr. Mayer's book provides a lot of wisdom about how that challenge can be met and managed more successfully."
—**Christina Maslach, PhD, Professor of Psychology, University of California, Berkeley**

"Essential reading for all clinicians who have been called to their work and are committed to creating a better practice environment for patients, their colleagues, and themselves."
—**Tait Shanafelt, MD, Chief Wellness Officer, Stanford Medicine**

"The emotional well-being of our physicians, nurses, other clinical caregivers, and first responders should be a top priority for our government and our society at large. Dr. Thom Mayer's excellent book is a timely and highly practical template for how to reduce the burnout burden."
—**Charles Stokes, RN, FACHE, Past Chairman, American College of Healthcare Executives, and former CEO, Memorial Hermann Health System**

"Thom Mayer's book is a timely and comprehensive overview of healthcare worker burnout. In addition to being grounded in current research, it also provides practical solutions for leaders who want to reduce burnout in their organizations. Using quotes and stories from literature and classic writers, it connects the issue of burnout and finding joy at work as part of the human condition throughout the ages. The book is inspiring as well as practical."
—**Jean Ann Larson, EdD, FACHE, Chief Leadership Development Officer, UAB Medicine, and Senior Associate Dean of Leadership Development, School of Medicine, University of Alabama at Birmingham**

"In *Battling Healthcare Burnout*, Thom Mayer turns his focus to a culture he's both role modelled and coached others to achieve through his career. Weaving together gripping firsthand stories and timeless philosophical truths with practical ideas, it's a terrific resource for all who are committed to improving the well-being of healthcare workers."
—**Craig Deao, Managing Director, Huron Consulting Group**

"Dr. Mayer provides an insightful view into the sources of burnout prolific in healthcare today, as well as a practical framework for better understanding, preventing, managing, and reversing burnout so our clinicians can get back to the love of their calling—caring for patients. This is an important read for any healthcare leader striving to create a culture where physicians, nurses, other clinical caregivers, and first responders across the board can not only do their best work but also thrive while doing so."
—**Carrie Owen Plietz, FACHE, President, Kaiser Permanente Northern California**

"We went into emergency medicine to help people and to save lives, but when burnout sets in we lose that focus and ourselves. This book helps us better understand ourselves and our teams and how to refocus on the job we love. An essential read for all frontline workers."
—**Mark Rosenberg, President, American College of Emergency Physicians**

Battling Healthcare Burnout

Battling Healthcare Burnout

LEARNING TO LOVE THE JOB YOU HAVE, WHILE CREATING THE JOB YOU LOVE

Thom Mayer, MD

Berrett–Koehler Publishers, Inc.

Berrett-Koehler Publishers, Inc.
1333 Broadway, Suite 1000
Oakland, CA 94612-1921
Tel: (510) 817-2277
Fax: (510) 817-2278
www.bkconnection.com

ORDERING INFORMATION
Quantity sales. Special discounts are available on quantity purchases by corporations, associations, and others. For details, contact the "Special Sales Department" at the Berrett-Koehler address above.

Individual sales. Berrett-Koehler publications are available through most bookstores. They can also be ordered directly from Berrett-Koehler: Tel: (800) 929-2929; Fax: (802) 864-7626; www.bkconnection.com.

Orders for college textbook / course adoption use. Please contact Berrett-Koehler: Tel: (800) 929-2929; Fax: (802) 864-7626.

Distributed to the U.S. trade and internationally by Penguin Random House Publisher Services.

Berrett-Koehler and the BK logo are registered trademarks of Berrett-Koehler Publishers, Inc.

Printed in the United States of America

Berrett-Koehler books are printed on long-lasting acid-free paper. When it is available, we choose paper that has been manufactured by environmentally responsible processes. These may include using trees grown in sustainable forests, incorporating recycled paper, minimizing chlorine in bleaching, or recycling the energy produced at the paper mill.

Library of Congress Cataloging-in-Publication Data

Names: Mayer, Thom A., author.
Title: Battling healthcare burnout : learning to love the job you have, while creating the job you love / Thom Mayer, MD, FACEP, FAAP, FACHE.
Description: First edition. | San Francisco : Berrett-Koehler Publishers, Inc., [2021] | Includes bibliographical references and index.
Identifiers: LCCN 2021005975 | ISBN 9781523089918 (paperback) | ISBN 9781523089925 (adobe pdf) | ISBN 9781523089932 (epub)
Subjects: LCSH: Medical personnel—Job stress. | Burn out (Psychology)—Prevention.
Classification: LCC R690 .M3523 2021 | DDC 610.73/7—dc23
LC record available at https://lccn.loc.gov/2021005975

First Edition

26 25 24 23 22 21   10 9 8 7 6 5 4 3 2 1

Book producer: Westchester Publishing Services
Text designer: Laurel Muller
Cover designer: Mike Nicholls

To my brilliant, beautiful, and always inspiring wife, Maureen
Our kind, thoughtful, generous, and loyal sons, Josh, Kevin, and Gregory
Josh's wife, Valerie, Kevin's fiancée, Nicola
Josh and Valerie's children, Eve, Audra, Clara, and Ryan
and
My patients, mentors, and colleagues,
Who have given me much more than I could ever give them

Contents

PART FOUR: Tools for Battling Healthcare Burnout

Battling Healthcare Burnout

Introduction
The Passion Disconnect of Burnout

In the middle of the road of my life
I awoke to find myself in a Dark Wood
Where the True Way was wholly lost.

DANTE, *THE INFERNO*[1]

How did we start on our journey in healthcare? Simple: it was passion that brought us here—a deep and abiding passion for the hard work of caring for others, whether as a physician, nurse, or healthcare leader. It is important to emphasize *hard work* because caring for ill and injured people on their journey back to health is never easy. What allows us to navigate this hard work is *passion*—without it, the work cannot be sustained, which is at the core of the burnout dilemma.

Early in my talks to healthcare leaders and teams, I use this image **(Figure Intro-1)**:

Then I ask them:

Is that you?

Going *in* to work?

Or going *home* from work?

Far too many times, it's how we feel going home. What a pity. Shouldn't we feel that way going into a calling in which people with pain and suffering invite us into their lives, share their stories, and allow us to attempt to alleviate those afflictions? Passion is essential to the work done in healthcare—only it can fuel the challenging work required of us. Burnout creates a passion disconnect, robbing us of the fuel needed to do our jobs effectively. This disconnect affects up to 50 percent of our teams. Burnout is thus a killer of joy, passion, delight, and contentment in our work lives. It creates a healthcare workforce composed of the *working wounded*, a group of people whose wounds come not from the demands of the patients but from the frustrations of the systems and cultures in which they work. An important tool in battling burnout is to "reverse the jump" so we jump for joy going in to work, not just going home.

The Supreme Allied Commander in World War I, French general Ferdinand Foch, famously noted, "The greatest force on earth is the human soul on fire."[2] Passion is the fire that brought us here, and it must burn within us at every level of healthcare, helping us through the stresses we inevitably face.

Deep Joy, Deep Needs

My brilliant wife, Maureen, and I raised three wonderful boys—now young men—and whenever I dropped them off at the school they attended, I always said precisely the same thing to them: "One more step in the journey of discovering where your deep joy intersects the world's deep needs." (As you might guess, they preferred to take the bus.) "Your deep joy" is simply the passion that fuels you. Once you know that, the rest of the "world's deep needs" are just details on the journey.

When burnout occurs, it requires a "passion reconnect,"[3] or a rediscovery of your deep joy, which is intuitive but certainly not easy, precisely because the way we're working isn't working. This simple statement—attested to by the high burnout rates just mentioned—contains multiple layers. The first layer is the obvious one: healthcare professionals need more coaching and mentoring in personal and professional resiliency to avoid burnout. But as we will see throughout the book, that is far too simplistic a view, and it is insufficient to fully address burnout. In fact, the "way we're working" is within a flawed culture and in systems and processes that are exacting a toll we can no longer afford to pay, personally, professionally, and institutionally. Yes, we need to work on ourselves first, but we must also work on changing the culture and the system. The results we're getting—including burnout in nearly 50 percent of our teams—are precisely what our current systems are designed to produce.[4]

Unfortunately, those systems are often changing for the worse. For example, the near-universal adoption of electronic health records (EHRs) has put increased stress on clinicians, robbing them of their passion. As one physician told me, "I used to love being a doctor. Now I'm just a 'data monkey' sitting in front of a computer." She understood that *anything that puts you closer to a patient is a good thing, and anything that takes you away from patients is a bad thing*—even if it is a necessary one. Solving the problems created by EHRs requires increasing personal resiliency and adaptive capacity. But it also requires courage from healthcare leaders to *adapt the system to the people, not just the people to the system.*[5] Even the most noble and well-intentioned efforts to improve healthcare will increase burnout if this is not kept in mind.

It has been my privilege to have spoken with tens of thousands of healthcare leaders from over 40 percent of hospitals and healthcare systems across the country. When I ask the audience, "How many of you *know* someone who is burned out?" every hand goes up. But when I then ask, "How many of *you* are burned out?" most of the hands fall, except for the courageous few who are willing to admit the burnout epidemic has infected them. Many feel a sense of failure and shame when they admit they are burned out, born from a sense of guilt that, "I'm not as good as I thought—this is starting to get to me." The goal of this book is to break that cycle so we can find our way out of the "Dark Wood" that Dante allegorically describes. Because, as I noted earlier, the fundamental truth of burnout is this:

The way we're working isn't working.

Burnout versus Burn-In

As the medical director for one of the largest fire department and emergency medical services agencies in the nation for over 15 years, I learned a great deal about fires, wildfires, and how things burn. The largest fires with the highest heat and intensity expand from the core, not the periphery. The term *burnout* implies that the "flames" are coming from the inside and consuming us as they burn outward. But what if we used our passion to "burn in" instead of burning out? What if we used the heat from the friction of job stressors to fuel the flames of passion to drive and sustain performance? Why not use both organizational and personal resiliency to redirect the heat to burn inside us, reigniting our passion? The heat from stressors is still there but is transposed from a negative to a positive. What gives light must endure burning, in this case burning with the intensity of passion.

The strategies in this book are designed to allow you and your team to "burn in" instead of burning out, redirecting whatever job stressors cannot be eliminated or ameliorated so that they protect your passion.

Protect Your Passion

Your passion cannot protect itself—you must do your part. Our passion, as strong as it is, must be nurtured and rekindled to sustain itself throughout the travails of our ever-changing, increasingly demanding work environment. Protecting your passion requires the application of the disciplines of personal resilience and the art of strategic optimism, which are discussed in Chapter 8. Make sure your energy and optimism are invested in protecting your passion and allowing it to reconnect.

Why I Wrote This Book

I have a deep and abiding passion for patients and the people who take care of patients—which means I *hate* burnout and the horrible toll it extracts from members of the healthcare team. The added stresses of facing down the horrific challenges presented by the SARS-CoV-2 virus only accentuated this issue.[5-6] So I *love* the chance to contribute, in ways large or small, to specific, pragmatic solutions to battle burnout, in hopes that it will ease the burdens of those whose passion it is to serve patients and their families.

A few words about the title, *Battling Healthcare Burnout*. It reflects my belief that it will indeed be a battle that each of us must fight for the remainder of our professional careers if we are to "save the people who are saving people"—the healthcare teams in our organizations. This book was years in the making but was completed during the horrific coronavirus crisis, in which thousands of healthcare team members were infected and some lost their lives in the battle.

I am loath to compare anything to the horrors of war and am not attempting to do so in a discussion of burnout. However, burnout is a scourge that must be battled if we are to decrease its toll; it will only grow if we do not do our part in leading change, within ourselves and within our teams. *The work begins within*—we must fight to develop the skills to lead ourselves and then lead our teams.

The book's subtitle, *Learning to Love the Job You Have, While Creating the Job You Love*, refers to the fact that we have to not only change ourselves through personal resilience but also change the culture of our organizations and the systems and processes of the work, thereby improving organizational resilience to decrease job stressors. Neither personal nor organizational resiliency alone is sufficient—both must be present to produce the needed change.

A failure of leadership is what got us here; since our current culture, systems, and processes produce burnout rates of 50 percent or more, there is something inherently wrong with them. That is a leadership responsibility. My fundamental belief is that every person in healthcare is a leader—we lead our own work and we lead the teams in which we work. "Lead ourselves, lead our teams" is a central theme of the book and summarizes my experience working in this space for over 30 years. We change culture and hardwire flow and fulfillment through systems and processes when we stop doing "stupid stuff" and start doing "smart stuff." This is the province of leaders at every level of healthcare. We cannot hope to gain the "passion reconnect" necessary to battle burnout without leadership. Because this is a book about how leadership must battle burnout, it presents a combination of cultural, strategic, and highly tactical solutions to the problems we face.

How This Book Is Organized

As an emergency physician, both anatomy (where things are) and physiology (how things work) are critical to me. Here is a primer on the anatomy and physiology of the book. Part One, "Understanding Burnout," starts with why burnout matters, which, succinctly stated, is that *every measure of quality in healthcare gets worse with burnout.* Chapter 1 defines the costs of burnout, both to the individual and to the organization, as well as building the case for viewing burnout solutions as a return on investment. Chapter 2 provides clear, brief definitions of terms, all in service of solutions, starting with defining burnout as a mismatch between increasing job stressors and the inability to develop the adaptive capacity or resiliency to deal with those stressors—resulting in the cardinal symptoms of burnout: emotional exhaustion, cynicism, and loss of meaning in work. Two essential corollaries are that we are all leaders, leading ourselves and leading our teams. The second is that we are all high-performing athletes, in need of the same performance and recovery principles as the men I care for in the National Football League, as the medical director of the NFL Players Association. The six Maslach/Leiter domains, which are used throughout the book and are described in Chapter 3, provide an excellent format to understand how burnout occurs.[7] Chapter 4 details the sources and etiology of burnout in physicians, nurses, and essential services team members and lays the foundation for how these will drive burnout solutions.

Chapter 5 introduces the concept that healthcare systems themselves are the proximate cause of burnout, which must be changed since, as Paul Batalden notes, "every system is perfectly designed to deliver precisely the results it gets."[8] Leadership at all levels is key to changing culture, systems, and processes. Organizational resiliency derives from changing to a culture of passion as well as hardwiring flow and fulfillment into the systems and processes of the organization. While the work begins within, leveraging personal resiliency alone will not be sufficient to change the culture and systems. Chapter 6 provides a model for change and accountability, which is a roadmap for reversing the problems that have created burnout and a path toward a culture of mutual accountability for solutions. Chapter 7 discusses why measurement matters and the existing survey tools to measure burnout, engagement, and fulfillment. As Peter Block says, "The useful aspect of measurement is that it makes explicit our intentions."[9]

Part Two, "Developing and Implementing Solutions," addresses the solutions to burnout by culture, systems and processes, and personal resiliency. Chapter 8 presents detailed means by which to reignite personal passion and resiliency. Leading ourselves comes before leading our teams, and multiple lenses are used to present solutions to this issue. Chapter 9 discusses how to change the cultures that have created burnout. If leaders proclaim they have a great culture, but that culture is burning out half its team, the culture must change. This chapter shows how *culture is the culprit* and details how to change the culture to one of passion and fulfillment. Chapter 10 delineates the concept of hardwiring flow and fulfillment into the fabric of the work by changing systems and processes to reduce job stressors and increase organizational resiliency. We must stop doing stupid stuff, thus eliminating waste, and start doing smart stuff, thus increasing value. It also emphasizes the importance of hardwiring fulfillment into systems and processes. Because EHRs are one of the main sources of job stressors causing burnout, Chapter 11 is dedicated to presenting ways to "take on the EHR" in meaningful terms to improve how the work is done.[10-11]

Part Three, "Other Voices," captures the voices and experiences of several nationally recognized healthcare systems in their burnout battle, including Novant Health System, Brigham and Women's Physicians Organization, Duke University Health System, Inova Health System, and Wellstar Health System.

Part Four, "Tools for Battling Healthcare Burnout," is one of the most important, since it is a compendium of the best solutions I have found in my work and that of others. Each tool is meant to be a practical pathway by which various aspects of the problem can be addressed. After presenting a format and framework for each of the tools, each of the three chapters of this part presents, respectively, the tools for personal passion and adaptive capacity, changing culture, and hardwiring flow and fulfillment.

Finally, the conclusion serves as a capstone to the message of reconnecting passion to purpose in service of our patients and those who care for our patients.

Each chapter has the following features.

QUOTATIONS

Each chapter begins with a quotation selected to highlight the theme therein. I have also liberally used quotes from the lives of great women and men within the text in hopes of further illuminating the points made. I hope you enjoy them. (As Teddy Roosevelt said, "Reading with me is a disease.")

CASE STUDIES

In my training in theology and while playing varsity football as an undergraduate, I discovered that I learned best by seeing practical application of the ideas we were taught, whether in the classroom or on the field. Stories well told and scrimmages were more important to me than readings and the film room, largely because once it was time to apply those lessons in life or on the field, I had already seen how things would happen and where the leverage was to succeed through positive mental imaging. I have generously used case studies to illustrate how burnout and its solutions have played out with others who have faced these challenges. All of them are true, although the names of the "players" and the "stadiums" in which they occurred have been altered. I hope they illuminate both the human suffering of burnout and the way these good people found their way out of burnout. That said, no work can fully capture every way in which burnout can occur or all the ways in which it can be battled. Your journey will in some ways be like others but will retain its own distinct elements. And yet the journey begins within . . .

HISTORICAL EXAMPLES

President Harry Truman said, "The only *new thing* in this world is the history you *don't know*."[12] Truman has the distinction of being the last US president who never attended college, yet he was a highly educated man who read history and literature voraciously, which helped guide his many wise decisions, including the Marshall Plan, the Truman Doctrine, the Berlin Airlift, the immediate recognition of Israel, the firing of General Douglas MacArthur, and the integration of the armed forces by executive order. His biographer, the incomparable David McCullough, notes, "Truman's profound sense of history was an important part of his make-up. He believed every President should know American history at the least, and preferably world history. A president with a sense of history is less prone to hubris."[12]

More recently, revered US Marine Corps general James Mattis, who was nicknamed "Monk Mattis" because of the large number of literature and history books he took with him on deployments, even in battle zones, made a similar point: "There is no substitute for constant study to master one's craft. Living in history builds your own shock absorber, because you'll learn that there are lots of old solutions to new problems. If you haven't read hundreds of books, learning from others, you are functionally illiterate—you can't coach, and you can't lead."[13]

Battling healthcare burnout requires more than a few "shock absorbers," so there are many historical examples in these pages, in the hope it will help you coach and lead your team, who desperately crave and need coaching and mentoring. About this, I am unabashedly unapologetic. I hope this approach works for you.

Good luck, good reading, good leading, and do not hesitate to contact me if I can be of help in any way.

Part One

Understanding Burnout

Effective definitions should drive solutions—practical and pragmatic ways in which to put those definitions to work in increasing resilience and decreasing burnout. There are three fundamental insights:

1. Every member of the healthcare team is a leader and requires leadership training—Lead Yourself, Lead Your Team

2. Every healthcare team member is a performance athlete, engaged in a cycle of performance, recovery, rest, and repeat performance—Protect Yourself, Protect Your Team

3. The work begins within—while organizational culture and systems need to change, we must always seek to reconnect our "deep joy" that brought us to healthcare in a "passion reconnect"

Chapter 1, "Why Burnout Matters," succinctly makes the case that every known metric by which to gauge quality in healthcare gets dramatically worse with burnout. Burnout itself is a ratio of increasing job stressors divided by the resilience/adaptive capacity to deal with those stressors. Resilience has many definitions, but the most pragmatic is that it is simply the adaptive capacity to deal with healthcare's abundant stressors. Christina Maslach and Michael Leiter's seminal work on burnout delineates the six domains of burnout: mismatch of workload demands and capacity, loss of control, loss of rewards and recognition, lack of community, lack of fairness, and loss of values. In order to devise solutions for burnout, it is important to understand the causes of burnout, include both commonalities and differences among physicians, nurses, essential services, and other team members. The cost of burnout is staggering and is delineated in detail, which helps those motivated to launch initiatives to battle burnout to make the case for a return on investment (ROI) to the leadership team.

All meaningful and lasting change is driven by intrinsic motivation and an understanding of "getting the 'why' right before the 'how.'" The most important reason to battle burnout and build resilience is that it makes our jobs easier while making our patients' lives better. Similarly, the most effective way to hold a team accountable is mutual accountability through leadership at all levels. Finally, in an age where metrics matter, a discussion of the measures of burnout and resiliency is presented in detail.

1

Why Burnout Matters

*Knowing what we know gives us peace. But knowing
what we don't know gives us wisdom.*

CONFUCIUS[1]

The Way We're Working Isn't Working

What if half of the physicians, nurses, and healthcare team members providing care to you and your family were burned out? How confident would you be that a team with half its members suffering from burnout would deliver optimal quality of care? That prospect is today's unsettling reality. Burnout has reached epidemic proportions, affecting up to 60 percent of physicians and 50 percent of nurses, depending on specialty.[2-6] The costs of burnout to organizations and providers are devastating, with negative effects on employee turnover, patient safety, quality, productivity, and personal health.[7] The challenge of dealing with the coronavirus pandemic did not create the epidemic of burnout, but it did accentuate it, as well as the necessity for actionable solutions.[8]

Simply stated, the way we're working isn't working. How could it be working when half of our team members suffer burnout and the consequences are so high? Our only hope is to exert inspired leadership to change these realities. The definition of burnout will be discussed in more detail later, but it can be succinctly stated:

Burnout is a mismatch between job stressors and the adaptive capacity or resiliency required to deal with those stressors, which results in three cardinal symptoms:

1. Emotional exhaustion
2. Cynicism
3. Loss of a sense of meaning in work[9]

In addition to this definition, this book relies on three additional insights:

1. Every member of the healthcare team is a *leader* who needs leadership skills to

- lead yourself, lead your team
- lead their team

2. Every member of the healthcare team is a *performance athlete* engaged in a cycle of performance, training, and recovery.
   - Invest in yourself.
   - Invest in your team.

3. *The work begins within.* Start with what you can control: you.

(As Marcus Aurelius noted, if you want good in the world, you must first find it in yourself.) Finally, as Bryan Sexton, a professor at Duke, points out, at a personal level, *burnout results in a diminished ability to experience the restorative effects of positive emotions*, as if a veil stood between us and our passion.[10]

Why does burnout matter? Is it simply an annoyance, or is it a deep problem infecting our ability to deliver quality patient care by committed, passionate clinicians and the team supporting them? How common is the problem, and what differences are there among our team members? How and why does it happen? How does it affect patients, those caring for patients, and the broader healthcare system? This chapter summarizes what is currently known regarding these questions, with the intent of helping guide solutions. It also lists what we don't know.

Burnout matters for five reasons:

1. Burnout is human suffering among our healthcare teammates, blunting our ability to feel positive emotions.

2. Burnout is common, affecting up to 50 percent of physicians and nurses.

3. Burnout is expensive, costing the healthcare system $4.6 billion per year.[11]

4. Every measure by which we monitor progress in healthcare gets worse with burnout.

5. There is no "meter" or "gauge" on our foreheads indicating, "Danger—this person is burned out."

Leadership is essential to preventing and treating burnout—lead yourself, lead your team.

Prevalence of Burnout in Healthcare

The prevalence of clinician burnout has been studied extensively, with most of the work with physicians and nurses. The simplest answer to "Who burns out?" is "Everyone, to varying degrees." Let's examine the data.

PHYSICIANS

Current data indicate that a minimum of 40–55 percent of physicians have experienced significant symptoms of burnout, with higher rates among physicians on the front lines of medicine who have extensive direct patient care responsibilities, including those in emergency medicine, family medicine, general internal medicine, critical care medicine, and neurology **(Figure 1-1)**.[12–14] Conversely, those physicians who rated themselves as the happiest are largely those off the front lines of medicine and in specialties in which patient care is more elective in nature **(Figure 1-2)**.[15] James Reason cites Shakespeare's *Henry V*, "We are but warriors for the working day," and then states that emergency physicians and nurses "stand on the front line between the hospital (the rear echelons) and the hostile world of injury, infections, acute illness. The nature and extent of these enemies are not really known until the moment of the encounter. And the encounter itself is brief, singular, hugely critical, largely unplanned and full of surprises and uncertainties. These skirmishes offer an almost unlimited number of opportunities for going wrong."[16]

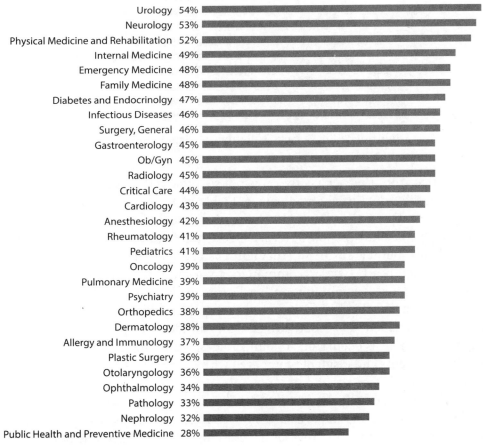

Specialty	Rate
Urology	54%
Neurology	53%
Physical Medicine and Rehabilitation	52%
Internal Medicine	49%
Emergency Medicine	48%
Family Medicine	48%
Diabetes and Endocrinolgy	47%
Infectious Diseases	46%
Surgery, General	46%
Gastroenterology	45%
Ob/Gyn	45%
Radiology	45%
Critical Care	44%
Cardiology	43%
Anesthesiology	42%
Rheumatology	41%
Pediatrics	41%
Oncology	39%
Pulmonary Medicine	39%
Psychiatry	39%
Orthopedics	38%
Dermatology	38%
Allergy and Immunology	37%
Plastic Surgery	36%
Otolaryngology	36%
Ophthalmology	34%
Pathology	33%
Nephrology	32%
Public Health and Preventive Medicine	28%

Figure 1-1: Burnout Rates among Physician Specialties[13]

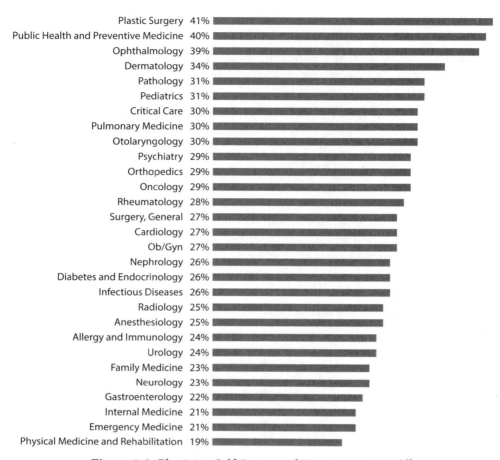

Figure 1-2: Physician Self-Ratings of Happiness at Work[13]

Viewed from this perspective, it is not surprising that we sometimes get it *wrong* on the front lines of medicine, but what is surprising is that we so often get it *right*.[17] Given the type and volume of stressors to which physicians and nurses are constantly exposed, it isn't surprising that nearly half of them have burned out—but it is surprising that figure isn't even higher.

Burnout is nearly twice as common in physicians when compared with other US workers after controlling for other factors, including work hours.[18] Recent data reiterate that this is the case, even though physicians have been shown to have higher resiliency,[19] accentuating the magnitude of the problem. It is alarming that burnout is occurring at younger ages, with a high prevalence among medical students and residents compared with people of a similar age pursuing other careers.[20]

This is undoubtedly due in part to the fact that medical students, residents, and recent residency graduates have more concerns regarding work-life balance and related issues than in previous generations. Chuck Stokes, one of the most trusted voices in healthcare leadership, argues that the younger generation of clinicians will have to "constantly reinvent themselves" over the course of their careers, evolving their areas of interest and their span of practice to avoid burnout and sustain their passion.[21]

While all of these prevalence rates will undoubtedly change over time—and hopefully some of the strategies designed to prevent and treat burnout will be effective—it is safe to say that no less than 35 percent and as much as 50 percent of physicians have substantial symptoms of burnout. It is a staggering insight when you consider that every other doctor may be burned out, particularly when the costs of burnout are considered, from decreased quality of care to effects on patient safety, even before financial costs are calculated.[22–24]

NURSES

Linda Aiken and her colleagues at Penn did the earliest and most extensive work on nurse burnout rates, which have typically been reported to be between 35 and 40 percent.[25–26] They noted in a 2002 study of over 10,000 inpatient nurses that 43 percent reported a high degree of emotional exhaustion.[27] (Most of the work done on nurse burnout has focused on the emotional exhaustion aspect of the Maslach Burnout Inventory, which arguably may skew the picture when comparisons are made to physician burnout data. For this and other reasons, further work is needed on nurse burnout, its sources, and solutions.) Some of the work on nurse burnout, particularly in the emergency department, focuses on the concept of "compassion fatigue," a close variant or cousin on the burnout spectrum, typically described as an erosion of the capacity to show empathy or compassion.[28]

The relationship between specialty area and burnout in nurses is less extensively studied, but there are some data that suggest higher rates in hospitals than in other settings and that nurses in high-stress settings such as ICUs and oncology units may have higher burnout rates, which, if borne out, may dictate targeted therapies for those groups.[29]

ESSENTIAL SERVICES: OTHER HEALTHCARE PROFESSIONALS

As a theology major in college, I was taught that all language has meaning and all behavior has meaning. One of the more disturbing things concerning the language of healthcare is how we refer to the members of the healthcare team other than nurses and doctors—those in the laboratory, radiology, finance/registration, environmental services, and others. In virtually every hospital and healthcare system in the nation, they are referred to as *ancillary services*. The word *ancillary* comes from the Latin word *ancilla*, the precise translation of which is "female slave."[30] *Webster's* definition is only slightly less demeaning when it comes to those with whom we work in healthcare: "subordinate, subsidiary."[31] The more accurate term is *essential services*, since we could not operate any area of healthcare without these teammates. *Stop allowing our team members to be called "ancillary"—they are essential to our work and should be recognized and treated accordingly.*[32]

Much less is known about the prevalence of burnout symptoms among our essential services team, including physician assistants,[33] nurse practitioners,[34] dentists, pharmacists, hospital support staff, and healthcare leaders/administrators. Research is under way in all these areas to quantify prevalence rates, including an ambitious effort by Mayer, Shanafelt, Trockel, and Athey to study burnout among members of the American College of Healthcare Executives.[35] While precise rates are not known, there is every reason to believe that the mismatch of job stressors and adaptive capacity that produces burnout is no less common in these team members, so solutions to prevent and treat burnout should be developed for them as well.

GENDER DIFFERENCES IN BURNOUT

Without question, the challenges facing women physicians are different from those faced by males, including a lack of role models; a lack of parity in compensation; a lower number of promotions to leadership positions; specific challenges of childbearing, child-rearing, and dual-career couples; higher rates of sexual biases and harassment; and a limited window of childbearing years. While gender alone is not yet a consistent predictor of burnout, some studies indicate that, after adjusting for personal and professional factors, women are at increased risk for burnout, perhaps by as much as 30 to 60 percent.[36-38] In 2017, a study of 15,000 physicians from 29 specialties found that burnout was self-reported by 48 percent of female physicians versus 38 percent in their male colleagues.[37] Whether this is due to a higher prevalence, the assessment tool itself, or a higher likelihood of women to report symptoms is currently unknown, but all should be subjects for further study.

Limited but intriguing studies indicate that there are subtly important differences in the ways that burnout is manifested, with women showing higher levels of emotional exhaustion and men with higher scores in cynicism/depersonalization.[39-40] Being a parent lowers the risk of burnout, which may be accounted for in many ways, including having higher adaptive capacity to deal with stressors.[41]

RACIAL DISPARITIES IN BURNOUT

Do people of color experience burnout differently or at different rates? Answers to these questions are of critical importance, and studies are only now being undertaken to find them. Initial reports are perhaps counterintuitive in that they show that physicians in minority racial or ethnic groups have considerably lower rates of burnout than their White counterparts.[42] In addition, favorable reports of work-life balance among Black physicians are perhaps due to better family support.[43] This is an issue that will be the subject of further study, as will whether there are differences in the symptoms of burnout and the resiliency of these physicians.

The racial disparity gap in healthcare outcomes is well documented and transcends income, geography, and social status. Alarmingly, the Football Players Health Study at Harvard, which is the "Framingham Study" of former NFL players funded by the NFL Players Association, shows dramatic gaps between White and non-White football players' health outcomes (including psychological maladies), even accounting for education and income.[44] Whether this proves true in physicians of color remains to be seen. During the COVID-19 pandemic, healthcare professionals of color contracted the virus at a rate 50 percent higher than their White colleagues, and studies are under way to understand the long-term effects.[45] How this affects burnout is the subject of ongoing research.

The Cost of Burnout

While there are clear financial costs from burnout, it is always critical to remember that the highest cost is the suffering it causes to the people on our teams. The human side of burnout is stark, raw, and all too real. Burnout's propensity to prevent us from enjoying the pleasures derived from caring for patients by blocking the ability to fully enjoy the positive emotions arising from clinical practice is a huge tragedy.

But there are also financial costs, and making the case for preventing and treating burnout will always have a fiscal dimension. At a time when healthcare reimbursement is declining, each healthcare expenditure undergoes scrutiny to determine its value and return on investment (ROI).[46–49] An exegesis of the costs of burnout makes the case for its effective recognition, prevention, and treatment, particularly when the costs to the individual, the team, the organization, and society are all considered.[47–49] The interrelatedness of these elements is shown in **Figure 1-3**. Burnout matters in all these areas, but they are deeply connected when it comes to calculating the cost of burnout and its total impact. Keep this in mind:

> Every measure of progress in quality in healthcare—however you define quality—gets worse with burnout.

Figure 1-3: The Costs of Burnout

THE COST OF BURNOUT: THE INDIVIDUAL

The costs of burnout to the individuals suffering from it are undeniable, persuasive, and devasting in their scope and effect. They include this haunting list:

- increased risk of cardiovascular disease[50]
- hypercholesterolemia[51]
- type 2 diabetes[52–54]
- musculoskeletal pain[55]
- prolonged fatigue[56]
- gastrointestinal disorders[57]
- respiratory illnesses[57]
- motor vehicle injuries
- suicide[58]
- depression[59–62]
- alcohol excess[63]
- drug use[64]
- residents—higher risk of needle sticks, bodily fluid exposures[58]
- occupational health issues

This litany is sad and unsustainable, and immediate action is needed to stem the tide of suffering for physicians. Burnout has a negative impact on nearly every aspect of an individual's physical, mental, psychological, and emotional health. The personal toll is apparent from these comments from my interviews with clinicians:

> As burnout set in and worsened, it seemed that whatever was "wrong" in my life got worse.

> It's just a downward spiral—things don't seem to get better.

> It's crazy—I'm a doctor, but my "numbers" on my blood tests just got worse and worse as the burnout symptoms got worse, even when I changed my diet and exercised more.

> I'm not doing *anything* I tell my patients to do when it comes to health—how pathetic is that?

> I can't eat, I can't sleep, I can't even seem to smile anymore at work. That's not why I became a doctor.

> I realized that if I was seeing in my patients what I was seeing in myself, I would tell them, "You *can't* keep doing this! This is horrible for your health at every level!"

As these quotes illustrate, burnout represents real suffering among people dedicated to preventing and relieving the suffering of others. Healthcare leaders have a duty to create cultures of passion and hardwire flow and fulfillment in their systems and processes to eliminate or reduce that suffering. Since we don't have a "burnout meter" embedded on our foreheads, we have to develop ways by which to measure our teams' status.

THE COST OF BURNOUT: THE TEAM

For teams as for the individual, the work begins within. The fundamental importance of teamwork is that it makes the job easier and is thus a source of intrinsic motivation. Nietzsche wisely said, "He who has a strong enough 'Why' can bear almost any 'how.'"[65] Teamwork helps us understand the "why" before the "how." *Leadership and teamwork are two sides of the same coin—the ability to make the job easier.* I will address the broader costs of the effect of burnout on the organization and society writ large later, but there is also undoubtedly a serious cost to the teams providing healthcare, over and above that seen at the macro level. Chapters 8–10 will address the importance of teamwork solutions to burnout. Ineffective teamwork leads to a higher, more complex workload, poor communication, a sense of unfairness, and a lack of clear values—all elements of the six domains of burnout defined by Maslach and Leiter and discussed in Chapter 3.

Teams are not just groups of people who work together to produce defined results—*teams are groups of people who trust each other.* The culture, systems, and personal passion disconnect that produce burnout fundamentally result in an erosion of trust, exemplified by a lack of effective teamwork.

> If I can't trust my teammates to take care of themselves, how can I trust them to take care of others?

Battling healthcare burnout requires innovation, and innovation can only occur at the speed of trust, since team members who cannot trust one another can't innovate. Prospective, nonrandomized studies indicate that turnover of any team member increases the likelihood of turnover of other team members within 12 months of the turnover, even when that team member is replaced.[66] All of this speaks to the contagious nature of burnout, which is attested to by the practical experience of leaders at all levels of healthcare. The cost to the team isn't just turnover—it is the insidious nature of the effects of emotional exhaustion, cynicism, and loss of personal accomplishment on the ability of the entire team to work as a high-performing group and its erosion of personal and team spirit.

The cost of burnout to the team also matters because team-based care has been shown to improve outcomes in each of the areas shown in the following list, which span a broad range of patients.[66-70]

- hypertension
- diabetes mellitus
- cancer
- geriatric care
- primary care clinics
- pediatrics
- emergency department
- joint replacement
- behavioral health care
- disaster medicine
- air medical care
- sports medicine

THE COST OF BURNOUT: THE ORGANIZATION

There are multiple costs to healthcare organizations and healthcare systems of burnout, each of which must be considered. This cost analysis is often important to justify the time and expense of the burnout and resilience initiative.

The Business Case for Burnout When considering the "business case for burnout," it is common to use the term *return on investment*. When considering the business of execution in healthcare, it is always both necessary and appropriate to consider not only whether something new actually works but also whether it can be afforded in today's capacity-constrained healthcare environment. It should also be asked, of all the things in which we *could* invest, why is preventing and treating burnout something in which we *should* invest? In the post-COVID-19 era, where the disease created tremendous stressors on the front lines of healthcare, Victor Dzau and his colleagues have argued persuasively for the prevention of a "parallel pandemic" of burnout threatening our workforce.[71] The business case for burnout shows that the ROI is dramatic, but also demonstrates that, in making the case, we move to a nonintuitive yet unavoidable answer.

Question: How can we *afford* to address burnout?

Answer: You can't afford *not* to address burnout!

Given the data supporting the costs of burnout at every level, healthcare leaders not only have a moral and ethical responsibility to address burnout, they also have financial and fiduciary responsibilities to do so. Let's look at the data that support this, which concern each of the following areas:

- turnover
- patient revenue and productivity

- quality
- safety: medical errors and malpractice risk
- patient experience
- absenteeism, presenteeism, and worker compensation issues
- branding and reputational costs

Turnover Nowhere are the burnout data clearer than in the direct connection between burnout and physician and nurse turnover within two years of its identification. Reports from Stanford, the Cleveland Clinic, the Mayo Clinic, and University of California–San Francisco show that physicians with burnout are twice as likely to leave their institutions.[72-75] Turnover of A-team members, both physicians and nurses, is devastating to any healthcare organization at every level. To lose the best of the team to burnout is even more concerning since in most cases it should be preventable or treatable. The connection between burnout and turnover is unquestioned. The odds that a physician intends to leave a job increase 200 percent with burnout. For each 1-point increase in emotional exhaustion on the Maslach Burnout Inventory or 1-point decrease in job satisfaction, there was a 28 percent and 67 percent higher level of work reduction effort and loss of productivity, respectively.[75]

John Brennan and his colleagues at Wellstar Health System in Atlanta have shown that the actual cost to the organization of the turnover of one physician exceeds $500,000 and is likely closer to $1,000,000.[76] Atrius Health reports the cost to replace a physician at $1,000,000 to $500,000.[77] Other studies indicate that it costs two to three times a physician's annual salary to replace that physician.[78] The cost of turnover among RNs has been estimated to be 1.2–1.5 times their annual salary.[79]

Patient Revenue and Productivity The loss of productivity at the national level has been estimated to be the equivalent of annually eliminating the classes of seven medical schools.[4] Without question, burnout is associated with decreased productivity in nurses and physicians, and it may also cause lost revenue, particularly in surgical specialties, during the time it takes to replace physicians.

Quality Several studies describe a link between the decline in quality indicators, including core measures, postdischarge recovery times, test ordering, prescribing habits, and patient adherence to medication recommendations.[80-83] Studies of both residents and attending physicians show that burnout is a predictor of failing to answer patients' questions and discussing treatment options with them. Nurse burnout negatively affects supervisor ratings of nursing performance.[84] The emotional exhaustion score among nurses increases the likelihood that patients will rate the hospital negatively, will not recommend the hospital, and will perceive their communications with nurses negatively.[84] Nurse burnout rates correlate with nurse ratings of the hospital's safety culture,[85–86] surgical site and catheter-associated infections,[87] and overall care quality.[86]

Safety: Medical Errors and Malpractice Risk The link between burnout and medical errors has been shown in multiple studies, including one demonstrating an 11 percent increase in medical error rates, poor communications between providers and patients, and increases in patient safety incidents.[80] In a study of 7,100 US surgeons, controlling for other personal and professional factors, burnout was tied to reporting a major medical error, as well as being involved in a medical malpractice suit. Major medical errors were also increased among internal medicine residents with burnout. Mean burnout levels in nurses were associated with higher rates of healthcare-associated infections. Perhaps most concerning are the data showing a direct link between burnout and malpractice claims.[82–83] Given all these data, who would want to be taken care of by a burned-out healthcare team?

Patient Experience The correlation between patient experience scores and burnout is intriguing. In environments where the numbers of patients seen per clinician per day are not subject to intense scrutiny, physicians with higher patient experience scores burn out at significantly lower rates. This includes emergency physicians and specialists in hospital medicine. (To be clear, both of these specialties have metrics to hardwire flow as a part of their practices, but they are not mandated to spend only a certain amount of time with their patients.)

However, among internists and family medicine practitioners, where the pressure to see more patients per day drives stressors, physicians with higher patient satisfaction scores have higher burnout rates. This is probably due to the increased pressure to see more patients and a change in their habit of spending more time with their patients. One of the most common and strongest causes of burnout among this group is the pressure to limit the time they spend with patients in the drive to see more patients per day.

I'll delineate this in detail in Chapter 8, but a key means to reduce burnout is to use evidence-based strategies to maximize the benefit of the time available with the patient. Simply stated, "It's not just how much time you spend with the patient—it's how you spend the time."[48]

Using time wisely by following scripts as evidence-based and survey-based language is a powerful way to maximize patient experience in a time-constrained environment.

Absenteeism, Presenteeism, and Worker Compensation Issues Unsurprisingly, the triad of emotional exhaustion, cynicism, and loss of efficacy often leads to physical and psychological illnesses that keep burned-out physicians and nurses from working. Absenteeism from work has a cascade effect, since either teams must work short (with less than a full complement) or someone from a call schedule has to work. When the call schedule is used too often, that has a further demoralizing impact of increased work hours and even resentment toward those who are absent. *Presenteeism* refers to team members working while ill and therefore at a reduced productivity level. However, working while burned out has an even deeper effect, given the psychological impact a negative team member has on the rest of the team. Absenteeism and presenteeism have been shown to dramatically increase in the presence of high burnout rates, as have worker compensation claims.[83–88]

Branding and Reputational Costs Building and sustaining a positive brand and a positive reputation in the community, region, and even nation has become an important focus for hospitals and healthcare systems.[89] Given the clearly demonstrated effects of burnout on negative aspects, outcomes, and ratings of care, it is nearly impossible to have a positive brand and reputation with a team whose burnout rates are excessive. Burnout and brand are thus on a collision course that is unsustainable over time, driving the realization that healthcare leaders cannot afford not to invest in programs designed to address burnout, including those that seek to change the culture, hardwire flow and fulfillment, and develop personal resilience and passion reconnect.

Calculating the ROI of Burnout Solutions At a time when healthcare reimbursement is under substantial scrutiny and terms like *mitigation*, *reductions in force*, *furloughs*, and *doing more with less* are rampant, all healthcare leaders must look at the investment of dollars and resources carefully, with the ROI lens front and center. However, the great news is that, given all the foregoing information, the math to calculate the effect of burnout interventions is not that difficult. The factors considered are the following:

- number of physicians or nurses
- turnover rate without burnout
- turnover rate with burnout
- cost of turnover per physician or nurse
- cost of the intervention

All of these data points are ones that should be tracked routinely in the burnout era and can be used to determine the effect of specific interventions. Here are the data needed in a sample calculation for a healthcare system with 500 physicians.

ROI Data Points for the Calculation

$$ROI = \frac{Net\,Return\,on\,Investment}{Cost\,of\,Investment} \times 100\%$$

Net Return on Investment = Return on Investment − Cost of the Investment

N = number of physicians in the organization
x = Turnover (TO) rate from HR data
y = Current yearly burnout (B/O) rate from survey data
z = TO rate in physicians with burnout = $2 \times$ those without B/O
    (from national benchmark data)
Cost of Burnout = $N \times x \times \$500,000$ (from conservative national
    benchmarks)

For an organization with 500 physicians and a turnover rate of 10 percent, turnover of physicians is 50 per year, with a cost of burnout of $25 million:

N = 500
x = 10%
Total Turnover = $50 \times \$500,000 = \$25$ million

The 10 percent burnout rate can be broken down between "normal" turnover and that from burnout, with national benchmarks indicating that the rate is twice as high in burned-out physicians, represented by z.

10% turnover = 50% non-B/O physicians (A) + 50% B/O physicians ($2A$)
10% turnover = $3A$
Turnover from non-B/O + A = 3.3%, or 17 of the total 50 physicians
Turnover from B/O = $2A$ = 6.7%, or 33 of the total 50 physicians

If the cost of intervention to prevent burnout of $500,000 results in a 20 percent reduction in burnout (from 50 percent to 40 percent), then the reduction in physician turnover of 20 percent relative risk would be 20 percent of 33 physicians, or 6.7 physicians per year, with a reduction in turnover cost of $3,350,000 (6.7 physicians $\times$ $500,000 cost of turnover per physician). The ROI calculation is as follows:

$$\text{ROI} = \frac{\$3,350,000 - \$500,000}{\$500,000} = \$2,850,000 \times 100\% = 570\%$$

Any good chief financial officer would tell you that is an investment worth making for any healthcare institution. You can plug your own numbers in to do an ROI calculation for an investment in burnout.

Tait Shanafelt and his colleagues have developed two worksheets, one to project the organizational costs of burnout and a second to determine the ROI of an intervention.[81] The following is a burnout assessment tool, the questions of which are a framework to assess an organization's efforts in investing in burnout recognition, prevention, and treatment.

Burnout Assessment Tool

- Are you investing (ROI) in preventing burnout and increasing resiliency or adaptive capacity?
- How *specifically* are you doing that?
- Is it working?
- How do you know it's working?
- What other investments should you make?
- What should you *stop doing*?

THE COST OF BURNOUT: SOCIETAL

Han and his team estimated that the societal cost of turnover and decreased productivity secondary to physician burnout may exceed $4 billion annually.[4] Add medical errors, threats to patient safety, malpractice risks, decreased quality of care, turnover, and so on, and the societal investment in the education, training, and development of physicians, nurses, and other healthcare professionals, which comes at least at some level from public funding, has its dividends seriously eroded by the scourge of burnout. All told, the societal, business, team, organizational, and personal toll of burnout among our team members must be addressed.

Implications for Solutions

With up to 50 percent of physicians and 40 percent of nurses experiencing symptoms of burnout, healthcare organizations simply cannot afford *not* to act in the face of this crisis. The good news is that two meta-analyses and systematic reviews show that organizational interventions can demonstrably reduce burnout, with even modest investments resulting in positive changes.[54, 88] What is most clear from these studies is that both organizational and personal strategies must be undertaken to fully address burnout recognition, prevention, and treatment.

PHYSICIANS

- broad, general strategies for all physicians
- targeted solutions for physicians by group—for example, emergency medicine, family medicine, internists, surgeons, and so on
- programs to reduce stressors and increase adaptive capacity
- teamwork skills with nurses
- specific strategies for women physicians (including leadership, gender bias, sexual harassment, peer communities, and mentorship training)
- changes to the structure of medical schools, residencies, and fellowship training to reduce burnout

NURSES

- discrete programs for nurses at highest risk (emergency department, critical care, oncology, newborn intensive care unit, pediatric intensive care unit)
- development of programs to combat "compassion fatigue" in nurses
- development and implantation of team-based skills and communications across boundaries

Patient Burnout

While our discussion has focused on the people providing care and the burnout they experience, a similarly grave problem exists but has not been discussed: *patient burnout.* Simply stated, the same systems, processes, and cultures that create burnout in healthcare professionals have also created a mismatch of adaptive capacity or resilience and the stressors of being a patient, which create exhaustion, cynicism, and lack of accomplishment—*patient burnout.* Patients have never been more frustrated with healthcare systems than they are currently, as multiple studies attest. At a time when mantras like "Patient first" and "Patient always" are proudly proclaimed, listening to the "voice of the patient" tells us that we have made access to care difficult, do not transmit information effectively or efficiently or in a way patients can understand, and even "torture" them by making it difficult for them to find a place to park to get to us. They often arrive in our treatment areas more anxious and frustrated than when they started and become even more so when they see a nicely framed expression of a mission, vision, and values that proclaims how dedicated we are to our patients—even as we have forced them through a gauntlet of obstacles to access to care.[89-90]

Patient burnout is subject to the same domains as provider burnout. As patients seek to navigate their way toward health, there is definitely a *mismatch* between the stressors in their healthcare journey and the adaptive capacity needed. Without question, they feel a *loss of control.* Far too often, there is a loss of a sense of *reward and recognition,* even when they are fully compliant and show improvement in key healthcare metrics. Ask your patients and they will often tell you that our healthcare system lacks a *sense of fairness.* Finally, when a sign proclaims the importance of the patient, but the patient waits hours, days, or weeks for access to care, the *values* are called into question.

While this patient is grateful for her medical care, the very process by which she receives it puts her at greater risk for a fall in navigating that care, as well as frustrating her tremendously. The culture and the systems and processes by which care is delivered seem to have been designed specifically to ignore the patient's needs and desires. I could provide thousands of similar cases in which patients are burned out with our healthcare system. As one patient told me, "Doc, if you call this a healthcare system, I think you need to look up the definition of those words. Isn't the patient the *only* reason you guys exist?"[91]

CASE STUDY

Maureen Vance is a 55-year-old female with a history of osteoporosis and hip, back, and extremity fractures. Her treatment requires an injectable synthetic parathyroid hormone to stimulate bone growth. The injections are given not by a physician but by a nurse practitioner. The healthcare system that provides her care has a main campus and multiple satellite facilities, one of which is 5 miles from her home. The main campus is 25 miles from her home, is undergoing construction, and is almost impossible to access easily. While valet parking is provided, the line to drop off a vehicle is over 30 minutes long and even longer when the vehicle is picked up, because of extremely limited parking and an understaffed, harried valet service.

Once the car is parked, it takes a 20-minute walk and three different elevators to get to the office. Once there, despite arriving 15 minutes early, she waits an hour to be put in a room, where she waits 25 more minutes. Once the nurse practitioner arrives, she hurriedly gives the injection, which takes less than 2 minutes, then leaves. Mrs. Vance waits 20 more minutes for a nurse to "discharge" her, which consists of having her sign some papers and giving her 10 dense pages of discharge instructions, which are not discussed with her. When she asks why the injection could not be given at the satellite facility near her home, she is told, "That's not our policy."

Recognizing that patients can burn out just as members of our team can should drive efforts to constantly change our systems to hardwire flow and value into every process *through the eyes of the patient*.

Once this concept of patient burnout is understood and the elements of it are recognized, it is time to move to a *therapeutic alliance* between the patients and their families and the care teams responsible for them. That starts with "making the patient a part of the team."[90-91]

MAKING THE PATIENT A PART OF THE TEAM

The concepts of teams and teamwork are essential to success in hospitals and healthcare systems, as I'll discuss in detail in Chapters 8–10. *A team is not a group of people working together; it is a group of people who trust each other.* I believe that the single most common problem in healthcare is *failing to make the patient a part of the team*. Shouldn't all healthcare teams make the patient not just a member of the team but the most important member of the team?

That statement, accusatory as it may unintentionally seem, requires exegesis. It starts with an understanding of the voice of the patient, which is distinct from, if related to, the provider's understanding of and empathy with the patient; both of the latter are important, but neither actually captures the voice of the patient.

Capturing the voice of the patient starts with moving from one question—"What's the *matter with you*?"—to another, deeper one: "What matters *to you*?" This is not verbal acrobatics, but rather a shift in focus from pathology to the patient's needs. Doing so starts the journey of transforming the patient from being a *recipient of care* to becoming a *participant in their care*.[91]

One additional part of making the patient part of the team comes from a British colleague who noted that the motto for patient-centered care should be "Nothing about me without me."[92]

PRECISION AND PERSONALIZED PATIENT CARE: A BURNOUT SOLUTION

Ralph Snyderman and Sandy Williams at Duke University School of Medicine first described the concept of precision and personalized medicine,[93] wherein the treatment of illnesses and injuries is specifically tailored to the unique needs of the individual patient, not just generically developed and implemented. Precision medicine begins with asking this simple question of every patient, every time: "What can we do for you to make this an *excellent* healthcare experience?" Note the pronoun *we*, which indicates the team nature of patient care. The focus is on "you," the patient, in an effort to discover what would be "excellent" (not just good or very good) *today*. I'll unpack this in more detail in Chapter 8, on personal approaches to improving care and resilience.

Summary

- The most important cost of burnout is the human suffering it produces in our team, with exhaustion, cynicism, and loss of meaning at work.
- Every measure of quality and safety in healthcare gets dramatically worse with burnout—we can no longer afford the cost, which may be as high as $4.6 billion per year.
- The business case for addressing burnout is impressive and far-ranging, and should include a calculation of the return on investment (ROI).
- Specific solutions should be targeted to physicians (including by specialty), nurses (including critical care and emergency department nurses specifically), essential services team members, and so on to ease human suffering while reducing the cost of burnout.
- Just as healthcare team members burn out, patients burn out as well, compounding the problem.
- Making the patient part of the team and employing precision and personalized patient care are two strategies that should be a part of every solution.

2

Defining and Modeling Burnout

Everything can be taken from a man but one thing—the last of human freedoms—to choose one's attitude in any given set of circumstances, to choose one's own way.
VICTOR FRANKL, *MAN'S SEARCH FOR MEANING*[1]

Definitions Drive Solutions: Burnout

I briefly defined burnout in the opening paragraph of Chapter 1, but let's look deeper. Burnout in healthcare is a mismatch between job stressors and the adaptive capacity or resiliency required to deal with those stressors, resulting in three highly negative, yet completely understandable and predictable, cardinal symptoms **(Figure 2-1)**:

1. Overwhelming emotional exhaustion

2. Cynicism born of detachment and depersonalization

3. Loss of meaning (or effectiveness, efficacy, or personal accomplishment) at work

This definition of burnout drives the solution of reducing burnout by decreasing job stressors, increasing adaptive capacity, or some combination of both. Adaptive capacity or resiliency involves elements of applied creativity, innovation to transcend adversity, and the ability to use the lessons of failure to fuel the battle against increasing job stressors. At a personal level, burnout results in a diminished ability to experience the restorative effects of positive emotions, as if a veil stood between us and our passion.

Resiliency includes a combination of organizational resiliency to change culture and systems and personal resiliency to adapt to job stressors. Both are necessary to battle burnout.

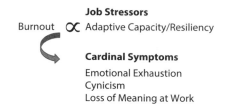

Figure 2-1: The Definition of Burnout and Its Symptoms

Symptom	**Strain Dimension**
• Exhaustion	• Individual Strain
• Cynicism	• Interpersonal Strain
• Loss of Meaning at Work	• Self-Evaluation Strain

Figure 2-2: Symptoms and Strains of Burnout

Exhaustion is the *individual strain dimension*, with the perceived depletion of mental, physical, psychological, and even spiritual resources available to deal with stressors. *Cynicism* is the *interpersonal dimension*, reflecting a negative, callous, and fundamentally detached response to those being served precisely while they are being served. Finally, *loss of meaning at work* is the *self-evaluation dimension*, often characterized by being excessively self-critical and reflected in feelings of incompetence, inadequacy, and lack of achievement (**Figure 2-2**). (The third symptom of burnout has variously been described as loss of efficacy, loss of effectiveness, loss of a sense of personal accomplishment, and loss of meaning in work. All are accurate, so I will refer to them interchangeably, depending on context. Each of these terms captures the *fundamental futility* that healthcare team members feel.)

Understanding what strains are associated with each symptom is critical to devising solutions tailored to the symptoms themselves. For example, elevated scores on the cynicism scale require strategies to increase a person's sense of connection, which decreases interpersonal strain, while the strategies targeting loss of meaning are more targeted to easing the torture of self-evaluation.

The Three-Dimensional Model of Burnout

Burnout is best considered a three-dimensional model of

- exhaustion,
- cynicism, and
- loss of meaning in work.

Symptoms of burnout can be classified as falling under one or more of these three categories (**Figures 2-3 and 2-4**).

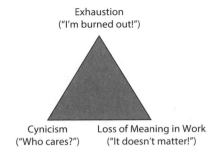

Figure 2-3: The Three-Dimensional Model of Burnout with Each Cardinal Symptom Diagnosed with Different Language

Figure 2-4: Symptoms of Burnout in the Three-Dimensional Model

Learning the pain of burnout is best achieved through interviews with those experiencing its symptoms. Or as Dante further said in *The Inferno*,

Death could scarce be more bitter,
But if I would show the good that came of it
I must talk about things other than the good.[2]

To fully understand burnout is to hear the words of those afflicted with it, or "things other than the good." The fact that you are reading this book suggests that you have heard similar statements.

EXHAUSTION

In interviews with hundreds of healthcare team members, these are typical descriptions I have heard:

I'm so burned out—I'm literally exhausted.

I can barely keep my head up at work.

First of all, I can't sleep, but even when I do, I wake up more worn out than when I went to bed.

I'm "running on empty," as the Jackson Browne song says, and it's not much fun.

I'm tired, but when I'm at work I try to kick into a higher gear—but there's no "higher gear" there.

At the risk of hyperbole, fatigue doesn't even begin to describe how I feel—it's an ache in my soul which drains everything I do.

I came home from work and my seven-year-old daughter said, "What did you do today, Daddy?" I felt so frustrated that I burst into tears, frightening both her and me.

The toll of burnout manifests itself in statements about how exhausting and energy-depleting healthcare work can become if we do not address burnout. As discussed in Chapter 1, a precision and personalized patient care paradigm should be tailored to eliminate the exhaustion resulting from burnout.[3]

CYNICISM

I thought I was going to save the world as a doctor—or at least my part of it. Honestly, at this point, who cares? It's all a myth.

If you had told me I would develop anger at my patients, I would probably have slapped your face. But that's what it has come to.

I read Cervantes in high school, and the image of the physician as "knight-errant" was very powerful for me when I entered healthcare. Now . . . well, that's gone and if I feel like anyone, it's Sancho Panza.

I knew I was in trouble when I started to realize that my patients had sometimes stopped being people to me and started seeming like "problems."

I was suturing a laceration the other day and I couldn't seem to calm the patient down—he kept squirming, making the job harder. I actually yelled at him—I'm embarrassed to say that—but I've never thought of a patient as depersonalized as I did that person. I immediately thought, "Something's got to change—I can't live this way."

I've noticed that I am actually withdrawing from my patients at times, because I feel like, "Who cares? Does it really make a difference?"

I would never have thought of myself as sarcastic, but that is what I have become. And I am ashamed to admit it.

When healthcare team members, particularly physicians and nurses, realize they have become cynical, it is a harsh awakening. As the great novelist Saul Bellow notes, "Reality greets these ideas the way a cement floor greets a dropping light bulb."[4] In my experience, cynicism is in many ways the hardest, most shattering reality of burnout with which to come to terms and requires aggressive solutions, which I'll detail in Chapters 17–19. For a healthcare professional, to admit they have become cynical is a low point—one they never thought they would reach. As Oscar Wilde notes, "A cynic is someone who knows the cost of everything . . . and the value of nothing."[5]

In order to "reverse the jump" when going to work in healthcare, will the staff be

- bathed in cynicism?
- or buoyed by hope?

One of the central goals of healthcare leaders is to create hope where hope is flagging, to create progress in the midst of cynicism.

LOSS OF MEANING IN WORK

I worked so hard to get into school, then through residency to become a "master clinician." Now I often think, "It doesn't really matter what I do."

It seems like I just don't have the bandwidth to make a difference, between exhaustion and spinning my wheels.

The more metrics they pile on me, the less effective I get.

Morale is at an all-time low—and it is going south.

The pressure mounts and mounts and my ability to produce is cratering.

Honestly, does it really matter anymore?

I always thought I had great coping mechanisms, but they left me behind a long time ago.

I'm spinning my wheels—just burning up effort and getting nowhere.

I am in a hole—and I can't stop digging.

Exhaustion and cynicism or depersonalization result in inevitable feelings of a loss of ability to make a difference in patients' lives—which is precisely what we all sought to do in the first place, fueled by a passion that now seems a distant memory.

Exhaustion, cynicism, and loss of effectiveness should be recognized as what they are—human suffering. Those who experience burnout are suffering from the cost extricated from them by the work they do. W. H. Auden captured it well in the first lines of "Musée des beaux arts":

> *About suffering*
> *They were never wrong, the Old Masters*
> *How well they understood*
> *Its human position.*[6]

Burnout should always be understood as *human suffering* among our team—our second greatest resource. And that suffering affects the care of our greatest resource—our patients. What could be more human than the suffering of those who entered their demanding careers precisely to decrease suffering?

The "Other Side" of Burnout: Passion, Engagement, and Resiliency

The psychological relationship of people to their careers can be conceptualized as a continuum, from the positive experience of passion and engagement to the negative experience of burnout:

Passion	Burnout
Energy	Exhaustion
Engagement	Cynicism
Making a Difference	Loss of Meaning in Work

Engagement is defined as a positive, energetic state of job involvement, with personal gratification enhancing one's sense of professional accomplishment or efficacy. Craig Deao of Studer Group/Huron Consulting describes engagement as being emotionally invested in the organization, being committed to creating value, and making discretionary effort when no one is watching.[7] To what extent are healthcare systems committed in meaningful, demonstrable ways to promoting passion's three core qualities of high energy, committed involvement, and maximum effectiveness? *A commitment to passion (and its three component areas) is a commitment to* **changing the job** *and its effect on the team, while focusing on personal resiliency alone leads to strategies to* **change the person**. Leaders must invest in both areas if burnout is to be combated.

Most hospitals and healthcare systems use staff and physician engagement surveys, but fewer survey for burnout.[8] This is more than a theoretical or research-based issue, since many studies may show a moderate to high level of engagement and yet still find unacceptable levels of burnout in the organization. Many hospital administrators prefer engagement or professional fulfillment scores over burnout surveys because the results are less explicitly negative.[9] The best approach combines well-crafted engagement surveys with burnout surveys.

While engagement is an important concept to consider in healthcare, as stated previously, *passion* is the real element that drives those in highly stressful environments, although that aspect is admittedly more difficult to capture. As Wilbur Wright said about the invention of human-powered sustainable flight, "Orville and I were having so much fun, we couldn't *wait* to get up in the morning."[10] That's precisely the type of passion needed to work well in every area of healthcare. Thus, mere engagement may be just a step away from the joy of passion to the tragedy of burnout.

Passion → Engagement → Burnout

Passion is the prize, not simply engagement. Considered in this light, the solution to burnout is restoring passion, not just attaining engagement. Engagement is thus a critically important step in the journey to passion, which is our ultimate goal.

Resiliency is defined as adaptive capacity or the personal and organizational qualities required to thrive in the face of adversity. Simply stated, resiliency is a measure of adaptive stress-coping capacity. The scale most commonly used to measure resiliency is the Connor-Davidson Resilience Scale, which began as a 25-element, four-point Likert scale but has since been shortened to 10-element and 2-element scales.[11] Most recent research uses the 2-element scale. From a broad perspective, the term *resiliency* is often used to refer to ways to combat burnout, which are addressed in detail in Chapters 8–11 but without using the term *resiliency* itself, since it is implied in the adaptive capacity to deal with stressors.

Recent research is concerning because it shows that burnout rates are higher in physicians than in the general working US population, even though physicians have significantly higher resilience than nonphysicians. Thus, although physicians have higher adaptive capacity, the job stressors are so high that they exceed physicians' innate resiliency. In fact, the specialty with the highest resiliency rate is emergency medicine, which also has the highest burnout rate.[12]

From a practical view, resiliency is the ability to "bounce back," to deform as needed to adapt to or "squeeze through" stressful situations and then re-form into a shape that allows us to move forward. As an experienced ER nurse once told me, "I have to be like Gumby—able to twist any way necessary to get through the day and then bend back into shape to face the next day!" That metaphor is an appropriate one for resiliency.

At its core, the commitment to resiliency or adaptive capacity is a fundamental human choice, as Frankl's words in the opening of this chapter attest. Resiliency is the ability to "choose one's own attitude in any given set of circumstances, to choose one's own way."[1] *Resiliency or adaptive capacity is not solely a matter of personal choice, but also requires leaders to ensure that the organization is committed to resiliency by changing the culture and systems that logically yet inexorably produce inordinate job stressors.* Frankl's words, properly considered, should produce a commitment to resilience from not only *each* of us but *all* of us—especially leaders.

Burnout versus "Rustout"

> *We must all wear out or rust out, every one of us. My choice is to wear out.*
>
> THEODORE ROOSEVELT[13]

Passion fuels us daily. When we experience burnout, we have a "passion disconnect," which leaves us without the necessary fuel to drive our engines. Perhaps a corollary to Ferdinand Foch's wisdom noted in the introductory chapter is, "To burn out, you have to have been on fire in the first place!" Some physicians, nurses, and healthcare leaders are perhaps less likely to burn out than they are to "rust out." Rustout is an appropriate metaphor for those whose passion has gradually atrophied such that the skills of adaptive capacity have frozen up, much like the Tin Man in *The Wizard of Oz*. These team members do not need a fire rekindled within them as much as they need the right "oil applied to their joints" to get them moving again. (It's important to note that joints are actually articulations, in the sense that they join parts of the body—or the organization—in close working proximity to each other.) Often, the "oil" that needs to be applied is the ability to articulate the importance of habits that prevent or treat burnout, and to reestablish the connection to the meaning and passion of caring for patients.

Rustout can also be considered a state of "uninterrupted ennui," a sense of acute and chronic boredom on the way to burnout. When we find that the work is no longer as satisfying as it was, we are seeing the first steps down the burnout path. Graham Greene captured this in the preface to his novel *A Burnt-Out Case*: "A doctor is not immune from the 'long despair of doing nothing well,' the same *cafard* that hangs around a writer's life."[14] The novel describes an architect who meets a physician in a leper colony treating advanced cases of Hansen's disease, whose disfigurement was such that "they were no longer recognizable—even to themselves." Victims of burnout in healthcare often say that about themselves—they no longer recognize their work lives, encompassed as they are by exhaustion, cynicism, and futility, often to the point that they feel the "long despair of doing nothing well." The term *cafard*, which means "pointlessness," comes from Baudelaire's poem "Les fleurs du mal."[15]

An experienced physician once told me, "I hate—and I mean truly hate—to admit this, but everything I do seems so pointless to me. I wish I could shake that feeling—but so far I can't."

The Role of Stress in Burnout: Eustress, Distress, and the Stress Tolerance Level

Since burnout is defined as an adaptive capacity mismatch between job stressors and the resources available to deal with such stress, it is important to recog-

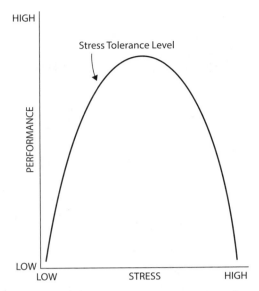

Figure 2-5: Stress, Performance, and the Stress Tolerance Level

nize the genesis of the concept of stress as *distress*, beginning with the work of Hans Selye.[16] While stress usually carries a negative connotation, Selye noted that there is good stress, or *eustress*, which is positive, motivational stress, driving us to higher performance. Working to get into medical, nursing, or hospital administration school; continually improving our practices by updating our knowledge base; and keeping mentally and physically conditioned to increase performance and recovery are all examples of eustress.

As **Figure 2-5** indicates, on the left side of the stress-performance curve, as stress/eustress rises, performance improves. Your stress response is a result of your experience and perception of stress and your ability to adapt adequately to it in positive ways. It is only when the ability to deal with stress reaches the stress tolerance level (STL) near the top of the curve that performance plateaus and then tumbles down the far side of the curve to distress or bad stress, where performance declines as stress continues to rise.[17] (I owe this insight to my late friend and colleague Joan Kyes, RN.)

Your colleagues, family, and friends know precisely how you look, sound, and feel when approaching the STL. If you have the courage to ask—and they have the courage to answer—they can be a rich resource for self-reflection on this matter. (As I will discuss later, developing the ability to recognize the signs and symptoms as we approach our respective STLs—both generally and in specific situations—is an essential strategy to prevent and treat burnout.) Increasing or continuing stress past this point results in negative distress and continuously declining performance.

Elite athletes famously thrive under pressure, some of which is a matter of recognizing its inevitability. Hall of Fame NBA player (and a source of both insight and wit as a commentator) Charles Barkley said, "Pressure? Isn't that something you put in tires?"[18] In my experience, great physicians, nurses, and healthcare leaders take the same approach, using the pressure of delivering results as eustress to fuel their passion, about which I will say a great deal more.

It is imperative to note that the concepts of eustress, distress, and STLs apply not only to individuals but also to organizations *writ large*, as well as the departments within them. Improving financial performance, adopting (and adapting to) electronic health records, developing patient safety initiatives, and instituting many other changes can give rise to positive stress as the system is improved. But be wary of reaching the STL of both the organization and those faithful team members who form the organization, which is a key leadership lesson. STLs represent an inflection point, where dealing effectively with stress improves performance and failing to do so causes a rapid decline in performance. Moving to the positive end of the curve is critical, and it can only be accomplished when you have a positive and proactive theory of change, fully believing that change is the only constant—in life and in healthcare.

As every amateur and professional athlete knows, improvement at any level requires the facility to change effectively, as well as a strategy, whether articulated or not, to deal with change. Domonique Foxworth, Pro Bowl cornerback, Super Bowl champion, and past president of the NFL Players Association, once told me, "Doc, as a cornerback, I have to run backwards and sideways as fast as the best athletes in the NFL, the wide receivers—and they know where they're going. I have learned to develop a strategy for change—because change is the only path to improvement if I'm going to stay with them. I also have a strategy for each situation, because my performance depends upon situational awareness. No two down-and-distance equations are the same. The first quarter and the fourth quarter are different, too."[19]

Dr. Evans's experience is quite common and illustrates both the chronic nature of the buildup of job stressors and the fact that solutions can be successful. She was recruited by the CEO to become the chief quality officer of the organization, where she is thriving both personally and professionally.

Burnout and Depression

Is burnout simply "depression at work"? The answer is, "Great question, but 'no.'" Depression is a context-free diminished sense of affective well-being, while burnout is a situationally specific, job-related diminished sense of affective well-being.[20] Both share a diminished sense of affective well-being, but the context, depth, and implications are distinct. *It is important to distinguish between burnout and depression, since their treatment is completely different.* Burnout requires solutions to reduce job stressors while increasing organizational and

CASE STUDY

Nancy Evans is a critical care physician with over 20 years of experience who had always been among the most highly rated and most respected physicians in her group, practicing at a level 1 trauma and tertiary care center. She had been, as she said, "through all the 'flavors of the month' of management styles." She had been through Lean, Six Sigma, total quality management, Continuous Quality Improvement, preferred provider organizations, health maintenance organizations, accountable care organizations, high-reliability organizations, and a new electronic health record. While she maintained a positive attitude throughout, she noticed her metrics on patient satisfaction and hardwiring flow had begun to erode.

Although she had previously had good scores on the Maslach Burnout Inventory across all measures, her most recent scores showed a marked negative change in emotional exhaustion and loss of personal accomplishment. When presented with these data, she said, "I thought, 'I can't be burned out—that's not me!'" In the midst of this trend, a new management team came to the hospital, proclaiming, "We're not putting up with the old, tired ways of doing things." But at a town hall meeting of physicians, she rose to tell the new CEO, "With all due respect, you've come in here telling us how bad we are—and you haven't even taken the time to get to know us. You should listen before you talk." Her colleagues cheered.

Because of her realization that burnout was setting in, she independently sought out training in personal resilience over a six-month period. Her performance metrics, Maslach Burnout Inventory scores, and sense of energy and personal accomplishment all improved steadily, after which she noted, "Burnout for me came on slowly and insidiously—I didn't see it coming, because it took years to develop. Once I recognized it and called it by name, I took the steps needed to deal with the chronic stresses of the job."

personal resilience, whereas depression requires medical treatment, ranging from various types of therapy to the use of medications. While there is certainly a link between these two conditions, not everyone who has symptoms of burnout will become depressed, and not everyone who is depressed also has burnout at work.[21] What evidence there is suggests that there may be an association between prolonged burnout and the future development of depression, but more work is needed in this area.[22]

Summary

- Burnout results from a mismatch between job stressors and the adaptive capacity or resilience to deal with them, resulting in a syndrome of emotional exhaustion, cynicism or depersonalization, and a loss of meaning in work.

- Engagement, while important, is only a step toward the real goal, which is reigniting our passion.

- Everyone in healthcare is a leader, and leaders must be as committed to *changing the job* (organizational resilience) as they are to *changing the person* (personal resilience).

- Rustout is as toxic as burnout.

- Being able to recognize your stress tolerance level and decompress from it is a critical skill.

3

The Six Maslach Domains

Though usually regarded as the result of trying to give too much, burnout in my experience results from trying to give what I do not possess—the ultimate in giving too little!

PARKER PALMER, *LET YOUR LIFE SPEAK*[1]

Burnout was first used nearly simultaneously in the mid-1970s by Herbert Freudenberger,[2] a psychiatrist working in an alternative healthcare clinic in the East Village, and Christina Maslach,[3] a social psychologist at Berkeley studying human emotions in the workplace. When Maslach described the phenomenon of exhaustion, cynicism, and loss of effectiveness to a female poverty law professor working under stressful conditions, the attorney exclaimed, "Oh my—we call that burnout!"[4] Thus, like many aspects of life, burnout was nascent, waiting to be described and given its name. (Freudenberger's mentor was Abraham Maslow, whom he met while taking night classes at Brooklyn College, illustrating Henry Adams's wisdom that "a teacher affects eternity. He can never determine where his influence ends."[5]) But the term *burnout* has seen a resurgence, particularly at a time when healthcare talent is at a premium and the cost of turnover continues to rise.

The Six Domains of Burnout (Maslach/Leiter): Definitions Drive Solutions

One of the most important elements of our understanding of burnout is the taxonomy developed by Maslach and her colleague Michael Leiter.[6] (In the remainder of the book, I have shortened this to "Six Maslach Domains" for concision and since the domains are widely known by this term.) This taxonomy indicates that burnout consists of the symptoms of exhaustion, cynicism, and loss of efficacy, which occur in six discrete domains:

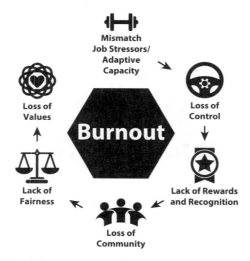

Figure 3-1: Maslach's Six Domains of Burnout

1. Mismatch in workload demands and capacity

2. Loss of control

3. Lack of rewards and recognition

4. Loss of community

5. Lack of fairness

6. Loss of values

This model **(Figure 3-1)** has distinct advantages for the diagnosis, treatment, and prevention of burnout. In diagnosis, consideration of these six areas of work life allows for a deeper understanding of what specifically *results* in exhaustion, cynicism, and the sense of loss of efficacy. But far more importantly, it serves as a blueprint for specific, targeted actions to blunt or reverse burnout through prevention and treatment, as Chapters 8–11 delineate.

(An alternate lens for classifying sources of burnout comes from the excellent work of Swensen and Shanafelt, reflecting the Mayo Clinic's approach, which lists six drivers that closely parallel the Maslach domains [**Figure 3-2**]. Both are effective ways of looking at what causes burnout and the solutions they drive. I have taught the Maslach/Leiter formulation for many years and use it in this book.)

MISMATCH OF WORKLOAD DEMANDS AND CAPACITY

Mismatches in workload occur when too many demands relative to the capacity to deal with them exhaust an individual's energy (and that of the team) to the point that recovery is difficult, if not impossible. This mismatch is a clear indica-

Maslach Domains of Burnout	Mayo Clinic Drivers of Burnout
1. Mismatch in Workload Demands and Capacity	1. Excessive Workload and Job Demands
2. Loss of Control	2. Lack of Control and Flexibility
3. Lack of Rewards and Recognition	3. Difficulties with Work-Life Integration
4. Loss of Community	4. Isolation and Loneliness
5. Lack of Fairness	5. Inefficiency/Inadequate Resources
6. Lack of Strong Values	6. Problems with Organizational Culture/Values

Figure 3-2: A Comparison of the Maslach Domains and the Mayo Clinic Drivers of Burnout

tor that job stressors have exceeded the individual's resiliency or adaptive capacity to deal with them. Thus, it's not necessarily the workload itself but rather the ability to deal with the workload that creates exhaustion. This is innately understandable to members of the healthcare team, where considerations of demand-capacity mismatches are a part of understanding flow. (See Chapter 9.)

These mismatches may involve physical, mental, and emotional demands, and the capacity to deal with them usually involves all three aspects to varying degrees, depending on the individual and the specific circumstances. Generally, workload mismatch is most directly related to the exhaustion aspect of burnout.

Dr. Davis's case is a classic one where the increased workload demands and decreased capacity to meet those demands result in burnout.

LOSS OF CONTROL

Healthcare systems often inadvertently create situations where the team and the members forming it have insufficient control over the resources needed to do

CASE STUDY

Sharyn Davis is an "internist's internist," widely admired by her colleagues and patients alike. She is a part of a large multispecialty group that has recently been forced to contract with several large insurance carriers, all of which have reduced payment to the group by nearly 30 percent while demanding the same high-performance metrics. As a result, she now has to see 25–30 percent more patients each day, which limits her time with them to 15 minutes for established patients and 30 minutes for new patients. The healthcare system has also mandated use of a new electronic health record. She says, "I am struggling to keep up—I feel like I can barely tread water against a strong current. I don't have the time with my patients to get to know them and their families. I feel like a machine, not a physician."

CASE STUDY

Jennifer Royalty is the patient care director of a busy emergency department (ED) in a 400-bed hospital, which suffers from a constant lack of beds and inefficient bed control. This results in large numbers of "boarders," or patients who lie in the ED hallways for hours, waiting for bed assignments. She and her nurses have to continually explain these delays to patients and their families, despite the fact that they have no control over bed assignments or the process of inpatient bed control and turnover. Despite many task forces and committees, the problem is getting worse and is outside the control of the ED staff. However, the CEO, chief operating officer, and chief nursing officer demand high performance on flow metrics, patient experience scores, and patient safety measures. Jennifer's nurses are starting to leave and pursue other jobs because of burnout with this problem and their lack of control over it. Many of her nurses tell her, "I am a critical care nurse, not a floor nurse. This isn't what I signed up for and doesn't use my talents and skills."

their work and have inadequate authority to obtain the necessary resources to do the work in the manner they would prefer. In working with the American College of Healthcare Executives Executive and Senior Executive Leadership program, I pose this question to the participants: "How many of you feel you are held accountable for a system over which you have no control?"[7]

Without exception, every hand is raised, enthusiastically, indicating that a loss of or lack of control is an issue in every healthcare system, where people feel their responsibility exceeds their authority over the results to which they are deeply committed. A mismatch in control is related to the loss of efficacy or reduced personal accomplishment aspect of burnout. As Maslach and Leiter note, "Control problems occur when workers have insufficient authority over their work or are unable to shape the work environment to be consistent with their values."[6] Unsurprisingly, when people have more control over their work, their actions are more freely chosen, which leads to higher engagement and a return to passion.

LACK OF REWARDS AND RECOGNITION

The third type of mismatch involves a lack of appropriate rewards and recognition for the work people do. In most cases, the lack of rewards is not primarily financial in nature but rather reflects a fundamental devaluation or lack of appreciation of the work and talents requisite to do such work. The lack of intrinsic rewards, such as a deep pride in doing something of importance extremely well, is often a part of this mismatch. Lack of rewards and recognition is closely

CASE STUDY

The team members of a critical care unit in a busy hospital provide care to high-acuity patients and are nearly always at 100 percent capacity. Unfortunately, the team feels taken for granted by their leaders, one of who remarked at a department meeting, "What did you expect when you signed up for a job in the critical care unit? That's where the sick patients come. Suck it up or we'll find someone who can."

associated with the "loss of meaning in work" portion of the Maslach Burnout Inventory.

Former French president Charles de Gaulle was surely correct when he said, "The cemeteries of the world are full of indispensable men."[8] Though few people working in a high-performance healthcare system consider themselves indispensable, nearly all consider their work *meaningful* to themselves and the lives of their patients, or they wouldn't be doing that work in the first place.

Lack of rewards and recognition creates situations in which the healthcare team is considered fungible, as this comment indicates: "This hospital doesn't consider me a professional—they consider me an FTE [full-time equivalent]." If senior leaders communicate—intentionally or otherwise—"If you can't do the work, I'll find someone who can," they are sending a clear message that the people doing the work are fungible. And the journey from "indispensable" to "fungible" is a sure path to burnout. As I will discuss in more detail, every day, leaders should say, "Thanks for doing a great job in tough circumstances!"

LOSS OF A SENSE OF COMMUNITY

The fourth type of mismatch occurs when people lose their sense of positive, proactive participation in a team or community in which they work. (Chapter 8 discusses teams in more detail.) People innately thrive in communities where praise, happiness, comfort, and even the trials of the job are shared communally. Sebastian Junger captures this well in his book *Tribe*.[9] The emotional exchanges and the sometimes sardonic repartee seen in healthcare teams are a part of their essential nature. As cynicism and exhaustion rise, the seams of the community are threatened, and people feel isolated, losing their sense of identity and connectedness in the process. In *Henry V*, Shakespeare captures this perfectly in Henry's speech (act 4, scene 3) before the Battle of Agincourt:

> *From this day to the ending of the world,*
> *But we in it shall be remembered—*
> *We few, we happy few, we band of brothers;*
> *For he today that sheds his blood with me*
> *Shall be my brother.*[10]

CASE STUDY

Timothy Seasons has had declining scores across all metrics measured in his family medicine practice. As his scores decline and his direct supervisor counsels him to "get your metrics moving," he withdraws even further at work, further worsening his scores. Nurses find him increasingly detached. Dr. Seasons is showing classic signs of burnout, particularly with regard to a lack of meaning at work, and his withdrawal may even signal the early stages of personal depression. A new leader becomes his supervisor and says, "Tim, you are an important part of the team and we will do anything we can to help you improve your scores. All of us are with you on this, so please let me know how we can help."

(There have been numerous comparisons of the COVID pandemic to the Battle of Agincourt.[11-12] However, it is wise to recall that Agincourt lasted less than a day, while the COVID-19 crisis has lasted many months with no end in sight.) Unfortunately, the fall from working with a "band of brothers" (and sisters) to "I'm working with a 'band of bothers'" is a treacherous one and marks a shift from community to isolation. The African proverb captures this well:

If you want to go fast, go alone.
If you want to go far, go together.

The further people withdraw from the team or community of caregivers, the more essential it is for leaders and other team members to make every effort to welcome them back on the team with encouragement, coaching, and understanding.

LACK OF FAIRNESS

Fairness is a fundamental human need, but it is also one that is felt even more acutely in professionals. Fairness communicates mutual respect, confirms self-worth, and creates a level playing field. Conversely, environments in which inequity rules are toxic by nature and dismissive to those required to work in them. A lack of fairness creates burnout both because it is exhausting and because it creates deep cynicism about the workplace and the leadership team responsible for it.

Unfairness is perceived when there are high demands for performance metrics but the means to attain those metrics are lacking, which can be termed "metrics mania without means." This exposes a patently unfair mismatch between what is demanded of us, the resources to attain the metrics, and even the assigned metrics themselves. Substantial experience shows that the first element to mark the descent to burnout in high-performing teams is the development

CASE STUDY

The ED of a community hospital has seen its annual patient volume increase by 35 percent, and the admissions from the ED account for over 70 percent of total hospital days. Despite the increase in the volume and acuity of patients seen, as well as the rising number of hospital boarders housed in the ED, multiple requests for additional staff and space have been denied, though construction dollars have been given to other areas of the hospital. The ED team members and their leaders are facing increasing frustration and burnout, particularly since they are held accountable for the same metrics targets.

CASE STUDY

Maribel Espinosa is a highly trained family medicine physician who has also done a fellowship in geriatrics. Because of a new contract with a large healthcare insurance company, her group practice has seen a dramatic reduction in reimbursement. As a result, she and her colleagues have a scant 20 minutes allotted for each patient. She notes that her geriatric patients require more than 20 minutes to deal with their complex medical problems and multiple medications. But her medical director and administrator both say, "That's just the way it is—you will have to make do with 20 minutes." Dr. Espinosa responds, "If that were your elderly mother or father, would 20 minutes be what you would want me to take with them?" Neither the medical director nor the administrator responded verbally, but their faces showed they understood.

of a sense of unfairness. When healthcare teams see what they perceive as unfair treatment, burnout almost always is a threat.

Both these case studies are classic examples of highly trained professionals having increased demands placed on them, despite increasing constraints on their time. These are issues of fairness, which can be a major driver of burnout.

STRONG VALUES

The sixth area of mismatch is a conflict of values or confronting realities where the stated mission, vision, and values are not matched by the resources necessary to attain them. Worse, in some cases, the values demonstrated by the leadership team conflict with the stated values of the organization. As a result of leading the efforts of the NFL Players Association to salvage an NFL season while keeping the players and their families safe during the COVID pandemic, I have been invited to speak to many audiences about leadership during a crisis.[13] I

> **CASE STUDY**
>
> A hospital states it values high-quality service and excellent patient experience, but the reality for the team is "Move 'em, move 'em, move the meat!" The conflict of stated values versus the reality creates deep cynicism among the staff. Some team members are actually ashamed of, instead of proud of, the stated values. If the leadership team communicates, directly or indirectly, "Get it done—I don't care how you do it," it further risks subjugating values for results.

always begin by pointing out that the midst of a crisis is a *terrible* time to be figuring out what your values are, since it is precisely those values that should guide your response to the crisis. The same applies to the burnout crisis—you should look to your personal and organizational values to guide your response.

An increasing amount of research shows that values affect multiple areas of the organization. This is important in both the diagnostic phase, where a discordance in values is a clear harbinger of burnout, and the treatment phase, where clear steps to realign culture and processes with values help move the team to a place where other burnout treatment strategies can be used effectively.

(I will discuss the concept of moral injury in more detail, but some have proposed that this term, which arose from the study of combat veterans whose values were potentially compromised by their actions, might apply at the extreme end of burnout. In this sense, moral injury may be an extreme and hopefully rare example of compromising values in pursuit of expediency.)

As I will discuss in more detail in Chapter 6, the culture of an organization is reflected less by "the words on the walls"—the stated mission, vision, and values—than by the "happenings in the halls"—what actually happens in the healthcare organization.

These six burnout domains form the basis of the specific strategies designed to address them, as indicated in Chapters 8–11. There are several other formulations regarding these domains, including those from the Mayo Clinic, Stanford, Duke, and other leaders in burnout research. However, they can all be related to the Maslach formulation, which is the foundation of our work on understanding the origins of burnout (Chapter 4) to determine solutions.

Leadership: Personal and Professional Skills to Battle Burnout

Burnout cannot be battled successfully without effective leadership at all levels of every healthcare organization. Why this statement is true relates to the very definition of burnout. We are all leaders charged with leading ourselves and our teams. As you recall, burnout occurs when job stressors exceed the adaptive capacity or resiliency of those experiencing those stressors, producing a syndrome of emotional exhaustion, cynicism, and a sense of futility. Any hope of decreasing the stressors and increasing adaptive capacity comes from leadership—both personally and professionally.

Without question, a failure of leadership is what created the burnout crisis. While this may seem a harsh judgment, the argument that increased job stressors were allowed to make their way into the fabric of hospitals and healthcare systems, creating a mismatch between those stressors and the adaptive capacity or resiliency to deal with them, is at the heart of understanding burnout. All of us who were charged with making changes—or allowing those changes to make their way into our systems—simply did not fully realize the impact they would have on our teams. That is meant not as an indictment of leadership but rather as an acknowledgment and acceptance of how we arrived at a place where half of our team members are burned out.

This is an unfortunate case where a respected leader did not see how deeply the adoption of a new system would affect the work lives of those he was responsible for leading. (I will discuss the impact of the increased demands and stressors of EHRs in Chapter 4 and solutions to them in Chapter 11.) The stressors of the EHR were deep, pervasive, and hugely influential, causing a motivated team to become demoralized and pessimistic. To be sure, healthcare *writ*

CASE STUDY

John Jones is a successful and highly respected chair of the ED at a high-acuity, level 1 trauma center. He leads a team of accomplished clinicians with talented associate medical directors, all of whom work closely and respectfully with their nursing colleagues. However, the healthcare system recently adopted an electronic health record (EHR) without the input of the staff. Because of the transition to the EHR, the superior metrics the ED had delivered quickly deteriorated. Sadly, so did the morale of doctors and nurses alike, as they now spend much more time in front of the computer than with their patients.

During a department meeting, after hearing considerable frustration and animosity about this issue, out of his own frustration, Dr. Jones says, somewhat angrily, "That's just the EHR—you're going to have to get used to it!" Morale plummeted further and confidence in Dr. Jones's leadership steadily eroded. A friend and mentor, showing personal leadership, advised him of this, and after reflection, Dr. Jones made a public apology, which included these words: "I share your frustration and I expressed that in a way I didn't intend. Let's work together on a plan that addresses these issues."

large did not anticipate just how much these systems would change the lives of our teams, but in Dr. Jones's case, the assertion that "you're going to have to get used to it" was viewed by many as a betrayal of his role as an advocate for emergency physicians, nurses, and the patients for whom they care. The stressors of the EHR vastly exceeded the adaptive capacity of the team members to deal with them. Dr. Jones's team felt he should have advocated more strongly for them (and their patients), instead of "giving in" to the IT department.

Is there evidence that improved leadership results in lower levels of burnout and increased fulfillment? While the number of studies supporting this is currently small, the data are nonetheless compelling. A study of 2,800 physicians practicing at the Mayo Clinic used a 60-point leadership scale to asses physicians' ratings of their leaders and compared it with burnout rates using a modification of the Maslach Burnout Inventory. Each 1-point increase in physicians' ratings on the leadership scale was associated with a 3.3 percent decrease in the likelihood of burnout. There was also a 9 percent increase in satisfaction for individual physicians, correcting for age, sex, and specialty. Further, 11 percent of the variation in burnout and 47 percent of the variation in satisfaction was tied to aggregate leadership score.[14] Other studies—and considerable practical experience—have shown remarkably similar results, so it can be confidently said,

Leadership is essential to battling burnout.

As the case study shows, the corollary of that statement is that poor leadership almost inevitably leads to burnout, although that has not been as well studied. Indeed, the very fact that the job stressors causing burnout were allowed to proliferate in our systems without considering the need for increasing adaptive capacity is testament to the role of leadership—and its failures.

Leadership is essential in all three areas in which I have framed burnout: creating a culture of passion, hardwiring flow and fulfillment (systems and processes), and reigniting passion and personal fulfillment. Leaders cannot shield their teams from all the increasing job stressors on the horizon, but they should at least anticipate them and consider ways to blunt their impact, as well as to increase organizational resiliency throughout the change initiative. They should also play a lead role in helping to increase personal resiliency and adaptive capacity along the way.

This wisdom is not unique to our time, since Machiavelli understood it long ago: "And it ought to be remembered that there is nothing more difficult to take in hand, more perilous to conduct, or more uncertain in its success, than to take the lead in the introduction of a new order of things. Because the innovator has for enemies all those who have done well under the old conditions, and lukewarm defenders in those who may do well under the new."[15]

As I will discuss in detail later, leadership includes as a core competency the ability to use effective change management techniques to anticipate and blunt

Leadership
- Envisioning
- Strategies
- Alignment
- Empowerment
- Direction Setting
- Execution

Management
- Planning
- Budgeting
- Organizing
- Staffing
- Controlling
- Problem Solving

Figure 3-3: The Skills of Leadership and Management

Leadership Goals for Burnout
- **Think** about burnout in a radically different way
- **Act** on those thoughts within the week
- **Innovate** to change culture, systems, and people

Figure 3-4: Leadership Goals for Burnout

the effect of job stressors to the extent possible while increasing both personal and organizational resiliency. While there are many books on healthcare leadership,[16-19] several concepts are essential, in addition to the importance of change management.

What is the distinction between leadership and management? John Kotter's work in this area is perhaps the best and clearest.[18-19] He notes, "The fundamental purpose of management is to keep the current system functioning. The fundamental purpose of leadership is to produce change, particularly non-incremental change. Most companies are over-managed and under-led."[19] Both leadership and management skills are required to deal with burnout, since management skills, which are different from leadership skills, will be required to keep the current system functioning *to the extent that the system is predictably and reliably producing value* (**Figure 3-3**). Leadership skills are necessary to encourage change whenever the current system fails to deliver value or causes waste, whether for the patient or the team itself.

Managers are maintainers, and leaders are innovators. To be successful in producing results while minimizing burnout, leaders must think, act, and innovate (**Figure 3-4**).

The first step is to help the team to think about burnout in a radically different way by using the definitions of burnout to guide solutions and getting them engaged from the start. Second, leaders must challenge their teams to act quickly, usually within a week after a solution is proposed, in order to show progress and generate hope. (Generally, if new ideas aren't acted on in some way, large or small, within a week, they aren't acted on at all.) Finally, leaders must be catalysts for innovative cultures, systems, processes, and behaviors to combat burnout and enhance both personal and professional resiliency or adaptive capacity, which is discussed further in Part Two. And as I have discussed, innovation occurs "at the speed of trust" among the team members.

Summary

- The six Maslach domains provide a taxonomy for understanding both the causes of burnout and their solutions:
  1. Mismatch in workload demands and capacity
  2. Loss of control
  3. Lack of rewards and recognition
  4. Loss of community
  5. Lack of fairness
  6. Loss of values
- Leadership skills at all levels are necessary to battle burnout—lead yourself, lead your team.
- To be successful, leaders must think, act, and innovate in understanding, preventing, and treating burnout.

4

Causes and Drivers of Burnout

The value is not in seeing much, but in seeing wisely.
SIR WILLIAM OSLER[1]

Unless we know what causes a disease, we can't effectively treat it. From Semmelweis to SARS-CoV-2, etiology drives treatment. Fortunately, we know a great deal about the etiology of burnout, starting with the calculus that, since burnout results from a mismatch of job stressors (the numerator) balanced by adaptive capacity or resiliency (the denominator), anything that increases job stressors without at least a commensurate increase in resiliency causes burnout. Two of the three areas of the causes of burnout are due to organizational stressors (culture and hardwiring systems and processes), which means leaders must embrace accountability for changing their culture and systems.[2-3] And yet far too many healthcare leaders still labor under the erroneous belief that burnout is a failure of the individual, without considering the system in which these individuals work.[4]

Because leadership is ultimately responsible for the onslaught of job stressors and the cultivation of organizational resiliency or adaptive capacity, leadership's failure to deal with those changes has been a root cause of burnout.[5-6] Unless and until leaders embrace their responsibilities to decrease or mitigate job stressors and increase adaptive capacity, nothing will change. Or at best we will have more resilient people leading themselves in a culture and with systems and processes resistant to leading their teams.

Two physicians from different organizations and in different specialties described the impact of job stressors due to changes of the system:

> I don't know who, why, or how this system was designed, but it seems they did it precisely to perfect the production of burnout.

> This change was handled with an uncommon degree of arrogance by people who have no conception whatsoever of the work we do, the

negative impact that this change has on our lives, and the distraction it creates from our goal of providing excellent patient care. Other than that, it's fine.

Fortunately, effective organizational and personal leadership offers a road-map to prevention and treatment once the causes of burnout are understood.[7–8] Faced with the cataclysmic pace of change that will unquestionably be our daily diet for the foreseeable future, leadership at all levels must have at the top of their list of core competencies the ability to anticipate the effects of job stressors and adaptive capacity, minimizing the former and maximizing the latter.

Notwithstanding the importance of changing culture and hardwiring flow and fulfillment, the *work begins within* precisely because we cannot lead our teams unless and until we lead ourselves. Again, if we want a good world, we must first look for good in ourselves.

Who Burns Out? The Paradox of Burnout

It is important to know *who* burns out if we seek to treat it. The people who burn out in healthcare are precisely those who care the most about their patients and how that care is best delivered—*those who have the most passion.*[9] As mentioned previously, the paradox of burnout is that it occurs predominantly in those who care the most—the A-team members. To burn out, you must have a fire burning within, and there are plenty of B-team members who are never "on fire" enough to develop that passion. B-team members, who complain constantly, are often those whose rhetoric is most inflamed regarding job stressors, but they lack the passion to lead themselves and lead the team. B-team members typi-cally have a victim's mentality, certain that the world is "doing them wrong," without taking the leadership challenge of changing themselves and changing the system. (The A-team/B-team concept is discussed in more detail in the next chapter.)

It is also clear that B-team processes can easily burn out A-team members.[10] Even if we have discovered our deep joy, the constant wear of job stressors can exhaust the best of us. That is why changing ourselves alone is not enough—we must also be committed to changing the culture and hardwiring flow and ful-fillment into our systems and processes.

Lead yourself, lead your team.

Common Causes, Diverse Dimensions: Specificity of Causes Drives Specificity of Solutions

While there are common causes of burnout throughout healthcare, there is vari-ability in the precise expression within areas and across categories of team members, as I discussed in the last chapter. The causes and job stressors of burn-out in an emergency physician whose daily workload comprises new, undifferentiated patients with which she has no previously established contact differ significantly from the job stressors of an internist who has met the vast majority of her patients and has had at least some opportunity to establish a relationship with them.[10] A pediatrician or family medicine physician has other discrete stressors, which differ from those of a surgeon.[11-12] Similarly, the job stressors for a critical care nurse differ from those of a community health center nurse (**Figures 4-1, 4-2, and 4-3**). To Osler's point, in seeking to reduce burnout, understanding *all* the possible drivers results in "seeing much," while understanding the specific causes in the individuals and groups suffering burnout allows us to "see wisely."[1]

This insight is critical to understanding both the common ground and the diverse needs each person within these groups will encounter in their journey

- Excessive work hours
- EHR
- Malpractice suits/litigation risk
- Productivity-based pay
- Doing more with less
- Call schedule/frequency
- Low self-compassion and perfectionism
- Ultimate responsibility resides with them
- Academic factors—"publish or perish"
- Witness to death and suffering—ultimately responsible
- Moral injury

Figure 4-1: Differential Causes of Burnout: Physicians

- Role ambiguity
- Lack of respect/acknowledgment
- Poor treatment by other team members
- Inadequate staffing (increased job stressor without increased adaptive capacity)—"short-staffing"
- Intense exposure to patients and family
- Witness to death and suffering
- Moral distress/injury
- Inadequate compensation
- Poor career ladder

Figure 4-2: Differential Causes of Burnout: Nurses

- Lack of thanks/appreciation
- Job security
- Limited career progression
- Inadequate compensation and appreciation
- Often understaffed
- Exposure to patients and family limited/circumscribed

Figure 4-3: Differential Causes of Burnout: Essential Services

back from burnout. Healthcare systems often embrace broad, interdisciplinary solutions that can be applied across boundaries, but many of these efforts are condemned to diffuse, ineffectual implementation and eventual failure, precisely because generic solutions cannot always address the specific drivers of burnout.[13] While the causes of burnout match the Maslach burnout domains, each area of the healthcare system should be queried (usually with free text questions and interviews) to determine the specific causes of burnout. (See Chapter 7 for more detail.)

The Causes of Burnout across the Six Maslach Domains

The drivers and causes of burnout can be classified in several different ways, but the simplest is to consider the six domains of burnout described by Christina Maslach and Michael Leiter, which were discussed in detail in the previous chapter **(Figure 4-4)**.[14] Because of the wide and pervasive impact of the electronic health record (EHR), it is mentioned in all the domains, but is discussed in more detail in Chapter 11.

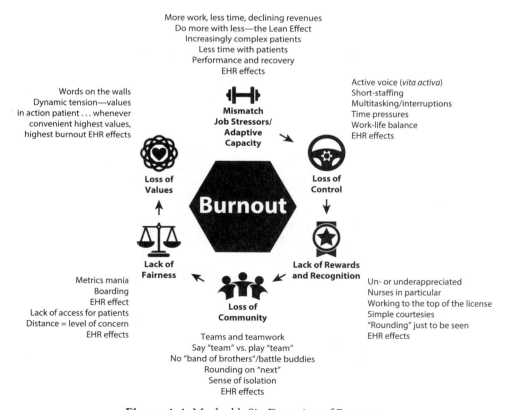

Figure 4-4: Maslach's Six Domains of Burnout

MISMATCH BETWEEN DEMANDS (JOB STRESSORS) AND ADAPTIVE CAPACITY

This first dimension goes to the heart of the causes of burnout, since it addresses both the numerator of job stressors and the denominator of adaptive capacity or resilience, including the following:

- too much work, not enough time, declining revenues
- "Use less, do more"—Lean without changes in systems and processes
- the paradox of time, since it takes more time to do the work (complexity of patients, EHR, documentation, regulatory requirements, etc.) precisely when we have
  - less time with the patient (our primary source of passion)
  - unmanageable work schedules (long hours, nights, weekends, and holidays; "doubling back" without sufficient recovery time)

The sad fact is that, far too often, productivity gains in healthcare have been attained by forcing providers to work harder in systems that demand even more from them, which produces burnout. These demands will become even higher as the population ages, as our patients will be not only older but more complex, on more medications, and with more medical problems. Indeed, the Institute for Healthcare Improvement states, "Lean means using less to do more," which is often not welcome news to team members.[15]

Just when the patient population's needs are increasing (increased job stressors), the capacity to deal with this complexity is under siege (decreased adaptive capacity). This includes an increase in administrative burdens, which create additional time pressures and complexity, particularly for healthcare clinicians **(Figure 4-5)**.[16]

The evidence that increasing workload increases work stress and burnout is well established and is not limited to healthcare.[17] In healthcare, in a survey of 7,288 physicians, Dyrbye and colleagues found a 2 percent increase in burnout for every hour over 51.8 hours per week worked,[18] which would be consid-

Clinical
- Searching for results (radiology, labs, consults, previous medical records, etc.)
- Documenting history, physical examination, progress notes
- Multiple "clicks" on multiple screens
- Fewer consultants

Nonclinical
- Billing requirements
- Documenting nonclinical issues
- Redundant documentation requirements
- Regulatory burdens

Figure 4-5: Mismatch of Demands and Adaptive Capacity: Administrative Burdens

ered a high workload in any job except healthcare. As the National Academies of Sciences, Engineering, and Medicine note, "For more than a century, the norm for healthcare professionals has been to work long intense hours and to selflessly put patients' needs above one's own."[19]

Elite athletes in all sports understand the clear balance between performance and recovery, as I will discuss in detail in Chapters 8 and 17. The science describing this balance is detailed and extensive and extends to mental performance.[20–21] Healthcare team members are "elite athletes" who need sufficient recovery to perform at the highest levels. Leaders must build "recovery time" into organizational resiliency (Chapters 9 and 10), but also at the personal resiliency level, which is discussed in Chapter 8. Healthcare leaders should invest in *peak performance*[22] of their teams and the individuals on those teams, not just simple productivity metrics. This entails a deeper dive into who performs well, why, how it can be improved, and under what circumstances that performance can be translated to other team members.

LOSS OF CONTROL

There are many reasons why people choose a career in healthcare, but among the most common is the desire to "make a difference in people's lives." That is a desire to live "in the active voice," undertaking positive, proactive, and deeply meaningful actions not for the good of the caregiver but for the good of the patient. This is our "deep joy."[23] The great philosopher Hannah Arendt called this the *vita activa*, a life of action engaged with others.[24] Perhaps no other profession necessitates a *vita activa* more than healthcare, where our work is always integrated with others in a passionate team dedicated to the service of patients. Clinicians in particular

CASE STUDY

John Jones is an experienced surgeon and one of the most trusted doctors in the hospital. His patient experience and flow metrics have always been the best. The migration to a new EHR was challenging for him, as for many others, and clearly slowed the pace at which he was able to see patients. Several new "evidence-based" clinical guidelines were recently implemented, none of which the clinicians had any voice in creating. Dr. Jones noted in an interview, "My dad was a World War II Marine, so I was raised with a 'bias toward action,' motivated by a desire to get things done for the good of others. But now it seems our entire team is 'under fire,' with constant changes to the way we practice, and which we had no voice in creating. Outside forces seem to control my practice. I show up and every day it seems I hear, 'We're down two OR nurses today, so suck it up.' It's incredibly frustrating and it's wearing me out."

enter their careers to "make things happen," not to "have things happen to them." When they feel a switch to "the passive voice," in which things are happening *to* *them* without a basic sense of control, burnout is the predictable result.

Dr. Jones is feeling is a fundamental loss of control over the way he practices his specialty. In interviews with his nursing and physician colleagues, they all expressed similar thoughts and emotions. Short-staffing, in which there are not enough team members to do the work designed for a full contingent on the schedule, is an extremely common phenomenon, and one that goes to the core of losing control. Working short of targeted staffing levels has major negative impacts on quality measures.[25–26] Nurse burnout increases significantly with "inadequate," "inappropriate," or "short staffing."[27] Rao and his colleagues surveyed 1,774 physicians and showed that inadequate staffing interfered with patient care, shifted the focus away from patients, and increased administrative duties.[28]

One of the most widespread issues arising from a lack of control is the nearly incessant plague of interruptions, which drives the need for clinicians to multitask in many settings. The paradox is that many members of the team often take great pride in their ability to multitask, when in fact the data clearly indicate that multitasking reduces performance, which is addressed in more detail in Chapter 17.

All of this leads to a mismatch in work-life balance, where the demands of work flow over into the personal lives of healthcare team members in ways that have a negative impact on their home lives.[29]

LACK OF REWARDS AND RECOGNITION

Healthcare teams are busier than ever, with more being demanded of them all the time. We are (or so it seems) so busy we are not taking the time to give rewards and recognition where they are due, either to ourselves or to others.

To a degree never seen before, people feel unappreciated or at the very least underappreciated.

> I didn't become a critical care nurse because I wanted "medals" or people to recognize me. But I did think there would be a fundamental appreciation for the long hours of training and education it took to get to this level. That rarely happens anymore.

While this is more common in nurses, it also happens with physicians and essential services team members. Changing culture, hardwiring flow and fulfillment through systems and processes, and cultivating personal resiliency are all at play here. Whenever we have professionals who are not "working to the top of their licenses," we are at risk for having people do work that, while unintentionally, may be slightly demeaning. We have countless checklists for safety, flow, and patient experience, but very few checklists for rewarding and recognizing our fellow team members. Henry Clay recognized the value of simple recognition over 100 years ago when he said, "Courtesies of a small and trivial character are the ones which strike deepest in the grateful and appreciating heart."[30]

Take a moment the next time you are at work to observe how people interact. Do they routinely smile, nod in acknowledgment, or give other verbal or physical signs of appreciation? Do staff routinely say, "Thank you"? Do leaders identify problems and then fail to follow through by fixing those problems? Do meetings start on time, every time, which is a simple sign of courtesy to those summoned to the meeting from their busy days? While these problems of a lack of rewards and recognition are often pervasive, they can be remedied, as I will discuss in Chapter 17, but *only if leadership is committed to doing so at every level of the organization.*

LOSS OF COMMUNITY

Lack of meaning arises from a loss of connectedness and community. Healthcare professionals all want to be a part of the "we few, we happy few, we band of brothers" that Shakespeare described.[31] Our middle son, Kevin, was a Marine infantry officer who completed two combat tours in Afghanistan during Operation Enduring Freedom. One of the core principles for Marines in combat is that of "battle buddies," in which members of the platoon are assigned to watch out for their team members. This is a concept we can use well in healthcare. But precisely when we need the skills of teams and teamwork most, there are forces that pull that sense of community apart.

> One of our best and most respected nurses has a well-deserved reputation for deeply caring about her patients. She has always made a point to call them or, if they are admitted to the hospital, go see them on the floor or ICU. But last week, she was "caught" by a supervisor rounding on a patient in the hospital and her job was threatened for "violating HIPAA rules." Have we come to the point we can't even stay in touch with our patients? What does that say about the culture and values of this organization?

We often "say 'team,'" but we more rarely "play 'team.'" If a nurse who has cared for a critically ill or injured patient in the emergency department can't round on that patient in the hospital without being made to feel like a criminal, something is wrong with our conception of teams and community.

> Dr. Robin Crantz is one of the most widely respected internists and geriatricians in the entire region, whose patients revere her for her wisdom and compassion. Recently, she reluctantly realized that continuing to admit her own patients was simply not feasible, given reimbursement levels, regulatory burdens, and other pressures. While she knew the necessity of this step, after six months, she said, "I thought I was ready for all the implications of having the hospitalists care for my patients.

But the one thing I didn't realize was that meant not seeing my colleagues in the hospital on a regular basis. The lack of camaraderie left me feeling alone and isolated in a way I couldn't have predicted."

The advent of hospital medicine has many important advantages, but as this physician learned, there are unintended consequences, including feelings of isolation and a lack of connectedness. As the complexity of healthcare systems rises, the culture and the systems and processes in which we deliver care have often developed substantial boundaries that both we and the patient must navigate to feel a part of the team. Fortunately, the CEO and chief medical officer recognized how important it was to keep primary care physicians and developed a special place for medical staff to eat adjacent to the hospital cafeteria, which was close to the physician office building, thus helping reestablish camaraderie. (And as we will see in Chapter 13, Brigham and Women's Hospital established the "Brigham to Table" program, providing meals for the staff to share twice a month.)[32]

LACK OF FAIRNESS

Healthcare team members are not only among the most fair and reasonable people I have ever met, they are also offended by unfairness in the care of their patients or when it is encountered by others. As job stressors rise and adaptive capacity fails to meet the pace of change, it becomes increasingly apparent when the scales seem weighted against fundamental fairness.

A simple example is the increasing focus on metrics-based measures to evaluate success and hold teams accountable for results. I have no objections to such measurement—in fact, I have advocated for it my entire career.[33] What I object to is what I've called "metric mania without means," a maniacal focus on metrics disconnected from the reality of what is required to obtain those metrics in the cauldron of patient care. Asking people to do more (better metrics) with less (reduced, curtailed, or changed resources) seems fundamentally unfair unless healthcare leaders ask for the voice of those held accountable in the design and implementation of the improved systems and processes necessary for that to occur.

Byron is a victim of *metrics mania without means* in that he is being held accountable for an element of the system (inpatient bed control) over which he has neither control nor a voice. Imagine if the operating rooms were cut in half, but the surgeons, nurses, and essential services team were all held accountable for the same flow, safety, and patient experience metrics. Yet that fundamental fairness is being routinely breached with the ED team when they have half the beds they need for their patients.[34]

Far too often, the adage that a leader's concern is inversely proportional to his or her distance from the source of the problem is true. In Byron's case, his chief nurse executive is perfectly willing to expose ED nurses to the indignities of patients boarding in the hallways for hours but is unwilling to have such

CASE STUDY

Byron Saxon is the nursing director of an emergency department (ED) with 90,000 annual visits of high acuity where 35 percent of patients are admitted to the hospital. Taking a team-based approach to lead across boundaries has resulted in top-decile metrics for the ED, which have been sustained over time. Unfortunately, a series of events outside the ED has resulted in nearly constant hospital boarders, who often stay in the ED for 8–12 hours waiting for an inpatient bed. Recently, over half of all ED rooms and hallway spaces were occupied by hospital boarders. In a meeting with his chief nurse executive, he was told, "Byron, your metrics are falling across the board. What is your plan to stop this 'freefall'?"

patients "board" in the hallways of the inpatient unit, which is a simple solution to off-load boarders from the ED. Understandably, to the ED nurses, this seems unfair—not to *them* but to their *patients*.

Patients' lack of access to high-quality clinical care is a significant source of burnout in healthcare. When staff sense that lack of or differential access is based on race, socioeconomic status, or country of origin, this is exacerbated significantly.

LOSS OF VALUES

Whenever the stated values of the healthcare organization are not matched by what occurs in the organization—or as I have phrased it previously, when the "words on the walls" don't match the "happenings in the halls"—burnout is a predictable outcome.[35]

This illustrates the importance of values and how the details of poor culture, systems, and processes can lead to values in reality that are different from those that are proclaimed. It's also an example of how fairness and values can collide if we don't match our commitments across all our boundaries.

Perhaps the most extreme example of how a failure to deliver on values can cause burnout is *moral distress or moral injury*.[36] Moral distress occurs either when people are asked to do something that offends their values or when they observe that the system in which they work fundamentally betrays its values, seemingly in a systematic way. Sources of moral distress differ between nurses and physicians:

Sources of Moral Distress: Nurses[37-38]

- poor communication
- inefficient input into clinical decisions
- clinical disagreements with physicians

CASE STUDY

John Brees is the medical director and Joan Smith is the nursing director of a busy ED. Their healthcare system proudly proclaims its primary value as "Patient always," which appears on every computer screen in the hospital, as well as on posters in each hallway. The system has its own employed medical group, including the broadest possible range of specialties, from primary to subspecialty and surgical care. Despite that, patients referred from the ED to the medical staff for follow-up routinely have to wait three to four weeks to be seen in physicians' offices. It is increasingly common for patients to return to the ED for their follow-up care, since, as one patient said, "They couldn't have cared less about getting me an appointment—I felt abandoned." Asked about this phenomenon recently, Joan and Dr. Brees noted, "Apparently the primary value isn't 'Patient always,' but 'Patient only when it is convenient for us.'"

- unsafe staffing
- unnecessary tests and procedures

Sources of Moral Distress: Physicians[39-40]

- excessive documentation
- lack of resources, compromising clinical care
- lack of administrative action
- 20 percent of physicians have considered leaving their jobs because of moral distress

Sources of Moral Distress from Patients: Primary Care Physicians[41]

- ignored advice
- noncompliance
- requesting unnecessary tests and procedures
- lack of respect
- threat of workplace violence

Moral injury is a term that was first defined in the context of combat veterans who witnessed events that violated their sense of ethics, ideas, or values in battle.[36] This left them unable to justify, process, or integrate those events into the fabric of their moral system, producing moral injury. This concept has been extended by some to healthcare, where many of the available choices appear to be "bad choices" that violate the moral system. Some of the events of the coronavirus pandemic fall into this category.

CASE STUDY

Dominique Stallworth is an experienced veteran ICU nurse, who often said, "I've seen it all." Her healthcare system was in the eye of the storm of the SARS-CoV-2 crisis, with ICUs filled with patients with the most severe type of coronavirus pneumonia, often called the "cytokine storm." Typically, ICU patients lie on their backs, facing up, so that the doctors and nurses can look into their eyes. But these patients were found to do much better when prone, allowing better ventilation and draining. Because of the highly transmissible nature of the virus and its devastating consequences, no visitors were allowed, even family.

Dominique said, "I've seen many patients die—hundreds of them. But at least I could look in their eyes and try to comfort them. At least their family could visit them and say their goodbyes, making peace, and sending them on their way. This was different—far more horrifying than anything I have ever experienced. Having to die alone and with a horrible sensation of suffocating . . . I'm not sure I will ever get over it."

Is moral injury an extreme form of burnout? Or is it a distinct entity unto itself, "beyond burnout"? While I suspect it is the former, regardless of how we classify it, we do need to recognize that it is a profound and seemingly lasting challenge to our moral code and must be anticipated and dealt with proactively when we see extreme situations. These nurses and physicians are at special risk because they have to process dealing with the unthinkable without having been adequately prepared.

Summary

- Leadership is essential to connect the causes of burnout with pragmatic solutions—lead yourself, lead your team.
- The "paradox of burnout" is that those with the most passion—the A-team members—are most prone to burnout.
- The specific causes of burnout differ between nurses and doctors, as well as by specialty or job area.
- Each of the causes of burnout can be classified under one of the six Maslach domains.
- EHRs as a cause of burnout cut across all domains.

5

The Calculus of Burnout and Leadership

Every system is perfectly designed to produce precisely the results it gets.
PAUL BATALDEN (ADAPTING ARTHUR JONES'S INSIGHT)[1]

In the Introduction, I discussed the concept of "burning in versus burning out" and the importance of reigniting our passion while protecting it. "Burning in" means using our passion to fuel the flames of our "deep joy" in caring for patients, using the heat of the friction between job stressors and resilience to power us. Reigniting your passion requires the application of the disciplines of personal resilience and the art of strategic optimism to protect that passion. Chapters 2 and 3 provided a taxonomy of burnout, with definitions driving solutions. These definitions create shared mental models, which form the basis of a deeply and widely understood foundation from which the entire team can work on burnout. Armed with these practical definitions and shared mental models, let us move to how to put those definitions to work in ways that make our patients' lives better, our jobs easier, and our teams less likely to burn out. That is the foundation for the following concepts:

Lead yourself, lead your team.

Protect yourself, protect your team.

The work begins within.

The Calculus of Burnout Results in a Passion Disconnect

The calculus for decreasing burnout is very simple: decrease the "numerator" of job stressors while increasing the "denominator" of adaptive capacity or resiliency **(Figure 5-1)**. Throughout the book, this "numerator"/"denominator" terminology is used to identify burnout problems, as well as the solutions necessary to deal with them. (Remember that resiliency and adaptive capacity are

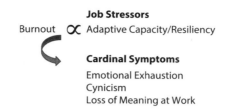

Figure 5-1: Definitions Drive Solutions

synonymous in the burnout definition and are used interchangeably throughout the book.)

Burnout results in a *passion disconnect*, and passion is the fuel that drives us in the difficult job of caring for patients. Without passion, we are truly "running on empty," in the words of singer-songwriter Jackson Browne. Decreasing job stressors while increasing resiliency is the path toward a passion reconnect, which "fills our tanks."

The framework for understanding burnout comprises three elements:

1. Instilling a culture of passion and professional fulfillment

2. Hardwiring flow and fulfillment into systems and processes

3. Reigniting passion and personal resilience

The cultures of our organizations and the systems and processes by which healthcare is provided are characterized by *organizational resilience*, while reigniting passion demonstrates *personal resilience.* I will discuss the roles each plays in battling burnout in detail. Ninety percent of the literature on burnout is focused on diagnosis, with a scant (but increasing) 10 percent focused on prevention and solutions.[2] Further, most of the work on burnout has concentrated almost exclusively on personal resilience, while far less focuses on the necessity of changing the culture and systems in which we work. When the system produces burnout in 50 percent of its talent, the *system* must be changed, not just the *people*. Paradoxically, the pathway to improving culture and systems arises from the personal transformations of individual team members, which is why I say "the work begins within." As those transformations occur, individuals, then teams, then organizations, then systems accelerate the pace of innovation.

One central message of this book is that, with effective, positive, and proactive *leadership* (at both the organizational and personal levels), the pathway to a passion reconnect is not only possible but predictable. Conversely, a lack of leadership is precisely how the scourge of burnout reached epidemic proportions. Battling healthcare burnout is one of the most important aspects of healthcare leadership, as well as a significant challenge.

My experience and that of many others, including national leaders like Tom Jenike at Novant (Chapter 12), John Brennan at Wellstar (Chapter 16), Steve

Motew at Inova (Chapter 15), and Nicholas Beamon at OneTeam Leadership (Chapters 12, 15, and 16), is that, as leaders, we should begin the work ourselves and extend it to the organization, not the opposite.

Changing Results Requires Changing the System: "Data, Delta, Decision"

Putting definitions to work requires a deep understanding of the role of systems in healthcare. It starts with a simple question: "Do you *love* the results of your hospital or healthcare system?" If the answer is yes, then you have a perfect system, designed to deliver precisely those results. If the answer is no or "It depends," then there is an inexorable corollary—if you don't love your results or you love some but hate others, *you must change the system to get different results.* You cannot hate your results and love the system—the system is designed to get precisely those results. As we will explore in more detail, change is often hard, so we must have a *system to foster positive change.* The Danish philosopher Søren Kierkegaard noted, "The most important questions in life are simultaneously those asked least often."[3] The important question of how to effectively and nimbly change the system may be asked least often—but it is at the heart of battling burnout. The three constant questions focus on the core of change **(Figure 5-2)**:

> What are the *data*?
>
> What is the *delta*?
>
> What is the *decision*?

"What are the data?" refers to the metrics of the measures by which we judge success. "What is the delta?" refers to the difference between our target metrics and the metrics obtained during the measurement period. "What is the decision?" is specifically how the system will be changed to obtain the target metrics, since the system as it operated within the measurement period was perfectly

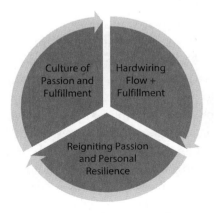

Figure 5-2: The Three Core Elements

designed to get precisely the results it got. Far too many leaders choose to "exhort the troops" to get higher metrics, instead of understanding that they are working in a flawed system that must be changed.

What does this have to do with burnout? First, the pressure to hit targeted metrics is in itself a stressor to those charged with reaching them, so the burnout "numerator" is higher. How can we change the system to increase the "denominator" of adaptive capacity in a commensurate fashion, so we don't produce burnout? The more that systems and processes are hardwired in an evidence-based fashion, the better it works for the patients and the people who take care of them. The three constant questions develop solutions that cut across all three core elements (changing the culture, hardwiring flow and fulfillment, and developing personal resiliency).

The Elements Necessary to Develop an Effective Change Strategy

How can we change the system itself to avoid burning out our teams? There are three important concepts:

- healthcare as a complex, adaptive system
- "connecting the gears"
- a pragmatic theory of *intrinsic motivation*, or "getting the 'why' right before the 'how'"

HEALTHCARE AS A COMPLEX, ADAPTIVE SYSTEM

The great leadership guru Peter Drucker[4] correctly noted that healthcare is a *complex adaptive system*, with multiple highly interrelated processes performed by professionals (physicians, nurses, and healthcare leaders) and essential services staff (laboratory, imaging, environmental services, food services, etc.). Sadly, Drucker's insight came only two years before his death, so we are deprived of an in-depth exegesis of healthcare from his highly analytical mind. Far too often it is subject to what Phillip Ensor originally described as *functional silos*,[5] in which interrelated processes are not sufficiently linked in a seamless fashion.

An example that demonstrates that healthcare is a complex, adaptive system comes from the work of Peter Senge, who was among the first to effectively articulate the critical nature of systems thinking.[6] Senge asked one of his colleagues, Daniel Kim, to devise a game that would demonstrate the concepts of systems thinking as a practical example of the way in which even seemingly disparate processes influence not just *other* processes but *all* other processes. The result was a game, which is still in use today, called *Friday Night at the ER*. Kim and his associates recognized that the complex, adaptive systems present in emergency departments were a way of teaching systems thinking to people while demonstrating the importance of moving from "silo thinking to systems thinking."[7] In healthcare, individual teams or units often attempt to maximize their results without sufficient thought of the impact on the overall system—or even the overall health of the patient. Leadership to improve burnout must emphasize the role systems thinking plays.

CONNECTING THE GEARS

Successful healthcare leadership requires disciplined strategies and tactics in the areas of most importance, which are, at a minimum, the following:

- clinical excellence
- patient experience
- patient safety—high-reliability organizations
- hardwiring flow for efficient, effective processes and systems

I call it "connecting the gears" **(Figure 5-3)**.[8] There are three important insights to this concept, the first of which is obvious and intuitive, while the second and third are less so. First, whenever we change any of the gears, it affects the patient. If moving one of those gears results in a negative impact for the patient, don't do it—or at a minimum rethink the change and how the negative impact could be removed.

The second insight is that each of those gears comprises a detailed, disciplined, and evidence-based set of systems and processes, not just "words on the walls." The challenge of leadership is not just to identify what success looks like and how it will be measured, but to enact an evidence-based path by which to get there.

Third, and this is the subtlest of the insights, is that you cannot move *any* of the gears without moving *all* the gears, since healthcare is a complex, adaptive system. For example, it is not uncommon in healthcare for teams to improve the results in their unit, while harming the results in others.

If we do not "connect the gears" in ways that are meaningful and actionable, both for the patient and for those who care for the patient, we inevitably create rework, inefficient and ineffective processes, poor results, frustration, friction, and burnout. But if each of those gears has a discrete set of disciplined, evidence-based solutions delineated, not only is burnout prevented, but passion can be reconnected.

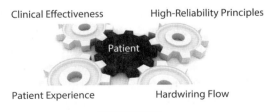

Figure 5-3: Connecting the Gears

CASE STUDY

An ICU team has been focused on reducing length of stay (LOS) as a key performance indicator. Working as a team, the ICU nurses and physicians have reduced LOS by 1.2 days, a metric that was celebrated at the hospital's management team meeting. However, shortly after, it was noted that there was a high rate of "bounce-back," in which patients are transferred out of the ICU who must be transferred back as a result of clinical deterioration, which was a source of dissatisfaction for all team members, the patients, and their families, as well as a risk to patient safety. It also resulted in an increase in total hospital LOS. The root cause in this situation was a failure to consider the systemic nature of patient care and the downstream effect that improving one metric may have on others.

GETTING THE "WHY" RIGHT BEFORE THE "HOW": AN INTRINSIC THEORY OF MOTIVATION

Highly trained and motivated members of the healthcare team always want to know, "*How* do we provide superior outcomes and a great experience for all of our patients?" That question, while understandable, misses Nietzsche's point that it is essential to discover the "why" that motivates professionals *before* the details of the evidence-based "hows" can effectively be put into action. Healthcare leaders should always start with the "why," as reflected in these common questions from the staff:

- Why are we doing this?
- Why are we changing?
- Why can't we keep doing what we're doing?
- Why is this change better than the way we're doing it?

The simplest answer, as noted throughout the book, is the following:

The way we're working isn't working.

Few healthcare professionals or leaders would claim that their systems are optimally designed, staffed, funded, resourced, supported, and maintained. The processes by which care is provided are often flawed and need improvement, as virtually all hospitals and healthcare systems operate in a significantly capacity-constrained environment. Evidence-based approaches make the job better by making the work easier. Successful implementation requires a disciplined approach applied to *every patient every time by every team member*. "Lead yourself, lead your team" is the key to that.

The "Why" Is That It Will Make the Job Easier In change efforts, failure occurs when team members believe the only reason to embrace excellence is that it is good for improving scores and building market share. (Try telling nurses on a busy unit that the reward for great patient experience is more patients. That won't seem like a reward to many of them.) Before asking others to master the "how-to," it is necessary for them to comprehend the "why-to."[9]

Why Get It Right? A-Team versus B-Team Members This question can be answered by asking the team to finish this sentence:

The number one reason to get things right in healthcare is . . .

Team members will state that it is good for the patient, the family, patient safety, risk reduction, market share, and metrics scores. These are all correct, but leaders must emphasize that the best "why" is this:

It makes your job easier.[10]

Like most people, healthcare professionals do not change easily. The most compelling, effective, and sustainable reason to change—for example, by improving patient experience, hardwiring flow, seeking clinical excellence, improving patient safety, or developing burnout solutions—is that it *makes the job easier* for the team. Providing quality clinical care at the bedside is a difficult job that seems to get more challenging every day. It should not be a surprise that team members push back when leaders say, "Oh, and by the way, get your scores up, too." For too many care providers, scorecards are just one more mandate among an already overwhelming list of "musts."

To demonstrate this concept, simply ask members of the team the question,

Do you offer quality, patient-centered care?

Some will say yes and some will say no, but the vast majority will say, "Sometimes" or "It depends." When the answer is "It depends," what does it depend on? The good news is that the team knows, as the following exercise shows. To determine the specific cause of this variability, consider asking the staff the following:

Are there days when you come to work, see the people you are working with, and say to yourself, "Bring it on! Whatever we've got to do today, these folks can make it happen"?

The answer will be yes. When asked to describe what they call the members of that team, they will answer, "the A-team." When asked, the team members will quickly list the attributes of the A-team:[10]

- positive
- proactive

- confident
- compassionate
- competent
- good communicators
- team players
- trustworthy
- do whatever it takes
- have a sense of humor

Now ask the team,

Are there also days when you go to work, see who you're working with, and think, "Shoot me, shoot me, shoot me. I can't work with them—I worked with them yesterday. Who in the world makes the schedule around here, anyway?"

That team is known as the B-team, and the staff will describe the characteristics of its members as follows:

- negative
- overreactive and hypersensitive
- confused about the team goals
- negative, backstabbing communicators
- lazy, shifting responsibility
- frequently arrive late to work
- always have an excuse about why they didn't . . .
- constant complainers with a victim mentality

Everyone on the team can name the B-team members—except of course the B-team members themselves. Amusing nicknames could be applied to members of this group.

- Nurse Ratched, the dour nurse from Ken Kesey's book *One Flew over the Cuckoo's Nest*, whom everyone recognizes (except, of course, Nurse Ratched herself)
- Tomas Torquemada, the grand inquisitor of the Spanish Inquisition . . . and it can feel as if one Dr. "Torquemada" can extract more pain in a single 10-hour day than Tomas Torquemada did in 10 *years* as the grand inquisitor
- Administrator Scrooge, the coldhearted, miserly "C-suite" member who immediately says "No!" to all ideas that don't have a guaranteed significant return on investment, strangling innovation and furthering burnout

Finally, ask the team members,

How many B-team members does it take to destroy an entire shift?

They will respond emphatically, in unison, "One!" One person can destroy, or at least dramatically lower, the morale of an entire, busy clinical unit. It happens every day. These insights point to ways to use the performance gap to drive intrinsic instead of extrinsic change.

The "Why" in Practice   Once the dichotomy of the A-team and B-team has been explained and demonstrated, there is an opportunity to make two important points. The "why" of change is that it makes the team members' jobs easier. If not, the change is not important. This point can be illustrated through the A-team/B-team exercise just described (and discussed in more detail in Chapter 17). The A-team attributes are evidence-based pathways to success; B-team attributes make the job harder for the rest of the team. All team members want to work with A-team members, all the time. If you can give them that hope, you will succeed.

The "why" of change also gives everyone hope that—finally—the B-team members will be held accountable for their actions, which affect our patients and their families and destroy our morale. Without this intervention, staff members are left to wonder when, if ever, we as healthcare leaders will enforce that accountability.

The role of the leader is to identify, accentuate, train for, and reward A-team behaviors while simultaneously searching for, confronting, and eliminating B-team behaviors, which should not be tolerated. *This is at the heart of why effective leaders have lower burnout rates among their teams.*

Leaders who accept the responsibility of ensuring patient focus and team collaboration and accountability tap into the brilliant wisdom of people like psychologists Abraham Maslow[11] and Eric Erikson[12] and psychiatrist Victor Frankl.[13] Each, in their own way, recognized this sage wisdom: "All meaningful and lasting change is intrinsically, not extrinsically, motivated."

Helping healthcare team members understand that the leadership team is fanatically dedicated to making their jobs easier not only communicates the "why" of change but also demonstrates that the leaders and their teams will be ready to bear almost any "how." The result of combined leader and staff buy-in is that metrics will rise and stay elevated because the "servant hearts" of the team will become intrinsically motivated to make their own jobs easier and make others' jobs easier as well. But far more important is the signal of hope it sends to team members that their jobs will be easier.

Then, and only then, is it appropriate to move on to the question of "how," as Peter Block indicates in the title of his provocative book *The Answer to How Is Yes: Acting on What Matters.*[14] Leaders are more successful when they focus less on the scores and more on the "why," asking,

What have I done today *that makes life easier for my team and my patients?*

In doing so, a powerful and sustainable force in your organization will be unleashed: intrinsic motivation for staff to *always* be members of the A-team.

Summary

- Since every system is perfectly designed to produce precisely the results it gets if healthcare leaders want to change the results, they must be courageous enough to change the system, since the way we're working isn't working.
- The three elements of a systems approach to burnout are the following:
  1. Instilling a culture of passion and professional fulfillment
  2. Hardwiring flow and fulfillment into systems and processes
  3. Reigniting passion and personal resilience
- Three questions should drive our conversations to change the system: "What are the *data*?"; "What is the *delta*?"; and "What is the *decision*?"
- Effective concepts to consider when developing change strategies are the following:
  - healthcare as a complex, adaptive system
  - "connecting the gears"
  - intrinsic motivation—getting the "why" right before the "how"
- The A-team versus B-team exercise demonstrates that "the number one reason to get this right is that it makes the job easier!"

6

A Model for Change and Mutual Accountability

Making shots counts. But not as much as the people making them.

MIKE KRZYZEWSKI, DUKE MEN'S
BASKETBALL COACH AND WINNER OF
FIVE NCAA NATIONAL CHAMPIONSHIPS
AND THREE OLYMPIC GOLD MEDALS[1]

A Model for Change and a Scorecard for Success

To conduct an assault on burnout, we need an effective model with which to frame the problem and a scorecard to monitor successes and the reasons for them. Our model starts with the assumption that the sources of burnout as a mismatch between job stressors and the adaptive capacity or resilience to deal with those stressors are twofold:

- personal factors (lead yourself)
- systemic/organizational factors (lead the team)

The journey begins with us since the work begins within. As personal transformation occurs, people are inspired to transform the culture and the systems and processes embodying the work we do. As noted previously, much of the current literature on burnout focuses on personal factors and how to improve personal resilience. But doing so exclusively ignores the critical role that our current *culture and system* have in producing burnout in the first place. More importantly, too much of the work to date has implied—if not explicitly stated—that *we* are the problem, instead of advocating the cultivation of personal resiliency by investing in the people themselves and not in what they can do for us.

Systemic/Organizational Factors: Culture and the Hardwiring of Flow and Fulfillment

The organizational factors producing burnout include the culture of the health-care system, as well as how effectively flow and personal and professional fulfillment are hardwired into the system.

I will define each of these elements shortly, but for now, let's simply focus on the role they play in producing burnout and the ways in which they can be changed to prevent or treat burnout. Culture and hardwiring flow + fulfillment are *organizational resilience*, or "creating the job you love," in the burnout equation.[2]

Personal Factors: Reigniting Passion and Personal Resilience

The power to reignite passion on a personal level cannot be overstated, which is why I start with "Lead yourself." It is by changing the way we're working at the systemic and personal levels that passion can be reignited and reconnected to purpose. *Personal resilience* is the foundation for the solution, but it is incomplete without changing culture and hardwiring flow and fulfillment—all three are needed for success. "The work begins within" and that work fuels us in making changes to the culture, systems, and processes.

The Model for Changing Burnout and Driving Fulfillment: Three Core Elements

These observations provide a framework of three core elements (**Figure 6-1**):

- creating a culture of passion and fulfillment
- hardwiring flow and fulfillment (systems and processes)
- reigniting passion and personal resilience

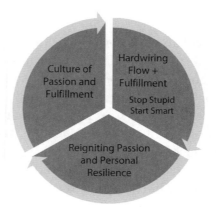

Figure 6-1: Three Core Elements of Addressing Burnout

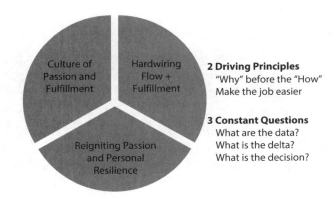

Figure 6-2: The Model for Decreasing Burnout and Increasing Fulfillment

This model demonstrates that culture, the hardwiring of flow and fulfillment, and personal passion and resilience are inextricably linked, with fully two-thirds of the burnout equation coming from how we work, and only about a third coming from personal issues. However, as I have noted, the best results occur in health systems that begin with facilitating personal resilience while working to change the culture and the system.

Let's consider how these three core elements combine to change the landscape of burnout and its solutions while maintaining an emphasis on getting the "why" right before the "how" by using intrinsic motivation and the three constant questions **(Figure 6-2)**. Combining these concepts creates the solutions discussed in Chapters 8–11, and the Mutual Accountability Jumbotron, which is discussed later in this chapter. This model provides a way to track progress toward the dual goals of systemic/organizational resilience and personal resilience, both of which increase the adaptive capacity of the system and the person to deal with job stressors.

CULTURE OF PASSION AND FULFILLMENT

The first core element is that the people and the systems and processes exist in an organizational culture, which must be based on passion and professional fulfillment. Regarding the successful transformation of that company, Lou Gerstner, former CEO of IBM, said, "I came to see in my time at IBM that culture isn't just one aspect of the game, it *is* the game."[3]

Culture is what people *do* in an organization, not just what they *say* they do. But it goes beyond that. It's also how people *think*—particularly how they think about change, improvement, and innovation, since those thoughts will change what they ultimately do. These insights are critical when considering burnout because the culture in which healthcare is provided will be quickly discerned by those providing the care. They know, before those in the C-suite do, when the "words and the music don't match." Here's a simple example, born from experience with the electronic health record (EHR).

CASE STUDY

Tamara Ellis is a highly rated and sought-after internist who specializes in hospital medicine, one of the fastest-growing specialties in healthcare. Her hospital introduced an EHR and mandated its use immediately. Unfortunately, the selection of the vendor was made without input from the line clinicians who would be using the EHR and was almost exclusively driven by the IT department. (To be fair, there were physicians on the committee, but none of them actively practiced medicine and they were widely referred to as "former physicians.")

Following the roll-out of the EHR, Dr. Ellis's productivity and patient experience scores fell dramatically. She became, in her own words, "more frustrated, cynical, and less effective." When she met with her service chief and expressed her frustration, he said, "That's just the EHR. You have to learn to live with it!" Shortly thereafter, she resigned her position to enter a concierge medicine practice, depriving the team of one of its "superstars."

There are many lessons to learn from this tale, but I will focus primarily on the culture of the organization for now. Let's start with the two driving principles:

1. "Why" before the "how"

2. Does it make the job easier?

In this case study, the "why" of the EHR appears to have been, "Because the boss says you have to do it." There was no serious consideration of involving clinicians in either the design or its implementation. As to the second question, far from making the job easier, it makes the work demonstrably harder, without consideration or explanation.

What other lessons can be gleaned from Dr. Ellis's experience and the culture in which it occurred? First, it illustrates that the organization does not have a change strategy in which those most affected by the change have a voice in the change itself. (If they aren't with you on the takeoff, they won't be with you on the landing.) In this culture, change is mandated from above. Second, the culture of the organization is siloed and does not take into account the fact that healthcare is a *complex, adaptive system*, where change in one area has predictable effects on others. Third, IT rules the roost in this culture, and the people caught up in the turmoil of the EHR change are left to fend for themselves. *This is a culture where the people serve the EHR, not the other way around.* (I will present solutions to Dr. Ellis's dilemma in Chapters 8 and 11.) Finally, despite what is proclaimed in the organization's mission, vision, and values, the culture in action is one where those providing care are treated as fungible instead of indispensable, even high performers like Dr. Ellis.

Culture in a Complex, Adaptive System Culture is continuously redefined and honed over time, and in response to a constantly changing landscape. The ability to develop the culture adaptively is perhaps the truest test of leadership.[4] Leaders who believe culture is fixed are doomed to failure, while leaders who see culture as an ever-adapting entity that reflects what actually happens, as influenced by a core set of values, can help guide their organizations forward.

Chapters 8–11 address how to use a matrix of questions to assess culture, the hardwiring of flow and fulfillment, and personal resilience, but here are some topline questions that help assess whether "the words and the music match" regarding culture:

- Is the person you report to passionate about their job?
- How, specifically, is that manifested?
- Does their passion help fuel your passion?
- Do they manifest behaviors that exemplify the culture?
- Do they demonstrate a commitment to their own wellness?
- Do they demonstrate a commitment to the team's wellness?

Words on the Walls versus Happenings in the Halls Chris Argyris notes that there is a fundamental difference between the "espoused theory," the theory promoted by leadership and management, and the "theory in action," which reflects how the organization actually operates.[5] Every healthcare system should carefully examine how closely its espoused theory matches its theory in action. What are the *actions* occurring in the interactions with each patient? Stated another way, pay attention to the "happenings in the halls instead of the words on the walls."[6] As lofty and noble as statements of mission, vision, and values can be, the true test is whether the "happenings in the halls" reflect those statements. Far too often, they don't and in some cases are diametrically opposed to the stated mission. Emerson said it well: "What you are stands over you and thunders so loudly I cannot hear what you say."[7]

In sharp contradistinction to the administrator in the previous case study, this CEO put the "why" of patient care ahead of the "how" of all the reasons it had never been done before. And the Boarder Patrol concept clearly made the job easier for the team—and improved the experience of the boarder patients. An essential part of the Boarder Patrol was using data on the number and types of boarders, the "delta" between the number of boarder hours and the target, and the concept empowered the morning huddles to make immediate decisions to reduce the boarder burden.

CASE STUDY

When I was the chairman of emergency medicine at a level 1 trauma center seeing over 100,000 visits a year, the emergency department (ED) was plagued by a massive "boarder burden," in which it was common to have one-third to one-half of the beds occupied by patients who had been admitted to the hospital but were waiting up to 12–18 hours to be placed in an inpatient bed. In the midst of one of our worst boarder days, I had a scheduled appointment with our CEO, Steve Brown.

Steve was a true "roll up his sleeves" executive who prided himself on exemplifying a lead-from-the-front style. I called Steve and said, "Boss, we need to do a 'walkie-talkie' today" (which meant that, instead of meeting in his office, we needed to walk and talk our way through the ED on rounds, a signature part of his leadership style). Instead of seeing statistics on boarder hours, Steve saw and met the patients boarding in the ED hallways.

We came to an 85-year-old lady, whose 92-year-old husband sat patiently at her side in a metal chair. Instead of just moving on, Steve insisted I introduce him. Once I did, he said, "Mrs. and Mr. Smith, my name is Steve Brown and I am the CEO—I run this place. I am so sorry this happened, but I promise you I will get you a bed and make sure this doesn't happen to anyone else in the future."

Steve was as good as his word and put the "Boarder Patrol" concept in place, which made the administrator on call responsible for meeting all boarders, whatever the time of day or night, to assure them they would get personal attention—and a bed.

This is as good an example as I have ever seen of making sure that the "words on the walls" match the "happenings in the halls." Without a commitment to a culture of passion focused on professional fulfillment, supported by timely patient rounding, Steve couldn't have heard Mrs. and Mr. Smith's voices. This story resonated through the halls of our medical center, proving that the leader meant what he said. Unfortunately, the opposite is also true far too often, as the following case study shows.

Based on these observations, I had to report that the organization's *espoused theory* wasn't matched by its *theory in action*—indeed, quite the contrary. What I observed was a persistent, pervasive demeaning pattern of interaction, which directly resulted in low team engagement, high rates of burnout, and low patient experience scores. This is an example of how a negative culture and the failure to hardwire flow and fulfillment produce frustrating—but predictable—results.

CASE STUDY

I was asked to work with a hospital's executive team, which had high aspirations for excellence and at least a "words on the walls" commitment to teamwork in service of a "through the patient's eyes with a servant's heart" mission. Despite their goals and stated commitment to hearing the voice of the patient, they were falling short and staff engagement surveys had turned downward in a dramatic fashion. After spending a week with the team, including watching them and their direct reports in meetings, on phone calls, and in the hallways, I was sorry to have to report this summary of what I observed:

- constant interruptions in meetings, a proclivity to debate instead of develop consensus, and a willingness to engage in confrontation that bordered on delight

- deep commitment to one's own proposed course of action instead of the team's

- inherent frustration in the inability to get a point across, regardless of how well reasoned and supported by data

- a "win at all costs" attitude that would have made Coach Vince Lombardi look like an amateur

- a tendency to interrupt the patient or family regularly in the uncommon instance in which an executive did round on patients

- communication that was nearly always one-way—a lot of talking, almost no listening

How to Move from the "Words on the Walls" to the "Happenings in the Halls" Once the difference between the "words on the walls" and the "happenings in the halls" is understood, how do we change this calculus to benefit the team?[8]

- Recognize it: Be clear in noticing the "delta" between what is said and what is done. Encourage others to do the same.

- Name it: Make sure the team understands this language and is attuned to it.

- Delineate it: State precisely what the disconnect is between the mission, vision, and values and the theory in use. Give examples.

- "Data, delta, decision" it: Use this format to drive the discussion down to the details.

- Resolve it by revisiting it: Constantly revisit the issue until it is resolved.

HARDWIRING FLOW AND FULFILLMENT: SYSTEMS AND PROCESSES THAT ADD VALUE, MAXIMIZE EFFICIENCY, AND DELIVER EFFECTIVE RESULTS

The second core element is assuring that all systems and processes are hardwired for flow and professional fulfillment by adding value, decreasing waste, maximizing efficiency, and delivering effective outcomes.

Defining and Creating Value My colleague Kirk Jensen and I coined the term *hardwiring flow* and wrote a book titled *Hardwiring Flow: Systems and Processes for Seamless Patient Care*,[8] designed as a practical guide to using an evidence-based, lean approach to improving flow in healthcare. We defined flow as follows: "*Flow* is defined as *adding value* and *decreasing waste* as our patients move through our service, processes, or behaviors by *increasing benefits*, *decreasing burdens*, (or both) when moving through our service transitions and queues." Simply stated, hardwiring flow means to "start doing smart stuff" that adds value, and to "stop doing stupid stuff" that creates waste. Flow and fulfillment are inextricable. We cannot attain fulfillment unless we hardwire systems and processes for smart stuff while eliminating stupid stuff **(Figure 6-3)**.

While some definitions of *value* stress that it is a ratio of healthcare *outcomes* divided by the *cost* of providing those outcomes, such formulations are not practical in assessing and delivering bedside care, particularly since "costs" are difficult to define, poorly understood, and largely beyond the control of those providing the care. What is the *cost* of an abdominal CT scan for a patient with abdominal pain? How does that relate to the *outcome*? What is the value of the abdominal CT relative to the number of negative CT scans necessary to identify one positive scan? How consequential does the CT finding have to be to be considered of *value*? How does any of this help doctors and nurses provide bedside care?

Very few people can hazard a guess as to the "cost" of an abdominal CT. Some might say, "Perhaps $3,000–$4,000?" But even if that number were accurate, that is not the "cost" of an abdominal CT. It is, at best, the "charge" for the

Hardwiring Flow

- Start Doing "Smart Stuff"—Adding Value
- Stop Doing "Stupid Stuff"—Decreasing Waste

Hardwiring Fulfillment

- "Fully Filling" Our Passion
- Fueling Our Fires to "Burn In"
- Stopping Burnout

Figure 6-3: Hardwiring Flow and Fulfillment

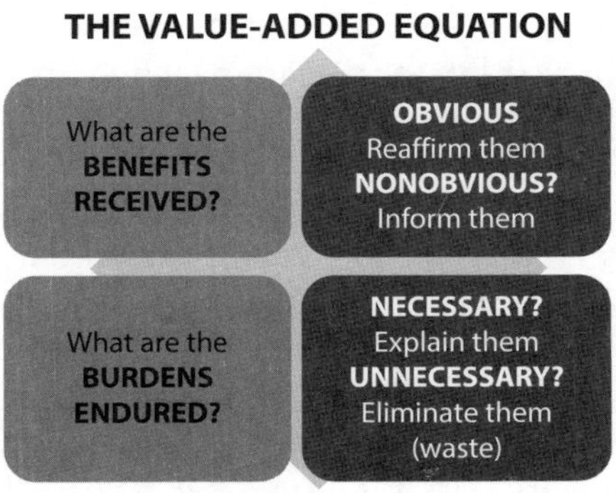

THE VALUE-ADDED EQUATION

Figure 6-4: The Benefit-Burden Ratio

procedure. (The marginal cost—the cost to do one more CT once the equipment and team members are in place—is nominal, perhaps a few hundred dollars. But the charge is many times that.)

Faced with these dilemmas of costs versus charges and trying to define outcomes in financial terms—which may well work in the macroeconomics of healthcare—we proposed a different definition of "value at the bedside": *Value is a ratio of the benefits received divided by the burdens endured to receive that value in the provision of quality care* (**Figure 6-4**).[8]

For a nurse or doctor at the bedside, this is a ratio that can be not only understood but also used to pragmatic effect for the good of the patient.

Value in Abdominal Pain A 32-year-old female presents to the ED with right-upper-quadrant abdominal pain, nausea, and vomiting. She has had two similar episodes of pain, but this is much worse. What value can her physician and nurse offer?

Aside from whatever broader equation is used for calculating value, the nurses and doctors in the ED can offer significant *benefits* with relatively few *burdens endured* to this patient almost immediately, including the following:

Benefits Received	**Burdens Endured**
Pain relief	Pain of starting the IV
Nausea and vomiting relief	Time to administer the meds
Rapid IV hydration	Time to obtain studies
Reassurance of the diagnosis	Anxiety until the diagnosis is made
Timely and efficient diagnosis	Several hours in the ED
Radiology and lab expedited	
Reassurance to the family	

This calculus of the benefit-burden ratio can be understood and used by the bedside caregivers—it doesn't require a PhD in healthcare economics to calculate *value.* Pain relief and stopping the vomiting are examples of *obvious benefits*, but they should still be reaffirmed with this language:

> *Your pain is likely coming from a gall bladder problem, but we can stop it with medication that works quickly and effectively, which I've asked the nurse to get for you. Your vomiting is coming from the same source, so he will get you a tablet you can put under your tongue, which works even faster than the IV route.*

Patients with nausea and vomiting are also dehydrated, which makes both the pain and vomiting worse. That is a *nonobvious benefit*, about which the patient needs to be informed, using scripts:

> *Ma'am, it's been my experience that people with pain and vomiting are dehydrated, which I confirmed by observing how dry your oral mucosa area is. We'll give you some IV fluid to "fill your tank" and the nurse will draw your blood at the same time so we don't have to stick you twice.*

The burden of anxiety can be eliminated early in the course of care:

> *Based on your symptoms and your physical examination, this is very likely due to your gall bladder, which is where your pain is, in the right upper area of your abdomen. When it goes into spasm, it can be quite painful and causes vomiting. In addition to the medications and IV fluid we are giving you, our team will bounce some sound waves off that area to see if the gall bladder wall is thickened or if there are stones in there, both of which are evidence of cholecystitis. You also have some "crackles" in your lung base over here, which are probably due to not breathing quite as deeply due to the pain, but since your pregnancy test was negative, we would like to do a chest x-ray just to make sure there isn't an infection. Does that all make sense? What questions do you have?*

An example of a *necessary burden* is the time needed to obtain the laboratory and imaging studies to confirm the diagnosis, which is a burden that should be explained. One of the best ways of doing that is a technique I learned from my colleague Ralph Badenowski from St. Vincent's Medical Center in Jacksonville, Florida, which led to me to refer to it as "Badenowski's Law."[9] It is a way of letting the patient and the family know that while they may spend several hours in the ED to obtain the studies to confirm or delineate the diagnosis, that time actually has a significant *value* compared with other settings in which the work could be done. Here's what Badenowski says to explain how the patient is getting "10 days of work done in about 4 hours":

> *Ma'am, we will take care of your pain and vomiting as fast as we possibly can, but the lab and radiology tests will take us about four hours to complete. But that's a real value where you get about 10 days of work done in*

about four hours, because, as you know, you didn't have to make an appointment to see me, you came right down to the ED. Many people wait several days to get an appointment with their doctor. And if you had pain in your doctor's office, they wouldn't be able to get the lab and radiology studies quickly like we can. You have to make an appointment and that takes several more days. We get the results of those studies within 30 minutes—you would have to wait a few more days to come back to the doctor to do that. So it will take about four hours, but we'll get 10 days of work done!

Badenowski's Law is a way of explaining obvious burdens to help create value from the patients' viewpoint. If burdens are unnecessary, they constitute waste and should be eliminated. For example, until recently, many radiologists and surgeons demanded that oral contrast be given to ED patients before obtaining abdominal CT scans, which delayed the study by as much as two hours per patient. However, except in limited circumstances, oral contrast was shown in numerous studies to be an unnecessary burden and was eliminated from the protocol, saving time, money, and discomfort for the patient.

Using the benefit-burden ratio to define value in healthcare drives decisions to the bedside, as well as encouraging the use of scripts as evidence-based language to help patients see the value they are receiving.

Using evidence-based disciplines to define value has three discrete effects:

1. It provides an actionable way to define and provide value at the bedside, by increasing benefits and decreasing burdens.

2. It leverages value as personally delivered through team actions tied to the systems in which that value is delivered.

3. It makes the job easier for the team by providing evidence-based disciplines by which to hardwire flow.

The third point is why I use the "hardwiring flow and fulfillment" formulation—because evidence-based, team-generated systems and processes to improve flow make the job easier and leverage the likelihood that professional fulfillment will be enhanced rather than diminished. If we are all collectively committed to adding value by increasing benefits and decreasing burdens, as well as eliminating waste, we are creating systems and processes of seamless care—good for the patient and good for those caring for the patient. When we hardwire flow through evidence-based leadership, we are also hardwiring fulfillment for those who provide the care.

Maximizing Efficiency and Delivering Effective Results The distinction between efficiency and effectiveness has been the source of debate and controversy. Archie Cochrane, in his book *Effectiveness and Efficiency: Random*

- Right resources (costs) for the . . .
- Right patient (core measures) in the . . .
- Right environment (bed) for the . . .
- Right reasons (evidence-based medicine) by the . . .
- Right team (best people) at the . . .
- Right time (flow metrics) . . .
- Every time! (high-reliability organizations)

Figure 6-5: Flow and the "Seven Rights"

Reflections on Health Service,[10] offers guidance on this subject. The fundamental question of *effectiveness* is simply, "Does it work?" In Cochrane's words, *efficiency* refers to the effect of "a particular medical action in altering the natural history of a particular disease for the better." This simple yet practical definition involves two parts:

- Does the action have a demonstrable effect? = Effectiveness
- Is the effect better? = Efficiency

Efficiency asks, "Is 'what works' worth the cost?" In this case, the cost is a calculus of dollars, time, and the effort requisite to produce the intended outcomes.

Jensen and I combined effectiveness and efficiency into the ability to use flow to produce the "Seven Rights" in healthcare, shown in **Figure 6-5**.

The *right resources* ensure that only the costs necessary are applied to the problem, whether clinical or administrative. The *right patient* ensures that core measures are used to define what measures will be used to gauge success. The right *environment* means that the MVP of the healthcare system, the bed, is used to the best advantage, and only for as long as the bed adds value.[8] The *right reasons* are the evidence-based protocols, open to iterative change as further evidence develops. The *right team* ensures that all those involved in the patient's care are operating at the top of their license and are best deployed to add value. The *right time* means that flow metrics are in place and monitored over time, so that flow, effectiveness, and efficiency are maximized. Finally, every patient, every time is an embodiment of the commitment to patient safety and high-reliability organizations. All of these "rights" are critical to both best outcomes and preventing burnout.

John Wasson at Dartmouth expressed this eloquently when he said, "They give me exactly the help I need and want exactly when and how I need and want it."[11] For those who think this an ambitious goal for all of healthcare, I ask this question: "If that were you, your spouse, your children, your mom or dad, your neighbor on that bed, isn't that precisely what you would not only *want* but *demand*?"

We must confess that the answer is "Yes!"

But the issue is not just whether we deliver value while maximizing efficiency and delivering effective results but also what the cost is—from the standpoint of stressors and the care providers' resilience or adaptive capacity to deal with those stressors. Does hardwiring flow and fulfillment enrich or deplete our teams and team members? One test of this is this question: "Are leaders willing to change processes and systems so their teams can stop doing 'stupid stuff' and start doing 'smart stuff'?" Are we able and willing to stop doing things we shouldn't be doing in favor of those things that are better for the patient—through the patient's eyes—while making the team members' jobs easier? A resounding "yes" gives hope we can reduce burnout and accelerate fulfillment. To "stop doing stupid stuff" requires the courage to state clearly that the ways we have been doing things aren't working . . . or at the very least aren't working well enough. That's the price of leadership.

REIGNITING PASSION AND PERSONAL RESILIENCE

While culture and the hardwiring of flow and fulfillment form the systemic/organizational sources of burnout and the resilience needed to combat it, the ability to reignite passion and develop and use the tools of personal resilience are the final third. This is the "learning to love the job you have" part of the equation. Chapter 8 covers this in detail, but the key is to use the six domains of burnout, as defined by Christina Maslach, as a format for building and maintaining personal resilience.[12]

- Diminishing stressors and increasing adaptive capacity: The domain of diminishing stressors is connected to changing culture and hardwiring flow, while increasing adaptive capacity develops both organizational and personal resilience.

- Seizing control: Seizing control starts with the personal and moves quickly to the organizational once the tide is turned, as we'll see in Chapters 8–10.

- Giving and getting rewards and recognition: Giving rewards always starts with the individual and stays with the individual, but it does redound to the broader culture.

- Returning community to healthcare: Community is a complex mix of individuals (and their resilience) coming together to form the broader culture and the systems and processes in which the community works.

- Demanding fairness in an unfair world: Fairness resides everywhere, all the time. If the system or those acting within the system act unfairly for one person, unfairness exists for all people. Fairness connects to all three core elements of burnout.

- Infusing values into your practice: This starts with individuals committing to their values in every action—including in leadership positions; their combined commitment to values defines the culture and hardwires flow and fulfillment.

A "Jumbotron" for Mutual Accountability

Success requires reporting efforts to address the three core symptoms of burnout, stating the effects on metrics for success, and noting progress made in the "data, delta, decision" format, all while using intrinsic motivation. Whether it is called a "Balanced Scorecard,"[13] "Pillar Management,"[14] or any of the other terms for the myriad ways of keeping score, measurement of important things matters, while measurement of trivial things does not—and the measurement of trivial things demoralizes and burns out those measured. Practicing medicine in the NFL is what I call "jumbotron medicine"—everything is up on the big screen for the entire stadium and all the viewers worldwide to see. (Before every Super Bowl, I meet with the team physicians, trainers, support medical staff, and referees. I always tell them the same thing, "Relax—there's only 80 million people around the world watching you.") It sometimes feels the same with our scoreboards in healthcare—everything measured is magnified, particularly when the metrics go south.

Begin by ensuring that those being measured have input on what is being measured. Be willing to toss out metrics that do not themselves *add value* by providing leverage in the "data, delta, decision" conversation. Make data conversations iterative—change data collection or data points in response to the changing needs of the complex adaptive system.

Keep in mind this wisdom: "What you permit, you promote."[15]

When systems, processes, languages, and behaviors contradict the "why" of the organization, leaders need to be courageous in correcting them. Otherwise, the team knows not only that the B-team has "gotten away" with it again but also that these behaviors are promoted when they are permitted to occur again and again. **Figure 6-6** shows how the jumbotron can be used with the three core elements and three constant questions to monitor the progress of action plans. This is described in more detail in Chapter 10.

The best jumbotron for burnout answers the three constant questions for each of the three core elements as they pertain to the area of focus. Using the examples in Figure 6-6, here is how the format can be used.

Culture of Passion and Fulfillment

Area(s) of Focus	Three Constant Questions
Passion/re-recruit A-team	Data? Turnover of A-team Delta? Difference between actual and target Decision(s)? Specific actions to re-recruit

Battling Healthcare Burnout
Mutual Accountability Scorecard

BURNOUT Organizational Personal	FOCUS	TOOLKIT
CULTURE • Passion • Fulfillment	PASSION	"Re-recruit" the A-team members
	PASSION FULFILLMENT	Servant leadership training, what kind of leader are you?
	PASSION	Appoint and fund wellness champions for each team
HARDWIRING FLOW + FULFILLMENT • Systems • Processes	EHR	Shadow shifting with A-team super users
	EHR	Unroof the "inbox abscess"
	FLOW	Stop doing stupid stuff, start doing smart stuff, send a signal of hope
	FULFILLMENT	Bounty hunt for unfairness, treasure hunt for fairness
	FLOW	Psychology of waiting tools and training
	FULFILLMENT	Develop and implement a "pain flight plan" champion
REIGNITING PERSONAL PASSION AND RESILIENCE	PASSION	"Love, hate, tolerate" tool
	RESILIENCE	ID stress tolerance level, disconnect hot buttons, don't let life be a surprise
	RESILIENCE	You are a performance athlete, do the things you tell your patients to do

Figure 6-6: Jumbotron for Mutual Accountability

Hardwiring Flow and Fulfillment

Area(s) of Focus	Three Constant Questions
Flow/treasure hunts for value, bounty hunts for waste	Data? Flow metrics, benefit-burden ratio Delta? Difference between actual and target Decision(s)? Stop doing stupid stuff; start doing smart stuff, send a signal of hope

Reigniting Passion and Personal Fulfillment

Area(s) of Focus	Three Constant Questions
Passion; love, hate, tolerate tool	Data? Burnout, resiliency, turnover Delta? Difference between actual and target Decision(s)? Accentuate "loves"; minimize "tolerates"; eliminate "hates"

Summary

- The model to address burnout involves three elements:
  1. Creating a culture of passion and fulfillment
  2. Hardwiring flow and fulfillment through systems and processes
  3. Reigniting passion and personal fulfillment
- The first two concern organizational resilience, while the third concerns personal resilience. All three are necessary to recognize, prevent, and treat burnout.
- Be aware of the trap of "the words on the walls" not matching "the happenings in the halls."
- *Flow* is defined as adding value and decreasing waste as our patients move through our services and processes by stopping stupid stuff and substituting smart stuff.
- *Value* is defined as a benefit-burden ratio, where value is increased as benefits increase, burdens decrease, or both.
- Flow depends on seven "rights":
  1. Right resources (costs) for the . . .
  2. Right patient (core measures) in the . . .
  3. Right environment (bed or facility) for the . . .
  4. Right reasons (evidence-based medicine) by the . . .
  5. Right team (best people for the specific job) at the . . .
  6. Right time (flow metrics) . . .
  7. Every time!
- The Mutual Accountability Jumbotron is needed to monitor progress.

7

Meaningfully Measuring Burnout

> *Not everything that counts can be measured. Not every-*
> *thing that can be measured counts.*
>
> ALBERT EINSTEIN[1]

Metrics and Leadership

Healthcare metrics have many positive but some negative attributes.[2–4] The positive attributes include the ability to establish baseline levels, the potential to use those baselines as a means to scientifically study evidence-based ways to improve outcomes, a pathway toward continuous improvement through best practices and the outcomes they produce, and, properly used in a positive culture, the intrinsic motivation of making the difficult job of healthcare fundamentally easier.[5] The negative aspects are not the measurements themselves but rather the ways they are used. When asked whether burnout surveys are good or bad, my answer is, "Like any intelligent question, it depends. What does it depend upon? It depends if you are going to use the survey as a 'tool' . . . or a 'club.'"[6]

Surveys should be used as a *tool*, a way of improving things not only from a metrics standpoint but also from a human standpoint. Are we using surveys solely for the sake of obtaining better *metrics*, or do they reflect better *outcomes* for the patients and for those who take care of the patients? Do the survey metrics lead to making the job easier for the healthcare team members? Do they provide a compass to find our way out of the barren territory of burnout? Do they create hope that things can be done in different, more fulfilling ways that help us reconnect to our passion?

Or are the surveys used as a "club," a blunt instrument to bludgeon the troops into a futile and seemingly never-ending pursuit of better numbers for the sake of numbers? Are they used to harass teams to obtain better scores than those of other units or sister hospitals, or even competitor healthcare institutions? This is a leadership issue—will the culture of your team allow the use of surveys as a tool, or will they be used as a club? Only leaders can make that choice, which must be made at the outset. Since the work begins within, look within yourself as a leader and ensure that *you* will use metrics as a tool, not a club.

Should we measure burnout? If so, what survey should we use? It depends on whether you want to make the problem better. If you do, commit to *measurement that matters*, meaning measurement specifically for the purpose of identifying sources of burnout and pathways to meaningful solutions to stop the toll extracted from our team members. Then act on them. If you don't want to make it better, just keep measuring and posting results, but don't lead the way in making meaningful changes to the culture, the systems and processes, or yourself. It's your choice.[7]

As a leader, if the level of burnout in your team breaks your heart because of the pain it is causing to the members of your team—and if you are committed to making a difference through the hard work of changing the culture, the system, and yourself—then by all means, choose a survey and implement it, but only if you have the will and tenacity to fanatically follow up on the results to tear down the obstacles to a passion reconnect. The most important question is not *which* survey to choose, but *whether you are committed* to acting on the stark results the survey will uncover. Are you and your team willing to use the results of metrics, including burnout and resiliency measures, to guide your efforts to stop doing stupid stuff and start doing smart stuff?

Very few things have the potential to inadvertently become more toxic to intrinsic motivation than "grades" or "scores," as Kohn,[7] Maslow,[8] Frankl,[9] Peters,[10] and many others have noted.[11-13] Many healthcare team members view metrics as "grades," largely because their leaders have used them as a club instead of a tool. The measurement of burnout is not immune to this and in fact is particularly prone to a paradoxical effect, since a baseline survey can be used by poor leaders to exhort the troops, "We need to improve our burnout results," which of course is often interpreted as meaning, "Stop being burned out." As Nicholas Beamon, CEO of OneTeam Leadership, says, "Are you serious? *I'm* the problem?"[14]

I admit to an evangelical commitment to the importance of the insight of Albert Einstein quoted at the beginning of this chapter, to which I add Peter Block's insight that "many people believe something doesn't meaningfully exist unless you can measure it. So much for love."[15] Measurement matters, but only when it is put in service of those being measured, so choose not only *what* survey to use but also *how* to use the survey for the benefit of those being surveyed. Harry Rhoads, cofounder of arguably the most successful speakers' organization in the world, the Washington Speakers Bureau, says, "The only reason for a person to give a speech is to help people."[16] The only reason to do a burnout survey is to help the people who are being burned out.

Factors to Consider in Selecting a Survey

When selecting a survey, there are several important factors to consider, each of which should undergo consideration by the team responsible for selecting the survey, after which a more informed decision can be made.

DIMENSIONS IMPORTANT TO THE STAKEHOLDERS AND TEAM MEMBERS

Does the survey instrument ask questions that capture the passion and interest of the team members? Are these the right questions to identify the right problems, or are they too abstract to be translated to practical solutions? Ask a core group of the team to rate the questions' ability to get to the right answers. "Survey the survey" by getting input from the team on the actionability of the survey in these areas.

ACTIONABLE ITEMS

Do the questions allow the team to devise strategies that can be put in action immediately? What would have to be true to take the responses to an actionable level? What needs to be done to remove obstacles to actionable items?

BALANCING SURVEY BURDEN WITH SUFFICIENT SPECIFICITY

The more questions, the longer the time and attention needed to respond. But does a one- to two-question survey give enough detail to lead to pragmatic solutions, or will it lead to vague actions with vague results? What is the "sweet spot" in this balance? Consult team members on this.

EASE OF ADMINISTRATION

Don't make the time and energy required by the process more burdensome than the results are worth. "Survey fatigue" is a very real phenomenon and should be expected. Don't burn out the team with a cumbersome survey on burnout.

SENSITIVITY TO DETECT CHANGES PRODUCED BY ENACTED SOLUTIONS

This is an emerging area but a critically important one. The focus is on solutions to battle burnout, but the survey (or the feedback from free-form questions and listening sessions with the team) must be able to connect actions with results. For example, if changes are made to systems and processes, will the survey be capable of detecting differences in burnout indicators? Similarly, when changes in culture occur, is the survey sufficiently sensitive to detect results?

STATISTICAL STRENGTH

While *face validity* is the most important factor, there will always be those in the organization who are focused on more detailed statistical analysis to ensure progress through benchmarking against norms.[17] When confronted with the dynamic tension between logic and the ability to show statistical proof, choose logic, as it will lead you to serving others faster and better.

FINANCIAL AND HUMAN CAPITAL COSTS

Nothing comes without a cost. Some of the surveys are not proprietary, especially for not-for-profits and research organizations, but the cost of administration of the survey and analysis of the results must be considered and calculated. How much staff time is needed for these functions?

Consider the cost of the proprietary Maslach Burnout Inventory (MBI) and the potential return on investment for the survey. The license to use and reproduce the MBI for a paper-and-pencil survey is $125 per 50 administrations and the manual (which is a succinct summary of burnout and the MBI survey process) costs $50, with volume discounts for large organizations.[18] For an organization with 500 physicians or 100 physicians and 400 nurses, the total discounted cost is less than $900, a largely insignificant cost given estimated costs of turnover in excess of $6 million if burnout issues are not addressed.[19] (See Chapter 1.) To the argument, "We can't afford the cost," my answer is, "You can't afford *not* to afford the cost."

Getting Started

Perhaps the hardest part of change is getting started. A compass helps, and the compass is the commitment to identifying the depth and breadth of the problem. Here are some suggestions for getting started.

- Start with the "why" of making the jobs of the team members easier by finding potential solutions, not just discovering the extent of the problem.

- Begin with a deep sense of humility. Remember that leadership failure is what led to burnout, at least on issues of organizational resiliency. Be prepared to face the raw truths of how the culture, systems, and processes have failed.

- If leaders are not committed to dealing with the problems the survey identifies, it is time to pull up and get that commitment either before or as a part of the rollout. Use return on investment as a lever to assist in securing that commitment.

- You are already surveying for measures on quality, safety, patient and team experience, engagement, and so on. Frame the addition of the burnout survey in the context of a commitment to improving organizational and personal resiliency. (Don't be surprised when the questions about metrics I posed earlier help focus metrics in other areas.)

- Experts in survey administration and interpretation, while helpful and perhaps essential, are not as important as making sure your team members are with you on the takeoff so they will be with you on the landing. This particularly includes key influencers, to whom the team will look for their reaction.

- Assure everyone at all levels that results will be transparent and focused on solutions. Think proactively about workflow and action plans to adapt to the results of the survey.

- Establish timelines for actions and follow-up.

- Who should be surveyed? Everyone in the organization. Full stop. At Best Practices, the physician group I founded, we had three rules:
  ○ Rule 1: Always do the best thing for the patient.
  ○ Rule 2: Do the best thing for those who take care of the patients.
  ○ Rule 3: Never confuse rule 1 and rule 2.[20]

- Surveying everyone ensures that you will capture responses from those who take care of the patient, as well as those essential service team members who care for the caregivers.

- How often should you survey? It depends—how much progress do you want? If you survey yearly, you will get yearly progress. If you want more frequent and consistent progress, then measure more frequently, even if not with a full-blown survey. My recommendation is to survey no less than annually but use free-form questions and listening sessions more often to maintain progress, particularly regarding advancing culture and hardwiring flow and fulfillment (systems and processes) issues.

- Monthly (or quarterly) team meetings should use the "three constant questions" approach (What are the data? What is the delta? What is the decision?). You are already integrating discussions of quality, safety, clinical guidelines, and patient experience into those meetings. Do the same with follow-up and feedback on burnout, ensuring that there is time to listen to the team's feedback on progress.

- During these meetings, start by being positive, accentuating progress, and thanking everyone for their feedback and hard work.

- Ask whether the action plans are generally moving in the right direction and what can be improved. Listening is critical for leaders, particularly early in the burnout efforts.

- There will be negative people with negative comments—expect them, but do not react to them. Let them know you appreciate their perspective and their willingness to share it, but ask for their solutions. Then ask whether they are committed to helping make the changes they suggest and what work they are willing to do to help. Above all, do not take it personally.

- When people are dominating the meeting (particularly with negative comments), simply say, "Thank you. Now let's get some other perspectives on the issue from those we haven't heard from."
- Recruit allies from the respected influencers on the team and enlist their commitment to speak up and lead improvement efforts.
- Don't get frustrated—and it will get frustrating. If you are making positive changes, you will be changing cultures, systems, and people, which is hard but worthwhile work. Without resistance, there is no meaningful and lasting change.[21]

Free-Form Survey Questions and Interviews

While the surveys listed shortly all have validity and are helpful, my experience and that of many others is that the use of free-form questions and interviews, in addition to the metrics from the surveys, is essential. Using the team members' own words is critical to capturing the fundamentally human cost of burnout and its effects on our team members. Leading ourselves and leading our teams through the fires of burnout requires as granular an understanding as possible of the sources and consequences of burnout. That requires "the voice of the patient," which in this case is the voice of the team members, since they are the "patients" suffering burnout.[22]

Free-form questions include the following:

- What are the biggest sources of burnout for you?
- What strategies have you used to battle burnout?
- What is the one thing that would reduce your burnout the most?
- How exhausted do you feel and why?
- Do you feel cynical about work? How could we work together to improve that?
- Do you feel a sense of meaning and purpose at work?
- What is your "deep joy," and have you been able to sustain that?
- What have been your biggest frustrations at work?
- What are your biggest job stressors?
- What could we do together to decrease those stressors?
- Do you feel you have enough adaptive capacity to deal with your stressors?
- What could the team work on to help increase adaptive capacity?
- What could you work on to help?

The only major drawback to free-form questions is that it is harder—but not impossible—to develop the answers into a statistical analysis. In my view, the richness of the answers and the ability to tie those answers to meaningful solutions far outweigh this.

Burnout Surveys and Burnout Plus Well-Being Surveys

Figure 7-1 summarizes the details of the available surveys, but a discussion of each is presented in this section. The National Academies of Sciences,

Survey Instrument	Strengths	Limitations
Burnout Surveys		
Maslach Burnout Inventory (Human Services Survey)		
22 items, 7-point Likert scale • Exhaustion • Cynicism/depersonalization • Personal accomplishment	Gold standard National database Detects effects of changes well	Fee for use Length of survey
Maslach Burnout Inventory (2 Items)		
2 items, 7-point Likert scale • "I feel burned out from my work" • "I feel more callous toward people . . ."	Stratifies elements Brief	Fee for use Questionably sensitive to change Limited benchmarks
Physician Worklife Survey (Mini-Z)		
10 items and 1 open-ended question, 5-point Likert scale *or* 1 item, 5-point Likert scale • "Overall, based on your definition of burnout, how would you rate your level of burnout?"	Scores correlate with outcomes of interest Relatively brief	Limited correlation with outcomes Limited to emotional exhaustion
Copenhagen Burnout Inventory		
16 items	All professions Very short Easy to do analysis Free	Length Rarely used in the US Limited benchmarks

(*continued*)

Oldenburg Burnout Inventory		
19 items	Free All professions	Complex to analyze
Burnout Plus Well-Being Surveys		
Well-Being Index		
7 burnout items and 2 items about satisfaction with work life and meaning at work • "The work I do is meaningful to me." • "My work schedule leaves me enough time for my personal/family life."	Free All professions Burnout and fulfillment	Fee for for-profits and online version Unclear relationship to solutions
Stanford Professional Fulfillment Index		
16 items, 5-point Likert scale • Professional fulfillment • Work exhaustion • Interpersonal disengagement	Brief Free for nonprofits/research Analysis is simple Burnout and fulfillment Sensitive to change	Moderate analysis complexity Moderate length Benchmarking data evolving

Figure 7-1: Strengths and Limitations of Burnout Surveys and Burnout Plus Well-Being Surveys

Engineering, and Medicine's 2019 report *Taking Action against Clinician Burnout* notes, "Although single-item measures of burnout are frequently used, the ability of such items to measure the holistic construct of burnout are unclear, their validity data are less robust, and their use cannot be recommended at this time."[23]

BURNOUT SURVEYS

Each of the following measures is designed to measure burnout exclusively.

Maslach Burnout Inventory (Human Services Survey) The most widely recognized and well-validated "gold standard" for quantifying burnout is the MBI, a proprietary survey with 22 questions on a seven-point Likert scale that takes 10–15 minutes to complete and integrates questions on emotional exhaustion, cynicism/depersonalization, and loss of efficacy or personal accomplishment.[24] (While there are three versions of the MBI—the Human Services

Survey, the General Survey, and the Educators Survey—research on burnout has focused on the Human Services Survey, so all subsequent references to the MBI are to that survey.) The MBI has the strongest construct validity data for use with physicians and other members of the healthcare team and has been in continuous use for over 40 years.[25] Since the MBI was developed in response to the definition of burnout that encompasses exhaustion, cynicism/depersonalization, and loss of personal accomplishment, its measures are directly tied to those concepts.

Burnout is most appropriately viewed as a continuous variable, ranging from low to moderate to high, and not a dichotomous variable that is either present or absent (although other surveys attempt to cast it as the latter).[26]

- High burnout: High scores on the *emotional exhaustion* and *cynicism* subscales and low scores on the *personal accomplishment* subscale
- Average burnout: Average scores across all three subscales
- Low burnout: Low scores on the *emotional exhaustion* and *cynicism* subscales and high scores on the *personal accomplishment* subscale[26]

Each of the three core symptoms of burnout should be considered, as well as their connection to the integrated model, using the six domains of burnout discussed in detail in Chapters 1 and 2.

Maslach Two-Question Survey Because of the time required to conduct and analyze the full 22-item MBI survey, West and colleagues[27] culled the two prompts from the MBI with the highest loading factor on the emotional exhaustion and depersonalization/cynicism subscales:

- "I feel burned out from my work."
- "I have become more callous toward people since I took this job."

The two-item survey has been shown to have high correlation with the full MBI on the emotional exhaustion and depersonalization scales and has been used in some healthcare systems to reduce responder burden. Others have used the full MBI initially, followed by the two-item scale for follow-up.[27]

Duke Modification of the MBI Based on the observation that the single most reliable indicator of burnout is measurement of emotional exhaustion, Bryan Sexton and his colleagues at Duke Health developed and validated a modification of the MBI, using five items of the original nine-item emotional exhaustion scale, and using a five-point Likert scale instead of the MBI's seven-point scale **(Figure 7-2)**.

The mean of the five items is converted to a 0–100 scale, with higher scores indicating more severe emotional exhaustion, and scores of greater than 50 used

The Duke Modification of the MBI
1. "I feel frustrated by my job."
2. "Events at work affect my life in an emotionally unhealthy way."
3. "I feel burned out from my work."
4. "I feel frustrated by my job."
5. "I feel fatigued when I get up in the morning and have to face another day on the job."

Figure 7-2: The Duke SCORE (Safety, Communication, Operational Reliability, and Engagement) Assessment

as a threshold for concern about emotional exhaustion and therefore burnout.[28] The tool is nonproprietary and therefore free for use.

Physician Worklife Survey (Mini-Z Full and One-Item) The Physician Worklife Survey (PWLS) or "Mini-Z" Burnout Survey was developed by Mark Linzer and his colleagues at Hennepin Regional Medical Center and is promoted by the American Medical Association's Steps Forward program.[29] It consists of 10 questions plus an additional, optional, open-ended question: "Tell us more about your stresses and what we can do to minimize them."

Some healthcare systems have used the single-item version of the PWLS: "Overall, based on your definition of burnout, how would you rate your level of burnout?" The responses are on a five-point Likert scale:

- "I enjoy my work. I have no symptoms of burnout."
- "I am under stress, and I don't have as much energy as I did, but I don't feel burned out."
- "I am definitely burned out and I have symptoms of burnout, e.g., emotional exhaustion."
- "The symptoms of burnout that I am experiencing will not go away. I think about work frustrations a lot."
- "I feel completely burned out. I am at the point where I may need to seek help."

Studies of the PWLS single-item survey have small numbers and included primary care settings almost exclusively. As its title indicates, it was designed for use with physicians. The single-item scores were associated with lower job satisfaction, greater likelihood to leave medical practice, medical error (self-reported), and less than optimal patient care practices. However, single-item scores from the PWLS do not correlate as well with the full MBI emotional exhaustion scale when compared with the original single-item MBI emotional exhaustion item.[30–31]

Copenhagen Burnout Inventory The Copenhagen Burnout Inventory evaluates personal work-related and client-related burnout. It comprises 16 data elements organized into three domains: *personal* (physical and psychological fatigue and exhaustion), *work* (physical and psychological fatigue and exhaustion related to work), and *client/patient-related*.[32] It is moderately complex to analyze. There are no national benchmark data in healthcare, and it is not widely used by healthcare systems unless they have had previous experience doing so.

Oldenburg Burnout Inventory The Oldenburg Burnout Inventory measures physical, cognitive, and affective exhaustion and disengagement from work, comprises 19 items, and can be used with any occupation.[33] It is free to use but has no construct validity in US physicians or other healthcare workers. For that reason alone, it is not likely to be a common choice for a burnout survey.

BURNOUT PLUS WELL-BEING MEASURES

Two measures are designed to combine dual measurement of burnout and professional fulfillment. Tait Shanafelt was instrumental in the development of both, the first while at the Mayo Clinic and the second with Mickey Trockel at Stanford.

Well-Being Index The Well-Being Index was designed by a team at the Mayo Clinic to identify distress as measured by burnout, fatigue, low mental or physical quality of life, depression, and anxiety or stress through what was originally a seven-item instrument, which was later expanded to nine items, with the additional two items intended to assess satisfaction with work life and meaning in work.[34] The last two elements were intended to identify individuals who were thriving. The original studies were done in medical students and residents and then extended to a comparison of 5,400 US workers and 6,900 physicians.[35] There is an effort under way to extend insights to nurses and advanced practice providers.

The questions include the following:

During the last month:
1. Have you felt burned out from your work?
2. Have you worried that your work is hardening you emotionally?
3. Have you often been bothered by feeling down, depressed, or hopeless?
4. Have you fallen asleep while stopped in traffic or driving?
5. Have you felt that all the things you had to do were piling up so high that you could not overcome them?
6. Have you been bothered by emotional problems (such as feeling anxious, depressed, or irritable)?
7. Has your physical health interfered with your ability to do your daily work at home and/or away from home?

8. The work I do is meaningful to me.
9. My work schedule leaves me enough time for my personal/family life.

The Well-Being Index is free for research use or for use by nonprofits for quality-improvement purposes. It can be accessed and information regarding cost can be found at https://www.mededwebs.com/well-being-index.

Stanford Professional Fulfillment Index   The Stanford Professional Fulfillment Index measures burnout and professional fulfillment in physicians, with the intent of extending it to other healthcare professionals.[36] The 16-item, five-point Likert scale survey was designed by the Stanford WellMD program.[37] The items fall into these categories:

- professional fulfillment (items 1–6)
- work exhaustion (items 7–10)
- interpersonal disengagement (items 11–16)

The questions are the following:

How true do you feel the following statements are about you at work *during the past two weeks*?
1. I feel happy at work.
2. I feel worthwhile at work.
3. My work is satisfying to me.
4. I feel in control when dealing with difficult problems at work.
5. My work is meaningful to me.
6. I am contributing professionally (e.g., patient care, teaching, research, and leadership) in the ways I value most.

To what degree have you experienced the following?
1. A sense of dread when I think about work I have to do
2. Physically exhausted at work
3. Lacking in enthusiasm at work
4. Emotionally exhausted at work

During the past two weeks my job has contributed to me feeling . . .
1. Less empathetic with my patients
2. Less empathetic with my colleagues
3. Less sensitive to others' feelings/emotions
4. Less interested in talking with my patients
5. Less connected with my patients
6. Less connected with my colleagues

The survey is available in Trockel and colleagues' article on it.[36] It can be used at no cost for nonprofit organizations for research or program evaluation.

Cost for for-profit use can be obtained from wellness.surveyteam@TheRisk-Authority.com. The Stanford Professional Fulfillment Index is currently in use by the Stanford Wellness Consortium, which comprises over 20 not-for-profit healthcare systems across the United States.[38]

Measuring Resiliency: The Connor-Davidson Resilience Scale The scale most commonly used to measure resiliency is the Connor-Davidson Resilience Scale, which began as a 25-element, four-point Likert scale but has since been shortened to 10-element and 2-element scales, the latter of which has been shown to be a validated and standardized measurement of the "bounce-back" and adaptability aspects of resilience and is the most widely used version in healthcare.[39–40] The two-question version consists of the following:

- I am able to adapt when changes occur.
- I tend to bounce back after illness, injury, or other hardships.

Scoring of the scale is based on the sum of scores for each item, ranging from 0 (the characteristic is not true at all) to 4 (it is true nearly all of the time), resulting in a total score ranging from 0 (the lowest resilience level) to 8 (the highest resilience level). More recent studies of resilience have used the two-question version.

Where Should We Go from Here?

If all this seems a great deal to process, it is. Get a team together (if your hospital or healthcare system hasn't already done so) and consider the options available. If your system already has a survey instrument in place, accept it, but you can also build from it in several ways. In some cases you can add additional questions to the survey to make them more specific and actionable for your team. If that isn't allowed, consider doing a separate survey for your team, focused on its unique opportunities and challenges. In my view, free-form questions and interviews are the single richest source of information on the discrete sources of burnout, they allow for development of solutions, and they create an opportunity to enlist the passion and talents of the team to battle burnout in their work life. Get the conversation started and make it easy to talk about burnout. Don't let it be a silent epidemic any longer. Transparency and integrity are key, and sunlight is a great disinfectant. Recruit a core group of passionate teammates who will be part of the guiding coalition to lead the effort to reduce job stressors while increasing organizational and personal resiliency or adaptive capacity. Create hope by fusing your commitment to change the organization with the team's commitment to lead themselves and their teams.

Summary

- To meaningfully measure burnout, use the surveys as a "tool," not a "club," which provides a clear path toward solutions rather than just identifying the incidence of burnout.

- Numerous factors should be taken into account in selecting a survey, including dimensions of importance to the team being surveyed, the balance between survey burden and sufficient specificity to drive action plans, ease of administration, sensitivity to detect improvements, and cost. The most important is ensuring the survey captures what matters to the team.

- Free-form questions provide a valuable tool for solutions.

- The "gold standard" is the Maslach Burnout Inventory, which is also the longest.

- Get started—get a powerful guiding coalition of influencers, stress transparency and integrity, "make the leap into the waters" of measurement, and create hope by developing action plans to decrease job stressors while increasing organizational and personal resiliency by leading yourself and your team.

Part Two

Developing and Implementing Solutions

Battling healthcare burnout can only be successful when our definitions drive solutions to decrease job stressors while increasing resiliency/adaptive capacity. The solutions fall into three broad dimensions and one that cuts across all the dimensions. The dimensions are as follows:

1. Culture of Passion and Fulfillment

2. Hardwiring Flow + Fulfillment
   - Stop doing stupid stuff
   - Start doing smart stuff
   - Decrease stressors by changings systems and processes

3. Reignite Personal Passion and Resilience—"The work begins within"

Successful solutions for each of these areas developed from work with hundreds of thousands of team members are presented in detail. The area that cuts across all three areas is the electronic health record, which has reduced massive stressors to every healthcare team member, for which many solutions are presented.

8

Sustaining Personal Passion and Resilience

*When we are no longer able to change a situation, we
are challenged to change ourselves.*

VICTOR FRANKL, *MAN'S SEARCH FOR MEANING*[1]

Reigniting Passion and Personal Resilience

Healthcare team members are artists, scientists, leaders, and tellers of the great stories of our patients. Our burning passion is to step into the lives of those we serve, in the hope of making those lives better or at the very least easier. The following two chapters focus on organizational resiliency (changing the situation), while this one, in Frankl's words, addresses the challenge "to change ourselves." The Stoic philosopher Hecato of Rhodes remarked, "What progress have I made? I have begun to be a friend to myself."[2] Beginning to be a friend to ourselves is an essential corollary to understanding that the work begins within.

In focusing on reigniting passion and personal resilience, two central ideas serve as the foundation:

1. Every member of the healthcare team is a leader and needs personal leadership skills to do their jobs. *Lead ourselves, lead our teams.*

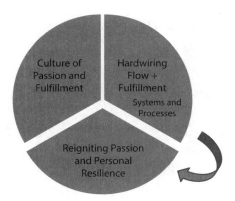

2. Every member of the healthcare team is a high-performance athlete, no less than the men and women at the highest levels of sport, and they thus require the same principles of performance, rest, and recovery. *Invest in ourselves, invest in our teams.*

All of us have a responsibility to "work on ourselves." That work takes different forms for different people but shares many common aspects that fuel our values and further our passion. This chapter focuses on strategies to reignite passion and personal resilience. As Tom Peters so eloquently notes, "You are the CEO of 'Me, Inc.'"[3] Make sure you are investing in yourself by reigniting passion and personal resilience—that will increase the shareholder value of "Me, Inc."

An important word of caution: even if your organization lags behind in doing its part to develop organizational resiliency, now is precisely the time to redouble *your* efforts to develop *your* personal adaptive capacity, since you will need it to deal with the job stressors of an organization not yet fully committed to increasing its resiliency.

However, what works magically for some people may not work at all for others. For example, pursuing "mindfulness" is one strategy discussed here that is commonly advocated as a solution to mounting stressors and burnout.[4] For some of you, it is an appealing strategy and one that you may have been considering or are beginning to pursue. For others, the response might be, "Oh no—not that 'touchy-feely' stuff again. If one more person tells me to be 'mindful' I'm going to scream." Given the breadth of background and interests of the members of the healthcare team, it's not surprising that one size never fits everyone. Without being encyclopedic, I have tried to share whatever solutions have been proved to have value by numerous healthcare sources. As in other chapters, I have classified these solutions according to how they best fit into the six Maslach domains.[5] However, six solutions cut across all the domains and are therefore presented first. These solutions are listed here, and the domains and the rest of the solutions associated with them are shown later in **Figure 8-1**.

- deep joy, deep needs
- throw guilt in the trunk
- make the patient part of the team
- precision patient care
- chief storyteller
- strategic optimism

Solutions across All Domains: The "Big Six"

Six solutions cut across all of the domains and should be used by all team members, regardless of where or what work they do. They are all leadership skills requisite for the demanding work of being a leader in healthcare.

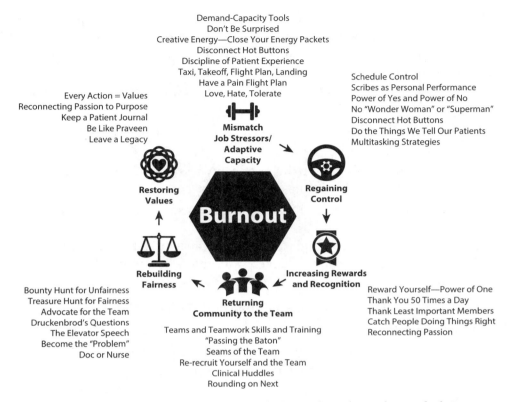

Demand-Capacity Tools
Don't Be Surprised
Creative Energy—Close Your Energy Packets
Disconnect Hot Buttons
Discipline of Patient Experience
Taxi, Takeoff, Flight Plan, Landing
Have a Pain Flight Plan
Love, Hate, Tolerate

Mismatch Job Stressors/ Adaptive Capacity

Schedule Control
Scribes as Personal Performance
Power of Yes and Power of No
No "Wonder Woman" or "Superman"
Disconnect Hot Buttons
Do the Things We Tell Our Patients
Multitasking Strategies

Every Action = Values
Reconnecting Passion to Purpose
Keep a Patient Journal
Be Like Praveen
Leave a Legacy

Restoring Values

Regaining Control

Burnout

Rebuilding Fairness

Bounty Hunt for Unfairness
Treasure Hunt for Fairness
Advocate for the Team
Druckenbrod's Questions
The Elevator Speech
Become the "Problem"
Doc or Nurse

Returning Community to the Team

Increasing Rewards and Recognition

Reward Yourself—Power of One
Thank You 50 Times a Day
Thank Least Important Members
Catch People Doing Things Right
Reconnecting Passion

Teams and Teamwork Skills and Training
"Passing the Baton"
Seams of the Team
Re-recruit Yourself and the Team
Clinical Huddles
Rounding on Next

Figure 8-1: Solutions to Reignite Passion and Personal Resilience by Maslach Domain

DEEP JOY, DEEP NEEDS

In the Introduction and Chapter 4, I briefly mentioned that I told our three sons each day when they were younger as I dropped them off at school that it was "one more step in the journey of discovering where your deep joy intersects the world's deep needs."[6] The consistent message to our sons was to begin with their "deep joy" as opposed to the "world's deep needs," since all of us must discover what we enjoy doing, where we enjoy doing it, the kind of people we want to share the journey with, and the circumstances under which all of this occurs. "Deep joy" is simply the passion that fuels you. Once you know that, the rest of the "world's deep needs" are simply details to be filled in over time. You can't give what you don't have, and you can't know what you have until you discover your deep joy.

Closely related to the concept of "deep joy, deep needs" is the importance of relationships, connectivity, and trust to health and happiness. Bob Waldinger is the fourth director of the Harvard Study of Adult Development. While that might sound a bit dry, it is the world's longest and most intense study of what makes people happy over time. In what are also known as the Grant and Glueck studies, since 1938 Harvard has been intensely studying 258 members of the Harvard sophomore class and 456 men from the Boston inner city to determine what factors were most responsible for health, longevity, and happiness. (As Waldinger notes, the men from the inner city always ask, "Why do you want to study me? My life isn't all that interesting." Waldinger observes, "The Harvard men never ask that question.")[7-8]

Among the many insights from the study, the two most powerful ones are these:

- Loneliness kills—it kills not just happiness but health and longevity as well.
- The single strongest predictor of happiness and a "good life" is having good relationships built on trust.

Everyone in healthcare whom I hold in esteem is someone I trust—and they trust me.

When job stressors grow and your adaptive capacity is thinning, reach back and rediscover your "deep joy." Chapter 17 discusses how to use the "deep joy" tool to do just that.

THROW YOUR GUILT IN THE TRUNK—LIGHTEN UP ON YOURSELF

We need to find a cleaner-burning fuel than guilt.

RICHIE CANTOR, PEDIATRIC EMERGENCY
PHYSICIAN AND TOXICOLOGIST[9]

Cantor is an expert on toxins. He also knows that among the most lethal of those toxins is guilt, which can extinguish passion in a flash if we let it. I ask people how they get to work and most answer, "I drive my car." I answer, "Do me a favor—next time you go to work, before you go in, open your trunk and throw all your guilt in there. Because it won't help you in any way when you are inside." This is a delicate balance, because as I've said before, guilt weighs heavily on those who admit they are burning out; they think they are too strong—or should have been—for that to happen. Nearly all victims of burnout think, "I can't believe I burned out—I thought I was better than that." We must all recognize that there's no shame in burnout. Leave the guilt behind; it only weighs you down.

The first step to throwing guilt in the trunk is recognizing it for what it is. Guilt comes from many places but almost always has its origins in how we grew up. There are always places deep in the psyche or soul that to this day cause us to feel badly. *Face, trace, and erase them.* The second step is to forgive yourself, regardless of how serious *you feel* your real or perceived transgressions may be. Remember, as Wayne Sotile, a pioneer in the study of physician burnout, says, "Self-care is critical care."[10] And yet most of us were taught that self-care was selfish. Third, remember that almost without exception, the events from which guilt arises weren't as bad as you remember. Or as Mark Twain wrote, "I have known a great many troubles, but most of them never happened."[11] Fourth, recall that "when you're in your own mind, you are behind enemy lines."[12] We would never judge others nearly as harshly as we have learned to judge ourselves. In fact, if we saw someone being that judgmental, most of us would confront that person and say, "You can't treat her that way—it's unfair." Don't treat yourself that way either.

Tom Jenike, the chief well-being officer at Novant Health, one of the nation's leaders in physician and team well-being, often says, "We have to be World Class at caring for ourselves and our team members so they can be World Class at taking care of our patients."[13]

MAKING THE PATIENT A PART OF THE TEAM

One of the tools that helps build personal resiliency the most is the concept of making the patient part of the team, which I introduced in Chapter 1 but is briefly summarized by these three points:

- Shift from asking "What's the *matter with you*?" to "What matters *to you*?"
- That helps move the patient from being a *recipient* of care to being a *participant* in their care.[14]
- The voice of the patient means, "Nothing about me without me."[15]

A constant focus on these areas makes the patient a part of the team and increases our personal adaptive capacity.

PRECISION OR PERSONALIZED PATIENT CARE

The concept of precision or personalized patient care, also described in Chapter 1, is another of the powerful tools to increase personal resiliency. As an emergency physician practicing in a 120,000-annual-visit, level 1 trauma center, I practice precision patient care by realizing that no two patients are alike, even with something as straightforward as an ankle sprain. That starts with always asking the same question of each patient: "What's the most important thing *to you* we can do to make this an excellent experience?"[16]

Precision patient care allows team members to tailor their care specifically to the person behind the disease, instead of focusing on a "one size fits all" approach. While the technical, clinical care may be the same for some patients, the precise way in which their care is managed after the diagnosis is made is at the core of precision patient care.

This is also true in diagnosing, preventing, and treating burnout and is much more than a theoretical distinction. For example, if a person's burnout symptoms reflect feelings of loss of meaning in work, should the presumption be made that treatment should focus only or largely on that aspect, or should it automatically be presumed that the patient had to have progressed through exhaustion and cynicism to get to loss of meaning in the first place? All three of the dimensions occur early, if differentially, in each person, and the treatment needs to be tailored to the needs of the person's burnout symptoms, based on surveys and open-ended conversations, as I discussed in detail in Chapter 7.

CASE STUDY

One evening, I saw a 15-year-old female lacrosse player with an inversion injury of her ankle. I performed a careful evaluation, during which I explained everything that I was doing, as well as the anatomy of the ligaments and bones of the ankle and first-, second-, and third-degree sprains. Although a fracture seemed unlikely, I described why we were obtaining an ankle radiograph.

When the radiograph was completed, I pulled the computer on wheels into the room, sat down, and demonstrated to the athlete and her family that the images confirmed my clinical diagnosis. I told them we would be discharging her soon and that she would be on crutches for several days and would need rest, ice, compression, and elevation during the next week. Asking what questions she had, I thought she was overreacting when she burst into tears.

It was then that I realized I had forgotten to use precision personalized care and had not asked, "What's the most important thing to you that would make this a great ED visit?" When I did ask that question, she told me she was a recruited athlete, the state championship was in four days, and several college coaches were going to be there to scout her. Playing in that game was the most important thing to her. I felt foolish. While I had made the correct clinical diagnosis, I had failed her by not considering what this injury meant to her.

I learned late, but not too late, what was most important to the patient and was able to arrange aggressive cold compression treatments, physical therapy sessions with the local professional team, and ankle taping by an athletic trainer. She was able to play in the state final in front of numerous women's college lacrosse coaches . . . and me.

CHIEF STORYTELLER, CHIEF SENSEMAKER

Reigniting passion and personal resiliency in healthcare requires the fundamental recognition that nurses and physicians have a nondelegable role as the "chief storytellers" for the patient and family.[17-19] *I believe there is no greater way to reignite passion and personal resilience than to control the narrative of your patients' care by accepting the dual roles of chief storyteller and chief sensemaker.*

Patients come to hospitals and healthcare systems because their lives are disrupted by pain, injury, and many other symptoms that they do not fully understand. Nurses and physicians have the role of the chief storyteller, who tells the story that otherwise the patient and the family may not fully understand. Doctors and nurses explain their symptoms and tell them the story of how the team will use diagnostic tools and studies to determine the etiology and devise the most effective treatment.

CASE STUDY

When our middle son, Kevin, was nine years old, I came home from work and found him nose deep in his literature homework. He asked whether I could help him. I read the passage carefully, thought for a minute, and told him what it said. His response was, "Dad, I know what it says. What does it mean?"

However, we not only need to tell patients the story of their care; we need to act as chief sensemakers as well. The chief storyteller tells the story of the symptoms, the diagnosis, and the proposed treatment, while the chief sensemaker integrates "the big story into the big picture."

If we want our patients to understand what their healthcare *means*, we must incorporate sensemaking into our storytelling. Sensemaking is layered over storytelling and provides the context of meaning. Sensemaking means navigating healthcare by means of a compass instead of a map. (And it is wise to recall Count Korzybski's caution that "the map is not the territory.")[20] The best compass is making the patient a part of the team so they can guide the journey with you. Karl Weick said it well when he noted that successful leaders capture both the big picture and the big story: "To lead in the future is to be less in thrall of decision-making and more in thrall of sensemaking."[21]

Reigniting passion comes from "guiding the journey" of patients and explaining what will happen to them through their healthcare peregrinations. That said, the story—and the sense we make of it—is always *mutually discovered*, a journey that is never one-sided but rather is cocreated by the team and the patient and their family.

STRATEGIC OPTIMISM

Are you an optimist or a pessimist? (Or a realist?) Do you see a glass half-full or half-empty? That test is often used to guide assessments of optimism versus pessimism. (Shortly before he died, I asked my father, known affectionately to everyone as "Grandpa Jim," that question. He thought for a moment, smiled, and answered, "It depends upon whether you're pouring . . . or drinking." It is always about perspective.)

Several years ago, I developed a concept known as *strategic optimism*,[22] which is the principle that life's greatest asset is our capacity for optimism, the ability to assess a situation and invest it with the most positive practical possibility. (There are many other definitions, but that is mine.) Since it is an asset, we should maximize the *return on investment* (ROI) to ensure we use it wisely and well and increase its "wealth." Despite our preconceptions, none of us have unlimited energy—and none of us have unlimited optimism, so it must be used wisely.

CASE STUDY

John Brown and Julie Broussard are both hospital medicine physicians in a level 1 trauma center with high volume and acuity. Long waits and delays are a daily occurrence for their patients, and hospital boarders range from 10 to 15 per day. The hospital has invested millions of dollars in a new electronic health record (EHR), with little advance training or support of the rollout.

Frustrations are extremely high among all the team members, including Dr. Brown and Dr. Broussard. Dr. Brown has chosen to spend a great deal of time complaining about the EHR, the boarders, and the stresses placed on him by administration to perform at a higher level. Recently, he vented these frustrations to a patient who complained about the long wait, saying, "Take it to the CEO—she's in charge here." When a nurse asked him whether he was being pessimistic, he said, "Why be pessimistic? It would never work." (And, no, he wasn't trying to be funny—he simply didn't understand the irony in his remark.)

Dr. Broussard has taken another approach by first admitting that the EHR is not going away, so she and the team would be wise to develop strategies to work with it and not against it. She volunteered to chair a task force charged with doing just that. Recently when the chief operating officer was rounding and asked about the boarders, she replied, "Thank you for coming to see us. I feel so badly for these patients and their families who wait for hours to days in the hallways on stretchers for a bed upstairs. And I'm concerned about our nurses, who are overburdened already and who are at risk for burnout if we can't work together to solve this problem. May I introduce you to Mrs. Woodyard? She's been waiting the longest for a bed upstairs. I'm sure she would love to hear your perspective."

Both Admiral James Stockdale and Senator John McCain were naval aviators during the Vietnam War whose planes were shot down, resulting in their being incarcerated for years at the "Hanoi Hilton." Both of them said it was their experience that the people who died first in that brutal environment were the "blind optimists," meaning the people divorced from reality who constantly felt they would be liberated "quickly, soon, or even the next day." They had not invested their optimism wisely, squandering it on an unreasonable belief, ungrounded in reality or reason. Stockdale called on what he described as "brutal optimism": "I never lost faith in the end of the story. I never doubted not only that I would get out, but also that I would prevail in the end, and turn the experience into the defining event of my life. This is a very important lesson. You must never confuse the faith that you will prevail in the end with the discipline to confront the most brutal facts of your current reality."[23]

To reignite passion and personal resilience, start with brutal optimism—a realistic assessment of the situation, confronting the "brutal facts of your current reality." Write those facts down. Now turn to the "faith that you will prevail in the end" to illuminate how you can invest your optimism to maximize your ROI. This is *strategic optimism*—since your optimism has boundaries and limits, use it to your strategic advantage by placing it in the right places at the right times for the right reasons for the maximum effect.

Both Dr. Brown and Dr. Broussard are extremely intelligent and talented physicians who are respected for their clinical acumen. But Dr. Brown has chosen to approach problems with a *victim's mentality*, believing that these problems are happening *to him*, and choosing to rail against the problem instead of finding solutions. He has chosen to adopt a negative leadership style, bathed in pessimism.

Dr. Broussard has chosen to invest a difficult situation with strategic optimism, choosing her words and actions to leverage a tough situation toward the most positive practical possibility. On self-evaluation, which doctor rates their energy level and attitude higher? Which one is rated extremely highly by the nursing team as a preferred physician with whom to work? Who is trending toward better scores on burnout and engagement indices? We all know it is Dr. Broussard, who has rejected a victim's mentality for the strategic optimism option. Her approach is not bathed in pessimism but is buoyed by hope.

Chandy John is a pediatric pulmonologist who wrote a thoughtful essay on her concept of "constructive worrying," defined as worrying only about those things that matter most and making positive and proactive plans.[24] Constructive worrying can be considered a corollary to strategic optimism in that it focuses worrying only on ways to improve, learn, forgive yourself, and then move forward. As she says, "So in fact, it's not just OK to worry, it's *good* to worry."

We all recall Hippocrates's dictum, "Primum non nocere" (First do no harm). But how many of us recall that the very next words are "Deinde benefacere" (Then do some good)?[25] Strategic optimism and constructive worrying help increase our personal resiliency by focusing on the good to be done.

As you assess your levels of the cardinal burnout symptoms of emotional exhaustion, cynicism, and a loss of meaning in work, where will you strategically invest *your* optimism? Will you invest it wisely, or will you squander it on false hopes and unreasonable expectations? And remember: the more wisely you invest your optimism, the more optimism you will have because of the ROI.

Solutions Focused on the Six Maslach Domains

Since the symptoms and consequences of burnout arise from a mismatch between increasing job stressors and the adaptive capacity to deal with those stressors, a critical part of the burnout solutions is to decrease the stressors, while increasing the adaptive capacity to deal with them.

- Demand-Capacity Tools
- Don't Be Surprised
- Creative Energy—Close Your Energy Packets
- Disconnect Hot Buttons
- Discipline of Patient Experience
- Taxi, Takeoff, Flight Plan, Landing
- Have a Pain Flight Plan
- Love, Hate, Tolerate

Figure 8-2: Solutions to Decrease Job Stressors, Increase Adaptive Capacity, or Both

DIMINISHING WORKLOAD DEMANDS AND INCREASING ADAPTIVE CAPACITY

Several highly specific strategies diminish workload demands, increase the adaptive capacity to meet those demands, or do some combination of both simultaneously **(Figure 8-2)**.

Using the Demand-Capacity Tools Personally While I will discuss the use of the five demand-capacity questions to hardwire flow and fulfillment in Chapter 10, these questions can be helpful in reigniting personal passion and resilience or adaptive capacity.[26]

1. Who is coming? (What are the demands?)

2. When are they coming? (What is the timing of the demands?)

3. What will they need? (What is the specific nature of the demands?)

4. Will we have what they need? (What capacity do we have?)

5. What will we do if we don't? (What is our adaptive capacity?)

In fact, I teach my residents and fellows to tell their patients, "We knew you were coming—we just didn't know your name."[27] This has several positive effects that increase personal resilience. First, it tells the patient that you have dealt with patients with their clinical problem and thus have experience with it. Second, it puts them at ease to know they have come to the right place with the right problem. Third, by saying "we" instead of "I," it communicates the team nature of the care they will receive.

For those in office-based practices where the appointments are known in advance, make time to review the schedule and put some thought into how you will approach those patients. Let them know you are happy to see them: "I was so pleased when I saw your name on the schedule today. It's good to see you. How have you been doing?" These tactics decrease job stressors by lowering anxiety and increase adaptive capacity. They are closely related to making sure you aren't surprised when you go to work.

CASE STUDY

Jon Myers has been the administrative director of a busy emergency department (ED) for 15 years. Nearly without exception, the ED is overcrowded, has multiple boarders, and has waits longer than he would like. He recently told me, "I have some staff—doctors and nurses—who have worked here as long as or longer than I have. Every day they come to work—mornings, afternoons, and nights—and it's always the same. Yet they look around and think, 'Where did all these people come from?' They're surprised. I'm surprised that they're surprised. How can they be surprised when that's all they see, all day, every day for the past 10 years?"

Don't Be Surprised Workload and adaptive capacity to deal with that workload are dependent on what we are prepared for as we approach our work. The good news is that, with some exceptions, most experienced physicians and nurses have an innately informed sense of what they will see during a typical day or night at work. Don't let work be a surprise—reflect on the way to work on the number and types of patients likely to be seen, what their likely expectations will be, and how best to positively and proactively care for them.

Don't let your work life be a surprise to you—think about what you are likely to see, the challenges you will face, and the tools and energy you will need to get through the day. You will need every ounce of your creative energy to get through the day.

Creative Energy—Close Energy Packets One of the most powerful personal solutions to reignite passion and personal resilience, known as "gaining creative energy by closing your energy packets," is also related to strategic optimism. One factor that determines workload demands and the capacity to deal with them is the amount of energy required to meet the demands (stressors) versus the energy available to you while at work (adaptive energy capacity). Just as exhaustion is an element of burnout, energy is the bellwether of passion and engagement. Joan Kyes, a registered nurse, had a wonderful concept she called "creative energy,"[28] which allows people to creatively invest their energy by completing tasks in a timely fashion, thus returning the energy so it can be used for other projects. Everyone knows someone who seems to have an inexhaustible energy reservoir—they are always ready to take on the next challenge—whereas those who are burned out always seem to have nothing left in their energy reservoir.

Kyes made the point that all humans have basically the same energy reserves and that when we take on a project, we take an "energy packet" out of the tank, with the size of the packet varying based on the magnitude and complexity of the requisite work needed to complete it. However, the energy expended on the task or project does not return to the energy reservoir until the task is fully completed. Thus, people who seem to have low energy levels have multiple "energy packets" out and open, depriving their energy tank of being refilled until those tasks are completed. Chapter 17 discusses how to use this tool.

Taxi, Takeoff, Flight Plan, Landing As a result of serving as the command physician at the Pentagon on 9/11, I have had several opportunities to observe naval aircraft carrier operations. On one of those trips, I had an epiphanic moment in which I realized that caring for patients is like performing carrier operations in that there is a discrete taxi, takeoff, flight plan, and landing:

- Taxi: Prepare to go into the room to see the patient, but with all pertinent information available before doing so.
- Takeoff: This is the most thrilling part of a flight and the first chance to make a great impression, so introduce yourself professionally and with energy to let them know you are pleased to be their doctor or nurse.
- Flight plan: Just as the F/A-18 pilots on the carrier know their flight plan for each mission, we need to know the "flight plans" for the most common clinical entities we will see in a day, including abdominal pain, chest pain, trauma, pediatric fever, hypertension, and well-child checks, all of which should reflect evidence-based team approaches, not just to clinical care and patient safety but to patient experience as well.
- Landing: Nailing the landing is key for aviators and for healthcare team members, so we need to prepare for how we will handle them.

More in-depth approaches are in Chapter 17, but remember that the workload is easier when we have well-developed and mutually shared approaches to patient experience.

REGAINING OR SEIZING CONTROL

Experience across many healthcare systems and all members of the team indicate that being held accountable for areas over which they have too little or no control is a major driver of burnout. **Figure 8-3** lists solutions to regain control, which are discussed below.

Regaining Control

- Gain Control of Schedules
- Scribes as Personal Performance Assistants
- Power of Yes and Power of No
- No "Wonder Woman" or "Superman"
- Disconnect Hot Buttons
- Do the Things We Tell Our Patients
- Multitasking Strategies

Figure 8-3: Solutions to Regain Control

Gain Control of the Schedule One of the areas where we feel loss of control is in the schedules we are required to work. Healthcare systems are realizing how important this is and have developed creative scheduling, such as self-scheduling, surge shifts, split shifts, and scheduling for circadian rhythms.[29] Take advantage of these opportunities where they exist and advocate for them where they don't. This is an important part of regaining control.

Scribes as Personal Performance Assistants: "Doing as Documenting" In several chapters, I have discussed solutions to the many stressors created by the necessity of dealing with the EHR, as well as the solutions needed to develop adaptive capacity to deal with them. One of those is the use of scribes, who should be viewed not just as individuals who record appropriate information but also as personal assistants who make the job easier in other ways. This includes enacting the concept of "doing as documenting." Imagine if doing the work were somehow magically translated into the medical record by the very act of performing it.

The "Power of Yes" and the "Power of No" to Regain Control Rob Strauss emphasizes the importance of "the power of yes," which recognizes that acknowledging a person's thoughts and feelings is not the same as agreeing with them or with the solutions they propose.[30] Tom Jenike, who developed and implemented the award-winning Novant Leadership Development Program described in Chapter 12, is often referred to as "Doctor Get to Yes" because of his similar focus on positive language and behavior.[31] "Yes" builds strength and trust without acquiescence. For example, if a patient requests an MRI scan of their knee at three o'clock in the morning for chronic pain, a typical response might be, "No, we don't do that study at three in the morning." Not only is the patient's request denied, but it is denied in a negative way, starting the interaction with "no." However, a more positive approach is to say, "Yes, I can understand that you would like to get the scan done immediately. However, for problems like yours, we've found that getting your physician's approval and coordinating with insurance actually ensures you aren't responsible for any unnecessary costs." The power of yes helps the workload by proactively using effective language to manage expectations.

Conversely, "the power of no" recognizes that we often take too much work on instead of reflecting on how the task fits with the others already on our plate or in the queue. Saying, "I would love to help, but I have to say no this time out of fairness to the other commitments I've already made."

No "Wonder Woman," No "Superman" Closely related to the power of no is the recognition that none of us are—or should try to be—superhuman action heroes, capable of accepting any and every challenge presented to us. First, it is unhealthy and frankly unnatural to take on all the world's work and make it our own. Second, while subtle, it bespeaks an arrogance that is ultimately unhelpful and can damage relationships if taken to an extreme, as if we are capable of things "normal human beings" are not.

When you notice, "Wow, I have a lot on my plate," be sure you show the maturity and common sense to say, "I would love that challenge and I am so pleased you thought of me, but I wouldn't be able to give the effort needed right now to do it justice. But please ask me another time and if I can help, I will." Show the self-awareness to know you are reaching your stress tolerance level, as discussed in Chapter 2. Most of us don't need a to-do list—but we do need a "to-don't" list.[32]

Disconnect Hot Buttons Everyone has "hot buttons," but not everyone knows what they are. If you don't know, ask the people you work with. Hot buttons are situations, types of interactions, or types of patients that get an involuntary, seemingly uncontrollable response from us that is invariably negative. Those responses increase our workload and reduce our resiliency, and they should thus be avoided. Leaving your hot buttons connected, particularly when you are experiencing symptoms of burnout, adds massive—and unnecessary—stress precisely when you cannot afford it. Chapter 17 discusses how to disconnect your hot buttons.

Do the Things We Tell Our Patients to Do Doctors, nurses, advanced practice providers, and other members of the healthcare team are extremely good at both *proscribing* things patients should not do and *prescribing* precisely what they should do. Are we following the same proscriptions and prescriptions for ourselves? The evidence is that we do not, which contributes to the epidemic of burnout.[33-34]

Recovery in High-Performance Healthcare Athletes The concept of recovery following high performance has strong scientific data to support it, as well as a massive body of experience in elite athletes.[35-37] However, recovery should also be used with members of our healthcare teams. The word *recovery* derives from the fourteenth-century Anglo-French term *rekeverer*, which means to return to health or a previous stable condition.[38] Modern sports science has clearly shown that effective recovery not only returns us to our previous stable state but also can increase performance over time, an important part of which is resiliency or adaptive capacity in all performance dimensions (**Figure 8-4**), including the following:

- mental
- physical
- intellectual
- psychological
- spiritual (connectedness, mindfulness, reflection)

Figure 8-4: The Cycle of Performance, Recovery, and Resilience

Properly understood, recovery has the potential to go beyond the prior state to a higher level of performance in each of these dimensions.[38] Drew Brees, who holds the NFL records for most passing yards and touchdowns, once told me,

> Doc, I am constantly committed to using whatever happens to me to get better. When I tore the labrum of my throwing shoulder when I was with the Chargers, there were plenty of people who told me my career was finished. I didn't think so and more importantly, the Saints didn't think so and I used every day of rehabilitation to improve. I still do that, every day, every play. As I tell my 3 boys every day, have an attitude of gratitude, humility, and respect and if you work hard enough at something you love, you can accomplish anything.[39]

While the physical toll of playing professional football is well known, the combined mental, physical, psychological, intellectual, and spiritual stress of working in healthcare is both cumulative and considerable. We need to use the principles of recovery to *recharge, replenish, renew, and restore*. The principles of sports science and recovery have made dramatic advances over the past 20 years, best summarized in the work of Mark Verstegen, the director of performance for the NFL Players Association, founder of EXOS, and the originator of the concept of *core performance*. EXOS's in-depth work on recovery is available free of charge on the company's website. It is common to hear, "This stuff is actually fairly simple." That is right, and as Verstegen says, "Simple things done savagely well."[40]

Breathe Of the things we take for granted in our lives, breathing is the most important and the most neglected. Obviously, it is the first step in oxygenating our tissues, but the way in which it is done can make a huge difference in performance and recovery. The children's book *Dinotopia* captures it well: "Breathe deep–achieve peace." How often did our parents tell us, "Take a deep breath"? It not only gives a moment's reflection but also allows tense muscles to relax and the rib cage to expand, increasing vital capacity. There are myriad ways to use breathing to perform and recover (including yoga breathing),[41-43] but two I find helpful are "6-4-10" and "6-3-6" breathing. "6-4-10" means to assume a comfortable position, then, while focusing on your breath, inhale for a full 6 seconds, hold it in your lungs for 4 seconds, then gently exhale for a sustained 10 seconds. Repeat this five times. I do it immediately after awakening, just before going into work, any time I encounter a stressful situation, and again at the end of the workday before I go home.

"6-3-6" breathing is a valuable tool for helping you prepare for sleep, as the shorter hold and exhalation prepares you for rest, not action. Do it 10 times and you will feel more restful. Invest some time in using your breath to your advantage.

Eat There are over 10,000 books telling you what, when, how, how often, and what not to eat, so I will only make a few points here:

- Do not skip breakfast. Without fuel, you are running an engine inefficiently and without the energy you need to do the hard work of healthcare.
- Think ahead. Part of the reason people end up eating junk food is that they haven't thought ahead to plan what and when they will eat. Take healthy meals and snacks (however you choose to define those) to work with you.
- Use food as a performance tool, not a reward.
- Eat colorfully. Make sure there are at least three colors per meal— that likely means you're getting the vitamins, minerals, and antioxidants you need. (And different colors of M&Ms and Skittles don't count.)
- Be aware of the glycemic index of foods and avoid refined carbohydrates.

Exercise Weight control largely comes down to calories in, calories out. Exercise is calories out. However, the benefits of exercise go far beyond weight control and include building muscle, improving aerobic metabolism, increasing endorphins, and increasing adaptive capacity or resiliency.[43-45] The effect on resiliency has been firmly established scientifically but is well known to athletes empirically. The following is a summary of thousands of pages of exercise advice:

- Treat exercise as a medication—because it is.
- You wouldn't skip your medications, so don't skip exercise.

- Put aerobic exercise sessions on your schedule for 50 minutes (plus stretching—see the next section) at least four to five times per week. Don't wait until it is convenient to work out, because it never will be.

- Recent work shows that exercise that involves reacting to the environment, making minute adjustments throughout (e.g., riding outdoors vs. on stationary bikes, running outside vs. on a treadmill), increases both athletic and mental adaptive capacity.

- The great news for gardeners is that working in the yard or garden for an hour burns 300 calories as an aerobic workout. Be sure to stretch afterward.

- The more burned out you feel, the harder it is to make exercise a habit, which makes it exponentially more important. When you find yourself thinking, "Seriously, does it really matter?" look in the mirror and say what you would say to your patients: "It matters, so get started."

Stretching High-performance athletes use stretching both before and after competition, and healthcare team members should too. Tom Brady has won six Super Bowls and was the MVP of four of them. He is still playing in the NFL at the age of 43. How has he maintained his high performance level so consistently and for so long? Over the course of a three-hour conversation, he summarized his approach:

> Doc, most of the strength and conditioning coaches in the NFL focus on lifting weights in various ways, all of which have the effect of building strength, but which also "tighten and shorten" the muscle fibers. That's not what a quarterback needs to do his job. I do the workouts I am told at the team facility, but then I go straight to my own facility with my own coach (Alex Guerrero), where we spend hours "lengthening and loosening" those same muscle groups, focusing on stretching and flexibility of the tissues. There are a lot of reasons I have been blessed with such a long career, but stretching is among the most important.[46]

Much of the work we do is physically demanding. Many nurses and physicians walk four to five miles per day on hard floors.[47] Surgeons and scrub nurses toil over the operating table for hours. Physicians and nurses in the ICU and offices are constantly moving from patient to patient and task to task. Unsurprisingly, this leads to a higher incidence of back pain in healthcare workers. Indeed, the work seems designed to produce lower back pain.

Much of this can be prevented with simple, brief stretching regimens focused on lengthening and loosening the hamstrings, which are the "silent villains" of lower back pain, since we tend to focus on our backs when they are tight, but hamstrings and hip flexors need to be stretched to relieve that pain.

Here are four stretches that can dramatically improve flexibility. I strongly recommend doing these stretches before, during, and after work, preceded by two to three sets of 6-4-10 breathing.

1. Hamstring and back stretch: Stand with your hips slightly wider apart than shoulder width. Cross your arms in front and gently bend at the waist, lowering your head until you feel a stretch in the hamstrings. Continue to breathe deeply and gradually continue to bend and drop your shoulders. Hold for three 6-4-10 breaths. (Most people feel a "popping" sensation in their back, which is just the discs coming out to a more physiologic length with nitrogen escaping and is nothing to worry about.) Do this before and after work and anytime you feel any element of back pain during work.

2. Hip flexor stretch: The hip flexors control a great deal of our mobility and also contribute to back pain when they are tight. Grab the back of a chair or desk to stabilize, which will engage your core muscles. Fold your right foot over your left knee while standing and gently begin to "sit," with your right hand applying gentle pressure on your knee. You will feel the gluteal muscles and the other hip flexors stretch. Over time you will be able to get your left knee at nearly a 90-degree angle. Hold for three 6-4-10 breaths. Now repeat with the left side. Do three repetitions on each side.

3. Single-leg glute, hamstring, and calf stretch: From a standing position, stabilize yourself by putting both hands down on a chair or desk. This will activate the core muscles that support your hips, torso, and shoulders. Extend the left leg forward and straighten it, placing your heel on the ground with your toes pointing up. Slightly bend the right leg and push your hips back. Hold this position for three seconds and then stand tall. Do 10 repetitions total, 5 on each side. This stretch should be felt in the glutes, the hamstrings, and the calf of the front leg as well as the triceps and core muscles.

4. Side stretch with rotation: Stand straight in a doorway. Move the left arm up the wall as if you were hanging from a monkey bar. Gently press into the wall with the palm, which will activate the core. Step back with the left leg into a gentle lunge, which will stretch the side and chest muscles. Challenge the position by bringing the left knee closer to the ground. While holding that position, stretch the right arm up and to the right. Lead with the thumb and look at the right hand, while limiting movement in the legs. Hold for three seconds and then return the arm to its starting position. Stand with shoulders back and spine straight. Repeat on both sides for five reps each.

The last two stretches are used with permission from Team Exos and can be viewed here: https://blog.teamexos.com/work-smart/hospital-staff-well-being.

Sleep Sleep plays a major role in intellectual, mental, and physical performance and recovery across all dimensions.[48-49] Sleep deprivation increases fatigue, impairs judgment, impedes physical performance, reduces reaction times, increases the risk of injury, and increases patient safety events. Sleep's effect on fatigue is particularly important—consider the words of Hall of Fame coach Vince Lombardi: "Fatigue makes cowards of us all."[50]

Investing in proper sleep length and architecture is one of the best strategies to increase personal resilience or adaptive capacity. Part of resiliency is the ability to "de-form" in order to squeeze through tough circumstances and then "re-form" to get back into action. Recovery and sleep are key to the ability to do this successfully. There are many ways to improve sleep quality, quantity, and architecture, which are briefly summarized here:

- Set a personal goal of getting seven to nine hours of sleep per day.
- If you know when you must get up, work backward from that point to help develop your "sleep ritual" and give yourself at least an hour to prepare for sleep.
- Melatonin is a naturally occurring hormone that regulates night and day cycles or sleep-wake cycles. Darkness causes the body to produce melatonin, so sleep in a cool, dark room.
- Light, particularly "blue light" such as light from computers, televisions, smartphones, and some e-readers, decreases melatonin production and signals the body to alertness. Avoid blue light for at least two hours before sleep.
- Exogenous melatonin (5–10 mg), even at the maximum dose, often has a half-life of four to five hours, causing people to wake up before a full seven to nine hours of sleep.
- Sustained-release forms of melatonin are designed to combat this effect.
- The amino acid 5-hydroxytryptophan, either alone or combined with melatonin, can be an effective sleep adjunct.
- More recently, research has shown that phosphatidylserine (100–200 mg at night) increases sleep architecture and duration, as well as increasing focus and attention span.
- For shift workers who rotate day, evening, and night cycles, there are excellent resources to guide effective sleep.

Sunlight For centuries, philosophers and poets have extolled the virtues of sunlight, including its ability to improve mood, attitude, and performance. My grandpa Jim always said, "It's easier to have an 'attitude of gratitude' when the sun is on your face." Scientific literature supports many positive effects of sunlight, mediated largely but not exclusively through vitamin D_3.[51-52]

All of this must occur with appropriate use of sunscreen to prevent skin cancers and melanoma, of course. But sunshine should be treated as a medication with many positive effects—because it is.

Pursuing Perfection or Pursuing Peace? Engaging the Mind, Body, and Spirit We are all leaders, and we cannot lead effectively without a clearly centered mindset of serving others. That requires finding a way to pursue our own peace. If you want to help others—and all of us do—you must do the work of pursuing not just perfection but peace. Without that core motivation and value, people are unlikely to follow you.

Countless people have informed the literature, art, and science of mindfulness, so to mention some of them risks raising the ire of those who are devotees of others. However, in my admittedly nonexpert study of mindfulness, several names that are most prominent are Michael Singer,[4,53] Jonathan Kabat-Zinn,[54] Daniel Siegel,[55] and from the Buddhist tradition, the Dalai Lama[56] and the Buddhist monk Thich Nhat Hanh.[57] I could not possibly do justice to summarizing their prolific work, but here is my summary of thoughts on mindfulness.

At its core, *mindfulness is a self-regulated focus of attention on the present moment, infused with curiosity, openness, acceptance, and surrender, but devoid of judgment, bias, and prejudice.* For me, the core of mindfulness is getting out of your own way.

A central feature of all mindfulness is the concept of having a clear understanding of what we control and what we do not control, since it is a waste of time to invest "strategic optimism" in things beyond our control.

Singer, author of *The Untethered Soul*[4] and *The Surrender Experiment*,[53] explains that we have little or no control over the "Outside World," despite what we might have learned from traditional teachings. This is in contradistinction to the "Inside World," over which we have complete control, which includes our minds, our emotions, and our thoughts. This is precisely what Epictetus said:

> Of things that exist, some are in our power and some are not in our power. Those that are in our power are opinion, choice, the things we do like, the things we don't like, and in a word, those things that are of our own doing. Those that are not under our control are our bodies, property, possessions, reputations, positions of authority and in a word, things that are not of our own doing. We must remember that those things are externals and are therefore not our concern. Trying to control or to change what we can't only results in torment.[58]

Singer correctly notes that we can choose to live inside a "beautiful, centered space"[53] if we can but focus on what we can control to the exclusion of what we cannot control. Let the "outside in"

- only as you want or need, and
- do so at considerable peril if you let it control what it clearly does not.

Admiral James Stockdale, whom I quoted earlier, was a navy fighter pilot whose A-4 Skyhawk was shot down over Hanoi, where he was the senior officer held as a prisoner of war. He said that as soon as his aircraft was hit, he thought, "I am descending into the world of Epictetus."[59] In battling burnout, never lose track of what you control—and what you don't. As Singer says, "The world can be a dangerous place . . . or a great gift."[4, 53] Balancing that choice goes to the heart of battling burnout.

Both Kabat-Zinn and Siegel have used fMRI to study the effect of mindfulness training and meditation on increasing the signal and capacity of the prefrontal cortex, the area of the brain that governs resiliency.[54–55,60] The following are the elements that Kabat-Zinn lists as the components of mindfulness:[54]

- beginner's mind
- nonjudging
- acceptance
- letting go
- trust
- patience
- nonstriving
- gratitude
- generosity

Call it what you will—mindfulness, reflection, focusing on what matters, source of being, place of peace—it can be a source of healing, but only you can determine whether it works for you. I confess that when writing this chapter, I was reviewing a video on mindfulness when my wonderful wife walked in and asked what I was doing. I said, "I am fast-forwarding through a lecture on mindfulness." So I am hardly one to tell you whether this will work for you. If you are so inclined, I recommend giving it a try.

Namaste Customs can have great power, and some of the most powerful are greetings. The traditional Sanskrit greeting, much used but less understood, is "Namaste." There are many interpretations of the term, including "The light in me honors the light in you." But my preferred translation, based on the wisdom of several colleagues who are fluent in Hindi or Sanskrit, is this, "I greet the God within you."[61]

I love that, and I think it is the best way to approach the hard work of healthcare. That is what we do every time we see a patient—we greet the God within them.

Duke WISER Web-Based Training The habits of mindfulness and meditation take time and the investment of energy to develop, as worthwhile as that investment is. Partially in response to this, Bryan Sexton and his colleagues at the Duke University Health System developed WISER (Web-based Implementation of the Science to Enhance Resilience). The program is described in more detail in Chapter 14, but WISER comprises 18 tools developed from the science of positive psychology and tested through a National Institutes of Health Research Project Grant that are designed to cultivate the behaviors of resiliency. They are enjoyable to use, are easy to access, have high utility, and have a quickly measurable but sustainable impact. In particular, I find that these tools are helpful: Three Good Things, Random Acts of Kindness, Gratitude Letter, and Awe.

Think, Laugh, Cry NCAA National Championship–winning men's basketball coach Jim Valvano gave one of the greatest speeches I have ever heard in accepting the Arthur Ashe Courage Award at the ESPN ESPY Awards. His body riddled with stage 4 bone cancer, he urged the audience to do three things each day: take the time to think, to laugh, and to be moved to tears. As he said, "If you do that, that's a full day."

Healthcare team members have the chance to experience things that make us think, laugh, and cry every day. But you must take the time to pause, reflect, and do those things.

Have a Multitasking Strategy

Effective executives do first things first and they do them one at a time.

PETER DRUCKER, *THE EFFECTIVE EXECUTIVE*[62]

While Drucker's advice came well before the "onslaught of electrons" in which our current lives are conducted, it is nonetheless sound counsel to avoid multitasking. While multitasking seems like an unavoidable occupational hazard in healthcare and many people take pride in their ability to multitask, the literature is quite unequivocal that *multitasking makes you stupid.*[63-64] The rates of errors, miscommunication, patient safety incidents, and even malpractice claims rise as the rates of multitasking and interruptions rise.

Follow these two principles:

1. Do everything possible to eliminate multitasking from your work.

2. Develop strategies and tactics to deal with multitasking.

Increasing Rewards and Recognition

- Reward Yourself—Power of One
- Thank You 50 Times a Day
- Thank Least Important Members
- Catch People Doing Things Right
- Reconnecting Passion

Figure 8-5: Increasing Rewards and Recognition Solutions

GIVING AND GETTING REWARDS AND RECOGNITION

If there is the feeling that team members aren't appropriately given rewards and recognition for the hard work done, if there is a mismatch between appreciation earned and appreciation received, the best way to fix that is to give rewards and recognition to others (**Figure 8-5**). While it also ties into values, a culture imbued with praise for others has an infectious effect on the entire team. Indeed, it also affects the patients, who invariably notice people who are gracious and kind toward others.

Take a minute to pause and reflect on the many great things that are done on behalf of patients by you and your immediate team members in just one day. Do the members on your team consistently thank each other for this great work? We need to build "thank-you pauses" into each day to ensure we are increasing rewards and recognition. Of course, we want to increase the amount and quality of the great work done, but why not increase praise for the work already being done?

Reward Yourself: The Power of One The first step in ensuring rewards and recognition is rewarding and recognizing ourselves. Many people live lives where they aren't ever sure whether they make a difference. That's not true for the healthcare team, demonstrating what I describe as "the power of one." When we go into a patient's room, we can confidently say, "We *will* make a difference. What will the difference be?" One doctor, one nurse, one team taking care of one patient—we *will* make a difference; of that there is no question. Rewarding ourselves by recognizing the control we have over our interactions with our patients and families is a powerful way to prevent and combat burnout.

Say "Thank You" 50 Times a Day Since rewards and recognition are contagious, one of the most obvious solutions is to ensure that routinely thanking others is a part of the work life, preferably in a disciplined, thoughtful way. If saying thank you 50 times a day seems a daunting task, consider this:

- Most physicians see at least 20 patients a day.
- Most nurses see at least 10 patients a day.
- The nurses spend more with the patient and the family.
- If each physician thanks the patient when they first see them, thanks them again when they leave, and thanks the nurse for their care, that is at least 60 times a day.

CASE STUDY

In my job as medical director for all 2,500 NFL players, I make a point to attend several training camps each year, meeting with players, coaches, athletic trainers, and the medical staff. When visiting the Denver Broncos several years ago, I was touring the training room with their venerated head athletic trainer, Steve "Greek" Antinopolis. I noticed that every door into or out of the training room has this sign above it: "You can easily judge the character of a man by how he treats those who can do nothing for him." I asked Greek about it and he said, "Oh, Coach Kubes [Gary Kubiak] feels very strongly that we're all a part of the team and he stresses this quote to the players constantly."

When I saw Coach Kubiak several hours later, I complimented him on it and asked where he first heard it. He said his dad told it to him every day. (As some of you know, that quote is from the German philosopher Johann Wolfgang von Goethe. Goethe's wisdom lives on in an NFL locker room.)

- If the nurse thanks the patient and the family when they arrive and when they leave and thanks the doctor and essential services team, they are past 60 times as well.
- And of course, the more "thank you" is said, the easier and more natural it becomes.
- "Thank you" provides the lubrication to treat "rustout."

Thank the "Least Important" Team Members We would all do well if that wisdom lived in the halls of our hospitals and healthcare organizations. Do you live by that wisdom?

All the members of our team should be thanked, not just the nurses and doctors, but the technicians, registrars, and environmental services (EVS) folks as well. Making sure to say thank you to all of them every chance you get is a sound investment in preventing and treating burnout. After a difficult trauma resuscitation, it's not uncommon for the nurses and doctors to thank each other for handling the patient well. But thanking the EVS folks who clean up the mess made during the resuscitation is also a discipline that should be developed. That reward and recognition is well deserved—and always noticed.

Catch People Doing Things Right So much of healthcare is based on a disease model that we often find ourselves focusing on what's wrong or what went wrong, instead of proactively focusing on what went right and should be celebrated. Unexpected rewards and recognition arise from "catching" people doing things right and publicly complimenting them on their work. No one is immune to the power of praise.

CASE STUDY

The chief nurse executive (CNE) is completing patient care rounding and is hurrying back to her office for a solid day of meetings and phone calls. As she looks back, she sees a wheelchair in the middle of the hallway unattended. As she begins to walk back, a busy nurse comes from a patient room, walks out of her way to get the wheelchair, wipes it with disinfectant, and puts it back where it belongs, never noticing that the CNE is there. The CNE approaches the nurse and says, "I just saw what you did. That was very impressive." The nurse smiles and answers, "Hey, you're just visiting, this is where I live—got to keep things squared away." Before starting her meetings, the CNE takes a moment to send a congratulatory email to the nurse director of the unit, praising the nurse by name. She also writes a personal note to the nurse saying, in part, "You reminded me of why I became a nurse."

Reconnecting Passion: Great Place to Work = Great People to Work With Reconnecting passion to the job requires a recognition that great places to work arise from the great people who do the work. There is nothing abstract about a great work environment—it is great people with great leaders doing great work in service to their patients. The more this is articulated in what is said and done, the more the team will reconnect their passion and feel appreciated. "You did a great job on that case. Well done!" is a powerful reward and recognition. Writing a letter or email commending the team and copying those in "the C-suite" is also effective, as mentioned in the preceding case study.

Recruiting members to the team is one of the most important investments of time and energy, since it increases the talent pool. Make sure "hire right" includes hiring for passion and an "attitude of gratitude" for the rest of the team.

RETURNING COMMUNITY TO THE WORKPLACE

Teams are a community of caregivers who trust each other, and it is critical to accentuate and nourish that sense of community (**Figure 8-6**). Healthcare is by

Returning Community to the Team

- Teams and Teamwork Skills and Training
- "Passing the Baton"
- Seams of the Team
- Re-recruit Yourself and the Team
- Clinical Huddles
- Rounding on Next

Figure 8-6: Solutions to Return Community to the Team

nature a team effort, but the language and the behaviors used should reflect a community commitment, since all healthcare is "cocreated" by the entire team.

If you want people to "say team," make sure you "play" team.

Use the words *team* and *teams* regularly, as in "nursing team," "EVS team," "nutrition team," and so on. *I* accepts responsibility if something goes wrong. *We* says team when creating expectations or sharing praise.

Re-recruit Yourself and the A-team A great deal of time, effort, and energy goes into recruiting, training, and orienting physicians, nurses, and the other members of the team. Far too little time, effort, and energy go into the process of "re-recruitment," in which the members of the team or community are continuously reminded of how valued their contributions have been and how critical they are to the success of the team.[65] In addition to changing the character of performance evaluations to consider how the work itself can be changed to make their lives easier, letting the A-team members know how much their efforts mean to the patients and the team itself is an important part of re-recruitment daily.

If you don't "re-recruit" your A-team, someone else will.

Far too few people are aware of this concept of re-recruiting your star performers.

"Huddle Up": Using Clinical Huddles to Reinforce Community Clinical huddles create teamwork in healthcare, sharing mental models and delineating specific contributions that will be made by team members for the good of the patient. They also ensure that the entire team interacts and prevent people from working in relative isolation through the course of the day. And they create common understandings among the team members, further reinforcing community.

REESTABLISHING FAIRNESS IN AN UNFAIR ENVIRONMENT

As much as values are critically important to preventing burnout, the domain of fairness is where burnout in hospitals is often first noticed. Because of the deeply egalitarian nature of healthcare, it is not surprising that this is the case. However, focusing on fairness also has tremendous leverage on reestablishing the team's and leadership's commitment to fairness, equity, and parity, both for the team and for its patients (**Figure 8-7**).

Rebuilding Fairness

- Bounty Hunt for Unfairness
- Treasure Hunt for Fairness
- Advocate for the Team
- Druckenbrod's Questions
- The Elevator Speech
- Become the "Problem" Doc or Nurse

Figure 8-7: Solutions to Rebuild Fairness

Mutual Accountability and the Language of Fairness Eliminating functional silos (first described by Phil Ensor in 1988)[66] and ensuring there is mutual accountability across boundaries is a clear way of ensuring fairness, since many people "say 'team'" but don't "play 'team.'" Mutual accountability involves eliminating statements such as, "Well, the physicians' patient experience scores are great. It's the nurses' scores that are pulling us down." Instead, an approach that focuses on fairness uses language such as, "We are all in this together. Let's see what worked in raising the physician scores and see if we can apply that in other areas." Accountability across boundaries is essential to creating transparent fairness.

The language we use also reinforces both community and fairness. Examples include the following:

- "That was an excellent job!"
- "You just saved this guy's life!"
- "Thanks! You made a B-team day into an A-team one."
- "What could I have done today to make your job easier?"
- "Anne picked up some very important information that is going to improve your care."
- "Isaac is our best advanced practice provider. You're fortunate he's here."

The more this language is used—and used across boundaries—the more evident fairness will be.

Druckenbrod's Questions Glenn Druckenbrod, the medical director of the Department of Emergency Medicine at Inova Fairfax Medical Campus, stresses the importance of the discipline of using three questions during the "landing" portion of the ED visit:

- "Have we met your expectations?"
- "What questions do you have that I can help with?"
- "How did we do?"[67]

These questions signal to the patient and the family that we are committed to fairness.

The Elevator Speech A medical director and her nursing director partner are waiting for an elevator to "round on next" on patients admitted from the ED. The elevator door opens to reveal the following people: the CEO, chief medical officer, chief nursing officer, chief operating officer, chief financial officer, and board chair, who are making their own rounds. Inevitably, they will ask, "How is it going today in the ED?"

The directors' response is their "elevator speech,"[65] which is a focused, insightful, succinct message of "the story of the ED." The physician and nurse should have their elevator speech prepared and they should have discussed it among themselves, since both will be in the role of "chief storyteller" in explaining the complex adaptive system that every ED is. The story should always begin and end with the patient, not the staff, since that is their main focus—and power. Committing the time and effort to coordinate an elevator speech focusing on the patient helps create a sense of fairness to those who hear it.

Become the "Problem" Doctor or Nurse This solution seems counterintuitive. However, it is wise to develop a reputation for being proficient at solving problems. Because the ED is a complex, adaptive system, problems are a part of its operations. Emergency nurses and physicians solve problems all day, every day, so it is a skill set that is very familiar to them. Being known as a problem-solver of the highest skill is an effective pathway toward building community, both within the ED and throughout the hospital.

REINFUSING VALUES INTO YOUR PRACTICE

The role of having honorable values in healthcare cannot be overstated, since the work is too hard without a clear connection to our core values of dedication to our patients and to our team members. **Figure 8-8** lists ways of doing this.

State Common Values While healthcare teams typically feel they have a set of values to which they hold themselves accountable, it is far less common for people to formally express what those values are. It is even less frequent that they commit those values to writing. Some go as far as to write their own personal vision statement. If we can't say clearly and succinctly what our values are, how will we or others know them? Stephen Covey wrote eloquently of the importance of this.[68]

Once you complete a personal vision statement, compare those values with the stated values of the hospital. Are the two sets of values consistent? If not, how do they differ? If the differences between your personal values and those of the hospital differ substantially, how will you reconcile them in your work? Does the experience at work lead them to believe that the actual values of the workplace are different from those proclaimed? After all, "the words on the walls aren't nearly as important as the happenings in the halls." Reflect on how they or the practice could change to better reflect the values to which the individual

Restoring Values

- Every Action = Values
- Reconnecting Passion to Purpose
- Keep a Patient Journal
- Be Like Praveen
- Leave a Legacy

Figure 8-8: Solutions to Restore Values

and their colleagues aspire. Until values are understood and articulated, it is difficult to embody them in action.

Keep a Patient Journal It is a natural human tendency, perhaps accentuated in professionals, to focus on the negative in hopes of finding ways to improve. But physicians and nurses aren't always great at recalling and reflecting on the good things they do during a normal day. This includes not just saving lives or making a complicated diagnosis but also the simple kindnesses we express to our patients and to each other. One way to ensure that these critically important moments are not forgotten is to write them down. Keep a journal in which you write a brief note—preferably at the end of each shift, but no less than weekly—recalling a patient and their family, or a nurse who made a great pickup, or a doc who was especially kind to others, or a technician who was mentored.

Remember that none of the works of the Stoic philosophers were written as books—most were journals. The most famous such philosopher is Marcus Aurelius, whose only work is *Meditations*, a collection of the journals he kept for himself—a compelling and lasting piece of literature.[69]

Don't be hesitant to praise yourself in thoughts and journal entries. Give yourself credit for what you do well—you deserve it! And don't be surprised if keeping this journal helps you adopt even more habits of kindness and gratitude.

Be Like Praveen Everyone has heroes in their work whose values inspire us to do better, care more, and care more often. One of mine is Praveen Kache, with whom I worked at Sentara Northern Virginia Medical Center. Praveen is one of the kindest people I know, but this story is about much more than kindness. He was working an overnight shift and an 85-year-old lady was brought in from Brightview, the nearby nursing home and assisted-living facility. She was mentally sharp and had a French accent, having lived in Normandy during the Nazi occupation in World War II. Praveen asked her, "What's the most important thing I can do for you to make this a great ED visit?" She replied, "Just get me well enough to go back to Brightview."

Praveen took great care of her, hydrating her and getting appropriate diagnostic tests. He also took the time to sit and talk with her, letting her tell her story. True to his word, he got her back to the nursing home, as she wanted. But one week later, I received a note from the woman (with the beautifully flowing penmanship that is no longer taught) expressing her delight with "Dr. Kache Praveen" (she reversed his name), who "couldn't have been kinder and got me back to the nursing home, as I asked." Enclosed was a check for $10,000 made out to the ED. To be honest, for a moment I saw that amount and thought, "That's a *lot* of money for someone living in a nursing home. Plus, she's 85 years old, maybe she mistakenly got the number of zeros confused when she wrote the check." Well, not only did the check clear the bank, when I spoke to her she said, "I only wish I could have given more."

We recognized Praveen at the annual medical staff meeting as an exemplary physician and commented on his taking the time to sit and talk with an old lady. He said, "Oh it was my privilege! I treat these folks like they are *time machines*. When I talk with them, I get to go back in time and experience what they lived through." He felt it was a privilege on that busy night to go back in time and learn what it was like in Normandy during the Nazi occupation and the liberation in 1944.

Be like Praveen.

Leave a Legacy Some people have jobs that make them wonder, "Do I *really* make a difference in what I do?" In healthcare, we don't have that problem—we know we will make a difference in peoples' lives by using "the power of one." But what will our *legacy* be? One of the most wonderful things about healthcare is that we can measure our legacy very easily—*one patient at a time*. Every time we have contact with a patient—no matter what we do in healthcare—we leave a legacy. Every time we interact with our team members, as we "pass the baton," we leave a legacy. Even to the people who see us doing our work, we leave a legacy. What an honor to have work that leaves a legacy.

Next time you finish work and get in your car to go home, pause for a moment before starting the engine and ask yourself, "What kind of legacy did I leave in there *today*?" Very few things are more effective at restoring values in work than considering the legacy you leave.

Summary

- Every healthcare team member is a leader and needs personal resiliency to lead. Every team member is a high-performance athlete who needs training and recovery.
- You are the CEO of "Me, Inc."—invest in yourself.
- The "big six" are the solutions to reignite passion and personal resiliency that cut across all six of the Maslach domains:
  - Deep joy, deep needs: Discover where your deep joy intersects the world's deep needs.
  - Throw guilt in the trunk—lighten up on yourself: "We have to find a cleaner-burning fuel than guilt."
  - Make the patient part of the team: Shift from "What's the matter *with you*?" to "What matters *to you*?"
  - Personalized patient care: "What's *the most important thing* we can do to make this a great experience?"
  - Chief storyteller, chief sensemaker: Tell the patient the story of their care and make sense of it.
  - Strategic optimism: Invest your optimism to maximize the ROI.

9

Organizational Solutions for Improving Culture

Culture eats strategy for breakfast.

PETER DRUCKER[1]

A culture committed to passion for patient care and professional fulfillment is critical to developing and sustaining organizational resilience. However, culture creates burnout when it espouses professional fulfillment but the culture "in action" is different, as Chris Argyris notes.[2] When the "words on the walls" aren't matched by the "happenings in the halls,"[3] burnout is inevitable. Culture is not just what people *do* in an organization, it is also what they *say they do*, as well as *how they think*, particularly how they think about *change, improvement, and innovation.* Few things further widen the gap between job stressors and the resilience required to deal with them than leaders who espouse one culture but embody another. Leaders who proclaim they have a great culture but have burnout rates of nearly 50 percent are disconnected from the reality of how burnout occurs. As Steve Narang, the president of the Inova Fairfax Medical Campus of Inova Health System, notes, "Culture comes straight from the airway of the organization."[4] Physicians and nurses all learn the "ABCs" of resuscitation, always

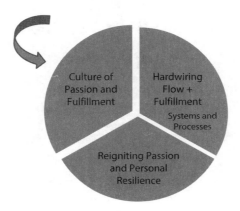

starting with *A*, the airway. Narang is precise in noting that culture constitutes the first and most important part of "resuscitating" organizations suffering from burnout. Similarly, Ed Schein famously noted that, "Leadership and culture are two sides of the same coin."[5]

Fortunately, the gap between job stressors and the resilience they require can be avoided because there is a suite of solutions designed to create a culture of passion and personal and professional fulfillment in healthcare **(Figure 9-1)**. These solutions cut across the Maslach domains, as shown in **Figure 9-2**.

- Leaders Everywhere at Every Level
- Leadership Candor Is Essential
- Look in the Mirror— Leadership Self-Assessment
- Leadership-Culture Realities
- Form Follows Finance
- Words on the Walls
- Leadership Development
- Limits Begin Where Vision Ends

- What Kind of Leader Are You?
- The Case for Servant Leadership
- Culture of Passion, Compassion, Appreciation, Transparency, and Growth
- Empowerment Solutions
- Stop Doing Stupid Stuff
- Take on the EHR
- The Chief Wellness Officer Dilemma

Figure 9-1: Solutions to Create a Culture of Passion and Personal Resilience

Figure 9-2: Solutions to Create a Culture of Passion and Personal Resilience by Maslach Domain

Leaders Everywhere at Every Level

In creating culture, "leadership" does not mean *just* senior leaders or department directors. Every time healthcare team members show up to work, they are responsible for *leading their part of healthcare*. Every doctor, every nurse, every lab technician, every imaging specialist, and every person in environmental services (EVS) leads themselves and those with whom they interact during the course of their work in creating a culture that day, that evening, that night. They create "happenings in the halls" that collectively define the organization and its culture.

> *In healthcare, leadership is for everyone because everyone leads.*
>
> *Lead yourself, lead your team.*
>
> *Leaders at all levels are performance athletes who need performance and recovery.*
>
> *Invest in yourself, invest in your team.*
>
> *The work begins within.*

Leadership Candor Is Essential

While leadership at all levels is essential to battling burnout, in the arena of culture, leadership is *the* issue.[6] This requires an unprecedented level of candor, precisely because it takes a tremendous amount of intellectual honesty to admit that our current culture is what *created*—or at the very least *allowed*—burnout to occur. To those who say, "We have a culture of passion and fulfillment," the logical question is, "Then why are half your team members suffering from burnout? If they trusted your culture, they wouldn't be burned out."

The role that leadership has inadvertently played in burnout's creation requires honesty and candor. The importance of candor is not to create a sense of guilt about how we got here, but to create hope in changing the culture for the future. It is important to reiterate that part of measurement is to assess, usually in a free text format, what the team members feel are the major issues regarding culture and organizational adaptive capacity. Ed Schein understood the importance of both candor and an iterative approach to leadership's role in culture: "The ability to perceive the limitations of one's own culture and to develop the culture adaptively is the essence and ultimate challenge of leadership."[5]

The courage to embrace input on the culture and its impact, including its unintended consequences, is fundamentally a commitment to hearing the following:

- the "voice of the patient" regarding what reality is for them[7]
- the "voice of the provider" regarding whether the culture results in burnout, to what extent, and what the specific reasons are

There are two important *dynamic tensions* regarding culture and burnout. To Narang's excellent point, culture is a primary function of leadership and its ability to frame the context in which healthcare work is done, as well as ensure there is sufficient organizational resilience or adaptive capacity to do so. At the same time, that adaptive capacity arises from the ability of the culture (as embodied by its leaders) to show iterative resiliency.

The second dynamic tension is that nothing can be *purely culture* since it can never be defined in the abstract or in isolation—it can only be discovered in the actions of the organization and its leaders.[7-9] Of necessity, changing culture has significant implications for both the hardwiring of flow and fulfillment and personal resiliency.[10]

Look in the Mirror: Leadership Self-Assessment

The key issue is how leaders at all levels embody the stated culture through their actions and decisions. That starts by taking a long, reflective look in the mirror. These questions are important to consider:

- Does your healthcare system invest in leadership development?
- Is leadership development focused on helping the individual or on how the individual can improve results for the organization?
- Do you promote those who promote personal and professional fulfillment through the leadership culture?
- Whose actions embody the positive aspects of your culture?
- Who is doing innovative and unexpected things to advance a culture of passion and fulfillment?
- What risks were they willing to take to be innovative?
- Is there a culture of appreciation or underappreciation in the system?
- Is there a deep and abiding sense of community and transparency?
- Does the chief wellness officer report to the CEO or the chief operating officer (COO)? If not, why not?
- Is your culture one where systems and processes change as a result of identifying burnout and its sequelae?

Now go back and give specific examples that support your answers. The self-assessment gets a lot harder when we are required to do this. I was a theology major when I was in college. At the end of my senior year, we had four hours to complete our written final exam, which comprised an envelope with questions and several blue notebooks in which to write. Fortunately, the exam was on an honor system, so you could open the envelope anytime and anywhere you wanted, as long as you completed it in four hours, based solely on your thoughts and without consulting notes, textbooks, or other people. I opened my envelope and the question read, "Discuss the Old and New Testaments. Give examples." I thought for a couple of moments and wrote, "The Old Testament says, 'It's the Law.' The New Testament says, 'It's a little more complicated than that . . .'" I would have been done, except for that pesky, "Give examples." That took a lot longer. And the "leadership look in the mirror" will take a lot longer when it comes to giving examples.

Form Follows Function, Form Follows Finance

While many people are familiar with the saying "form follows function," most are perhaps less so with the phrase "form follows finance." Both are applicable to the inextricable relationship of leadership and culture. To an increasing degree, leaders are also guided by the *financial aspects*—how much and for what each area is reimbursed. For a typical department in a large hospital or healthcare systems, there are vice chairs or associate medical directors for the following:

- quality
- patient safety
- patient experience
- performance improvement/flow

Is there a vice chair or associate director for wellness and resiliency? If not, why not? The "business case for battling burnout" is clear and shows the return on investment (ROI) for investing in such a position and giving that person an appropriate budget and authority to make changes to the system, which is producing precisely the results it is designed to. Another way of thinking about this is the adage often used by my colleagues Liz Jazwiec and Craig Deao, "What gets rewarded gets repeated."[11]

Under the assumption that a leadership position is some sort of reward, create a position of vice chair or associate medical or nursing director for wellness and resilience with the appropriate protected time, compensation, and authority. The broader dilemma of the chief wellness officer is discussed later in this chapter.

Words on the Walls, Happenings in the Halls

Leaders must be fanatical about looking for examples where the "words on the walls" are not matched by the "happenings in the halls." Use the process described in Chapter 6 to close this gap.

Leadership Development to Battle Burnout

The single most important concept in creating a culture of passion and fulfillment is that every team member at every level in every healthcare organization is a leader. Each of us is responsible for leading ourselves and our teams through our words, thoughts, and actions. Hospital medicine physicians are leaders creating a culture for that day for the team members and patients for which they are responsible. Nurses, even if they are not the charge nurse, use leadership principles to manage their patients. The essential services team leads the way in providing imaging, laboratory, registration, and environmental services, and they collectively create a culture through these actions. Make sure your teams at all levels understand this and that your organization invests in leadership skills for everyone, not just those with formal titles.

If every team member is a leader, every team member requires leadership training to battle burnout, first within themselves, then within the team. Across healthcare, training is essential but too often neglected. As Sir Richard Branson, founder of Virgin Airways, said, "Train people well enough they *can* leave. Treat them well enough so they *don't want to.*"[12] Coaching is an important part of leadership training, as John Wooden, UCLA men's basketball coach and winner of ten national championships, noted, "I was never much of a game coach, but I was a pretty good practice coach."[13]

All healthcare systems have some level of leadership development training, but few have a specific focus on educating leaders on the definition, effective treatment, and prevention of burnout.[14]

DEFINING BURNOUT

Effective leadership for burnout should start with a common definition, which should be known throughout the organization. This simple step is too often overlooked. As you may recall, here is our definition:

> *Burnout is a mismatch between job stressors and the adaptive capacity or resiliency required to deal with those stressors, which results in three cardinal symptoms:*
>   1. *Emotional exhaustion*
>   2. *Cynicism*
>   3. *Loss of a sense of meaning in work*

Ensure the definition is universally known and understood and that it is a part of leadership development training and team meetings.

JOB STRESSORS

Leaders should be "data and information mavens," constantly seeking to understand the job stressors for each unit for which they are responsible; the variable stressors for nurses, doctors, and essential services members; and how the teams' efforts to battle burnout are faring "down in the trenches." While Chapters 17–19 discuss the tools for battling burnout in detail, one specific tool can be extremely helpful in identifying and ameliorating job stresses: the "love, hate, tolerate tool." In team meetings, the concept should be introduced, and team members should be encouraged to reflect on their answers, both individually at first and then in subsequent team meetings **(Figure 9-3)**.

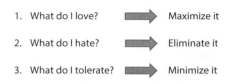

1. What do I love?   ➡   Maximize it

2. What do I hate?   ➡   Eliminate it

3. What do I tolerate?   ➡   Minimize it

Figure 9-3: The "Love, Hate, Tolerate" Tool

Asking people what they love and maximizing it is a step toward helping people reclarify the passion that brought them to healthcare.

To be sure, Dr. Knight wasn't able to completely eliminate the intrusion of the EHR, but she was able to decrease it and her burnout symptoms improved dramatically. (I will discuss the use of scribes and virtual scribes in Chapter 11.)

Leadership exists at every level, in every person, with every patient in healthcare. There are no unimportant members of the team. As a result of Earl's report to the leadership team, the culture of the organization changed, since everyone began to thank the EVS team members whenever and wherever they saw them. Disciplined leader rounding can also be an effective tool to learn job stressors and gather thoughts on how to reduce or eliminate them. Regardless of what methods are used, leaders at every level of healthcare should actively seek to learn and more fully understand the job stressors their team members face and how they are changing over time.

ADAPTIVE CAPACITY OR RESILIENCE

Increasing organizational adaptive capacity and resilience combines elements of culture and the hardwiring of flow and fulfillment by changing the systems and processes that are needed.[6,10] Leaders should be taught the tools needed to provide their teams with those same tools, including stakeholder analysis,[15]

CASE STUDY

Sharyn Knight is a family medicine physician who is considered by her patients and her peers to be among the kindest, most committed physicians in the healthcare system, but she admits that the stressors she faces are challenging. When asked to do the "love, hate, tolerate" exercise, her eyes flooded with tears as she said, "I love sitting and talking with my patients and their families, getting to explore how best I can help them through their lives." What she hates is the "distraction and intrusion of the electronic health record [EHR]," which she said is "like this monster of an obstacle between my patients and me." As she worked with her leader on these issues, maximizing her "love" and eliminating her "hate" led to her experimenting with using a medical scribe to interface with the computer/EHR, allowing her to focus on interacting with her patients.

CASE STUDY

Earl Thomas is the director of EVS for a large hospital. He decided to do the "love, hate, tolerate" exercise with his team, which required translating it into several different languages, because of the cultural diversity of his staff. The CEO was impressed that Earl had done this and asked him to present his results to the entire leadership team at their monthly meeting.

A naturally shy yet very articulate man, Earl started by saying how humbled and honored he was to speak to the group and then told the assembled crowd the results of the exercise.

"What our team loves is the chance to participate in some way, no matter how small, in helping our patients get well and back to their families. That and the occasional smile and kind word the doctors and nurses give them make it all worth it.

"What our team hates is when people walk past them in the hallways and don't even acknowledge them with a nod, a smile, or even the rare 'thank you.' To be ignored is what they hate.

"The rest they just tolerate as the price they pay in doing the job."

If I told you there wasn't a dry eye in the house, I wouldn't be exaggerating. Some of the nurses and even a few physicians were sobbing, since they had never realized they were sometimes walking past members of the EVS team without even acknowledging them.

boundary management,[16] communication skills,[17] and the tools of teams and teamwork.[18-19] Learning to provide a sense of balance between organizational and personal resiliency is also important. Leader rounding and the "love, hate, tolerate" exercise are both helpful here as well.

RETURNING FROM BURNOUT

Despite leaders' best efforts to prevent burnout, there are times when job stressors (and the changes creating them) will exceed resiliency's ability to counteract them, resulting in exhaustion, cynicism, and loss of meaning at work. Leaders must be masters at helping their team members in their "journey back from burnout." The first step in that journey is creating a culture that understands how and why burnout occurs and in which compassion is a constant. As I've discussed, there is always some element of shame for those who suffer from burnout, so compassion and understanding are requisite to guide the journey back to reconnecting their passion.[20-21] Coaching and mentoring not only should be core values of the culture but are disciplined skills that must be taught to all leaders at all levels of the organization.[22-23]

REDESIGNING PERFORMANCE ASSESSMENTS

Too many hospitals and healthcare institutions have performance assessment processes that reek of hierarchical, authoritarian interactions and too little chance to compare the demands of the job with the resources needed to complete the tasks. As Peter Block,[24] Tom Peters,[25] and Peter Drucker[26] have noted, the sessions often have an almost neocolonial feel, as professionals feel they are fundamentally being told the following:

- "Here are your deficiencies."
- "Here are the data supporting your deficiencies (which you had no voice in generating)."
- "Here's the timeline for reassessing your deficient performance."
- "Fix it!"
- "How do feel about your deficiencies?"
- "Oh, by the way, I basically own you."

A far more productive approach is to use these assessments as a means of coaching and mentoring team members, including by addressing where they stand on burnout (both objectively and subjectively). This would involve addressing both ways individuals can augment their capacity to deal with job stressors and ways the job itself can be changed to make it less stressful and more manageable. (What a revolutionary concept—a performance assessment that takes into consideration both how the person is performing and *how the job is performing for the person*.)[27]

ITERATIVE APPROACH

As we navigate the "perpetual whitewater of change,"[17] it becomes increasingly apparent that the only constant is change. Leaders should have a change management strategy, of which there are numerous examples, such as those in the work of Kurt Lewin,[28] Abraham Maslow,[29] William Bridges,[30] Elizabeth Kubler-Ross,[31] and John Kotter.[32] It matters less what change model is used, but it matters greatly if leaders have not thought out which model will guide them and their teams. Not surprisingly, to help others with adaptive capacity requires an ongoing, iterative approach to dealing with changing job stressors.

LEADING FROM THE FRONT

Leadership development programs should always stress the critical importance of "leading from the front." Leaders who share and understand the travails of those they lead are universally more successful than those who fail to understand this insight.[33-34] There is a rich history of this concept, particularly in the military, from the Greeks and Romans to Grant and Lee to numerous World War II generals, including George Patton, Bernard Montgomery, Terry Allen,

Norman Cota, Teddy Roosevelt Jr., "Brute" Krulak, and Charles de Gaulle.[35–37] (Patton always either walked or rode in an open staff car on his way to the front with the Third Army in France but always flew back to headquarters by plane or in an enclosed car, so he would not be seen by his men as "retreating.")[38]

For healthcare leaders and managers, this means spending as much time as possible, particularly in times of change, on the front lines with physicians and nurses providing care. Ask open-ended questions like these:

- "What could I do to make your jobs easier and your patients' lives better?"
- "Whom should I compliment today?"
- "Which patients should I listen to today?"
- "What job stressors are particularly meaningful today? What can I do to help?"

While leaders may not always be able to end job stressors immediately, they can put them in perspective and seek to increase adaptive capacity.

Limits Begin Where Vision Ends: Using Vision to Create Culture

Successful leadership does not occur without developing and communicating a clear vision of what constitutes success for the team and their patients. On May 6, 1954, Roger Bannister, then a medical student at Oxford University studying exercise physiology, ran humankind's first sub-4-minute mile, covering the distance in 3 minutes, 59.4 seconds. In a way that can scarcely be imagined over 65 years later, this event truly stunned the world, despite the fact that Bannister and two other runners, American Wes Santee and Australian John Landy, were each working furiously to do so.[39] Many of the most sophisticated medical experts of the time had said that the feat was simply impossible—the human body was incapable of attaining it, and a man would die in the attempt.[40] The accomplishment was treated, as well it should have been, as a triumph not just of athleticism but of the human spirit. (When Bannister finished his earth-shaking feat, he thanked three groups of people. The first were his pacers and training companions Chris Chataway and Chris Brasher. The second was his mother. The third was a man named William Morris, the groundskeeper at Iffley Road Track, who Bannister felt had played a critical role in having the track in pristine condition.[40] There are no unimportant people.)

However, 27 months after May 6, 1954, 10 runners had run sub-four-minute miles. In fact, one year and two weeks later, three men, in the same day, in the *same race*, did so. Something had happened that had never before happened in human history and that was felt by many to be physiologically unattainable— and yet, once the *vision* became a reality, it almost became commonplace. In fact, by 2012, 1,000 men had run a sub-four-minute mile. This is precisely what is meant by "limits begin where vision ends."[41]

If there is a shared vision expanding the limits of the organization, one of the most fertile areas to explore is the experience of other leaders committed to creating a culture of passion and fulfillment. Make sure you are regularly reaching out to them to share experiences in battling burnout. Bannister, Santee, and Landy were competitors, not collaborators. They were not sharing the lessons learned in their quest, which might have increased the pace of progress for all of them. And don't forget that one year and two weeks after Bannister ran his race, three men broke the four-minute barrier *in the same race.* It is a testament to the power of people to pull others along with them to achieve seemingly impossible things together. Use your colleagues to help fuel your quest.

The Case for Servant Leadership

The pioneer of servant leadership was Robert Greenleaf, who is among the most influential people in the field of leadership. Simply stated, servant leadership focuses not on the leaders and their needs but rather on those being served and whether they grow and develop in the course of being served.

In a penetrating 1969 essay that dramatically changed the way leaders were viewed, Greenleaf wrote,

> A fresh critical look is being taken at the issues of power and authority, and people are beginning to learn, however haltingly, to relate to one another in less coercive and more creatively supporting ways. A new moral principle is emerging, which holds that the only authority deserving one's allegiance is that which is freely and knowingly granted by the led to the leader in response to, and in proportion to, the clearly evident servant stature of the leader. Those who choose to follow this principle will not casually accept the authority of existing institutions. Rather, they will freely respond only to individuals who were chosen as leaders because they were proven and trusted as servants.[42]

Greenleaf recognized that such a concept would not be welcomed in the existing corridors of power, where too few view themselves as servants and too many have viewed leadership as exerting power and authority over those who are led. The servant leader is always a *servant first,* then a leader. These are understandably extreme ends of the leadership spectrum, between which, as Greenleaf noted, "are shadings and blends that are part of the infinite variety of human nature."[42]

Servant leadership presents a dynamic tension between a call for service and the legitimate need to exercise accountability. Leaders and managers are called on, by the very nature of their duties, not only to lead but also to hold those led to accountable and measurable results. This trend in healthcare is accelerating, not declining. Leaders and managers are accountable for producing results as a part of their contract and their performance plans. In this environment, how can one emphasize servant leadership?

Consider the following two quotes, which highlight this dynamic tension between servant leadership and accountability. The first answers the question, "What is the best test of the servant leader?"

> Do those served grow as persons? Do they, while being served, become, healthier, wiser, freer, more autonomous, more likely themselves to become servants? And, what is the effect on the least privileged in society?[42]

Greenleaf's focus is on those who are being served, as opposed to those who are leading, and our ability to expand their capabilities. While Greenleaf was not speaking specifically of healthcare leaders, one can't help but be impressed at the applicability of what he says to what healthcare leaders do daily, which is serve others, help expand their capabilities, and consider "the effect on the least privileged in society." Contrast this with these words, which speak to the use of power and accountability among servant leaders:

> I cannot conceive why anyone would want to be in a position of leadership anywhere unless one is comfortable with getting and using power. The wear and tear on the individual who leads is too great, and nothing, in my judgment, but the satisfaction of using power would compensate for the personal investment.[42]

While there are many descriptions of servant leadership, none is better than that of Frances Hesselbein, former CEO of the Girl Scouts of America, Presidential Medal of Freedom winner, and one of the great leaders of our time: "Leadership is a matter of *how to be, not what to do.*"[43]

Recall that teams are not groups of people who work together—they are groups of people who *trust each other*. So the core competency of servant leaders is the ability to engender and cultivate not just trust in themselves but also the team members' mutual trust of each other. As healthcare leaders and managers, we must be able to create teams capable of serving first but serving consistently and accountably as well. As Spinoza said, "Excellence is what we strive for, but consistency is what we demand."[44]

The dynamic tension that Greenleaf identifies between servant leaders and their use of power is apparent when we consider that all leaders seek to provide medical and service quality in each encounter by every team member, but reaching that end requires "getting and using power" to ensure accountability by teaching and developing the disciplines needed to achieve those scores through intrinsic motivation. Greenleaf notes, "Every achievement starts with a goal—but not just any goal and not just anybody saying it. The one who states the goal must enlist trust, especially if it is a high-risk or visionary goal, because those who follow are asked to accept the risking with the leader."[42] Leaders who wish to embrace their role in creating culture must have the ability to tie the passion and dedication of the team to the goals. Greenleaf says it best: "Not much happens without a dream. And for something great to happen, there must be a great dream. Behind every great achievement is a dreamer of great dreams."[42]

My advice is simple: *Dream great dreams and create a great culture.*

Culture of Passion, Compassion, Appreciation, Transparency, and Personal and Professional Growth

Passion is the key to both professional and personal fulfillment, so a culture of passion is essential to create the *passion reconnect* needed to battle burnout. The values of passion for the job; compassion and appreciation for ourselves, our patients, and our team members; transparency of results communicated in a timely manner; and a commitment to personal and professional growth and development are all essential to a successful healthcare organization. This includes a commitment to the following:

- ourselves
- our patients
- our team

A COMMITMENT TO OURSELVES

It might seem counterintuitive to begin with our commitment to ourselves to create a culture through daily action. But unless we can express our own passion and have compassion and appreciation for ourselves, we can't begin to truly have it for others.

Not to be overly critical, but the nurse's response inadvertently deflects the praise the trauma surgeon is sending her way, possibly because of a lack of ability to accept a compliment. "Thank you. I thought it went well, too. I'll tell the team you said that," might be a bit better in treating herself to the deserved praise sent her way. This might seem a fine point, but look for this on leader rounds.

Unless we can be compassionate to ourselves, unless we can genuinely forgive ourselves, we have little hope of forgiving others. And forgiving others is a

CASE STUDY

Sara Scott is the chief of trauma surgery, and she is called to the emergency department trauma resuscitation area for a "code blue," the highest level acuity for a trauma patient. The resuscitation is long, complex, and difficult, but the patient is finally stabilized enough to be taken to the operating room.

As she prepares to head to the operating room, Dr. Scott turns to the charge nurse, who ran the nursing side of the team, and says, "Great job. That was a tough one, but you handled it superbly." The nurse says, "Thanks, but it really wasn't anything."

part of our daily work. Simply stated, we will never be able to treat our patients and our teammates well if we can't find it in our hearts to treat ourselves well.[44]

A COMMITMENT TO OUR PATIENTS

Passion for our patients is obviously what brought us to healthcare and sustains us in difficult times. (And these days, they *all* seem to be difficult times.) I discussed this in detail in Chapter 1, but these are key parts of a culture of passion, compassion, appreciation, and transparency regarding the patient:

- making the patient part of the team
- moving from "What's the matter *with you*?" to "What matters *to you*?"
- patients as *participants* in their care, not just *recipients* of their care
- "nothing about you without you"

With every patient, we should encourage ourselves and our team to think, "How does what I'm doing reflect passion, compassion, and appreciation?"

A COMMITMENT TO OUR TEAM MEMBERS

With extremely rare exceptions, all of healthcare is a team sport. The care we provide is always provided with the help of others, without whom we couldn't serve our patients. This accentuates "the seams of the teams," which are the many handoffs and transitions that occur during care. The way we treat each other is a strong signal not just to the team members but also to the patients, families, and others who observe our interactions. I will discuss the concept of "leading up/managing up" in Chapter 10, but this is the skill of making those with whom we work start their interaction in a positive fashion, especially in the course of transitions of care from one person to another or one service to another.

A culture of appreciation always begins with personal praise at the patients' bedside but extends into how we treat each other and some of the small symbols and gestures in our interactions. Henry Clay said, "Courtesies of a small and trivial nature are the ones which strike deepest in the grateful and appreciating heart."[45]

One simple way in which appreciation can be expressed is to heed the age-old wisdom that breaking bread builds bonds of fellowship. Many healthcare

EXAMPLES OF "LEADING UP"

Hospital medicine physician to patient: "John is your nurse, and he's one of the best we have."

Nurse to inpatient: "Your hospitalist has requested a consult with the cardiologist, Dr. O'Brien. He's not only a great doctor but a great person as well. I know you will like him."

systems have leveraged this by providing meals to facilitate these communications. Brigham Health has implemented the "Brigham-to-Table" initiative, which provides meals three times per week to its patient care units, in an attempt to bring their teams together for meals and conversation. One colleague described his system's efforts to show appreciation through paid communal meals by saying, "We went from 'Breaking Bad' to 'Breaking Bread.'"[46]

All of this requires a fundamental value of integrity, which has many definitions, and about which much has been written. Cheryl Battle at Inova Health System defines it as follows: "Integrity is what you do when there is no one else around."[47] I can't improve on that and I know no one who can.

Empowerment Solutions

Empowerment is one of the most overused and least understood terms in healthcare. Detailed service and healthcare research indicates that no service leader, within healthcare or other industries, has ever succeeded without a deep culture of empowerment. Indeed, world-class organizations such as Mayo Clinic consider it a central tenet of their culture.[48] *Empowerment means that those providing the service have the ability to change or improve the service or processes if it better meets the patients' needs or expectations to improve patient experience.*[17] Easily said, but much harder to deliver in a practical fashion.

At a large, prestigious healthcare system with a reputation for having empowered programs, I posed this question: "Are you empowered?" The silence, frankly, was a bit disquieting, until a small voice from the back of the auditorium said, "They *tell* us we are." If the team is told they are empowered but the reality of that empowerment isn't clear, it's time to start over.

POINT-OF-IMPACT INTERVENTION

The best empowerment tool is point-of-impact intervention, which is a combination of the concepts of empowerment and negotiation. It begins with the insight that in patients who registered a complaint about their care, when their caregivers were asked whether they had any notion that the patient was unhappy at the time, 92 percent said yes. In other words, the majority of the time, when complaints occur, the staff know at the time there was a problem.[17] Point-of-impact intervention simply recognizes this fact and puts a tool in the hands of the caregiver to resolve the problem at the patient's bedside, the "point of impact." The tool consists of the following steps:

1. Identify the problem and address it immediately.

2. Establish the fact that you know there has been a breakdown.

3. Wipe the slate clean.

4. Establish their expectations—what's the delta between their expectations and their experience?

5. Negotiate and resolve issues.

6. If possible, meet their expectations.

7. Offer reasonable alternatives.

8. When all else fails, offer an alternative person to talk to.

These eight steps simply represent a disciplined approach to ensuring that we address the patient's expectations in real time so that we do not make the incident report bigger than the incident itself. Of particular significance is step 4, because many times the patient feels the staff has not met their expectations. Ensuring that the team goes back to the patient to reestablish their expectations is key to point-of-impact intervention, which dramatically reduces patient complaints by addressing them at the bedside, before the patient leaves the emergency department.

HARVESTING COMPLIMENTS, CULTIVATING COMPLAINTS

What causes compliments and complaints? For compliments, it is real or perceived A-team behaviors or processes; for complaints, it is B-team behaviors or processes. Leaders and managers must "harvest compliments" to discover what A-team behaviors and processes result in exceeding expectations and creating a positive patient experience. And they must "cultivate complaints" to understand the source of B-team behaviors and processes, which cause a failure to meet expectations. For this reason, all compliments and complaints should be discussed openly at team meetings so that group learning can occur.

Start Doing Smart Stuff, Stop Doing Stupid Stuff: Start Creating a Signal of Hope

Since the emergence of the science of performance improvement, lean management, and patient safety, leaders have come to understand the reality that many of the systems and processes by which healthcare operates produce inefficient, suboptimal results with unintended, wasteful consequences. Simply stated, we do a lot of "stupid stuff." "Stop doing stupid stuff" should be a model for all healthcare leaders, since this sends a signal to the team that its leaders are serious about creating a commonsense culture where systems and processes not only produce results but also allow for personal and professional fulfillment of the team.

Have the Courage to "Take on the EHRs"

Another area where both culture and systems and processes intersect is the EHR, which has been a major source of burnout, particularly with physicians and nurses. Chapter 11 addresses the specific strategies and tactics for taking on the EHR. Leaders must start this process by showing the courage to stop saying,

"That's just the EHR. You have to get used to it," and stand up for those who are forced to use it. That's a cultural issue, not just an operational one. Start with a clear and transparent commitment on the EHR that makes it clear that leaders recognize the horrible impact it can have on our teams and their tendency to burn out.

The Chief Wellness Officer Dilemma

One indicator of the seriousness with which a healthcare organization is taking the burnout epidemic is the appointment of a senior-level person whose responsibility it is to coordinate the diagnosis, treatment, and prevention of burnout. For most organizations that have chosen this path, the title for this person is usually chief wellness officer (CWO). It is currently not known how many healthcare systems have created such a position, their qualifications, their span of control or influence, or their impact, although a group of clinicians affiliated with the National Academy of Medicine's task force on wellness has issued a call to action for the creation of this position.[49] Stanford's WellMD program offers a course for CWOs,[50] and the Massachusetts Medical Society and Massachusetts Health and Hospital Association have made hiring a CWO one of their three recommendations to combat burnout.[51]

The arguments for such a position are straightforward and include the following:

- the moral imperative to address burnout
- the negative impact of burnout on quality measures
- the ROI from a financial perspective
- the ability and experience of senior-level leaders to address quality (chief quality officer), information technology (chief information officer), and even patient experience (chief experience officer)

(The impact on quality is a powerful argument. Tolerating the conditions that produce burnout requires being able to state, unequivocally, "I am willing, as the CEO [or COO, chief medical officer, or chief nursing officer] to accept inferior patient care!" That negative consequence is as unavoidable as gravity.)

Should healthcare organizations make such an investment? As a former theology major, I was always taught that the answer to any intelligent question is, "It depends." In this case, my view is that it depends on the following:

- Who does the CWO report to?
- What are the qualifications?
- What is the job description?
- What is the budgeted amount of time for the position?
- What is the budget for the program, or is it just one person?

REPORTING RELATIONSHIP

If CWOs report to anyone but the CEO (or perhaps the COO), they will lack senior-level commitment to making effective changes. Think about the fact that culture, the hardwiring of flow and fulfillment (systems and processes), and personal resiliency will all need to be addressed for the CWO to be successful. For example, if it is discovered that the culture and the systems and processes by which care is delivered are producing unacceptable levels of burnout, how can changes be made in those core aspects of the enterprise without the considerable leverage of either the CEO or COO? I would not advise someone to take on this role unless they report to the top. Anything less is a recipe for failure and frustration.

QUALIFICATIONS

Does the CWO have to be a physician? No, because the skills needed to succeed are neither innate nor exclusive to physicians. But if the organization has a culture in which physicians will not effectively listen to anyone other than a physician to make fundamental changes, then the answer is yes. (Which of course suggests that the culture needs to be changed.) Two of the best CWOs I know have PhDs in psychology (Bryan Sexton at Duke and Ryan Breshears at Well-Star). In practice, about two-thirds of CWOs are currently physicians, with the rest being nurses or behavioral psychologists. Some organizations have both a nurse and a physician working together in the role. The most important qualifications are significant experience in a clinical role, to engender the required respect of the team, and a deep and abiding passion for the plight of those who are burning out.

JOB DESCRIPTION

The National Academy of Medicine has provided a template for a set of responsibilities for the CWO (**Figure 9-4**). This and other descriptions often speak to the need to facilitate, coordinate, and work closely to make system-wide changes, including the implementation of evidence-based interventions to enable clinicians to do the following:

- effectively practice in a culture promoting their well-being
- develop personal resiliency as a priority

While those are worthy goals, I confess to uneasiness when I hear the term *facilitate*, as it connotes a frustration and futility that places that person in an untenable position. If it is that person's job to facilitate, is it the responsibility of the other C-suite members (and their direct reports) to "be facilitated"? Do those people have language in their job descriptions to the effect that being facilitated and cooperating with that facilitation is an important part of their job? I doubt it. This is not meant as pessimism, or even a healthy dose of much-needed reality,

CASE STUDY

Gretchen Nordstrom accepted the position of CWO at a large healthcare system, which recognized it had a problem with burnout and turnover of its physicians and nurses. After three months on the job, she discovered that the culture and the systems and processes were directly related to the increasing issue of burnout. She pointed out, privately and in meetings, that unless the culture and the systems were changed, it was unlikely that burnout could be prevented or treated. In a meeting of the senior leadership team, the COO said, "Your job is to facilitate and coordinate, not to make decisions—that's my job. Besides, our operational metrics are the best they have ever been."

but a realization that the metrics for wellness and burnout must be a significant part of the organization's scorecard to allow the "data, delta, decision" approach I have proposed. Finding the sources of burnout alone is ineffectual unless changes can be made at the top levels of leadership to change the system.

In this case, the COO seems to be willing to trade the costs of the suffering of burnout for the expediency of short-term results. It will be difficult or impossible for Dr. Nordstrom and her colleagues to change culture and systems in such an environment.

Any job description that translates to a passionate, empowered, and influential central advocate for the health and wellness of the workforce is the key to success.

BUDGETED TIME

For all but the smallest of healthcare systems, if the problem is significant enough to warrant a CWO and senior management and the board have recognized the ROI of effective burnout solutions, the position warrants at least a 75 percent time commitment, as well as support staff necessary to conduct and analyze burnout and fulfillment surveys and conduct leadership and resiliency training. Some systems have dedicated a full-time commitment and commensurate salary. (CWOs should always maintain some clinical responsibilities, partially because that maintains a sense of verisimilitude among one's clinical colleagues.) A colleague who burns with passion on burnout and resiliency recently asked my opinion on whether the CWO job she had been offered could be done "with a 0.5 FTE [full-time equivalent] time commitment." I responded, "What the organization is telling you is 1) they view the position as an FTE, not a passionate person committed to make meaningful change, and 2) [they have] a half-time commitment to solve about half the problems . . . Which half?" She declined the "opportunity."

Reports to

Senior Leadership (CEO, President, or Dean)

Minimum Requirements

Resources, including them members, to (i) implement and evaluate evidence-based interventions at the individual, group, and system level; and (ii) ensure implementation and continuous feedback.

Coordinates with other executive leaders (e.g., CQO) to ensure well-being is prioritized and integrated into executive leadership activites.

Works closely with marketing and/or communications team to ensure that community-wide messaging is supportive of the well-being for the community served.

Specific Responsibilities

- Provides strategic vision, planning, and direction to the development, implementation and evaluation initiatives to improve health and well-being outcomes
- Regularly monitors and reports outcomes, including measures of engagement, professional fulfillment, health and well-being, return on investment, value on investment, and tracks how they change with the introduction of interventions
- Raises awareness and provides education about the impact of professional burnout and the benefit of building resiliency and coping skills in clinicians
- Implements effective evidence-based individual-level interventions, group-level interventions, and system-wide interventions
- Implements system-level interventions on efficiency of practice, participatory management, and empowering of healthcare professionals to develop their voice on culture

- Pursues/advances well-being research efforts where appropriate
- Coordinates and works with mental health leaders to decrease stigma and improve access to and awareness of mental health services
- Creates a culture of wellness to improve organizational health and wll-being at the system level
- Conducts evidence-based quality improvement efforts that support clinician well-being
- Oversees the business plan development for implementation and delivery of programs and services that support clinician well-being

Figure 9-4: Sample Job Description for Chief Wellness Officer Position

BUDGET

The ROI for well-being programming in both healthcare and other industries has been proved in several studies, with effects on quality, productivity, turnover, malpractice cases, and employee satisfaction and fulfillment.[52-53] Data from the Ohio State University are particularly encouraging.[54] These results are unlikely to occur without the appropriate budget to include, at a minimum, administrative support, decision-support access, staff to administer and analyze data, and sufficient support for ongoing training across the institution.

SUMMARY

While there is a great deal of enthusiasm regarding the appointment of CWOs, it remains to be seen whether they will have the intended effects or whether Merton's law of unintended consequences will apply. For example, if the CWO is unable to make necessary changes in culture and the hardwiring of flow and fulfillment (systems and processes), then it is highly likely that the team will view this as a failed effort—at best—and yet another unfilled promise or management style du jour at worst, further increasing frustration and causing even more burnout.

This is not to say that these positions cannot be highly successful, but rather that the mere creation of the position alone is not nearly enough to ensure success. Reporting to the CEO is ideal, but COO reporting will probably occur in most organizations. There could be real battles there, with a dynamic tension between the financial and infrastructure needs identified and put forward by the CWO and the financial reality that the COO will, in almost all healthcare systems, have to find ways to finance such activities in a revenue-neutral fashion, given the significant financial constraints facing hospitals and healthcare systems.

Most healthcare systems have chief quality officers and chief information officers. One test of how easily accepted the CWO position will be is how easily the chief quality and chief information officers were accepted by the leadership team and the medical and nursing staffs. Were they viewed as a welcome addition that added value to the work and the team who does that work? Or were they viewed as "yet another C-suite member to oversee my work"? The answers to those questions are good barometers of the likely success of the CWO.

Using the Love of Meaningful Work or "Deep Joy"

An intriguing idea that represents a fundamental change in culture (as well as personal resiliency) is tapping into the individuals' "love" responses from the "love, hate, tolerate" tool to identify what they feel is the most meaningful work they do. Stated another way, "What is your deep joy?" Tait Shanafelt and his colleagues studied the extent to which individuals can focus their primary efforts on the self-identified aspect of work they found most meaningful.[55] They found that if their group of academic faculty were able to focus 10–20 percent of their time on the self-identified meaningful work, the burnout rates dropped by 50 percent. As they said, "This suggests that physicians will spend 80% of their time doing what leadership wants them to do provided they are spending at least 20% of their time in the professional activity that motivates them."[55] Tapping into self-identified meaningful work, passion, or deep joy could be highly effective means of using intrinsic motivation as an important part of the culture.[55] While this work was done in an academic faculty environment, I have found it a useful way to help team members (not just physicians) identify what motivates them and ensure that they have commitment from the organization to help them pursue this. I have called it "singing with all your voices," meaning developing an understanding that in healthcare, all of us have a wide range of professional tasks and areas of expertise. A commitment to understanding what we love—the most meaningful part of the work we do—and developing that passion is important, even as we retain an understanding that there are other parts of the job we don't love. And we do have "other voices," meaning other talents and the sense of meaning deriving from them, but we must be attentive to discovering them.

Summary

- A suite of solutions assists in creating a culture of passion and personal resilience.
- All healthcare team members are leaders of their part of healthcare all day, every day.
- Redesign performance assessments to shift them from "neocolonialism" to meaningful coaching, mentoring, and transparency.
- Lead from the front to change culture.
- Embody servant leadership in all actions.
- Dream great dreams to create a great culture.

10

Hardwiring Flow and Fulfillment

We are what we repeatedly do. Excellence is not a virtue, but a habit.

ARISTOTLE, *ETHICS*[1]

If Aristotle is correct and we are what we repeatedly do, then what we do at work is guided by the systems and processes in which we do them. Much of the work on burnout has focused on personal resilience to the relative exclusion of changing the nature of the work and its consequences. *Having a good or even a great attitude about doing work that burns us out should not be the primary solution—fixing work that produces a 50 percent burnout rate should be.*

This requires changing the systems and processes by hardwiring flow and fulfillment into the work. Kirk Jensen and I coined the term *hardwiring flow* in 2009, defining it as follows: "Flow exists to the extent that value is added and waste is reduced to a product or service during a patient's journey through the queues and service transitions of healthcare."[2] We titled our 2009 book *Hardwiring Flow: Systems and Processes for Seamless Patient Care.* We knew, based partially on Mihaly Csikszentmihalyi's work,[3] that flow as an optimal healthcare

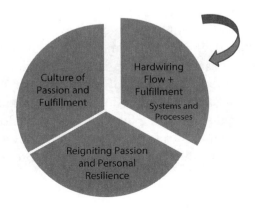

Culture of Passion and Fulfillment

Hardwiring Flow + Fulfillment
Systems and Processes

Reigniting Passion and Personal Resilience

Hardwiring Flow
- Start Doing "Smart Stuff"—Adding Value
- Stop Doing "Stupid Stuff"—Decreasing Waste

+

Hardwiring Fulfillment
- "Fully Filling" Our Passion
- Fueling Our Fires to "Burn In" Instead of Burn Out

Figure 10-1: Hardwiring Flow and Fulfillment

experience was attainable by concentrating on adding value and decreasing waste, which allows those working in the system to focus their talents to the maximum effect. But the subtitle is equally important, because it is the systems and processes that guide what we repeatedly do. Hardwiring flow means doing "smart stuff"—the stuff that adds value—while ceasing to do "stupid stuff" that creates waste, both of which allow us to use our talents more effectively and in a more fulfilling way. Flow and fulfillment are inextricable. We cannot attain or sustain fulfillment unless we hardwire our systems and processes for both flow *and* fulfillment. While it is common to measure flow exclusively by time, quality, and safety metrics, we must move to considering how our systems and processes affect fulfillment as well **(Figure 10-1)**.

Applying those disciplines consistently to allow patients to flow through the system is the province of *leadership*, which should identify the best practices to add value and decrease waste. But it cannot be done without the *followership* of those doing the work. This is true both because the people doing the work best understand the specific systems and processes and because they are the ones who most fully understand the details that produce burnout. Hardwiring flow and fulfillment into the systems and processes of the daily work is an important path to increasing organizational resilience.

Fulfillment in Healthcare

Curiously, a literature search for "fulfillment in healthcare" sends you to reams of articles on how *fast* one can get a product or service to a customer, not the deep personal sense of fulfillment needed to fuel our work. (Indeed, there is much more written in the "mindfulness" literature on fulfillment than in healthcare or scientific journals.)[4–5] Yet this concept of "fully filling an order" may have some attractiveness as we define fulfillment in healthcare. In our case, what "order" are we fully filling? Fulfillment of what—and why? Our fulfillment is "filling the order" of our deeply held passions and our deep joy—what brought us to healthcare originally and is the fire that fuels our efforts. It allows us to use the flame to "burn in" instead of burning out. Fulfillment also entails an intense clarity about worthwhile goals and values that provide a connection to the patient.

The thousands of healthcare team members I spoke with about this issue consistently told me that these are the elements that give them fulfillment:

- connection with patients
- making meaningful differences for their patients
- clear, honorable goals
- clarity of the challenge as well as the impact of their work
- rapport with colleagues
- challenging cases that match abilities with the work needed
- the ability to focus on difficult tasks and accomplish them
- constant upgrade of skills to meet the constantly changing challenges
- doing difficult work aligned with their values

These and other responses fit well into the concept of flow as optimal experience that Csikszentmihalyi described. Later in this chapter I will discuss the concept of working "at the top of your license," which is a clear example of professionals staying sufficiently challenged to experience flow at work. Critical care professionals such as emergency, ICU, trauma, and surgical physicians and nurses tell me without exception that their best days have been in the midst of crises and disasters, probably because of the challenge, clarity, and commitment needed to do the work. My experience and that of all of the people with whom I worked at the Pentagon on September 11, 2001, was that, as bad as that day was, it was the most satisfying day of our careers. In his great book *Tribe*,[6] Sebastian Junger notes the same phenomenon among survivors of the Afghanistan war and Bosnian conflict. Those who worked on the front lines in caring for patients in the coronavirus pandemic in 2020 also describe feelings of flow and satisfaction when asked about that challenging time.[7–8]

Hardwiring Flow and Fulfillment Solutions

With our definition of hardwiring flow and fulfillment in mind, let's proceed to how this concept can be used practically with specific strategies to increase organizational resiliency. These are listed by the six Maslach domains[9] **(Figure 10-2)**:

- diminishing workload demands and increasing adaptive capacity
- regaining or seizing control
- increasing rewards and recognition
- returning community to the team
- reestablishing fairness in an unfair world
- reinfusing values in the workplace

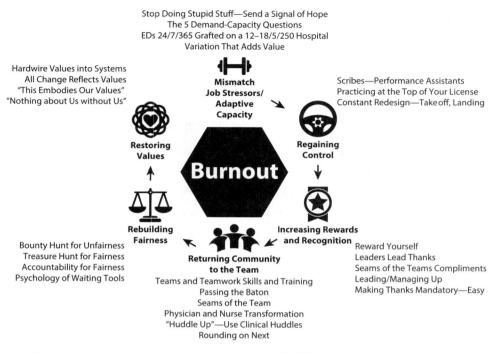

Figure 10-2: Solutions to Hardwire Flow and Fulfillment Matched to Maslach's Six Domains of Burnout

Because of its dramatic, universal, and powerful effect on burnout—and because it cuts across all of the domains—taking on the electronic health record (EHR), the subject of Chapter 11, is perhaps the most powerful set of solutions to hardwire flow and fulfillment in healthcare. Finally, several of the solutions apply both to organizational resilience, because of their effects on systems and processes, and to personal resilience, so they are listed here and in the following chapter, where the emphasis is on how to use them personally to fuel our passion.

DIMINISHING WORKLOAD DEMANDS AND INCREASING ADAPTIVE CAPACITY

Designing and implementing solutions to improve systems and processes in order to diminish workload stressors while increasing the team's adaptive capacity provide high leverage strategies to increase resilience and decrease burnout. **Figure 10-3** shows these solutions.

Start Doing Smart Stuff, Stop Doing Stupid Stuff: Send a Signal of Hope

Hardwiring flow and fulfillment involves doing "smart stuff"—the evidence-based best practice systems and processes that produce superior flow metrics and allow the team to feel fulfilled. The concepts of lean healthcare and hardwiring flow have as their fundamental insight that improvement of the systems

- Start Doing Smart Stuff
- Stop Doing Stupid Stuff
- Send a Signal of Hope
- 5 Demand Capacity Questions
- ED 24/7/365 in 12–18 /5/250
- Variation That Adds Value

Job Stressors
Adaptive Capacity

Figure 10-3: Solutions to Decrease Job Stressors and Increase Adaptive Capacity

and processes is not only possible but essential to healthcare leadership, as we lead ourselves and lead our teams.[9]

One of the hardest things for leaders at all levels to accept is that a lot of the things we do in healthcare simply don't make sense—either to the patient or to the people who take care of the patient. "Stop doing stupid stuff" is a way of harvesting "low-hanging fruit," fixing problems that everyone can see but few have had the courage to correct. Most importantly, it creates hope that leaders are paying attention and are serious about creating a commonsense culture. There are countless examples of stupid stuff, including these:

Many mornings in the emergency department (ED), patients wait in line to be triaged when there are rooms, doctors, nurses, and essential services staff in the back waiting for them. They wait in a line when there should be no line.

Patients sit in waiting rooms for hours throughout the healthcare system, looking at a vision statement that proclaims, "Patient first." Many of them have appointments but are still waiting for long periods. They can't help thinking, "Really? Because I don't feel 'first.'"

Nursing units operate with fewer nurses than scheduled but are expected to produce top-decile metrics. They use the same systems and processes when "working short" that they use when fully staffed. And we are somehow surprised when they think, "Seriously? You know we need this level of staffing, but nothing gets done."

A medical patient needs a physical therapy appointment before being discharged, which is identified as a rate-limiting step on rounds. However, instead of having a team member immediately call for the appointment, the team waits until rounds are completed before anyone calls physical therapy. By that time all the appointments for the day are taken and the patient cannot be discharged until the next day.

Patients "board" in ED hallways for hours (sometimes days) and are taken care of by ED nurses, who are thus unavailable to care for incoming ED patients. Once a bed is identified in the hospital, it takes hours to have it cleaned, and almost as long from the time it is cleaned until the inpatient team is ready to take the patient.

An orthopedic surgeon is on call over a busy holiday weekend, when there is a highly predictable number of patients with orthopedic problems who will require follow-up the next week. Instead of ensuring that there are a certain number of designated appointments for these patients, the surgeon's schedule is filled, meaning the patients from the on-call schedule won't be seen in a timely fashion.

One of the most critical rate-limiting steps in healthcare is the bottlenecks that occur in surgery, with delays between cases and surgeries requiring critical care unit beds "stacked" on days that create ICU overuse and backups for critical care patients admitted from the ED or transferred from other hospitals. Scientific surgical smoothing principles have not been applied to relieve the problem.

This list could go on, but each is an example of what appears to be stupid stuff, which we nonetheless continue to tolerate. The solution is to start doing smart stuff. Each of these problems can be fixed with relatively simple actions that change the systems and processes by which patients are cared for. Instead we create a culture where stupid stuff is tolerated. *Leadership at all levels must seek out and resolve stupid stuff whenever and wherever it is identified.* The first step for leaders to create a culture of hope and hardwire flow and fulfillment is to start doing smart stuff and start fixing stupid stuff. Fortunately, doing so sends a jolt of hope to the team, who think, "Well, I'll be darned. Maybe they are finally serious about correcting things around here."[10]

The impact on the staff of sending a signal of hope cannot be overstated. Team members are usually aware of the plethora of stupid things being done in the name of "That's the way we've always done it." When leaders begin to change these flawed systems and processes, it sends a signal of hope to the team that things don't have to stay mired in the status quo ante, unleashing the huge potential of innovation and creativity.[11]

The Five Demand-Capacity Questions   One of the key tools of hardwiring flow is the use of demand-capacity tools, including the five demand-capacity questions Jensen and I describe, which can also be used to allow us to understand patient demands, the expectations that accompany them, and the capacity to deal with them.[2] By applying these questions in our work, we can increase our adaptive capacity by understanding the demand-capacity curve.[2,12]

1. Who is coming? (What are the demands?)

2. When are they coming? (What's the timing of the demands?)

3. What will they need? (What is the specific nature of the demands?)

4. Will we have what they need? (What capacity do we have?)

5. What will we do if we don't? (What is our adaptive capacity?)

Within each shift, these tools should be used to maximize adaptive capacity to the workload and the stressors the workload entails.

Emergency Departments as 24/7/365 Grafted on a 12–18/5/250 Hospital EDs work 24 hours a day, 7 days a week, 365 days a year (24/7/365), which produces a workload that is predictable yet unrelenting. We can and should use the demand-capacity tools to inform us of who is coming and what

CASE STUDY

Dr. Andrew Mathews and Nurse Ann Corrigan have worked the last three shifts in the ED together, starting with a day shift on Thursday. Today is Saturday and they are working the evening shift. On Thursday, they had a patient they cared for together, a 35-year-old lady with vague symptoms of chronic back pain, for which she had been seen multiple times, both in the ED and by an orthopedist. When Dr. Mathews examined her, he noticed a vague fullness in the paraspinal area and an equally vague sense that this area was warmer to the touch. At three o'clock that afternoon, he requested a gadolinium-enhanced MRI scan of the lumbar spine, which was performed within two hours and showed a spinal epidural abscess, which was drained in the operating room that evening.

It is now nine o'clock on Saturday evening and he and Ann see a 50-year-old lady with the acute onset of bladder incontinence and the beginnings of paresthesia in the "saddle" region. They suspect these could be early manifestations of spinal cord compression known as cauda equina syndrome, which, if present, is a neurosurgical emergency. Forty-five minutes later Dr. Mathews is informed that the MRI technician says that he must speak to the radiologist before the study can be done. He pages the radiologist, who doesn't answer for another 45 minutes, but says, "Have you consulted neurosurgery to have them approve the MRI? We don't do MRIs on the weekend unless neurology or neurosurgery approves them." Dr. Mathews takes a deep breath and says in a measured voice, "Rodney, I would like you to take a moment and consider if this were your wife who had these symptoms, suggestive of the beginnings of spinal cord compression. Would you want us to jump through all these hoops and delay her care?" The radiologist approved the study, which indeed showed acute spinal cord compression. It was immediately decompressed surgically, and the patient made a full recovery, which might not have been possible if the MRI had been further delayed.

they will need. But it needs to be recognized that the hospital does not, by nature, operate with all its resources, facilities, and staffing at the same level 24/7/365. Many of the resources needed to care for the ED's patients—including MRI, consultative services, physical therapy, behavioral health services—are only available 12–18 hours a day, 5 days a week, 250 days per year (Monday through Friday, with holidays off or at limited staffing).[13]

This case study reflects the details (except for the names) of actual cases, and it is a clear example of two standards of care—one for daytime, weekday hours and a second one for nights and weekends. As a result of the second case, despite its good outcome, a change was made in the policy for ordering MRIs, with a clear set of evidence-based protocols developed and approved by the emergency physicians, radiologists, neurologists, and neurosurgeons. The better the organization understands this demand-capacity mismatch and is prepared to deal with it by developing proactive strategies, the more their adaptive capacity increases.

Variation That Adds Value: Different Strategies for Different Realities

What is true in the morning is a lie by the afternoon.

CARL JUNG[14]

The concepts of hardwiring flow often stress reducing variation whenever possible, but the more penetrating insight is to recognize variation that adds value. For example, at ten o'clock on a weekday morning, the ED may use a process of "direct bedding" or "triage bypass," in which patients are taken directly back to an ED bed instead of getting delayed at triage.[15] But once the beds are all full, that process no longer works, and a different set of processes must be in place, including advanced triage orders for certain patients or, if beds will not be available for extended periods of time, physician or provider at triage.

Specialists in hospital medicine are familiar with the times of day when admissions come into the hospital, including the rates from the ED and from physician offices, as well as transfers. The best of them treat these patients expeditiously, often coming to the ED before all lab studies are completed, effectively working "in parallel" instead of sequentially. All of these are examples of teams prospectively understanding that in some cases variation adds value because the flow circumstances vary. This concept increases capacity in the face of increased demands (job stressors) and smooths workload.[2,10,16]

This case study is a clear example of how variation in flow patterns and demand-capacity principles drove a change in systems and processes during a single day in the ED. These principles apply across the healthcare system, where variation can add value.

REGAINING OR SEIZING CONTROL

In healthcare it seems that control over our daily lives has gradually been eroded, both for leaders and for all team members. When I speak to large audiences of

CASE STUDY

The ED team at Inova Fairfax Medical Campus were innovators in developing solutions to hardwire flow and fulfillment. Using data on arrivals and the five demand-capacity questions, teams of physicians, nurses, and essential services staff designed systems and processes to address each of the "flow realities" that occurred over the course of a typical day. In the mornings, there were available beds and staff, so the process known as "triage bypass" or "pull until you are full" was implemented, where patients went directly to open beds instead of waiting in a line to be triaged. When all the beds in the ED were full, the process needed to be different to meet the different circumstances. Advanced triage or advance initiatives were developed so the triage nurse could implement standing orders to begin the patients' diagnostic work-up and begin the treatment for certain conditions. Later in the day, there were predictable times when the "boarder burden" of patients waiting for hospital beds caused delays because the ED beds were full. A system known as "team triage" was developed where an emergency physician, nurse, scribe, registrar, and technician were deployed to the triage area so patients could immediately be evaluated by the team and their diagnosis and treatment could begin. Over 30 percent of those patients were diagnosed, treated, and discharged without ever needing an ED bed. Both flow metrics and team and patient experience scores improved with each of these processes.

healthcare leaders and providers across the country, I always ask them this question: "How many of you feel that you are held accountable for a system over which you have little or no control?"[17]

Unsurprisingly, every hand goes up. Each of these strategies helps regain control (**Figure 10-4**).

Scribes as Personal Performance Assistants One of the most consistent aggravations for physicians and nurses in EDs is the necessity of dealing with the EHR. The issues of EHRs and scribes are addressed in Chapters 8 and 11, but note that one solution to this is the use of scribes, or "personal performance assistants," who are specifically trained and tasked with ensuring that the EHR needs are met, but that the physician's or nurse's interaction with the EHR is confined to value-added situations. This fundamentally changes the workload, freeing professionals to work at the "top of their license" instead of being glued to the computer screen.[18–19]

Practicing at the Top of Your License Practicing at the top of your license means that all team members work to the full extent of their education, training, and experience and are not forced to perform tasks that can easily be done by

- Scribes as Personal Performance Assistants
- Practicing at the Top of Your License
- Redesign Systems and Processes with the "Takeoff" and "Landing" Approach

Regaining Control

Figure 10-4: Solutions to Regain Control

other team members with lower levels of training. It means that doctors do "doctor stuff," nurses do "nurse stuff," and so on through the team. Control is regained when systems and processes change to ensure that our skills, talents, and passion are harnessed to what we were trained to do. When staff at every level of the organization are surveyed regarding professional fulfillment, they universally and emphatically state that they want to spend their days doing work they are trained to do and not get bogged down with tasks and processes that could easily be done by those with lower levels of education and training.

The use of well-trained emergency department technicians to perform EKGs, start IV lines, do discharges for patients with minor illnesses and injuries, and handle other tasks allows higher levels of fulfillment.[20] In EDs with the best practices, it is rare for an emergency physician to suture a laceration, since the advanced practice providers not only are capable of doing this procedure but are also often better at it because they do it more often and do not have the same time pressures as the physicians. Over 15 years ago, I surveyed the senior, experienced nurses in our level 1 trauma center concerning which tasks they would be happy not to have to perform, and starting IVs was at the top of the list. Having technicians or EMTs working in the department take over those responsibilities increased satisfaction and fulfillment in both groups. Practicing at the top of the license is a way of hardwiring flow by decreasing the waste of doing a task that others could do equally well or better. It also is a more cost-effective means of resource utilization and efficiency for payers.[21]

Redesigning Systems and Processes with the "Takeoff" and "Landing" Approach One of the most powerful strategies to regain control is to ensure that all of our teams know that systems and processes are subject to constant reexamination and improvement. Further, each reexamination of systems and processes should be driven by the approach that "if they aren't with you on the takeoff, they won't be with you on the landing," which is an essential component of regaining control.

REWARDS AND RECOGNITION

Rewards and recognition cut across all three dimensions of culture, personal resiliency strategies, and the hardwiring of flow and fulfillment. It is essential

**Rewards &
Recognition**

- Reward Yourself
- Leaders Lead Thanks
- Seams of the Team
- Leading Up/Managing Up
- Making Thanks Easy

Figure 10-5: Solutions to Increase Rewards and Recognition

to hardwire gratitude, generosity, and thanks into our systems and processes **(Figure 10-5)**. (Specific personal strategies are discussed in Chapter 8.)

Leaders Lead the Way in Saying Thank You It starts at the top—if healthcare leaders at all levels constantly exhibit the behaviors and language of thanks, the rest of the team will follow. Think of your most valued mentor. Didn't she give you thanks often, which inspired you to do even better? Didn't she see more in you than you saw in yourself? Didn't she help you set guilt aside and thank yourself instead of being excessively self-critical? As Max DePree, former CEO of Herman Miller, says, "The first responsibility of a leader is to define reality. The last is to say thank you. In between, the leader is a servant."[22]

The best place to say thanks is at the bedside or in the work environment, where the praise was earned and others can witness it. One of the most enduring ways for a leader to say thanks is vastly underused but always deeply appreciated: a brief handwritten note. I use four-by-six-inch notes, which require brevity and clarity but also fit into a pocket quite easily. I have found that many people do just that, carrying a note with them at work to keep it close for inspiration during challenging times. The paper I use simply has a name at the top, no titles, which stresses that it is a *personal note*, not from "the boss" but from a person who is thankful to work with you. What do you write in the note? Just open your heart and write that in the note. No need to overthink it. When should you write it? Whenever you think of it. Leaders should treat rewards and recognition as a discipline, as a regular part of the day. Just as you should say thanks every day on leader rounds and in the course of your work, you should also return from rounds, sit down, pull out at least one card, and think, "Whom do I need to thank today for doing a great job? To whom am I particularly grateful today?" President George H. W. Bush was a prolific note and letter writer, not because it was a leadership tool or PR trick but, as he said, "because that's how I was raised and because it made *me* feel better."[23]

Reward Yourself We will never be fully able to reward and recognize others unless we can accept rewards and recognition ourselves. It is a curious phenomenon that many healthcare professionals, who have chosen their careers to serve others, nonetheless are sometimes reluctant to serve themselves through self-recognition of a job well done.[24] In designing and redesigning systems and processes, look for subtle opportunities to build rewards and recognition into them. Hint: anytime we transition service from one person or system to another, there is an opportunity to give rewards and recognition, as I will discuss next.

Seams of the Team and Harvesting Compliments One of the most important insights in hardwiring flow is the importance of adding value and eliminating waste during the service transitions of healthcare. An equally important insight is that there are far more service transitions in healthcare than we often realize. I'll discuss this in more detail in "Passing the Baton," but as leaders look at systems and processes, they should look for the "seams of the teams," which are the seams of transitions, and find ways to ask, "How can we build thanks, rewards, and recognition into each of them as a standard way of operating?"[25] One of those ways is by "leading up" through language.

Leading Up or Managing Up A critical leadership tool to hardwire flow and fulfillment into systems and processes is a concept I have referred to as "leading up" or, as the Studer Group refers to it, managing up.[26] *"Leading up" or "managing up" refers to empowering others by using verbal service transitions to ensure the patient is led to expect excellence from the person or groups who will next care for the patient.* While the primary benefit of leading or managing up is that it prepares the way for a smooth service transition from one person and one service to another, it also serves to "lead up" the person to whom care will be transferred in that it helps them to understand that a great deal will be expected of them, given their superb introduction to the patient and family.

The following are some examples:

- "Janet is your nurse today, and she's the best."
- "Jim is the orthopedic technician, and he will put your splint on and teach you to walk with your crutches. He's actually better at this than I am."
- "Let me introduce you to Dr. Smith, my partner, who will be taking over for me. I have briefed him on all the details and he will take great care of you."
- "The x-ray shows that your bone is fractured, so I spoke with your physician, who recommended I call the orthopedic surgeon. His name is Dr. Theiss and he will be in to take care of you soon. He is excellent and will do a great job!"
- "As I said earlier, we will need to admit you to the hospital today, so I have called your doctor, who asked that we admit you to one of our hospital specialists in hospital medicine. Dr. Gonzalez will be admitting you today and will keep your doctor informed of your care every step of the way."

Making Thanks Mandatory Makes Thanks Easy It seems that giving thanks, rewards, and recognition should be the easiest thing on the planet, doesn't it? Why is it so rare in our daily lives, particularly in healthcare? As you approach your day, closely observe your teams. Do they thank each other often or rarely? Which is more commonly heard, "Thanks, that was a great job," or "Why did you make that mistake?"? On balance, is there more praise or blame in your day? The ratio of praise to blame is the inflection point between burnout and fulfillment.

"Making thanks mandatory" doesn't necessarily have the ring of a servant leadership culture. But if rewards and recognition are a part of "the way we do things here," saying thanks becomes the norm, not the exception—and it makes it easier to say thanks. The more the team does it, the more they will reconnect to their passion.

RETURNING COMMUNITY TO THE TEAM

> *We can confidently assure that in healthcare, you will be taken care of by a* team of experts. *But we can less confidently assure that you will be taken care of by an* expert team.
>
> THOM MAYER[27]

Healthcare is, by nature, a team sport—it can only be provided by a group of people who work together for a common goal. That said, a team is not a group of people who simply work together; it is a group of people who *trust each other while they work together.* The primary teamwork goal of leaders seeking to hardwire flow and fulfillment to battle burnout is to foster and develop trust among the team members and to exhibit language and behaviors to engender trust.

In addition to the foundation of trust, teams in healthcare share a definition and a set of teamwork skills **(Figure 10-6)**.[27]

Teams and Teamwork Skills and Training Teams have four fundamental characteristics. First, they have a common sense of clearly defined purpose that the team had a role in generating ("takeoff" and "landing"). Clarity of purpose is essential to flow. Second, trust and a deep sense of respect for *all* team members

- Teams and Teamwork
- Passing the Baton
- Seams of the Team
- Physician and Nurse Transformation
- Huddle Up
- Rounding on Next

Restoring Community

Figure 10-6: Solutions to Restore Teams and Community

and the unique roles they play is a core aspect. Third, hardwiring flow and ful-fillment focuses on ensuring there is a system of value-added processes, with a focus on the "seams of the teams" during which transitions occur. Finally, there must be a culture of celebration of *team success* while providing *individual coaching and mentoring*.[27]

Fortunately, in addition to this definition, there is a set of time- and experience-tested tools of teamwork (further discussed in Chapters 17 and 18):

- making the patient part of the team
- hire right!
- the seams of the teams
- dyad/triad leadership
- mutual accountability
- a culture of coaching and mentoring
- anticipation
- demand-capacity leadership
- empowerment
- high-reliability organizations
- reliable and redundant communication
- clinician huddles

Passing the Baton   Jensen first pointed out to me that at the 2008 Beijing Summer Olympics, the US men's 4×100-meter relay team comprised the best athletes in the world—some say it was the best relay team in the history of the sport. Their goal was clear: to win the gold medal. Their path was also clear: to advance through successive rounds to the finals. They were the best individual athletes in their sport, so much so that it was difficult to decide which order to run them in, since the anchor, or final runner, is usually the fastest. Did they win the gold medal? No, they did not. In fact, they didn't make it out of the quarterfinal round. Why? They dropped the baton.

At that level of sport, with athletes that good and that experienced, this may seem hard to believe. But it was not a failure of the athletes but rather a failure of coaching. They had been coached to run fast *individually*. But the goal of a relay team is to run fastest *as a team*. These were good men who had trained their entire lives to reach the pinnacle of the Olympic Games—but the team had been assembled only a relatively short time before the Olympics. Perhaps if the coaches had them spend more time on the baton passes, the results would have been quite different.

The point is that leaders must recognize the multiple service transitions that necessarily occur in healthcare—the passing of the baton and the seams of the teams. In healthcare, perhaps the "baton" that is being passed is our patients.[3,9]

When we figuratively drop them by not focusing on the handoffs, we not only fail to serve them well, but we also inadvertently create burnout among the "great athletes" forming our teams. Coach your teams to "pass the baton well," not just to attain individual results.

Physician and Nurse Transformation An important transformation is under way in healthcare in which physicians, as well as nurses, are moving from a position of authority to being a part of a team in partnership with the patient and family. In the past, physicians were expected to be authoritarian, authoritative sources of wisdom and knowledge to whom patients came for answers to their needs. Of course, they were also expected to be compassionate caregivers. Osler's wisdom was always correct: "It is better to know what sort of patient has the disease than what sort of disease the patient has."[28]

The transformation among physicians and nurses also includes placing them in roles as "chief experience officers" and "knowledge translators." Physicians and nurses are the primary determinants in the creation of a positive experience for their patients, which means they need to be not only excellent clinicians but also experts at creation of the experience for the patient and the family, which combines the art and the science of medicine and nursing.

While the authoritarian models of the past placed an expectation of almost encyclopedic knowledge and wisdom on the part of the nurse-physician dyad, today patients are so well informed in many cases that doctors and nurses effectively become "knowledge translators" whose role it is to make sense of the data and interpret its meaning for the patient and family, integrating what the data have shown into an understandable whole.

This transformation can be a source of frustration and therefore burnout if it is not understood, embraced, and anticipated. It redefines how the team acts as a community in this new environment. If this is understood, it can help create a new sense of community and teamwork, preventing burnout.

Huddle Up: Using Clinical Huddles to Reinforce Community Chapter 19 discusses the role of clinical huddles in creating teamwork in healthcare. These huddles develop *shared mental models*[29] by which community is reinforced on a regular basis, as well as delineating specific contributions that will be made by team members for the good of the patient. They also ensure that the entire team interacts and prevent people from working in relative isolation through the course of the day. And they create common understandings among the team members, further reinforcing community.

Rounding on Next Rounding is an important tactic within the organization that ensures that information is shared across boundaries and communication is enriched. It owes its origins to the concept of "management by walking around," originally described by Tom Peters and Robert Waterman in *In Search of Excellence* and further examined by Peters in *The Excellence Dividend*.[30–31]

Rebuilding Fairness

- Bounty Hunt for Unfairness
- Treasure Hunt for Fairness
- Accountability and Language
- Putting the Psychology of Waiting to Work

Figure 10-7: Solutions to Rebuild Fairness

The rounding concept should be extended to "rounding on next," which refers to rounding on patients admitted from the ED to the hospital.[32] Keeping a log of patients each physician and nurse admits and having them visit the patient on the inpatient unit has incredible value in helping them understand their important role in the healthcare community. It is also deeply appreciated by the patient and family, increasing gratification and preventing burnout. An additional way to "round on next" is to place follow-up phone calls to discharged patients. While this has clear value in reestablishing community, it is less effective than the face-to-face interactions of rounding on inpatients.

RESTORING FAIRNESS IN AN UNFAIR ENVIRONMENT

Healthcare team members are driven by a profound belief that what is provided to their patients should be eminently fair. While some refer to this as healthcare equity, in the trenches it comes down to a tacit determination of "Is this fundamentally fair to the patients and to those who take care of the patients?" **(Figure 10-7)**.

Conduct a Bounty Hunt for Unfairness and a Treasure Hunt for Fairness
As much as values are critically important to preventing burnout, the domain of fairness is where burnout in healthcare is often first noticed. Because of the deeply egalitarian nature of physicians and nurses, it is not surprising that this is the case. However, focusing on fairness also has tremendous leverage on reestablishing the team and leadership's commitment to fairness, equity, and parity, both for the team and for its patients.[9] Look at each aspect of hardwiring flow and fulfillment and every system and process. For each, conduct a "bounty hunt" for unfairness and eliminate it. Have a "treasure hunt" for fairness and celebrate it.

Mutual Accountability and the Language of Fairness
Eliminating functional silos[33] and ensuring there is mutual accountability across boundaries is a clear way of ensuring fairness, since many people "say 'team'" but don't "play 'team.'"[27] Mutual accountability involves eliminating statements such as, "Well the physicians' patient experience scores are great. It's the nurses' scores that are pulling us down." Instead, an approach that is focused on fairness uses language such as, "We are all in this together. Let's see what worked in raising the physician scores and see if we can apply that in other areas." Accountability across boundaries is essential to creating transparent fairness, as well as team trust.

The language we use also reinforces both community and fairness. Examples include the following:

- "That was an excellent job!"
- "You just saved this guy's life!"
- "Thanks! You made a B-team day into an A-team one."
- "What could I have done to make your job easier?"
- "Anne picked up some very important information that is going to improve your care."
- "Isaac is our best advanced practice provider. You're fortunate he's here."

The more this language is used—and used across boundaries—the more evident fairness will be. A core concept in fairness is ensuring that the B-team members are held accountable for their actions, language, and behavior. Failing to do so massively erodes trust in leaders, since the team feels, "There are two sets of rules here—one set of rules for the B-team members, who 'get away with it,' and a second set of rules for the A-team, who are held accountable."[32]

Putting the Psychology of Waiting to Work One of the things that seems most unfair to patients is how long they are forced to wait in healthcare. Most people consider time to be one of their most valuable assets, so wasting time is not only rude and unconscionable, it also wastes a valuable asset that cannot be recaptured. Jensen first pointed out to me that the psychologist David Maister recognized there is science behind how waiting can be managed in an effective fashion.[34] Hardwiring flow and fulfillment requires designing systems and processes to minimize waiting when possible and to use the skills listed in **Figure 10-8** when they can't.

RESTORING VALUES INTO THE WORKPLACE

Very few things cause more moral dilemmas resulting in burnout than situations where team members witness the contrast between stated values and actions that are diametrically opposed to those values. It has been my experience that the more focused and pristine the stated values, the more potential for actions that don't fit those values. Values like "Patient first" and "Patient always" are excellent, clarion calls to action, but leaders who seek to hardwire flow and fulfillment should constantly reexamine processes and systems to assess how they reflect those values (**Figure 10-9**).

Constantly Apply the "Connect Systems and Processes to Values" Test At each level of the healthcare organization, leaders at all levels should ask these questions:

- How does this system or process actively reflect our stated values?
- If it doesn't reflect those values, what changes need to be made to correct that?

Unoccupied time feels longer than occupied time
- TVs, magazines, health care material
- Company—friends and family
- Review-of-systems forms, kiosk, pre-work
- Frequent "touches"

Pre-process waits feel longer than in-process waits
- Immediate bedding
- No triage
- AT/AI (Advanced Treatment/Advanced Initiatives)
- Team triage

Anxiety makes waits seem longer
- Making the customer service Dx and Rx
- Address the obvious—pre-thought-out and sincerely deployed scripts
- Patient and leadership rounding

Uncertain waits are longer than known, finite waits
- Previews of what to expect
- Expectation creation
- Green-yellow-red grading and information system
- Traumas, CPRs—informed delays
- Patient and leadership rounding

Unexplained waits are longer than explained waits
- In-process preview and review
- Family and friends
- Patient and leadership rounding

Unfair waits are longer than equitable waits
- Announce codes
- Fast-track criteria known and transparent

The more valuable the service, the longer the customer will wait
- The value equation: maximize benefits for the patient and significant others + eliminate burdens for the patient and significant others

Solo waits feel longer than group waits
- Visitor policy—the deputy sheriff takes a furlough
- Managing the family's expectations
- It's OK to leave for a while
- On-stage/offstage

Figure 10-8: Putting the Psychology of Waiting to Work

Restoring Values In Work

- Constant "Connect Systems and Processes to Values" Test
- All Change = Values
- "This Embodies Our Values by…" Test
- "Nothing about Us without Us"

Figure 10-9: Solutions to Restore Values

- Who will be responsible for those changes?
- When should we expect the changes to occur?
- How will we know the changes have reconnected our values to the systems and processes?
- Do these systems and processes promote a "passion reconnect"?

Regardless of the model of change or performance improvement used, these questions are essential.

All Change Is Tied to Values The only constant in healthcare is change, and we find ourselves in the "perpetual whitewater of change." Having an organizational and a personal change strategy is a core element of battling burnout. Imbedded in those change efforts should be a constant view toward how each change reflects—or contradicts—the values we embrace.

In Every Action, Encourage Team Members to Be Able to Say, "Yes, This Embodies Our Values" Systems and processes are the cauldron in which values are reflected, but so are the actions, behaviors, and language of the individual team members who enact them. Team members should be encouraged to continually reassess not only how to hardwire flow and fulfillment but also how their own actions embody those values.

"Nothing about Us without Us" One of the bedrock elements of "making the patient a part of the team" is the principle of assuring the patient we are committed to the ideal of "Nothing about me without me."[35] Leaders should extend that concept to apply to every team member in making changes to the system. Far from being disruptive, it conveys to team members that their input will be sought, that input will be considered, and that the team writ large will follow the new system in service to its values.

Summary

- Hardwiring flow means building into systems and processes the ability to add value and reduce waste during the patients' journey through our healthcare systems.

- Hardwiring flow and fulfillment means starting to do "smart stuff" (which adds value), ceasing to do "stupid stuff" (which creates waste), and "fully filling" our passion by burning in instead of burning out.

- Solutions to hardwire flow and fulfillment should be grouped according to Maslach's 6 domains.

- Constantly test whether your systems and processes reflect or contradict the stated values.

- All change must be tied to values. Do the changes provide a path to "passion reconnect"?

11

Burnout and the Electronic Health Record

> *I've come to feel that a system [the EHR] that promised to increase my mastery over my work has, instead, increased my work's mastery over me.*
>
> ATUL GAWANDE[1]

Electronic health records (EHRs) are now a part of daily life for virtually every healthcare team member and yet constitute a significant cause of burnout.[1-4] The issues attendant to the use of EHRs cut across all areas of organizational and personal resiliency, as well as all six of the Maslach domains, so EHR problems and solutions warrant a separate chapter. At the outset, giving teams the ability to "take on the EHR" in a positive, constructive fashion is an extremely strong symbol that leadership is committed to a culture of adaptive change or resiliency.

Taking on the Electronic Health Record: A Leadership Mandate

EHRs produce burnout precisely because they create significant job stressors without an increase in adaptive capacity to deal with those stressors. The question is not, "What should be done?" It is, "Will leaders have the *courage to do what must be done*?" Unfortunately, far too often the answer has been no. "That's just the EHR. You have to get used to it" is heard far too often—and all of us know that EHRs are here to stay in healthcare. But the fact that they *have to be dealt with* should not mean that this *has to be done the way it is currently being done*, since the consequences of the status quo ante are unacceptable levels of burnout, much of which is EHR-driven. In Chapter 8, I noted the importance of physicians and nurses being the chief storytellers and chief sensemakers for the patient, but we often feel more like the chief electron collectors and recorders. To paraphrase Gawande's excellent point, that is why the EHR has increased our work's mastery over us.[1]

Leading ourselves and leading our teams requires the courage and capacity to take on the EHR so that it does not continue to extract its current toll. Doing so protects ourselves and protects our teams by simplifying our work and increasing our recovery and performance. And taking on the EHR is work that begins within.

While EHRs have existed in various forms for decades, passage of the Health Information Technology for Economic and Clinical Health Act, which was part of the American Recovery and Reinvestment Act of 2009, massively accelerated healthcare systems' migration to the adoption of EHRs.[5] Among many potential positives, EHRs were said to do the following:

- increase efficiency
- enhance quality
- promote patient safety
- reduce cost

However, the speed at which Congress was allocating and releasing funds and the regulatory mandates for adoption simply did not result in a framework promoting interoperability, much less allow clinicians to absorb this massive change in their work lives.[6] There were many downstream effects of this, but at the core was a fundamental, if unintended, sense of arrogance toward clinicians and the disruptions this would cause in their daily lives in delivering care to their patients. (Indeed, even the name of the act drips with an arrogance born of excessive confidence in information technology [IT] to deliver "economic and clinical health.") In fact, many members of the healthcare team hear the term *meaningful use* and think, "The only *meaningful* things are that physicians and nurses were *meaningfully* strong-armed into use, the vendors got *meaningfully* rich, and some leaders *meaningfully* crowed about how seamless the transition to EHRs was."[7] However, it can reasonably be said that it couldn't have been foreseen how deeply "the rise of electrons" would both improve and disrupt our work lives.

But the reality did not live up to the promises made regarding EHRs—in fact, it did not come close. Physicians, nurses, and healthcare team members across all disciplines share this frustration.[8-11] Susan Sadoughi, a respected and productive internist in Boston, has referred to the EHR as "a massive monster of incomprehensibility."[12] A study from the Massachusetts Medical Society showed that the biggest single "pain point" for physicians is the travails of dealing with the EHR.[13] "In the future all businesses will be run by a man and a dog. The purpose of the man is to feed the dog. The purpose of the dog is to make sure the man does *not* touch the equipment."[14]

Unfortunately, we have created a system where physicians and nurses seem to "touch the equipment" (the EHRs) all day, every day. That must change if we are to successfully battle burnout, which the solutions discussed in this chapter will help do. (Many of the insights in this chapter come from conversations with colleagues, the most important of which arose from my friends and colleagues Andrew Miner, Todd Taylor, and James McClay.)

To be sure, the supposed benefits of using IT in the form of EHRs were projected to be, but often fell short of, the following:[15-17]

- easy retrieval of timely, accurate, reliable information
- easy transfer of information to other clinicians
- charting
- clinical orders (computerized physician order entry)
- patient safety
- coding
- billing and regulatory compliance
- decision support analysis
- artificial intelligence solutions
- improved workflow based on data

However, far too often, members of the healthcare team heard their leaders say some version of, "That's just the EHR. Get used to it." That statement is a testament to the failure of the leaders, whose job it is to help develop and implement a culture as well as systems and processes that not only improve patient care but also make the team's jobs easier. (Without question, leaders at the unit level rightly note that statements about the inevitability of the EHR arose from *their* leaders and that they were simply passing the message delivered to them.) Many wonder whether those who designed the EHR ever actually used one, given the level of burnout they have engendered. A better sense of the history of change would have served the healthcare industry and its clinicians well, particularly the insights of Robert Merton, who in 1936 described the "law of unintended consequences."[18] Among the many unintended consequences of the near-universal EHR adoption are the following:

- creation of "click storms," meaning that care of the patient requires multiple "clicks" in the IT system
  - Current EHRs require no fewer than 33 clicks to order and record a flu shot.[19]
  - Emergency physicians and nurses on average endure the burden of having to perform 4,000 clicks per day at work.[20]
  - Internal medicine and family medicine physicians in an office setting perform over 2,700 clicks per day.[21]
  - Hospitalists require over 8,000 clicks per day to care for their patients.[22]

- ° Nurses have nearly the same "click burden," depending on the setting in which they practice; even operating room nurses are not immune from this plague.[23]
- creation of "note bloat," meaning that the medical record contains lots of words but very little meaning
  - ° Many EHRs use templates to complete history, physical exam, and other data, but these do not account for the uniqueness of the patient encounter.
  - ° Substantial time is required to wade through the medical record to find pertinent data.
  - ° The concept of "one size fits all" in EHRs, while intended to help simplify and standardize operations, has instead resulted in a situation where every patient sounds nearly the same. This creates the unintended consequence of a serious lack of personalization precisely when we are attempting to increase a focus on precision, personalized medicine.
  - ° "Screen switching" is common, requiring multiple efforts to move from one screen to another to coordinate information on a single patient encounter.[24]
  - ° Physicians and nurses alike have to use handwritten notes to capture the information on one screen before switching back to the previous screen.
- diversion of time away from bedside patient care and patient or family interaction
  - ° Surveys of physicians and nurses across specialties indicate that 44 percent of time is spent interacting with the EHRs, leaving only 28 percent for direct patient care and the remainder on technical activities.
  - ° Many clinicians feel they have become "data monkeys" instead of professionals.
- creation of significant work-life balance issues[25-26]
  - ° The inability to complete data tasks during the workday has created the need to "work from home" after hours. (This is more of a problem for physicians than nurses, the latter of whom simply stay at work longer to complete their tasks.)
  - ° This results in "pajama time," where physicians return to their computers at home to finish their work.
  - ° Other have described this as "date night with the computer."[27]
- creation of significant obstacles to teamwork among physicians, nurses, and essential services staff

- ° Team members are more focused on the computer than on their patients or interactions with each other.
- ° Time for discussion and professional interchange is decreased.
- creation of workflow issues causing waste
  - ° To retrieve information, clinicians must make trips to the printer (which are often distant from their workstations).
  - ° Interruptions and multitasking are built into the workflow.
  - ° In many systems, two people cannot enter information into the system simultaneously.
  - ° Ineffective functional silos are created.
  - ° Workflow must be interrupted to communicate.
- decrease in face-to-face time between nurses and physicians as well as the quality of those interactions
- inability to capture the "story of the patient" instead of a "flood of electrons"[28]
  - ° The medical record should be a story of the complex interaction of the patient's clinical, social, behavioral, and psychological needs, but it has largely become a cacophony of seemingly unrelated facts that far too often fail to "paint a portrait of the person."
  - ° EHRs should use plain, understandable English that paints an evocative picture of the patient, the patient's suffering, and its effect on the patient's life and that of his or her family, not the disembodied "computer voice" of our current medical record.

This list could go on for several pages, but the common feature to all of these issues goes back to the definition of burnout: a mismatch between job stressors (all of the foregoing items and more) and adaptive capacity or resiliency to deal with those job stressors.[29] Most physicians and nurses across specialties name dealing with the EHR as a significant cause of burnout in their practices.[30-31] Whatever the origins, the clear and widely known result has been throwing fuel on the fire of burnout.

While the toll extracted by EHRs has been and often continues to be substantial, there is significant evidence that a more enlightened approach where the IT system has to adapt to those using it, instead of the opposite, can have dramatic results, which I will delineate later in this chapter. EHRs can evolve from a necessary evil to an effective tool, an instrument panel and control center by which to improve the patient encounter, including through refinement of the utility and usability of "patient portals."[32] Three vendors control 70 percent of the entire healthcare system EHR market (Epic 28 percent, Cerner 26 percent, and MediTech 16 percent), and for hospitals with more than 500 beds, Epic (58 percent) and Cerner (27 percent) control the market.[33]

Solutions

When it comes to the EHR, the way it's working isn't working. That much is clear. These solutions are not quantum physics—they are commonsense ways to reduce the job stressors of the EHR while increasing resiliency. They make the computer work for us instead of us working solely for the EHR. But they all require the courage of leadership. Christine Sinsky and her colleagues propose a set of principles to guide this process **(Figure 11-1)**.[30] While the following solutions do not precisely follow that format, they are nonetheless sound ones to consider.

IMPROVE COACHING, MENTORING, AND EDUCATION FOR THE EHR

- As I've noted repeatedly, leadership is the key to battling burnout, and nowhere is it more important than with the EHRs. Lead from the front by listening to the frustrations and feedback from your team, then make an action plan with IT to address it.

- While it is always best for the system to be highly intuitive, that goal is not currently attainable in all systems. When it isn't intuitive, leverage coaching from experienced clinicians who have done it and seen it.

- During orientation, and periodically thereafter, budget for "at your elbow" coaches who "shadow shift" for several hours to help work through solutions.

- As Taylor and McClay note, physician and nurse champions at the unit level are the single most important predictors of the successful use of the EHR.[34]

Patient-Centered Design
1. EHRs should add value for the patient
2. The primary function for the EHR is evidence-based clinical care

Health Care Professionals
3. EHRs should improve or at least not reduce the well-being of clinicians
4. EHRs should align work with training of the team members
5. The EHR is a shared informational tool for patients and population health

Efficiency
6. EHRs should reduce waste while increasing value (Lean principle)
7. Electronic workflows should align with clinical work
8. Many forms of information flow are necessary (including nonelectronic)

Regulation and Finance
9. Resources (adaptive capacity) must match the new work (job stressors)
10. Evidence should guide changes, not just regulatory or financial issues

Figure 11-1: 10 Principles of EHR Solutions

Adapted from Sinksy et al.[30]

- At the Brigham and Women's Physicians Organization (a case study of which is presented in Chapter 13), one of the most successful solutions regarding Epic, their version of the EHR, was to provide one-hour, one-on-one "at the elbow" consultations with experts in physicians' specialty areas to observe workflow and customize solutions to match the individual physician's practice needs, as well as daytime access to a help line to solve problems.

SENIOR LEADERSHIP EFFORTS

- Ensure that there are EHR optimization teams both at the organizational and at the service unit levels, with a focus on making the EHR work for the team members, instead of the team members working for the EHR.
- Meet at least quarterly with the optimization teams at the unit level.
- Ensure that units and service lines have EHR optimization champions.
- To the extent possible, allow flexibility in scheduling or self-scheduling.
- Make progress transparent to everyone involved.

TYPE, POINT, AND CLICK AND "CLICK STORMS" MUST GO

- This area requires leadership's focus for many reasons, but the SARS-CoV-2 COVID-19 outbreak raises the issue of computer keyboards and their role as potential fomites for viral or bacterial transmission.
- Speech recognition and natural language processing (NLP) systems (e.g., Dragon and M-Modal) must be used to replace type, point, and click or typing into the computer, but efforts to reduce the 5–10 percent error rates must be aggressive and ongoing.[35]
- Personal performance assistants (scribes) and virtual scribes should be used to decrease the time that physicians and nurses spend in front of the computer.
- Data have shown repeatedly that if physicians see 1–1.5 more patients per shift, the cost of scribes more than offsets the cost in return on investment.
- Personal performance assistants and virtual scribes also "force" physicians to verbalize the results of the physical exam and the treatment plan, as well as the reasons for diagnostic tests, to the patient and the scribe, which improves patient experience.
- If sensitive information needs to be shared outside the room, the clinician and scribe can discuss this outside.

- While scribes have sometimes been described as a medieval solution to a modern problem, they are likely to remain part of the solution until better ones are developed, tested, and implemented.

- Don Berwick called for a 50 percent reduction in mandatory measurement in three years and a 75 percent reduction in five years.[36] That article was written in 2014, so three years was 2017, and five years was 2019—and no such reductions occurred. Healthcare systems must work to reduce regulatory requirements for mandatory measurement without meaning or added value. This will also help address the "note bloat" issue.

- Look for bottlenecks where interaction with the EHR seriously delays care and flow—these are areas where scribes may be used to ease rate-limiting steps.

- For example, triage in the emergency department can be a rate-limiting step for effective patient flow. Consider using a scribe with the triage nurse at peak hours of the day.

USE IT TO ALLOW "SHOW ME . . ."

- Speech recognition technology should be used to allow interfaces where the physician simply says, "Show me . . ." to pull up CT scans, MRIs, consultant reports, laboratory data and trends, and so on.

- If Siri and Alexa can do this, so can EHRs.

REDUCE SCREEN SWITCHING

- Allow multiple screens for computer stations, which allows clinicians to view different fields to make decisions.

- This allows much more use of the gestalt sense when, for example, CT scans and lab data can be juxtaposed.

- Some programs, such as Evidence Care, have developed automatic treatment pathways to reduce cognitive time and improve care that address this issue.

UNROOF AND DRAIN THE "ABSCESS OF THE INBOX"

- The "inbox" for most EHRs has gotten out of control, holding clinicians hostage to a barrage of messages.

- Sort what adds value and what is waste. For example, messages from physicians, nurses, labs, imaging services, and certain consultants are all value-added messages.

- Too many nonessential messages, memos, and announcements crowd our inboxes. We even get messages scolding us for not opening previous non-value-added messages.

- The inbox truly seems like an abscess, laden with things that fester with time, continuously growing and distracting us from important issues.
- Leaders must work with IT to drain the inbox of things that don't clearly add value to the care of patients.

TEAMS AND TEAMWORK

IT often distracts from the ability of the team to work together, pulling us apart and creating multiple distractions. If we are going to "say 'team,'" we have to "play 'team,'" including through these steps:

- Move physician and nurse workstations together.
- Use clinical huddles to improve communication and make it more consistent across team members.
- Build "decisions = doing" into clinical rounds by ensuring that someone with a "computer on wheels" captures orders, notes, and other EHR necessities.
- Move printers into workstations so the staff don't have to walk to get papers.
- Decrease interruptions and multitasking while clinicians are in the IT workstation.
- Only allow "value-added" interruptions (e.g., critical lab results, time-dependent results or issues).

ADDRESS WORK-LIFE BALANCE ISSUES

The C-suite must have a commitment such that the EHR and the IT leadership are charged with serving the patient and the people who take care of the patient, not the "false god" of IT itself.[37] The work that physicians in particular do should be able to be completed within the work hours designated for it, including ensuring that "deciding = doing = documenting." There must be a stated goal to reduce or eliminate the following:

- pajama time
- date night with the computer
- distractions from the family at home

USE AUGMENTED INTELLIGENCE AND APPLICATION PROGRAM INTERFACES TO LIBERATE YOUR TEAM

While the term *artificial intelligence* is widely used, in the case of EHRs the more accurate term is *augmented intelligence*.[38] Almost no one would deny that the initial roll-out of the EHRs from different companies shared both a certain rigidness regarding "That's just the way it's done" and an attitude of "Sure, we can interface with your lab, imaging, etc. programs." Over time the industry has moved toward the use of application program interfaces, which are a rich source to improve the usability of EHRs.[39] This accelerates the following:

- increase use of application program interfaces
- use physician and nurse builders—local solutions guided by national experience, passionate expert talent in your own shops
- leverage the 21st Century Cures Act of 2016 mandating the use of open healthcare apps

Epic's App Orchard is a step toward this usability through customization and should be further developed and implemented.

CONTINUE TO DEVELOP CLINICAL DECISION SUPPORT, INCLUDING USING AUGMENTED INTELLIGENCE

- Clinical decision support is an area rich in potential, under the right circumstances, which include using evidence-based principles (but without suffering from "analysis paralysis" or being slowed unnecessarily by the need for specialty society development).
- Augmented intelligence has an extremely important place in this process but is just now gaining significant traction. The pace will be improved as augmented intelligence is used to analyze data in real time to drive decisions, as occurred in the COVID-19 pandemic and previously in the inhalational anthrax crisis in the nation's capital.
- A practical example is the development by the physician group Best Practices of evidence-based evaluation and treatment guidelines for the 10 highest-risk yet common presentations to emergency departments, known as "Creating the Risk-Free ED" (**Figures 11-2 and 11-3**).
- Use the "5 Rights of Clinical Decision Support"[40] in the process:
  - right information to the . . .
  - right person in the . . .
  - right format through the . . .
  - right channel at the . . .
  - right time in workflow
- Use available sensor technology (e.g., Whoop, Zebra, or Catapult) to capture step counts, movement patterns, and other data to help guide ways to decrease unnecessary movements in hardwiring flow.

1. Acute Myocardial Infarction
2. Appendicitis
3. Meningitis
4. Chest Pain (Acute Chest Syndrome and Other)
5. Traumatic Wounds
6. Abdominal/Pelvic Pain
7. Pneumonia
8. Spinal Fractures
9. Acute Aortic Aneurysm
10. Acute Testicular Torsion

Figure 11-2: The Risk-Free Emergency Department Top 10 List of Risk

✓ **Best Practice #1**

Ensure any patient with acute onset of testicular pain and clinical findings of torsion has:
- IMMEDIATE call to Urologist
- Attempted manual detorsion

Treatment is immediate surgery

✓ **Best Practice #2**

Every patient with acute onset of testicular pain, <u>but</u> with equivocal findings of testicular torsion receives a color flow Doppler ultrasound

✓ **Best Practice #3**

Ensure any patient with <u>acute scrotal pain</u> and <u>negative imaging study</u> receives:
- Urologic consultation
- Admission, placement in observation unit OR follow-up with urologist in AM
- Careful discharge instructions

✓ **Best Practice #4**

Ensure prospective, proactive discussion with both radiology and urology regarding the use of color flow Doppler ultrasound

Figure 11-3: Creating the Risk-Free Emergency Department: Testicular Torsion

INCORPORATE "THE STORY OF THE PATIENT" INTO THE EHR

- At precisely the time we are seeking to ensure that clinicians take a personalized and precision approach to the patient, the "one size fits all" nature of the EHR and many templates inadvertently create a monotone record in which the contextual, personal nature of the patient is lost.

- Whether through scribes, virtual scribes, voice recognition, or other means, we need to capture the patients' voices, their fears, their sufferings, and what our plan is in a more narrative, empathetic fashion.

EXPLORE THE USE OF MOBILE PHONES TO SIMPLIFY ACCESS

- Like many things in the "electron culture," the use of mobile phones to remotely access EHRs will likely be a mixed blessing.

- Being able to enter orders and access records will likely help streamline patient care and improve flow.

- At the same time, being constantly connected has its downsides as well.
- That said, more access, careful controlled, is likely a part of the future use and availability of the EHRs.

CONCLUSION

All of these solutions and many more will be necessary to reduce the job stressors and increase both organizational and personal resiliency when it comes to the burden of EHRs.

Summary

- Physicians and nurses list the EHR as the single largest source of frustration and burnout.
- Leaders at all levels must be prepared to take on the EHR to ensure it works for the team members, while understanding these technologies are a part of modern healthcare.
- While the problems are pervasive and extract a high burnout toll, innovative solutions are being put in place in many healthcare systems to reverse the issues.
- Hope is on the horizon if leaders empower their teams to take on the EHR.

Part Three

Other Voices

The value of another's experience is to give us hope, not to tell us how or whether to proceed.

PETER BLOCK, *THE ANSWER TO HOW IS YES*[1]

Whether they are called case studies, benchmarking, or lessons from the literature, the experiences of those who have done the work are invaluable in battling burnout and building resilience, not because they tell us precisely what to do or what not to do, but because they give us hope that the difficult work not only *can be done* but also *must be done*. While there are many courageous innovators and educators working in this space, I have selected the ones featured in this part primarily because of their deep passion as well as their commitment first to the members of their healthcare teams (lead yourself, lead your team). All of them clearly understand that in healthcare, we can no longer sustain the cost that providing excellence in healthcare extracts from our team members; they know that those teammates are performance athletes in whom we must invest, since improving their lives is essential to improving their patients' lives. For all of them, the work begins within.

All of the healthcare systems that have tackled burnout have certain characteristics in common:

- They all began with leaders understanding their personal journey of burnout and their obligation to act on behalf of their teams—"The way they were working wasn't working."
- They all understood the importance of a passionate, powerful guiding coalition.
- They all state some version of "The work begins within," meaning a primary focus on investing in the individuals first.
- They share the importance of leading yourself, then leading the team.
- They all share an appreciation for the fact that team members are performance athletes.

I know you will enjoy learning from their work.

12

Novant Health System

Tom Jenike, MD, Chief Well-Being Officer and Senior Vice President, Novant Health, Charlotte, North Carolina

Case Study of a Burned-Out Doctor: How the Journey Started

I am a physician and the son of a physician. I chose a career in medicine because I wanted to help people get better and stay well. Somehow, along the way, *I* got worse. In medical school, residency, and practice, I took tremendous pride in being a part of what I thought of as a lifelong, worthy mission. I was determined to be the best . . . at any cost. In many ways I was doing justice to my goals. My practice was extremely successful, and I was one of the highest-rated and busiest family medicine physicians in Charlotte, North Carolina. I volunteered for numerous committees and was viewed as an emerging leader at Novant Health, the healthcare system in which I practiced. My patient satisfaction scores were soaring.

But my "family and personal satisfaction" scores were at rock bottom. My joy in practicing medicine had faded. I was overwhelmed with countless hospital initiatives and committees. I felt as if I was letting down my patients, my colleagues, and my family. My most important relationships and my own sense of health and well-being were suffering. In my mind, I had become a victim of the "medical machine," putting myself and the people in my personal life at the end of a long line of never-ending commitments. The way I was approaching my work was siphoning away the joy of being a doctor. Despite being not just a doctor but a *good* doctor, my personal fulfillment was being eroded by the daily grind.

Despite this, I *never* considered quitting, which is part of the dilemma of physician burnout. By and large, you don't make it through the gauntlet of medical training in any specialty by adopting a mindset of quitting. At the same time, however, many people check out without leaving the profession. They "retire on the job," by simply showing up without passion and with a victim's mentality, both of which jeopardize quality, safety, patient safety, and every other metric by which we measure success in healthcare. I was afraid of falling into that same trap.

I knew I was not alone in feeling burned out, but that was hardly comforting. Doctors all over the country are expected to deliver world-class clinical care while facing the economic, technological, regulatory, financial, and organizational stressors that combine to make being a physician harder and harder. As common as these experiences are among my colleagues, I noticed that no one talked about it openly and from a personal perspective. Physician burnout is a silent epidemic that poses serious challenges to patient health and our healthcare system. Most importantly, I have personally experienced the cost of depression and burnout as my close friend in medical school and then a partner in practice have both died of suicide.

Something had to change . . . I decided it had to start with me.

It Started at a Batting Cage

During this time, my son Jake was a competitive baseball player and I was his team's coach. In order to improve his batting skills, we met with a hitting instructor. He had a highly effective coaching style and a magnetic ability to connect with others. His name is Nicholas Beamon, and not only was he a great hitting instructor, I subsequently learned he was an executive coach, and a founding partner of OneTeam Leadership, a widely recognized executive and leadership coaching company based in Charlotte. During one of Jake's lessons, I mentioned my professional struggles and how they were affecting my life. After a few more sessions in the batting cage, I hired Nicholas to be my executive coach. Through our work together, I gained insights on how my approach to succeeding in medicine was affecting my experience of my work and my life, and most importantly I gained clarity on what was important to me as a physician, as a father, as a friend, as a colleague, and as a husband.

Based on the transformation I had been coached through, I began to reflect on this question: "Why can't this same approach be used to help other physicians become better leaders of their lives and their teams?" It came from a premise that if I was having great professional success and I was projecting to others that life and work were awesome but the way it *felt* was not at all awesome, then certainly I had colleagues with the same dilemma. I became deeply committed to helping others not simply survive through a career in medicine but actually thrive while doing so. Nicholas and I worked together to design and implement what came to be known as the Novant Physician Leadership Development Program, which is the foundational element of Novant's System Approach to Well-Being, Resiliency, and Performance. To use a familiar sports analogy, "The best defense is a good offense." Defending against burnout requires an effective offense to create a strong foundation of well-being, resiliency, and leadership skills requisite for professional fulfillment in what we all can agree is an extremely demanding environment. We also knew that old patterns have a strong gravitational pull, particularly in times of stress, so the leadership solutions needed "staying power." It was based on a combination of my experiences, Nicholas's expertise in executive coaching, and the Novant Health philosophy.

The Novant Health Philosophy

Novant Health operates 15 medical centers and 700 locations across the states of North and South Carolina, Virginia, and Georgia, with 30,000 employees and 1,800 physicians as part of its medical group. Leadership training and development are at the heart of Novant's journey for well-being and resiliency, and all such training reflects the philosophy, mission, vision, and values of the organization. In its simplest form, Novant's philosophy rests on this fundamental principle: "We will become world-class at caring for our people, so that they can be world-class at caring for our patients."

Stated in more detail, Novant Health has a deep commitment to the well-being of its providers and team members. Foundational to the approach is the philosophy that in order to successfully achieve our mission and vision and perform at the highest level, we must have an engaged and healthy team. We believe there is a direct correlation between our system performance in all areas (such as patient satisfaction, clinical quality, patient safety, and employee engagement) and the well-being of the people providing care to our communities.

In service of this philosophy, we have a long track record of investing in the professional and personal development of our people. Among the senior leaders such as our CEO, Carl Armato, there is an understanding that having a robust well-being platform is key to running a successful modernized healthcare system. Novant invested in senior leadership in the form of the position I originally held, senior vice president, chief human experience officer. This innovative position tied together the experience of all of our providers and team members and that of our patients and families. To further create infrastructure, strategy, and a culture of well-being, I now have the title of senior vice president, chief well-being officer, and report directly to the Novant Health chief operating officer, which gives direct access to decision-making, allocation of resources, and the matching of our work to the key strategic objectives of the mission, vision, and values of the organization. Leaders across the organization recognize the importance of the health of their teams and are held accountable to their people's engagement and well-being.

To provide the best healthcare, we must *care for ourselves and each other.*

That philosophy drives a definition of organizational resiliency and performance as intentionally creating a culture that directly aligns team member well-being with organizational health and performance. But it is important to note that the journey started with a commitment to develop a means by which personal leadership and transformation leads to personal well-being. That was the genesis of the Novant Physician Leadership Development Program—the focus on doing something for the physicians leading Novant as opposed to improving operational efficiency itself. Three insights helped drive the program:

- The program is focused on "you" versus "what you can do for Novant," a true investment in the lives of the people so committed to helping others.
- When your overall life is healthy, everything you touch reflects that health.
- The redemptive power of "I choose to . . ." versus "I have to . . ." helps participants to create a mindset of empowerment rather than that of a victim and leads to becoming reenergized and refocused.

Many people enter wondering what Novant will ask for in return.

- There is no "payback," yet they emerge more engaged and committed to the organization.
- People are empowered to ask themselves what can be done to make their work easier and better for themselves and their colleagues.
- Part of the intent of the course was to create a safe space where it was not merely "OK" to talk about the challenges and sacrifices of being a healthcare professional; we *must* talk about them.

We were also aware that, in our view, too much of the work on resiliency in healthcare has been focused on the perceived failings of the individuals who are burned out, as if they weren't tough enough or skilled enough or were skilled in insufficient ways. Those approaches can lead to the team member thinking, "Oh, so *I'm the problem*?" Therefore, there must be fundamental improvements in the way the system works for the individual. It was important to us to keep the focus on developing skills that would be a choice. Doug Collins, a four-time NBA All Star, US Olympian, and coach, commentator, and executive with the NBA, famously talks about the importance of "choices and voices," by which he means the choices you make and voices to whom you listen in life. Both the voices and choices have consequences. One of those choices is whether to continue as a physician or to continue working where you are. It is important to communicate, "You don't have to stay here unless that is your choice. You don't have to keep working the way you have been unless that is your choice."

The Genesis of the Novant Physician Leadership Development Program

After getting clear on the key elements of burnout and determining that the program's fundamental purpose would be to address this issue, we presented the concept to the CEO of Novant Health, Carl Armato. Carl knew not only that going on offense to address well-being was the right thing to do and completely consistent with the Novant philosophy, it was also the smart decision as a way to run a modernized healthcare system. He pointed out that taking our company where he wanted to go would be near impossible if half of those with the most important job function, physicians, were burning out. Further, the return on investment on decreasing physician turnover and strengthening recruitment would in itself justify the expense. He quickly and enthusiastically agreed to piloting a program, after which we approached and enrolled a number of key physician leaders at Novant Health. We thus established a powerful guiding coalition in support of the work, which is a key element of the success of any new and innovative program.

The initiative consisted of prework for the participants, a multiday retreat, one-on-one coaching, and mentoring opportunities, all designed to help our physicians have a significantly enhanced experience of their professional and personal lives. This included rediscovering their core values and purpose; developing stronger leadership skills; engaging more effectively with their families, peers, and patients; and helping them develop better work-life integration. Fundamentally it was a means of allowing important conversations to happen freely and openly that had not been happening.

The Nine Elements of the Novant Physician Leadership Development Program

The premise for the course was simple: "Lead the self, lead the team, and lead the organization." While the work requires deep reflection and a strong commitment to the process, it was designed to create physician collaboration in an environment that encourages new ideas and innovation. It included these nine critical elements:

1. To learn how to operate from a deepened sense of purpose

2. To develop a keen sense of personal awareness and understanding of how unconscious patterns of bias, behaviors, and thinking contribute to burnout

3. To focus on creating an "attraction to well-being" beyond a solution to burnout

4. To develop a new mindset, new habits, and a commitment to living like "healthcare athletes," which includes the concepts of work, rest, recovery, and rejuvenation (the last of which literally means to "restore youth")

5. To focus the training on being fully present and aware—or operating from one's fundamental personal core beliefs

6. To develop a deep understanding of "influential leadership" as a skill and learned ability

7. To become a more effective person through the intentionality of daily living

8. To redefine the medical group culture by establishing a strong community of physician support, communication, camaraderie, and teamwork

9. To mobilize participants as champions to address organizational forces causing burnout

The first cohort, which comprised 32 physicians, including key influential leaders in the organization, attended a three-day intensive course. The reception to the program was beyond our expectations, and the results were dramatic in numerous ways, which are delineated shortly. However, the most important results were the spontaneous comments of the attendees, which included the following:

"I wish I had words to express and quantify the impact this has had on me as a person and a leader, but sometimes the most vital and impactful things that happen in life are too great for human words to describe."

"I walked away feeling more personally fulfilled with my life and my work."

"I was more energized than I have been with medicine in years."

"Because of this program, I am a better physician, friend, father, husband, and son."

"My life has changed significantly since participating in the physician wellness program. I have learned how to take control of my happiness and have a much brighter outlook."

"The program made me realize that I wasn't truly getting to know my patients and I wasn't mentally available to my wife and children, even when I was physically present with them. Now that's changed and even the mood in my office is improved."

"This program saved my career. But what's really important is that it saved my marriage, my relationships with my kids, and most likely MY LIFE."

Results

In addition to these comments, from the first cohort of 32 participants to now, when we have had over 1,000 physicians (over half of our medical group) participate, we have seen consistently positive results. Our research shows that those who participated in the program scored higher than nonparticipants—

Results of Resiliency Program Investment

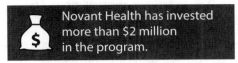

 Several initiatives have been launched as a result of the program's dialogue.

▶ Participants have become **champions** of critical programs and processes. Novant Health has developed an **EMR optimization team.**

▶ A yearlong **on-boarding program** has been launched for all new physicians. The program incorporates wellness, resiliency, and empathetic communication skills.

 Participants scored higher—often by more than **50 percent**—than others on many key measures:

+ personal **fulfillment**
+ **alignment** with the health system's mission
+ **positive attitudes** toward the organization

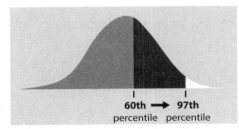

60th ➤ 97th
percentile   percentile

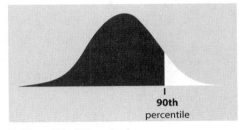

90th
percentile

Participants rank in the 97th percentile in both **engagement** and **alignment** with the organization. Prior to the program, scores were in the 60th percentile.

Novant Health's medical group, as a whole, now ranks in the **90th percentile** nationally in physician engagement.

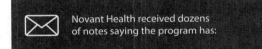 Novant Health received dozens of notes saying the program has:

+ **reignited passion** for medicine
+ improved **personal well-being**
+ **saved** marriages

Figure 12-1: The Results of the Resiliency Training Program

sometimes more than 50 percent higher—on several key measures, including personal engagement, alignment with the health system's mission, and positive attitudes toward the organization and its team members. Participants ranked in the 97th percentile in Press Ganey for engagement and alignment scores, up from the 60th percentile. As a whole, Novant Health's medical group now ranks in the 90th percentile in engagement, suggesting that the program may have had an effect even on those who have not yet participated in the program (**Figure 12-1**).

Changes Arising from the Work

While the most gratifying results from the program are the personal stories of those whose lives were changed positively, numerous initiatives have been launched in response to the experience, including the following:

- an electronic health record optimization team, led by prior participants of the program with a passion for making the electronic record more amenable, more accessible, and less frustrating for the team

- expansion of the program to include advanced practice providers and nurses (for which faculty from those areas were recruited; the core elements required some adaptation, but perhaps less than one might think, because the program is focused on both the human suffering caused by burnout and the universal nature of the leadership principles at its core)

- integration of the work to include physician recruitment and onboarding programs, so the elements are known from the outset of contact with the organization

- major efforts to change the culture, systems, and processes of the organization to improve fulfillment

- coaching and mentoring initiatives, led by prior participants, for other physicians, nurses, and advanced practice providers

- as a result of the challenges of the coronavirus crisis, acceleration of our remote learning skills and abilities, which allow for unique opportunities

Because of the success of the program and the universal nature of the tension between burnout and the leadership skills needed to combat it, we have been approached by several health systems and organizations to extend our work beyond Novant, which we have done, including facilitating programs in our ongoing partnership with Nicholas Beamon and OneTeam Leadership for the American Hospital Association.

Most importantly, we have been thrilled to extend the foundation within Novant Health to all its team members, reflected in its System Approach to Well-Being, Resiliency, and Performance.

The Novant Health System Approach to Well-Being, Resiliency, and Performance

As the Novant Physician Leadership Development Program evolved, so did a specific approach to well-being, resiliency, and performance across the entire organization. We refer to Novant Health's System Approach to Well-Being, Resiliency, and Performance as "inside out." This guides all our efforts and is critical to understanding the broad, system-based efforts to assist our team members. It begins with personal well-being and builds outward from there **(Figure 12-2)**.

PERSONAL WELL-BEING

It is important to have a strong foundation, which in our case is the focus on the individual, the source of the transformation. Comprehensive personal well-being is fostered through self-awareness, behaviors that promote self-care, personal and professional growth, and compassion for ourselves and others.

Figure 12-2: The Novant Health System Approach to Well-Being, Resiliency, and Performance

Its central tenet is, "Lead yourself first." In healthcare, this is somewhat counterintuitive, in that it focuses on personal well-being first, but with the goal of service to others. For example, many organizations, including ours, have a primary focus on the patient. But to serve the patient, we must have the skills and abilities to manage ourselves first.

COMMUNITY

A second nonintuitive insight is that the focus on personal well-being leads proximately and inexorably to the concept of "community." Armed with our strong focus on well-being, we progress to developing opportunities for connection points that foster community and collegiality among our team members. We move from cultivating personal skills to cultivating team or community skills and opportunities to work together for the good of others—in our case, our patients. Further, community and connection provide an important resource of resiliency.

OPERATIONAL EFFICIENCY

A team or community of caregivers, each armed with the tools and skills of personal well-being, can now focus their collective efforts on operational efficiency, providing wellness advocacy to make process improvements specifically targeted at facilitating efficiency and performance for team members, each of which reduces the barriers to doing the core work in the most effective and efficient fashion. (In the context of hardwiring flow, this means "stop doing stupid stuff and start doing smart stuff.") For each of the systems and processes by which we provide care, what is the smartest way of doing the work at the least risk of burning the team members out? Change the systems and processes to make the work serve not only the patient but also those serving the patient.

INFLUENTIAL LEADERSHIP

Leading yourself, leading your team, and leading your organization is the foundation of "influential leadership," where leadership engagement and skill development ensure specific, evidence-based behaviors that demonstrate support, appreciation, and professional growth for all team members. Influential leadership does not require an official title, is the antithesis of authoritarian or power-based leadership, and relies on the ability of each individual using his or her influence for improvement. "Do it because the boss says so" has no place in a community of influential leaders. Instead, senior leaders serve to convene conversations among members of the team to make positive changes.

ORGANIZATIONAL RESILIENCE AND PERFORMANCE

Only when all of these component parts are fully in place and influencing all the other parts do we arrive at what for many would be the primary goal, *organizational resiliency and performance*, which is intentionally creating a culture that directly aligns team member well-being with overall organizational health and performance (**Figure 12-3**). As Aristotle noted, the whole is truly more than the sum of the parts. In our view, starting with a focus on personal well-being and developing the team members' individual leadership skills, behaviors, and

Personal well-being: Foster personal well-being through self-awareness, behaviors that promote self-care, personal and professional growth, and compassion for ourselves and others.

Community: With a strong focus on wellness, intentionally develop opportunities for connection points that foster collegiality among our team members.

Operational efficiency: Provide wellness advocacy for process improvements that facilitate efficiency and performance for team members and reduce barriers to core work.

Influential leadership: Leadership engagement and development ensure behaviors that demonstrate support, appreciation, and professional growth for team members.

Organizational resilience and performance: Intentionally create a culture that directly aligns team member well-being with organizational health and performance.

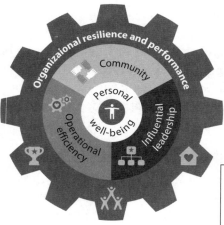

Figure 12-3: Organizational Resilience and Performance

abilities is the primary focus, not jumping to organizational performance, which is where many organizations start.

ADDITIONAL DEVELOPING PROGRAMS

Bringing this approach to life includes deepening our support and capabilities to reach all our team members. The following are some practical ways for our people to access programs and initiatives centered on well-being and resiliency. More detail on these programs is available on Novant Health's website.

- Thriving Together—Novant Health's platform for comprehensive support services
- Novant Health Leadership Development Program (signature program)
- Team Member Resiliency Program (one-day program)
- Odyssey Program (provider one-year onboarding)
- Provider Mentoring Program
- New Leader Immersion
- Clinic Administrator Development Program
- Provider Leadership series (Level-Up Leadership for lead clinicians)
- Novant Health Reads
- Team dynamics, health/culture development
- Empathic Communications Training for providers
- Mindfulness/Stress Reduction series
- Human Experience Leadership training/development

The Odyssey Program, which creates a one-year onboarding and coaching/mentoring program, has been particularly successful. The majority of coaches and mentors are former participants in the Novant Physician Leadership Development Program who have a passion to "pay it forward" to others.

As the Novant Health well-being and resiliency efforts have grown, additional programs have been and will continue to be developed.

IMPLEMENTATION TIPS

For health system leaders or medical groups considering developing their own resiliency and wellness programs, consider the following:

- *Do you have buy-in from senior leaders?* If those running the organization do not believe in this concept and are not willing to lead from this position, it will be hard to have sustained success. With the ever-changing landscape of healthcare as well as the head winds of financial strain, a deep commitment is required. At Novant Health our CEO, Carl Armato, calls this work his proudest leadership legacy.

- *Who on your staff will "own the program"? Can one individual be assigned to do this?* Someone needs to lead and be the symbol of the work. In our case at Novant Health it is the chief well-being officer, in direct partnership with the chief operating officer. Whoever is responsible needs to have sufficient authority to empower others to make changes that will change the culture, systems, and processes, not just the people.

- *What is the correct amount to budget for this type of program for your organization?* Understanding the critical importance of this effort to our system's success, we budget $3,600 per physician and $400 per nurse participant, which to us is a very sound investment in the future of our teams and team members. The program is accredited for 36 category 1 continuing medical education hours for physicians and 10 hours of Certified Nursing Units for nurses, which is considered an important benefit.

- *What metrics are used to assess the financial and nonfinancial return on investment?* In addition to the Press Ganey metrics on alignment and fulfillment, we look at the impact of the resiliency and leadership program on recruitment and retention. We have seen a 300 percent growth in our physician group since the inception of the program and a drop in turnover. Since physician replacement costs are conservatively estimated at three times their salary, turnover not only disrupts operations and causes increased stress, it also has a financial impact.

- *Does improving resiliency and well-being affect patient experience scores?* Our metrics show that patient experience scores do improve as a result of the programs, which also has an impact on many reimbursement models.

Additional Readings

Armato CS, Jenike TE. Physician resiliency and wellness for transforming a health system. *NEJM Catalyst.* May 2, 2018. https://catalyst.nejm.org/doi/full/10.1056/CAT.18.0188#:~:text=Reprints-,Physician%20Resiliency%20and%20Wellness%20for%20Transforming%20a%20Health%20System,their%20personal%20and%20professional%20lives. Accessed October 15, 2020.

Mahoney D. Novant Health's wellness program keeps physician burnout at bay. Press Ganey Blog. July 22, 2016. https://www.pressganey.com/blog/novant-health's-wellness-program-keeps-physician-burnout-at-bay. Accessed October 15, 2020.

Berg S. 1 part of physician burnout fix: help doctors develop as leaders. AMA Rounds. February 10, 2020. https://www.ama-assn.org/practice-management/physician-health/1-part-physician-burnout-fix-help-doctors-develop-leaders. Accessed October 15, 2020.

Summary

At Novant Health, we have learned that an intentional and deliberate focus on wellness, resiliency, and leadership development and engagement is critical to operating a high-performing and change-ready health system. We also learned that it is the responsibility of the executive leadership to encourage and enable staff to engage their own wellness and resiliency, demonstrating that it is not only possible but necessary to do the following:

- Slow down, press "pause," and be intentionally present in all areas of life, not just work.
- Recharge and maintain our batteries by building an intentional time to recover and rejuvenate (literally "re-youth") ourselves and our team.
- Acknowledge that improving ourselves is the access point to improving our life and the lives of those around us.
- Be realistic about expectations for ourselves and others—you cannot help anyone unless you start by being kind to yourself.

This is the path to leading yourself, leading your team, and leading your organization.

13

Brigham and Women's Physicians Organization

Jessica Dudley, MD, Former Chief Medical Officer,
Chief Clinical Officer, Press Ganey, Inc.

Sunil Eappen, MD, Chief Medical Officer

> *Each individual burns out in different ways.*
>
> SUNIL EAPPEN

> *Happy families are all alike; every unhappy family is unhappy in its own way.*
>
> LEO TOLSTOY, *ANNA KARENINA*

Starting the Journey

Brigham and Women's Physicians Organization (BWPO) began its journey to reduce or eliminate physician burnout while increasing fulfillment in 2016 through three primary initiatives:

1. In local department initiatives, chairs worked with faculty to engage in wellness efforts.

2. There was an identified need for institution-wide effort.
   - A physicians council and frontline physicians identified key priorities.
   - A decision was made to formally survey physicians for burnout and fulfillment.

3. A governance and accountability structure was established (**Figure 13-1**).
   - The BWPO Executive Committee created a wellness measure.
   - A wellness task force was established with the physician organization and the hospital that included the chief medical officer, the

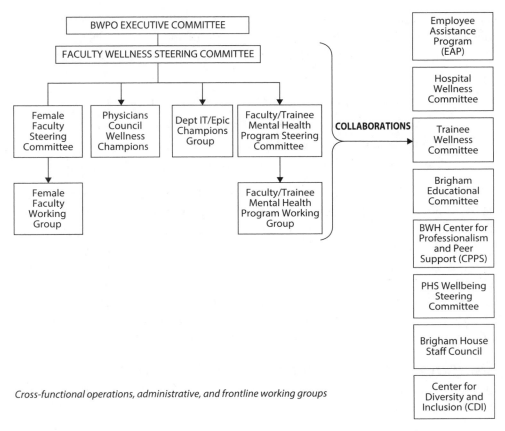

Figure 13-1: Governance Structure of the Brigham and Women's Physicians Organization Faculty Wellness Steering Committee

chief nursing officer, and HR representatives from both groups. This partnership was critical in responding to the needs of the frontline physicians.

BWPO had a rich history of investing in leadership through a physician leadership development program designed and implemented with Harvard Business School, the Brigham Leadership Program. In addition, a culture of fostering innovation through the Frontline Innovation Program and the Brigham Care Redesign Incubator and Startup Program is a part of the organization. This culture of leadership and innovation made the burnout initiative easier, given the background of change, innovation, and leadership tools already present.

Governance Structure

Governance structure is always important in an academic medical center. The Faculty Wellness Steering Committee consisted of 12 physicians and one additional administrative executive, including department chairs, hospital and physicians organization chief medical officers, and leaders from various other departments. The committee reported directly to the BWPO Executive Committee, emphasizing the importance of the initiative. Four groups report to the steering committee:

- Female Faculty Steering Committee
- Physicians Council Wellness Champions
- Department IT/Epic Champions Group
- Faculty/Trainee Mental Health Program Steering Committee

All these efforts worked in coordination and collaboration across the medical center's boundaries, including with the Employee Assistance Program, the Center for Diversity and Inclusion, the Center for Professionalism and Peer Support, and others. This governance structure was critical to ensuring that all voices were sought in the design and implementation of the program and that efforts were collaborative in nature, thereby reducing resistance to change.

BWPO did not create a position of chief wellness officer or chief human experience officer, instead assigning accountability to the steering committee, which worked with the chief medical officer and the president of BWPO.

Defining and Measuring Burnout and Fulfillment

BWPO employed the classic Maslach definition of burnout as a syndrome of the following:

- emotional exhaustion
- cynicism or depersonalization
- personal accomplishment

Professional fulfillment was defined by Tait Shanafelt as "happiness or meaningfulness, self-worth, self-efficacy and satisfaction in work."

MODELS, MEASUREMENTS, AND RESOURCES

As the BWPO burnout journey progressed, outreach efforts were made to learn from other leaders and organizations. Tait Shanafelt, then at Mayo Clinic and now at Stanford, met with members of the BWPO physicians' council to share background and experiences from Mayo, including the importance of engaging in regular measurement, addressing burnout openly, and sharing successes, as well as the critical nature of leadership accountability. Additionally, the physicians' council reached out to Stanford—which had developed its own model, called the Professional Fulfillment Index (PFI)—regarding use of its survey tool, which addressed both burnout and professional fulfillment. This survey was valuable because it also included questions to help identify drivers of burnout and professional fulfillment that were grouped into the areas of (1) culture of wellness, (2) efficiency of practice, and (3) personal resilience. The decision was made to use the Stanford Wellness framework and the Stanford Wellbeing survey tool. The Stanford survey was selected specifically because it encompassed both burnout and professional fulfillment measures and was designed to identify potential drivers of both. The PFI was included in the Stanford Wellbeing survey. The PFI is a 16-question, five-point Likert scale. The scale measures the following:

- professional fulfillment (6 questions)
- work exhaustion (4 questions)
- interpersonal disengagement (6 questions)

After review and edits from the physicians' council and Medical Executive Committee, in 2017, the first Brigham Wellbeing Survey (Stanford Wellbeing survey including the PFI, with some adjustments in response to feedback from the Brigham physician community) was conducted and the decision was made to join the National Physician Wellness Academic Consortium with the intent of learning along with others across the country and allowing for national benchmarking.

INITIAL (2017) SURVEY RESULTS

The results of the initial 2017 survey were striking in many ways. First, the response rate to the burnout survey was 64 percent, double the typical response rate from previous surveys. The high response rate was driven by several factors:

- chair and leadership commitment to the importance of physician burnout
- incentive program for leadership driven by metrics of completion
- presentation at faculty meetings
- inclusion of all faculty (including research and clinical)
- physician perception of the importance of this topic

Second, the burnout and fulfillment rates varied widely by department, from a high of 54 percent to a low of 21 percent, with a mean of 37 percent, reiterating that every individual burns out in his or her own way. Third, the survey process itself served a *convening function*, in that it served notice that burnout was important to the leaders **(Figure 13-2)**.

Conversely, fulfillment ranged from a high of 70 percent to a low of 29 percent, with a mean of 42 percent **(Figure 13-3)**. Interestingly, there was not a clear inverse relationship between burnout and fulfillment; in fact, some physicians with the highest fulfillment had high rates of burnout, potentially indicating that the job stressors for those physicians were excessive. (Resiliency was not measured in the surveys.)

The free text responses from the survey were particularly instructive in designing solutions, in both positives and negatives. The most common negatives

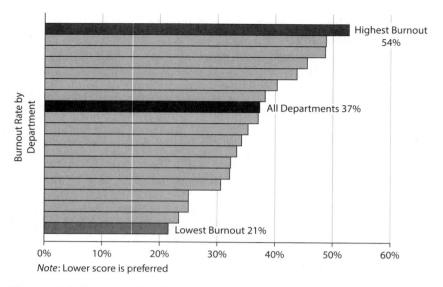

Figure 13-2: Burnout Distribution across All Brigham Health Departments

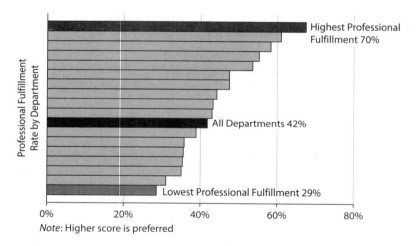

Figure 13-3: Professional Fulfillment Distribution across All Brigham
Health Departments

raised were the electronic health record (EHR) (Epic), high work volumes, and
lack of appreciation, while the top positives were interaction with colleagues, a
stimulating research environment, and the passion for caring for patients.

SIGNIFICANT GENDER GAP IN BURNOUT AND FULFILLMENT

Of considerable concern was the finding that female physician faculty had substantially higher burnout rates and lower professional fulfillment scores when
compared with their male counterparts **(Figure 13-4)**. Based on the 2017 survey, female physicians had a burnout rate of 44 percent and male physicians had

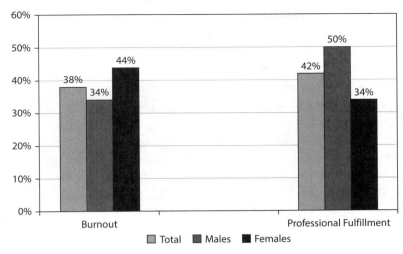

Figure 13-4: Brigham Health, All Departments: Burnout and Professional Fulfillment by Gender, 2017

a rate of 34 percent, while professional fulfillment was higher among male physicians, 50 percent compared with 34 percent in females. These findings led to a concerted effort to address these data with the Brigham and Women's Female Faculty Initiative (see later in this chapter).

INITIAL SOLUTIONS AND FUNDING

Initial funding for the burnout and wellness initiative came in fiscal year 2017 for $1.6 million and covered the following:

- Epic 1:1 "at the elbow" training
- launch of the Departmental Wellness Accelerator program
- initiation of planning for the Faculty/Trainee Mental Health Program
- Female Faculty Engagement Program
- launch of B-Well Brigham pilot projects

A return-on-investment approach was used to secure funding, focusing on the impacts of burnout and taking into account the known literature (at the time) that indicated that burnout increases medical error rate, decreases professional effort, and decreases productivity.

Fundamental Dichotomy in Defining Burnout

Among all the data from the surveys on the prevalence of burnout the single biggest driver of burnout was a fundamental dichotomy between the following:

1. The defining image of what life as a physician should be
2. The reality of what current physician practice comprises

The image that most physicians had in entering medicine was one of autonomy in service of caring for patients under humane and scientific principles (as well as teaching and research) in a milieu of respect and appreciation. The reality, however, was found to be different and consisted of feeling a constant pressure to do more with less while being compensated less for more stressors. As the stressors mount, the days grow longer and yet less satisfying with less professional fulfillment.

As disconcerting as that insight may be, having a clear understanding of it is essential to designing effective solutions. What is clear is that the goal of the work of decreasing burnout and increasing professional fulfillment is to reconnect physicians with their passion for patient care, teaching, and research while making their workdays better, easier, and shorter. It is both that simple—and that difficult.

T. S. Eliot notes in "The Hollow Men,"

Between the idea
And the reality,
Between the motion
And the Act,
Falls the shadow

The dichotomy between the perception and the reality of current daily practice casts a shadow over physicians, which increases burnout and decreases fulfillment. It is our task to remove that shadow, to the extent possible, which the initiatives were designed to do.

Summary of Initiatives

As the work of the steering committee progressed, a strategic approach was taken to decreasing burnout and increasing fulfillment, which included the following:

- *regularly measuring well-being* (burnout and professional fulfillment) using the PFI as a validated statistical survey with external benchmarks

- *creating a governance and accountability structure with financial resources* for reducing burnout and advancing faculty well-being

- *adopting and adapting the Stanford Professional Fulfillment Model well-being framework* to address three main areas of focus:
  - *culture:* leadership development, appreciation, community, Brigham to Table (see later in this chapter)
  - *operational efficiency:* Epic/EHR solutions, practice operations, administrative burden
  - *personal well-being:* Faculty/Trainee Mental Health Program, yoga, massage, mindfulness, and other resources

- *addressing the identified gender gap* through the Female Faculty Initiative, which focuses on advancement, flexibility, and respect

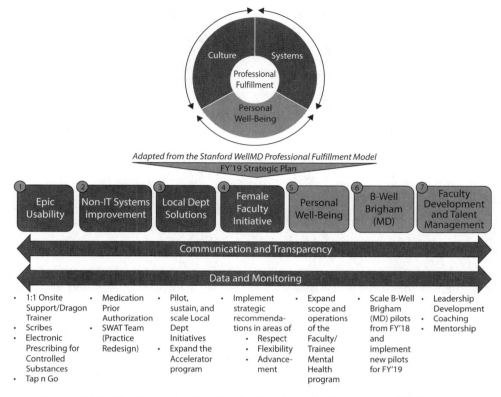

Figure 13-5: The Strategic Plan for the Faculty Development and Well-Being Effort, Fiscal Year 2019

- *funding pilot programs* that are department-specific and institution-wide, scale interventions that work—for example, B-Well Brigham modules and website access
- *participating in benchmarking* with the national consortium and across Partners Healthcare to share learning and identify best-practice solutions

The faculty development and well-being strategic plan for fiscal year 2019 is summarized in **Figure 13-5**. The budget for the program grew from $1.6 million in fiscal years 2017–2018 to $3 million in 2019, of which $1 million was spent and the remainder rolled over into the 2020 and 2021 budgets, with funding expected to remain at the same level, pending results.

ELECTRONIC HEALTH RECORD (EPIC) SOLUTIONS

The free text responses to the initial survey matched interviews with staff in identifying issues with the EHR—in our case, Epic—as the single biggest cause of stress and burnout. Accordingly, a number of solutions **(Figure 13-6)**

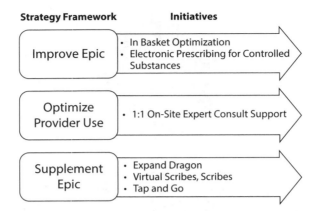

Strategy Framework   Initiatives

Improve Epic
- In Basket Optimization
- Electronic Prescribing for Controlled Substances

Optimize Provider Use
- 1:1 On-Site Expert Consult Support

Supplement Epic
- Expand Dragon
- Virtual Scribes, Scribes
- Tap and Go

Figure 13-6: Epic Usability: Decreasing EHR Burden for Providers, Fiscal Years 2018–2019

designed to make the EHR more accessible were implemented, including the following:

- one-on-one, one-hour "at the elbow" on-site consultation with an expert in the physician's specialty area
- trials of scribes and virtual scribes
- Dragon voice-recognition training
- electronic prescribing for controlled substances
- "Tap and Go"

Later a daytime EHR hotline was set up to deal with immediate Epic issues to gain resolution. Of these solutions, the "at the elbow" program to allow customization of physicians' workflows and the hotline were deemed to have been most widely used and successful. Scribe programs are still undergoing rollouts and have been particularly well received in dermatology and emergency medicine.

FEMALE FACULTY INITIATIVE

As a result of the gender gap identified in the initial survey, a consultant was engaged to review the survey and conduct focus groups to further delineate the problem. The physician focus groups included 80 faculty, and an additional 22 senior leaders were consulted. The Female Faculty Working Group and the Female Faculty Steering Committee developed draft blueprints for action based on the findings. Following this, the Faculty Wellness Steering Committee developed a strategic framework for action that was presented to the BWPO Executive Leadership group, which approved the budget and actions of the initiative.

The overall goal of the Female Faculty Initiative was *to find opportunities to advance female faculty in each department, implement an intervention, and measure the outcomes.*

The proposed interventions included the following:

- Work with departments to create a process for posting open leadership positions under Association of American Medical Colleges guidelines and developing standard work templates. Audit the process at least once.

- Pilot a coaching program to support female faculty performance and career advancement.

- Collaborate with the Office of Women's Careers to create a dashboard for female faculty career development to allow the team to identify opportunities within departments and track progress.

Unfortunately, despite all these focused efforts to deal with the unique stressors of female physician faculty members, the repeat survey performed in 2019 showed that in the intervening two years, burnout in female physicians *increased* (from 44 percent to 48 percent) and professional fulfillment *declined* (from 34 percent to 28 percent) **(Figure 13-7)**. During the same time frame, burnout and professional fulfillment rates did not significantly change in male physicians. (Burnout rates in males went from 34 percent in 2017 to 32 percent in 2019, while fulfillment went from 50 percent to 47 percent. Sample size and response rates did not change, indicating face validity and statistical similarity.)

There may be several explanations for this. First, the increase in organizational focus on burnout and fulfillment may have resulted in increased reporting, although that effect would have to have been differential for females versus males. This effect has been seen in some other surveys. Second, despite the focused efforts of the initiative, job stressors may have increased at a faster pace than adaptive capacity or resiliency. Third, factors and stressors arising

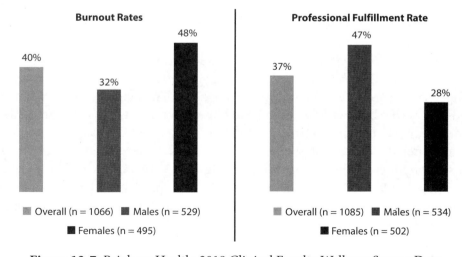

Figure 13-7: Brigham Health: 2019 Clinical Faculty Wellness Survey Data

from work-life balance in females may have increased differentially in the two-year period between the two surveys. Fourth, other institutions have noted a "penumbra effect," meaning physicians become aware of the importance of burnout and professional fulfillment yet are caught in the penumbra between awareness of the problems and the solutions needed to correct them. Compounding this would be the fact that the programs, although initiated, were not in place long enough to have a measurable impact. Finally, it is possible the focused efforts simply were not effective, but this is not borne out by personal conversations with those engaged in these efforts. Clearly, more data will be needed to resolve these questions, but there is full commitment to the Female Faculty Initiative.

FACULTY/TRAINEE MENTAL HEALTH PROGRAM

One of the more innovative and successful programs arose out of the survey and interview process. While the well-being survey did not specifically evaluate for mental health diagnoses, physicians are known to have higher rates of depression than the general population. In addition, review of the Brigham Emergency Action Plan utilization revealed low rates of use by physicians. Discussions with outside organizations, including Oregon Health and Science University, revealed models that had been developed specifically to support physician trainees and faculty. The Brigham physicians organization and hospital cofunded the Faculty/Trainee Mental Health Program. The program team comprised a psychiatrist and a psychologist who were hired specifically to support the program. These clinicians were experienced providers committed to addressing the mental health needs of physicians, trainees, and research faculty. The program was done by self-referral with an initial visit to discuss symptoms and determine whether the individual would benefit from ongoing treatment. If ongoing treatment was indicated, individuals could receive up to six confidential sessions to discuss these issues. The sessions were covered under the employee benefit program.

Feedback from the psychiatrist-psychologist team and the users of the program indicated that the perceived value of these sessions was high and that they ranged from coaching or mentoring through more formal therapy sessions. In addition to the therapeutic value, offering this resource was viewed as an important culture change, indicating that BWPO "truly cared and valued" its physicians. After the end of the six sessions, if necessary, a referral is made to an outside provider or alternative provider **(Figure 13-8)**.

Between May 2018 and August 2019, 159 people participated in the program, resulting in 672 visits, 21 percent of which were with faculty. Participation by department ranged from 2 percent to 10 percent. Females were 65 percent and males 35 percent of the visits.

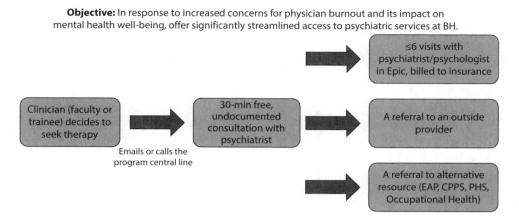

Figure 13-8: Personal Well-Being: Faculty/Trainee Mental Health Program

B-WELL BRIGHAM

B-Well Brigham is a pilot program designed to develop and implement well-being resources for the faculty, including a Faculty Development and Wellbeing website (http://fdw.brighamandwomens.org). The topics include reducing administrative and regulatory burdens, navigating Epic, managing high work volumes, and handling perceived lack of appreciation. A "Monthly Wellbeing Newsletter from the BWPO" was also developed and distributed (https://conta .cc/2m6qrcl).

BRIGHAM TO TABLE

The Brigham to Table program leverages the wisdom that those who "break bread together" work better together by providing lunches paid for by the department three times per week and reimbursing faculty for meals in which two or more faculty members gather to discuss physician well-being. Any opportunity to create communities for interaction combats burnout, and thus other means to bring people together should show equal value and be encouraged.

LOCAL DEPARTMENT SOLUTIONS

The top themes of work done to improve systems and processes to hardwire flow were improving scheduling flexibility, addressing staffing, redesigning workflow, working to understand and solve problems around the physician-nurse dynamic, and providing a 360-degree review process.

What Worked Best?

Feedback from the faculty and the steering committee indicated that some solutions were more effective and better accepted than others. First, the one-on-one "at the elbow" Epic consultations were extremely well received and effective from a practical standpoint, as well as emphasizing a change in culture toward one that invests in Epic workflow changes customized by individual and specialty. Second, the Epic/EHR hotline was also very successful for the same reasons, but more focused on real-time problems with real-time resources. The Faculty/Trainee Mental Health Program, while not used by a majority of faculty, was felt to provide significant value to those who did use the service and has supported many trainees. The trials of scribes, virtual scribes, and voice-recognition technology were effective, particularly in dermatology, where the cost of the programs was offset by increased productivity.

What Worked Less Well?

In general, programs such as yoga classes, meditation, massage, and mindfulness training were less effective. Many felt that work redesign to make clinical practice more effective and efficient was more important, since getting out of work earlier would allow the physicians to use their own resources for these programs. The Brigham to Table program was more used in primary care specialties than in general surgery and surgical subspecialties.

What's Next?

BWPO is committed to decreasing burnout and increasing physician fulfillment and will continue both its efforts and the benchmarking work nationally and across Partners Healthcare. As new data and innovative programs evolve, they will guide our further efforts. In addition, the work will be coordinated with the hospital and the healthcare system.

Additional Readings

West CP, Dyrbye LN, Rabatin JT, et al. Intervention to promote physician well-being, job satisfaction, and professionalism: a randomized clinical trial. *JAMA Intern Med* 2014; 174 (4): 527–533.

Trockel M, Bohman B, Lesure E, et al. A brief instrument to assess both burnout and professional fulfillment in physicians: reliability and validity, including correlation with self-reported medical errors, in a sample of residents and practicing physicians. *Acad Psychiatry* 2018; 42: 11–24.

14

Duke University Health System

Bryan Sexton, PhD, Director, Duke Center for Healthcare Safety and Quality, Duke University Health System

Jonathan Bae, MD, CPPS, Associate Chief Medical Officer, Patient Safety and Clinical Quality, Duke Center for Healthcare Safety and Quality, Duke University Health System

> *The negative screams at you while the positive only whispers.*
>
> BARBARA FREDRICKSON

Dr. Sexton's Story

I am a psychologist by training, with a focus on psychometrics and the role it plays in helping people help others—which is the core of healthcare. I am fascinated by the reasons why healthcare professionals follow evidence-based protocols, particularly in patient safety, but also across healthcare broadly. I was increasingly convinced that the primary obstacle to adopting positive change was not resistance to change but personal burnout. In other words, the best predictor of professionals' willingness and ability to participate in meaningful changes in quality improvement and patient safety is the extent to which they have the energy and resiliency to do so. Simply stated, did they have the "gas in the tank" to fuel the journey from where we are to where we need to be?

In 2009, I was fortunate to have an extremely secure position at one of the most widely respected academic healthcare systems in the United States, which I had held for 12 years. We were working on reducing bloodstream infections in hospitalized patients, with a focus on ICUs. I was bombarded with requests to take on additional work, speaking engagements, and projects. It seemed I was incapable of saying no, and this was part of the reason I became burned out. As Alexander the Great famously said, "The people of Asia became slaves because they could not pronounce the word *no*."

However, despite my great job at a major university, and a great wife, three lovely kids, and a fourth child on the way, I realized that I was burned out. The work was no longer fun, I was emotionally exhausted, I had become cynical, and the work had less meaning to me, all classic signs of burnout. I was confused about why I was so behind at work and everyone else seemed to be fine. During this personal crisis, the pressures at work increased, to the point where I was told, "Bryan, you're either on the train or you're off the train. Get on the train!"

Fortunately, I was actively recruited at that time by my current work home at Duke University as director of quality improvement and patient safety, where the leadership had a clear goal: to become the world's leader in healthcare quality and safety. The organization's leaders had a deep and fundamental humility and were deeply supportive of my ideas to develop well-being and resiliency resources as a foundational prerequisite for the team's efforts in quality, safety, and patient engagement efforts. During the interviews, I expressed these ideas and Duke said, "Bryan, come to Duke and help us do what you are describing." I was charged with a wonderful challenge: to develop and implement relevant ways to encourage well-being that resonated—personally and professionally—with a talented and motivated team of professionals.

My wife and I enthusiastically embraced this challenge and picked up the family and moved to Duke. This chapter summarizes the work our team, including Jon Bae, has done over the past 10 years. It is a story that says less about the negative consequences of burnout, as real and pervasive as they are, and instead focuses on reestablishing and rejuvenating the ability to experience the restorative effects of the positive emotions so abundant in healthcare and in life. Burnout is not inevitable but in fact can be prevented and treated with the use of the tools we and others have developed.

Dr. Bae's Story

My relationship with Duke University began when I was an undergraduate and has continued for 19 of the past 23 years, interrupted only by 4 years of medical school at the Medical College of Virginia. I returned to a combined internal medicine–pediatric residency, including a chief resident year under the guidance of now dean but then chair of medicine, Mary Klotman, who taught me the critical importance of leadership and the skills it entailed. In my clinical work as an internist and a hospital medicine physician, I use those leadership skills daily.

As the associate program director for quality and safety for the medicine residency program, I was responsible for encouraging our trainees to participate in our survey on the organizational culture of safety, which included a measure of burnout. This was the first time the survey had been administered to trainees, and over 80 percent of medicine trainees completed it. When the results showed over 80 percent of our trainees had scores suggesting mild to moderate burnout, I did not know what to do! I had the great good fortune of taking Bryan's course, which had a huge impact on my entire view of healthcare and helped me realize I too was intermittently experiencing burnout personally and professionally. We began work in the residency program—which now has burnout scores that are less than half as high as those in the early 2010s. The work has been extended across the organization since that time. It has been my good fortune to have become the associate chief medical officer for patient safety and clinical quality at the Duke University Health System (DUHS), working closely with Bryan, which has allowed me the privilege of advancing this work for the organization. Developing resiliency and well-being while battling burnout for the people on the Duke team helps them improve their care of our patients. It is a key part of Duke's strategic plan and I am honored to be a part of the work.

The Duke University Health System Story

At DUHS, our strategic plan for the last five years has been "advancing health together." At the core of this plan is the idea that supporting our people and the environments in which they work is foundational to all else. To advance health together, we focus on one employee at a time, by attracting, developing, and retaining a talented workforce that improves and saves lives. This focus on the importance of people is represented at its best by Healthy Duke, which has the goal of creating the healthiest campus in the country, inclusive of the entirety of our health system, physician practice, and all of our schools, undergraduate and graduate. The core belief is, "A healthier Duke starts with us." That is why we have made the well-being of the Duke family one of our top strategic priorities. We are engaging students, faculty, and staff across the Duke community to help each of us live healthier, improve our quality of life, and realize our full human potential.

In keeping with DUHS's goal to be a zero-harm system, we are creating a culture that fosters well-being and puts people first. In defining burnout, we use the symptoms of emotional exhaustion, depersonalization/cynicism, and a reduced sense of personal accomplishment, which in sum lead to the inability to experience the benefits of positive emotion in our personal and professional lives.

Defining burnout as a diminished ability to experience the restorative and rejuvenative effects of positive experiences and the emotions they generate puts the cardinal symptom of emotional exhaustion at the center. This understanding led to the development of tools and strategies to help individuals and teams return to experiencing those positive effects and emotions—and therefore enjoy the passions that a career in healthcare uniquely offers. The drivers of burnout include work unit, organizational, national, and individual factors. The first three of these represent two-thirds of the factors, while individual factors drive a third of them. But developing personal well-being and resiliency is essential to being able to change the other factors and is thus a foundational concept. It is also important to acknowledge that emotional well-being is a spectrum ranging from burnout to thriving; our goal at DUHS is not to eliminate burnout but rather to promote team members who are thriving in their work.

As a reflection of the importance of burnout and culture on the care we deliver to patients—places with more burnout have worse outcomes across the board—we include team member well-being as a critical aim of our quality mission. Caring for those who care for others as part of our pursuit of the "quadruple aim" is one of our most important strategies to keep patients safe and to lead in the delivery of the highest-quality, patient-centered care.

DUHS's framework for this work rests on five key concepts, each of which is discussed in more detail:

1. Assess and create awareness.

2. Care for each other.

3. Harness the power of leadership.

4. Improve the work.

5. Find joy, meaning, and purpose.

1. Assess and Create Awareness

The first step in the framework is to both assess the awareness of burnout and well-being and enhance and expand that awareness. The assessment of awareness derives from the survey tools used, including a formal survey that taps into the emotional exhaustion symptom of burnout and is derived from the Maslach Burnout Inventory (MBI) and "pulse" surveys, which allow for more proximal feedback.

MEASURING BURNOUT WITH THE DUKE TOOL FOR 10 YEARS

A detailed list of burnout surveys is presented in Chapter 7. One of the earliest efforts we undertook at Duke was also one of the most important. Based on the observation that the single most reliable symptom of burnout is emotional exhaustion, we developed and validated a modification of the MBI, using five items of the original nine-item emotional exhaustion scale and a five-point Likert scale instead of the MBI's seven-point scale:

1. "I feel frustrated by my job."

2. "Events at work affect my life in an emotionally unhealthy way."

3. "I feel burned out from my work."

4. "I feel frustrated by my job."

5. "I feel fatigued when I get up in the morning and have to face another day on the job."

The mean of the five items is converted to a 0–100 scale, with higher scores indicating more severe emotional exhaustion and therefore burnout. The tool is nonproprietary and free for use.

This measurement tool has been continuously used for the past 10 years (with minor modifications) and is the foundation for leaders in the health system, who have found it invaluable for leading their change efforts. Leaders throughout the health system routinely ask prospectively for the data, which help them tailor solutions for the work they are doing.

PULSE SURVEYS

Every 18–24 months, we measure employee engagement, the culture of safety, and workforce well-being, including with some of the scales referenced. We have done this for over 10 years and in the last 3 years have combined these approaches into a single survey instrument: CulturePulse. This survey has a reach of over 27,000 DUHS team members and has a response rate of greater than 70 percent. This has allowed us a real-time sense of the "pulse" of the organization, which allows us to pivot as needed to meet its needs through action planning both organizationally and at the unit or clinic level. It also helps assess not just the "macroculture" of DUHS but also the "microcultures" of the teams within the system.

CREATING AWARENESS

Awareness of the importance of well-being, resiliency, and burnout comes from many sources. To that end, we have enhanced communication to our team members through multiple modalities (newsletters, blogs, and social media campaigns) about the importance of a focus on our people and well-being. One of our main strategies has been the Well-Being Ambassadors course, which set out to identify leaders—formal and informal—to serve as culture change agents from the ground up. The program, described in greater detail shortly, has four goals for its participants:

1. Be a champion for well-being within your teams.

2. Role-model healthy behaviors for well-being.

3. Implement strategies locally.

4. Act as a culture change agent.

Bringing the concepts of well-being and resiliency to these ambassadors has allowed us to spread the concepts far more rapidly.

THE DUKE WELL-BEING AMBASSADOR COURSE— ENHANCING CAREGIVER RESILIENCY

Perhaps the biggest single impact of the work at Duke comes from the use of two-day and one-day courses to teach the resiliency essentials needed to do the hard work of patient safety and quality improvement teams. The "graduates" of these courses become Well-Being Ambassadors who are passionate advocates for teaching resiliency within their respective units. This is not a requirement for taking the course, but an overwhelming number of people become leaders in their own units.

Two-Day Course Description: Resiliency Full Course Before we care about quality, we must care about our work, and before we can care about our work, we have to take better care of ourselves. For decades, clinicians have been taught that self-care is selfish, which is simply not the case. The growing consensus in the peer-reviewed literature is that burnout levels in healthcare workers are reaching the breaking point. Quality improvement efforts frequently ignore the need to make sure that caregivers are ready for the next big initiative, and rarely do they first build up the resilience of staff before expecting even higher levels of quality and safety to be delivered.

For some, jumping into innovation is a reasonable first step. But for many individuals and work units, there needs to be a focus on the caregivers and their needs, to build capacity and bounce back from burnout, before providing the training and the tools to improve quality in a sustainable way.

The Enhancing Caregiver Resilience course is designed to meet the needs of our patient safety and quality improvement communities. The course is designed for caregivers in formal or informal leadership roles, but participants include executives, staff physicians, and nurses. Over 300 team members have taken the course, and each of our three yearly sessions of 70–80 participants is fully enrolled.

In this course, we provide participants with real-time feedback on burnout, depression, health behaviors, human limitations, and human nature. Participants are given protected time to practice and to work on themselves and their units. This is an intense and rewarding experience for participants, full of self-reflection, validation, coaching, and recharging those nearly dead batteries. The course is taught on-site for two consecutive days, followed two weeks later by a two-hour webinar for three days of continuing medical education / continuing education unit credit.

One-Day Course Description This is a special course at the center. Based on our two-day courses, this primer on resilience covers five modules:

- prevalence and severity of burnout
- fatigue management
- mindfulness techniques
- dealing with difficult colleagues
- coping with change

"Enlightening," "refreshing," and "interactive" are the most common descriptors participants use to describe this course. Tune in, charge up, and go forward. This course is taught three times yearly.

2. Care for Each Other

Duke's resources for well-being and resiliency are comprehensive:

- Healthy Duke (healthy.duke.edu)
- Duke Center for Healthcare Safety and Quality
- Duke Integrative Medicine
- Duke PDC Provider Empowerment Program
- Personal Assistance Services
- Human Resources—Live for Life
- Voices of Duke Podcast
- Provider Empowerment Program

The following resources are specific to the Duke Center for Healthcare Safety and Quality:

- Duke Health Well-Being Toolkit for Leaders (https://www.hsq .dukehealth.org/well-being-toolkit)
- Enhancing Caregiver Resiliency—full Duke Ambassador course
- Essentials—Duke Ambassador course
- WISER (Web-Based Implementation of the Science to Enhance Resilience)
- Resilience Adventures (bit.ly/resilbite)

WISER: The 18 Tools to Cultivate Resilience Building on Duke's commitment to safety, quality, and investigation of the ties between burnout and resiliency, and assisted by a $3 million National Institutes of Health Research Project Grant, we built an online set of tools known as WISER. WISER has the following features, each of which was viewed as essential to the work of the group:

- The evidence base for the utility of the tools was extremely strong.
- The tools have a very quickly measurable (and sustainable) impact.
- There is a low barrier to entry to accessing and using the tools.
- The tools are enjoyable, beneficial, and almost addictive in their simplicity.

Interventions last between 3 and 15 days, with participants receiving prompts for the tools via email or text message. Participation enhances well-being by building skills and contributes to ongoing research on interventions for health-care burnout. They are designed to cultivate the following:

- joy and playfulness (bit.ly/joyreflections; 2 minutes; 8 days)
- awe (bit.ly/awetool; 10 minutes; 2 days)
- gratitude (bit.ly/grattool; 10 minutes; 2 days)
- humor—three funny things (bit.ly/start3ft; 2 minutes; 8 days)
- work-life balance (bit.ly/wlbtool; 2 minutes; 4 days)
- hope (bit.ly/fwdtool; 2 minutes; 8 days)
- engagement (bit.ly/inttool; 5 minutes; 3 days)
- mindfulness—three good minutes (bit.ly/3goodminutes; 3 minutes; 8 days)
- perspective (bit.ly/doortool; 10 minutes; 2 days)
- ability to uplift others (bit.ly/posfbtool; 3 minutes; 8 days)
- kindness (bit.ly/kindtext; 3 minutes; 8 days)
- kinder internal voice (bit.ly/selfcomptool; 10 minutes; 2 days)
- routines and rituals (bit.ly/serenitytool; 2 minutes; 4 days)
- your signature strengths (bit.ly/strengthstool; 3 minutes; 8 days)
- rest and sleep (bit.ly/sleeptool; 2 minutes; 8 days)
- three good things—uplifts (bit.ly/start3gt; 2 minutes; 15 days)
- WISER—sampler of uplift tools (bit.ly/3wiser; five-in-one tool; 10 days)
- your burnout story—healing through reflective writing (bit.ly/storyburn; 20 minutes; 3 days)

Tens of thousands of people, both at Duke and outside the institution, have availed themselves of the WISER tools, the feedback from which has been over-whelmingly positive.

Bite-Size Resilience Adventures Many people in healthcare are so stressed and with such large work-life balance problems that they felt they could not even afford the time to invest in the WISER tools, as brief as they are. However, the research is clear that even brief expressions of gratitude lower stress, increase levels of well-being and resiliency, and produce less depression and burnout. Albert Schweitzer told us that sometimes our own light goes out and must be re-kindled by the lights of others.

With these insights, we developed a series of brief resilience activities for healthcare team members struggling with burnout or work-life balance who might need "bite-size resilience adventures" to get them started. These include short exercises on the following:

- awe (I saw something amazing)
- acts of kindness (I noticed something kind)
- relationship resilience (I noticed a good chat)
- looking forward (I see good things in the future)

Participants select the area in which they are most interested, which takes them to a brief video, a short activity, and a reflection. They are "bite-size" because they take a short investment of time but have a large return on investment in fostering well-being and resilience. Many people who access this series go on to access the other exercises or even the WISER resources.

3. Harness the Power of Leadership

Leadership matters at all levels of the organization, and the pathway to well-being and resiliency goes through investing in personal and professional leadership training. Leaders are the key to building optimal work environments. We have included in our training for leaders and managers—the Guide to Managing at Duke—a focus on resilience and well-being. Moreover, a focus on your team member well-being is a regular part of performance reviews. Leadership rounding has been a key strategy for us for over a decade. Other tools that have been created include simple strategies to regularly incorporate well-being into meetings, as well as a well-being toolkit for managers.

WELL-BEING TOOLKIT FOR LEADERS/MANAGERS

Creating a culture that fosters well-being and puts people first does not always come easily or naturally. The toolkit provides ideas and resources to do just that. Each of the suggestions therein is a tried and tested way to put more "gas in the tank" so team members are better equipped to meet the demands of the day. Well-being encompasses several dimensions that are highly interconnected in pursuit of a broader view of health to help us live healthier, improve quality of life, and realize our full human potential. There are five pillars of well-being:

1. Food and nutrition
2. Mental and emotional well-being
3. Physical activity and movement
4. Fulfillment and purpose
5. Environment and culture

Each of these five pillars seeks to use evidence-based approaches and tools to create actions that build a culture addressing these areas:

- Build resiliency.
- Humanize the work.

- Strengthen your and your team's leadership style.
- Cultivate community.

The toolkit is iterative in nature and is continuously being improved and expanded based on feedback from our teams.

RESILIENCY WEBINARS

In addition to the online resilience tools and the Duke Health Well-Being Toolkit, Duke Health has also developed a series of online webinars available to hospital associations, groups, and individuals through a subscription service. The current webinar series comprises 12 modules designed to be viewed monthly for a year, but is being expanded to a full 24 webinars to be viewed over 24 months. Individuals can join in any month and view all 12 webinars. Both continuing medical education and continuing education unit credits are offered as a part of the program. The following is the current content:

- **January**—*Prevalence and Severity of Burnout: Workforce Resilience as Care Quality.* Burnout is increasingly common, compromises clinical and operational outcomes, and is treatable. What happens in our heads when we burnout is discussed.
- **February**—*Enhancing Resilience: The Science and Practice of Gratitude.* This session demonstrates a simple, enjoyable, and effective tool for improving well-being by cultivating gratitude, with improvements in resilience, sleep quality, and depression.
- **March**—*Measuring and Understanding Health Care Worker Resilience, Work Life Integration, and Burnout.* The absence of something bad (burnout) is not the same as the presence of something good (resilience). We demonstrate the links between well-being metrics and show how they vary at the individual and the work levels. Burnout may have more to do with colleagues than previously thought.
- **April**—*Enhancing Resilience: Three Good Things.* The most popular and effective of the burnout tools is a simple, enjoyable, and remarkably effective tool that can be done for 10–15 days—but with effects that last up to a year. Each night, reflect and write down three good things that happened that day and what role you played in making them occur.
- **May**—*Enhancing Resilience: Practicing Safe Stress and the Science of Sleep.* What should you eat on a stressful day? How long is a good nap? The answers might surprise you. Here we recognize, anticipate, and respond to the human limitations of sleep deprivation.
- **June**—*Psychological Safety: The Predictive Power of Feeling Supported When Things Go Wrong.* "Better to be silent and thought a fool than

to open your mouth and remove all doubt." This session demonstrates the concept of psychological safety, cultivating voice, and understanding what we can do to make it easier for others to speak up with concerns and comments.

- **July**—*Being Present: The Science of Mindfulness.* The data are clear: mindfulness matters. We demonstrate what it means to be in the "present moment," or mindful; review the research on mindfulness for well-being; and discuss how mindfulness can help communication and relationships.

- **August**—*Relationship Resilience: The Science of How Other People Matter.* This session describes how cultivating meaningful relationships is a health behavior, and how loneliness puts us at risk for lower satisfaction at work and in life, poorer immune system functioning, and even reduced longevity. It is the quality, not the quantity, of our relationships that matters most.

- **September**—*Collaboration versus Dealing with Difficult Colleagues: Assessing, Understanding, and Improving Teamwork in a Work Setting Near You.* This session guides you through the prevalence and severity of disruptive behavior, as well as its correlates and consequences. Institutional and individual strategies for dealing with difficult colleagues are discussed.

- **October**—*Science of Wow: Cultivating Awe and Wonder as a Resilience Strategy.* A feast for the eyes, this highly visual and image-driven webinar summarizes and demonstrates the benefits of the emotion of awe, including increased life satisfaction, greater sense of meaning, and a desire to connect with others.

- **November**—*Positive WalkRounds: Leader Rounding to Identify What Is Going Well—Links to Quality, Culture, and Workforce Resilience.* An institutional intervention to enhance workforce resilience is discussed, demonstrating how traditional WalkRounds identify bright spots, and how each contributes uniquely to quality and safety, but also to workforce resilience.

- **December**—*Enhancing Resilience: Survival of the Kindest.* This summarizes the research to explain that there are demonstrably powerful benefits to being altruistic and provides a framework for how to use random acts of kindness in individual and work settings.

4. Improve the Work

As much as building well-being and personal resiliency are critical to success, it is important to understand that resiliency is the foundation for improving the work we do as well. The more resilient your team, the faster and more effectively they will be able to come together to redesign the systems and processes to make the work better for those who do it. At the same time, the work we do has an impact on the resilience of our teams. Having great, resilient team members work in poorly designed jobs that erode their well-being is no way to build a sustainable culture. To that end, we have embarked on a journey to drive engagement of our people to see and solve problems that are getting in the way of delivering patient care as an engagement and well-being strategy. The Duke Quality System uses the concepts of a lean management system to create a team of over 20,000 problem solvers and is rooted in the foundational concept of respect for our people and the work they do.

Numerous additional efforts are under way at DUHS to address this, including the following:

- workflow improvements in the electronic health record
- dictation services
- electronic health record optimizations
- provider efficiency reports

When our teams are burned out, not only does it negatively affect every metric in healthcare, it makes it difficult, if not impossible, to implement change, which is central to improving the work.

5. Find Joy, Meaning, and Purpose

The first four steps are in service of increasing our team members' sense of joy, meaning, and purpose in the sacred work they do. Too often, healthcare systems have assumed that this sense of purpose is innate in providers. At DUHS, we have designed several ways to harvest and reinvest the stories of the courageous heroes who walk our halls and create miracles every day. Here are some of them:

- Gratitude matters! Duke has numerous reward and recognition programs, including the Good Catch Award, High Five Award, and Strength, Hope, and Caring Award.
- The DUH Safe Choices Training improves understanding of human error, at-risk and reckless behavior, and the impact of personal choice in preventing patient harm.
- *Voices of Duke Health* is a podcast featuring Duke Health providers, staff, students, trainees, patients, and visitors in one-on-one conversations about what is meaningful in their lives, work, and relationships. A link to the site is available to all team members, who can also sign up to record their conversation in the listening booth (www.listeningbooth.info).

- Compassionate Care Conferences are monthly gatherings that discuss the human side of delivering care.

- Efforts to understand, listen, and make meaningful changes in the area of racial disparities and social injustice have been led by our chancellor of health affairs, Eugene Washington, who has been at the front of the rallies and listening sessions.

- Social media efforts to thank the "heroes we work with" include #ThankYouDukeHealth.

Ensuring not only that team members are appreciated but that they *know they are appreciated* requires leadership by every team member at every level of the organization.

Advice for CEOs

Maladaptive leadership is largely responsible for the epidemic of burnout in healthcare, but effective leadership can turn the situation around. The single biggest piece of advice to the team in the C-suite is this: *Take your foot off the accelerator as a default maneuver of leadership.*

There is an understandable tendency to want to produce results quickly, since once people arrive in senior leadership positions, they think, "Finally, it's *my turn* to turn this ship around." We have found that enlightened healthcare leaders are moving away from thinking, "Is it really my job to deal with a bunch of burnouts?" Instead, they genuinely seek solutions that invest in the individuals and allow for time to pause, reflect, and consider how best to arm the team members to experience positive emotions. The tools we have listed are an effective way to begin that journey and certainly worth the investment of time and energy.

What's Next?

While human existence at its foundation has certain constants, the circumstances in which we live and the complexity thereof are constantly changing, as the recent pandemic showed all too clearly. We will continue to expand, adapt, and innovate at Duke to improve the well-being and resiliency resources for our team members so they can better serve our patients.

Additional Readings

Adair KC, Kennedy LA, Sexton JB. Three good tools: positively reflecting backwards and forwards is associated with robust improvements in well-being across three distinct interventions. *J Posit Psychol* 2020; 15: 613–622. doi: 10.1080/17439760.2020.1789707. Accessed November 3, 2020.

Adair KC, Rodriguez-Homs LG, Masoud S, Mosca PJ, Sexton JB. Gratitude at work: prospective cohort study of a web-based, single exposure well-being intervention for health care workers. *J Med Internet Res* 2020; 22 (5): e15562.

Rehder KJ, Adair KC, Hadley A, et al. Associations between a new disruptive behaviors scale and teamwork, patient safety, work-life balance, burnout, and depression. *Jt Comm J Qual Patient Saf* 2020; 46: 18–26.

Sexton JB, Adair KC. Forty-five good things: a prospective pilot study of the Three Good Things well-being intervention in the USA for healthcare worker emotional exhaustion, depression, and work-life balance and happiness. *BMJ Open* 2020; 9: e022695. doi: 10.1136/bmjopen-2018-022695. Accessed November 3, 2020.

15

Inova Health System

Steve Motew, MD, MHA, FACS, Chief, Clinical Enterprise, Inova Health System, Falls Church, Virginia

Inova Health System is a five-hospital, not-for-profit health system serving over 2 million patients in northern Virginia and the National Capital Area through its 2,000 beds and, most importantly, its over 18,000 team members, including more than 400 members of the Inova Medical Group. All Inova hospitals carry a five-star rating from the Centers for Medicare and Medicaid Services. Like most successful health systems, Inova believes deeply in the importance of mission, vision, and values to guide all our efforts (**Figure 15-1**).

Our approach to burnout and resiliency reflects our deep commitment to Inova's "people strategy," which arises from our belief in the importance of the people who are aligned in high-performing teams to deliver excellent care to our patients. We simply cannot provide "world-class healthcare, every time, every touch," without investing in the leadership skills of all of our people at every level of the organization, including both personal skills of resiliency or adaptive capacity and the skills of teamwork.

Inova's journey toward leadership development and resiliency training was launched systematically just before the emergence of the coronavirus pandemic. The rising stressors in healthcare were already creating burnout among the team, but the pandemic served to accentuate its importance. As our community looked to Inova clinicians to care for them in the crisis, it became the latest and most acute of a seemingly never-ending list of requests, responsibilities, and pressure points that burdened caregivers with the weight of consistently and persistently going above and beyond the call of duty to serve our patients. While the pandemic did not cause us to engage in the work, it certainly accentuated its importance.

Before accepting my current position as chief of clinical enterprise for Inova, I had the honor of serving as senior vice president of Novant Health with responsibility for five hospitals in the Winston-Salem/Brunswick markets with 1,400 beds and more than 150 physician clinics. In that role, I was deeply familiar with Novant Health's approach to burnout and resiliency (Chapter 12)

Figure 15-1: Inova Health System's Mission, Vision, and Values

and worked with Tom Jenike of Novant and Nicholas Beamon of OneTeam Leadership, whose work deeply influenced my thinking. In fact, Inova has engaged Nicholas in our work, as I will explain later.

In addition to the importance of this work to our people strategy, two key aspects of our organization are the concepts of triad leadership and organization into service lines across all hospitals and outpatient practices. Inova's concept of triad leadership expands the dyad concept of having physician and nursing leaders working together across boundaries and extends the team to include a coequal leader from hospital administration. This structure allows improved leadership, management, and most importantly, innovation.

Inova is organized into 11 distinct but interrelated service lines across the organization and its sites:

- Cancer
- Heart and Vascular
- Medicine
- Surgery
- Musculoskeletal
- Women's Health
- Neurosciences
- Pediatrics
- Behavioral Health

- Primary Care
- Clinical Platforms

The primary intent of the service line and triad structure is to focus all resources on the patient, with leaders working across boundaries. Inova's work on resiliency is an integral part of the broader people strategy and the service line and triad leadership systems. Our leader, Stephen Jones, who is the president and CEO of Inova Health System, was deeply committed to the effort and ensured that the entire senior leadership team was as well.

Early Work at Inova Health System

When I arrived at Inova, there were multiple groups of passionate people, all trying to provide resources for burnout and resiliency. However, their excellent work lacked central coordination, so an initial goal was to pull these passionate people into a team with a cohesive purpose. Much of the early work centered on "affinity support solutions," such as education, massage therapy, and yoga resources. A behavioral health psychologist was engaged in the work, but with no scientific analysis at that time. The biggest problem was not a lack of purpose or enthusiasm, but that the team was being bombarded with wellness efforts done with perfectly good intentions but not in any unified and meaningful way.

We decided that a powerful guiding coalition of five to six passionate people was needed to crystallize the work and give it direction. We knew that it was imperative for our teams across all hospitals and service lines. One of the earliest innovators in this work was Lucas Collazzo, then president of the medical staff at Inova Fairfax Medical Campus, which is the largest of the Inova hospitals and a tertiary-care academic medical center. He brought enthusiasm and passion to the work and quickly agreed to attend a seminar sponsored by the American Hospital Association taught by Tom and Nicholas. He returned even more enthusiastic, proclaiming, "I am totally in. Let's do this work."

The Inova Health System Leadership Development and Resiliency Program

Working with our guiding coalition, we engaged Nicholas to assist in designing and delivering a four-day initial cohort, similar to but not precisely the same as the Novant work, focused on helping the participants "dive into self" in ways that changed perceptions, opened attitudes, and provided resources to increase resilience. It allows participants to "press pause" in their busy professional and personal lives and examine their current experience of their work and personal lives. The introspective but proactive process reveals internal biases, barriers, and patterns that interfere with the team members' ability to rejuvenate themselves from the demands of work to launch themselves toward greater fulfillment.

Several concepts formed the foundation of the work. The first is the importance for physicians, nurses, and other team members to rediscover their sense of joy, meaning, and purpose and the actions embodying them. Second is the development and cultivation of intentionality, which is the discipline of paying attention and choosing actions that reflect intentionality by focusing on what we control as opposed to what we do not control. Third is the importance of influential leadership, which grows from a commitment to lead yourself, lead your team, and lead your organization. Fourth is the core belief that the focus is on investing in the individual team members and their leadership and resilience skills. Finally, these skills are not "nice-to-have" elements in healthcare but rather are vital foundational tools if we are to recruit, retain, and keep healthy our team members. We did not engage in the work to improve results but rather to improve our people's ability to return to the passion that brought them to healthcare originally.

The journey begins with a rediscovery of what brought us to healthcare and can be described in many ways, such as "core purpose," "True North" (as Steven Covey calls it), "deep joy" (as discussed in the Introduction and Chapters 4 and 8), or "true self." Regardless of the terminology, it is a reflective exercise that at a minimum asks these three questions:

1. What brings me true joy?

2. What brings meaning in my life?

3. What acts, actions, and commitments most reflect the purest version of my true self?

Intentionality takes those answers and develops the training and discipline to focus on choices that fuel joy and meaning through the actions of our day, paying particular attention to the things we control and excluding those we do not, thereby avoiding a victim's mentality, where things are seemingly always happening *to us*, instead of being *chosen by us*. Our true or deep joy is the compass by which we steer, guiding the choices we make. By working on personal leadership skills and the ability to build adaptive capacity in the face of tremendously stressful work environments, we develop influential leadership, which is based on the concept of leading yourself, leading your team, and leading the organization by choosing actions that reflect your true self and thus empowering yourself but also your teammates and the entire organization. The word *influence* derives from the Latin *influere*, which means "to flow into," an apt metaphor for a leadership style that uses personal transformation to "flow into" the efforts of the team by leveraging our efforts where they will produce the most impact.

Participants in the First Presentation

The people invited to the initial cohort were selected from among leaders and emerging leaders, or those known to be experiencing significant stress, and were selected from across the system. The attendees were told that we were passionately declaring that resiliency and leadership training were a core part of our people strategy. It was designed as an investment in them as people and as leaders, and not as a means to specifically attain higher metrics or performance results.

Beginning in August 2020, 30 people were part of the initial group invited to a local resort and conference center. The group was heavily but not intentionally weighted to physicians. Based on our engagement surveys, our physicians were below the national mean. The message was clear: Inova is committed to taking care of its people who take care of patients—every touch, every time. Yet the focus was on investing in them to lead themselves, then lead others, and the broader organization only secondarily.

Response to the Inova Training

Almost all attendees had an enthusiastic and appreciative response to this training. Many members of the cohort expressed gratitude, with the terms *insightful* and *meaningful* most often used. This was viewed as a major change in the Inova culture, with more than a few expressing, "I can't believe that you would do that for us!" In that respect, the initial effort was successful in initiating change in our culture and investing in our people.

There were some members who were less transformed than others and who maintained a certain wariness about the intent of the work, but they represented a minority of the attendees. Perhaps most important is that several months after the meeting, most team members have used the training to become more intentional in using their influence to improve their own lives and the lives of their team members and patients.

Future Steps in the Journey

We used the feedback, both positive and negative, to guide changes in the subsequent cohorts, the second of which occurred in November 2020, after which the leadership team pulled up to "do a biopsy" on the efforts to further improve our ability to deliver on our commitment to invest in our people. All "vital signs" to date point to changing the culture effectively, as well as the systems and processes in which our people work, in addition to investing in their personal leadership skills. Without question, investing in leadership development and well-being training will be a key piece of Inova's ongoing people strategy.

16

Wellstar Health System

Jill Case-Wirth, MHA, RN, BSN-SVP, Chief Nurse Executive

Ryan Breshears, PhD, ABPP, Chief of Behavioral Health

John Brennan, MD, FACEP-EVP, Chief Clinical Integration Officer

LeeAnna Spiva, MSN, PhD, AVP, Nursing Practice

I see it every day. . . . I see it in their eyes, I hear it in their voices, I feel it in our teams.
JILL CASE-WIRTH (DESCRIBING THE RESULTS
OF THE WELLSTAR RESILIENCY AND
LEADERSHIP DEVELOPMENT EXPERIENCE)

At Wellstar, our patients are the center of everything we do. Nationally ranked and regionally recognized for our high-quality care, inclusive culture, and exceptional doctors and team members, Wellstar Health System is one of the largest and most integrated healthcare systems in Georgia. Our state-of-the-art facilities include 11 hospitals, 300-plus medical office locations, nine cancer centers, 55 rehabilitation centers, three hospice facilities, one retirement village, 21 imaging centers, 15 urgent care locations, and five health parks. Every day, our team of 24,000-plus healthcare professionals provides personalized care for patients at every age and stage of life.

As a not-for-profit health system, our passion for people extends beyond our system and into the communities we serve. Each year, Wellstar thoughtfully reinvests in the creation of healthier communities through prevention and wellness programs and charity care for eligible patients. Our efforts at building resiliency and well-being among our team start with our mission and vision:

Our mission: To enhance the health and well-being of every person we serve.

Our vision: To deliver world-class healthcare to every person, every time.

"Every person we serve" includes all of our team members, whose health and well-being are threatened by the accumulation of stress from internal and external drivers. Left unchecked, these can lead to burnout. If we want them to be able to deliver world-class healthcare to every person, every time, we must invest in their personal well-being, resiliency, and leadership development. Wellstar Health System is actively pursuing strategies to ensure that our physicians, nurses, and caregivers have the tools for a successful work-life balance. In fact, we have expanded the Triple Aim (high quality, improved access, and affordability) to include caregiver wellness for a Wellstar Quadruple Aim. Patient outcomes improve when caregivers are engaged in and invigorated by their work. To help us exceed the expectations of our patients and consumers, we are partnering with our physicians, nurses, and other caregivers to improve their wellness and resiliency via the Wellstar Physician Resiliency and Leadership Development Experience and a Wellstar Nursing Resiliency and Leadership Development Experience, both of which launched in 2018. Each of these programs is a critically important part of our journey, and both were influenced by the work done at Novant Health and OneTeam Leadership, led by Nicholas Beamon, who was critical in our work.

Wellstar Nursing Resiliency and Leadership Development Experience

At Wellstar, nurses are not only our largest workforce, with over 7,300 nurses, but also the essential, vital contact with our patients. Nurses lead "from the bedside to the boardroom" throughout the organization. We consider them to be "the heartbeat of healthcare." Nonetheless, as Ryan Breshears, chief of behavioral health at Wellstar, pointed out early in our efforts, the work they do extracts a significant physical, mental, emotional, and even spiritual toll, which we believe requires a rethinking of the investment needed in their resiliency and personal and professional leadership training. Rest, recovery, regeneration, and self-care are all required components in order to care for patients and experience greater life fulfillment.

While the demographics are changing, nursing is currently overwhelmingly a female profession and therefore deeply influenced by an ethos of caring first for others, and only then caring for yourself. We knew we had to change that mindset, so the patient was still our primary focus, but without putting ourselves last or—sadly—sometimes never. We began our journey with the individual, assuming, "If we can't care for ourselves, we can't care for others."

EXECUTIVE REGISTERED NURSE TEAM THREE-DAY RETREAT

The three-day immersion program, followed by a one-day capstone, included an off-site retreat designed to help participants rediscover their core purpose, develop stronger self-leadership skills, and establish a foundation of personal resilience to support achieving better whole-life balance (**Figure 16-1** lists program objectives). We began by convening a cohort of 25 senior executive nurses

Three-Day Program	One-Day Program
• Learn how to operate from a deeper place of personal purpose and core clarity. • Develop a keen sense of personal awareness and understanding of how one's unconscious patterns of behaviors, inner dialogue, and choices can contribute to burnout. • Focus on creating an "attraction to wellness" rather than a solution for burnout. • Develop a new mindset, new habits, and a commitment to living like "healthcare athletes," which includes the concepts of repetitive cycles of work, rest, recovery, and rejuvenation. • Develop a greater ability to lead oneself and therefore have a greater ability to influence the team and the culture in a positive manner.	• Gain insights into the power of self-leadership: awareness of patterns, biases, mind frame, and in-the-moment presence. • Develop the ability to make intentional decisions and act in service of improving one's quality of life. • Develop the ability to consistently restore physical vitality and energy. • Improve the ability to consistently restore emotional resiliency and access full engagement in every dimension of one's life. • Develop the ability to consistently access one's A-game, best self, and best life. • Create equilibrium within the eight dimensions of the My Life Balance Dashboard: (1) Professional (2) Health and wellness (3) Finances (4) Personal growth (5) Spiritual (6) Significant other (7) Fun and recreation (8) Family and friend

Figure 16-1: Program Objectives, Three-Day and One-Day Programs, High Level

from across the system. (We have intentionally kept the training sessions at about 25 members to maximize their intimacy and effectiveness.) Our chief nurse executive, Jill Case-Wirth, worked with Nicholas Beamon to devise the curriculum and models and they led the rollout together. The focus was on helping individuals rediscover their fulfillment in work through an understanding of the role that personal leadership plays as the essential pathway to professional leadership. It begins with a deep self-awareness journey toward building and sustaining a strong foundation of personal resiliency. This approach supports individuals as they build a new overall life strategy and mindset regarding personal wellness. This strategy includes specific rituals that allow individuals to rejuvenate their physical energy, emotional state, mental alertness, and inner spirit. "Lead yourself before leading the team" was a foundational concept, as we sought to create a culture of developing and aligning personal values first. Only after that transformation is made in an intentional way can it be applied to aligning them with professional values.

We found that many participants came to the course expecting the "usual suspects" from traditional leadership development courses but were surprised when it became apparent that the work focused on them and was an investment in their personal lives. Many of them were excited when they completed the retreat, but they were also anxious, wondering, "Are we up to the journey and the challenges it represents?" For most, this was the first time they had attended leadership development that was designed for them personally, which was a surprise. One nurse leader said, "In 30-plus years, never—not one single time—has Wellstar taken the time to invest *in me as a person*, to help me prioritize my values, my choices, and consistently be my best self."

Follow-up from the one-day retreat was performed at one-month, six-month, and one-year intervals. The one-month single-day sustainability retreat is particularly critical to the success of the program, as it reinforces both the curriculum and the organization's commitment to the individual and his or her personal development. The following data were gathered from participants:

- 98 percent reported being able to enjoy personal time without focusing on work matters.
- 87 percent reported being able to disconnect from communication during free time.
- 83 percent reported being able to free their minds from work when they are away from it.
- 98 percent reported being able to see every patient or client as an individual with specific needs.
- 96 percent reported being able to care for all patients or clients equally, even when it is difficult.
- 100 percent reported that their work is meaningful.
- 79 percent reported that they rarely lose sleep over work issues.
- 98 percent reported that the work they do makes a real difference.

The following quotes from participants demonstrate the impact of the course:

- "A life-changing experience!"
- "This was a fantastic program, helping me to be the best me, so I can be the most effective for those around me (home and work)."
- "The approach taken during this entire retreat was wonderful and very effective in delivering the message of being in the moment, how to balance the life wheel and discussing finding effective ways of contributing and engaging in my team at work."

- "This conference did an excellent job of helping me be aware of my own biases and filters and how to remove them to be my most relaxed, present, authentic self."

Following completion and initial feedback from the first course, the three-day program cascaded to the 63 executive directors and directors of nursing of the Wellstar Health System, with minimal changes.

THE SECOND ROUND

Designed to bring resiliency support to nurses at the bedside, a one-day format has been designed to support an additional 250 nurse managers, assistant nurse managers, and professional charge nurses. We recognized the tremendous challenges that these frontline leaders face as they are unwavering in their commitment to our patients, our communities, and the teams they lead. The work is both physically and emotionally demanding, creating vulnerability for distress and burnout. The one-day format was designed to support team members as they began their personal wellness journey. These one-day wellness workshops include follow-up support and are designed to allow team members the opportunity to explore the primary external and internal components that lead to burnout, fatigue, and disengagement. Participants explore their current level of physical wellness, mental wellness, and the conditions that have affected both. This self-reflective and insightful look allows a critical mass of nurses to take the initial steps required to build a sustainable model of professional success and personal satisfaction. The primary focus of these workshops is to support nurses in building a solid foundation of self-leadership that allows them to proactively manage the demands of their work and create a reliable process of rejuvenation. Participants receive both preparatory and postcourse assignments designed to assess their current state of wellness and begin the process of making adjustments to create greater clarity, greater wellness, and a sustainable approach to working in healthcare. (Figure 16-1 lists the program's objectives.)

IS THE TRAINING "WORKING"? MEASUREMENT AND RESULTS

While we are in the process of studying changes in resilience and leadership styles, which will be discussed later, the free-form feedback and check-ins at the intervals described have shown extremely positive responses. On rounds, it is impossible to overstate how many times people have commented on how meaningful and helpful the training has been in their personal and professional lives. As the quote beginning the chapter indicates, the impact has been profound and lasting. While we certainly expect some "drift" or erosion of the skills over time, our experience so far has been encouraging in the extreme.

The following data were collected from participants:

- 100 percent reported that the workshop has put them on a path to strengthen their personal resiliency.

- 100 percent reported that the experience will have a positive impact on their personal life.
- 98 percent reported that the experience will have a positive impact on their professional life.
- 100 percent reported that the facilitators of the workshop were effective and engaging.

The following quotes from participants demonstrate the impact of the course:

- "Thank you to Wellstar for recognizing the value and importance of taking care of myself. This exemplifies why this is such a wonderful place to work."
- "I feel very encouraged that my organization is promoting a healthy work-life balance."
- "I really enjoyed this training and found several takeaways to apply to my work/home life."

CHARGE NURSE TRAINING IN LEADERSHIP STYLE AND RESILIENCY

The charge nurse has a critical role in the organization, stretching across all inpatient units and emergency departments, but receives little time for development or training opportunities. To create a healthy work environment and advance role effectiveness, it was critical to provide charge nurses training. Because of this, we created and studied the results of a two-day resiliency and leadership development program for our charge nurses. We partnered with Catalyst Learning to execute NCharge, an evidence-based curriculum using a classroom-based, instructor-led training model. The leadership class was 8.5 hours, including 7 continuing education unit credit hours. Course content included supervisory skills (including communication styles, managing conflict, and accountability) and critical thinking skills. Charge nurses attended the one-day program described earlier and outlined in Figure 16-1.

Measuring Resiliency In order to assess changes in resiliency, we used the 25-item Connor-Davidson Resilience Scale, including personal competence, trust in own intuition, acceptance of change, control, and spiritual influences, rated on a five-point Likert scale, with a potential total score of 100, with higher scores indicating higher resiliency. While data analysis is ongoing for all but the charge nurse group, the charge nurses showed a statistically significant increase in resilience from pre- to postintervention ($P = .003$).

Measuring Leadership Style We used the Multifactor Leadership Questionnaire, which is a 45-item survey that measures leadership styles as transformational, transactional, or passive avoidant and also measures leadership outcomes. Charge nurses who attended the training showed a statistically significant increase in transformational and leadership outcomes. Charge nurses expressed verbally and in writing that the leadership and resiliency courses would help them in their effectiveness in leading their teams, improving quality, reducing costs, and achieving greater employee engagement. As one charge nurse stated, "My biggest takeaway was self-reflection—just making sure before I interact with my team that I am in the right professional space and that I am ready to take on the challenge because I know that others are looking to me for guidance."

We set the vision that our organization would become one that develops nurse leaders and supports their progression from charge nurse all the way to the level of chief nursing officer. As with the charge nurse development program described earlier, we embarked on a journey to develop a comprehensive nursing leadership development strategy for our nurse managers and assistant nurse managers. We offered a comprehensive leadership development program, strength-based coaching, and one-day resiliency program to these leaders over the course of a year and measuring leadership style and resiliency. We began data analysis in the summer of 2020, but those efforts have obviously been affected by the enforced "COVID pause." We look forward to sharing those data when they are analyzed.

HORIZONS: WHAT'S NEXT?

We continue to analyze responses and interpret data, but our organization at the highest system levels supports the necessity of well-being and resiliency training for all our staff as an integral part of our future. Perhaps our highest priority post-COVID is to extend this valuable training to our bedside nurses, who are among our most valuable resources. We anticipate this to have the same fundamental focus on the personal journey of the individual but will certainly have certain modifications. Major questions are how we can scale it and how we can maintain progress over time.

We have already seen a coaching and mentoring effect from the initial cohorts in that many of the attendees have a burning desire to participate in the ongoing rollout of the work. We anticipate harnessing their passion as a way of continually completing the work. A "shepherd model" will guide that work.

We are also at work on integrating the nursing and physician work (described shortly) on resiliency and well-being in meaningful ways. Since Nicholas Beamon and his colleagues at OneTeam Leadership have been integral to the development and presentation of both efforts, we are confident this will be a seamless process.

Finally, Ryan Breshears has been working on dealing with burnout and the effects on moral distress and moral injury in the post-COVID period, so we anticipate developing solutions on that front as well.

Wellstar's Journey toward Physician Wellness

Conceptualized over a century ago, the Yerkes-Dodson law illuminates the dynamic relationship between the level of stress an individual is experiencing and the quality of his or her performance. What we sometimes neglect to consider is how these interactions apply at higher systemic levels (e.g., stress as a mediator of the relationship between a person and his or her direct supervisor) as well as within micro-systems (e.g., the extent to which stress catalyzes changes in the nervous system or contributes to impaired functioning in a particular organ). Further, we also sometimes fail to understand how individual and system-level protective factors and vulnerabilities intermingle to either contribute to clinical phenomena such as burnout or mitigate the probability of their expression.

To understand Wellstar's journey into physician resiliency requires some appreciation of system-level contextual factors. In April 2016, Wellstar completed the acquisition of 6 new hospitals, expanding from a 5-hospital system in the northwestern Atlanta suburbs to an 11-hospital system and the largest within the greater Atlanta area. This growth occurred following months of exploration and planning and was preceded by an anticipated merger with a large academic healthcare system (Wellstar terminated the partnership in the final hours). Not to be missed, the strategic shifts and incremental growth came on the heels of a system-wide transition to a new electronic medical record platform. In sum, by mid-2016 our physician workforce was under a prolonged phase of stress and uncertainty, with external drivers that included rapid organizational growth, the infusion of new clinical and executive leaders, increased patient population demands and a shifting payer mix, adoption of new practice habits via the electronic medical record, and the inherent challenges of integrating disparate organizational cultures as we transitioned into a One Wellstar system. These were stressors external to the individual physician, representing threats to autonomy and order. The result: ours was a system with prodromal symptoms of burnout.

Recognizing that these macro-system and external drivers were increasing stress on our physician and advanced practice provider (APP) workforce, Wellstar prioritized physician burnout as the central theme in our spring 2017 Medical Staff Leadership retreat, which was attended by over 250 physicians and APPs. Dike Drummond, a nationally recognized expert on physician burnout, provided the keynote address. Just before that event, Wellstar sent three physician leaders to Novant Health to participate in its physician immersion program and to bring back insights regarding the value of developing our own physician resilience program. This initial anthropological study was described as a "life-changing" experience for our physician attendees, propelling Wellstar to accelerate our own programmatic efforts.

WELLSTAR PHYSICIAN RESILIENCY AND LEADERSHIP DEVELOPMENT EXPERIENCE

At the recommendations of our physician leaders who partook in the physician immersion program, in March 2017, Wellstar formalized a partnership with Novant and OneTeam Leadership, leveraging the understanding and expertise of their program leaders, Nicholas Beamon and Tom Jenike (senior vice president and chief well-being officer), in development of the Wellstar Physician Resiliency and Leadership Development Experience. An initial focus group of select medical staff leaders was assembled to understand the perceived needs of our physician workforce. Subsequently, an initial cohort was assembled of 20 Wellstar-employed and Wellstar-affiliated physician leaders who volunteered to undergo a three-day off-site immersion experience. Volunteering physicians represented a cross section of medical specialties and ranged in experience from early career to 25-plus years of professional practice. Pre-retreat, physicians participated in individual 30-minute intake/coaching calls with Jenike and Beamon and completed pre-reads and exercises that oriented them to thoughtful self-reflection regarding personal values and formative autobiographical experiences that have shaped their characters and personal drives.

Understanding Burnout in Relation to the Individual System Implicit in the Wellstar–OneTeam Leadership approach to physician resiliency is the recognition that internal psychological needs and goals must be explored in relation to the expression of general stress and burnout symptomatology. For physicians with strong needs for personal autonomy, for example, emotional distress (e.g., anger or frustration) is more likely to manifest in the context of loss of decisional rights. And those clinicians with strong needs for order would be considered more vulnerable under conditions of change and uncertainty. These foundational understandings help to place the program in context and address the real-time stress drivers. The OneTeam facilitators emphasize the contributions of individual personality leanings, learned experiences, and core values—and how these factors influence physician behavior, including stress responses, both personally and professionally. The objective is not to subject participants to group counseling, but there are therapeutic benefits in response to this intentional process of self-reflection and the deepening of insights about oneself. Since August 2017, 138 physicians and advanced practitioners have elected to participate in the Wellstar–OneTeam immersion program. One participant described the impact of the program as follows: "I have become the real 'me' again." Another stated, "This was a fantastic program, helping me to be the best me, so I can be the most effective for those around me (home and work)." Post-retreat outcomes corroborate the subjective benefits, as demonstrated by the following:

- 98 percent reported being able to enjoy personal time without focusing on work matters.

- 87 percent reported being able to disconnect from communications during free time.

- 83 percent reported being able to free their mind from work when they are away from it.

Addressing Organizational Contributions to Burnout The positive impacts of Wellstar's immersion program have been well documented by attendees. After program completion, a significant number of participants from the initial cohort, for example, made monetary contributions earmarked for physician resiliency through the health system's foundation. And although the anecdotal reports have been almost uniformly positive, as a system Wellstar is attuned to our need to address the prominent front-end drivers of burnout as well. Following the lead of renowned experts such as Tait Shanafelt, Wellstar's conceptualization of wellness encompasses a holistic model in which clear and effective communication, lean process improvement initiatives throughout the continuum of care, electronic medical record optimization, and physician leadership development programming converge to increase professional enrichment and eliminate stressors that create vulnerabilities in our clinicians.

Wellness during COVID

The COVID pandemic was novel, but recent history offered insights about the potential challenges Wellstar team members could face. For example, in 2003, following the SARS outbreak in Canada, 29–35 percent of healthcare workers reported high levels of emotional distress.[1] These effects persisted for more than 24 months postoutbreak, with downstream impacts on burnout, reduced work hours, and reduced patient contact hours.[2] Risk factors included professional identity as a nurse, having children at home, and working in close proximity to SARS patients. In early 2020, research from Wuhan generalized these predictive factors to COVID-19.[3]

Anticipating the impact of COVID on our Wellstar clinicians, we redeployed underutilized behavioral health team members and established a method to stratify Wellstar clinicians on the basis of two empirically supported risk factors: professional identity as a nurse and increased exposure to COVID patients. Second, we developed a menu of resources customized to professional identities (nurses, physicians, and so on) and organized based on intended impact contingent on the distress risk **(Figure 16-2)**.

- Primary resources: Options for asymptomatic team members who could benefit from preventive strategies to sustain personal well-being throughout the pandemic

	Primary	**Secondary**	**Tertiary**
Methodology	Preventive	Preventive or responsive	Responsive
Provider distress	Minimal	Mild	Moderate or severe
Resources	Internal	Internal	External

Figure 16-2: Resources Coordinated to Intended Impacts

Menu of Resources	**Primary**	**Secondary**	**Tertiary**
1. Frontline provider outreach calls	+	+	+
2. Provider wellness toolkit	+	+	+
3. Apps and web-based tools	+	+	+
4. Behavioral health podcast series	+	+	+
5. Stress management video series	+	+	+
6. Mindfulness groups	+	+	+
7. Spiritual health care support		+	+
8. Peer/colleague support line		+	+
9. Debriefings (crisis/noncrisis)		+	+
10. Counseling services		+	+
11. Medication management			+

Figure 16-3: Menu of Wellstar Wellness Resources

- Secondary resources: Tools for team members with mild to moderate symptoms of emotional distress, or team members working in closer proximity to COVID patients who could become vulnerable over the course of the pandemic

- Tertiary resources: Resources for team members with moderate to severe symptoms of emotional distress who were in need of more rigorous interventions, including outside referral to a treating behavioral health provider

A menu of wellness resources (**Figure 16-3**) was developed by Wellstar's Psychological Services team, which leveraged the evidence base of the biopsychosocial model.[4] In partnership with nursing leadership, physician leadership, and Wellstar's communication and Human Resources teams, a multimodal approach was utilized to ensure that team members were aware of available resources and resources were readily accessible. External referrals for mental health services, for example, were driven through a methodological approach of identifying community-based behavioral health providers who were willing to allocate predetermined availability to focus on healthcare workers' distress. This emergent network of providers was quickly leveraged to provide a range of support for Wellstar team members to complement the in-house services offered by Wellstar-employed psychologists and other team members. Through this internal-external partnership, Wellstar physicians, nurses, and leaders were offered access to on-site crisis debriefings for entire teams and virtual counseling services—made more accessible through behavioral health copay waivers for all Wellstar employees.

A multifaceted communication strategy was developed in collaboration with senior leaders. Methods of resource deployment included virtual "state of the system" meetings, biweekly clinical communication calls with Wellstar medical staff members, and a consistent cadence of email communications that called attention to the wellness resources offered to Wellstar clinicians. Links were made accessible through the electronic medical record homepage, and wellness efforts were championed by Wellstar's senior physician and nursing leaders. Other methods included marketing of wellness resources via prominent visual cues, such as screen savers on Wellstar computers, and leveraging of the Wellstar intranet homepage. To further infuse clinician wellness into the organizational culture, wellness was prioritized as the topic of emphasis at Wellstar's annual 2020 Nursing Leadership retreat as well as the fall 2020 Medical Staff Leadership retreat.

Removing Barriers

What can we do to get physicians to access these resources?

INTERNIST

Interestingly, I've spoken with a number of colleagues who voiced hesitancy about considering attendance to this program. They're missing out!

UROLOGIST

Lack of time, competing priorities, stigma, and lack of resources are often cited as primary barriers to utilization of wellness methods. While Wellstar addressed the last of these reasons through the acceleration of our internal and external resources, our leadership recognized the importance of making access easy for our clinicians. We recognize that healthcare workers often subjugate their own wellness and prioritize the needs of their patients. And our leaders realized early that passive access was unlikely to meet team member needs, particularly in the context of increased workload. Thus we designed and deployed two proactive outreach methods, which distinguishes our model from many others:

1. Outreach calls to frontline nurses and respiratory therapists: Personal phone calls to frontline nurses and respiratory therapists by licensed behavioral health providers. In each call, a single distress question is asked and resources offered. Team members with elevated subjective ratings receive a follow-up contact within 30 days of the initial call. All calls are followed by a personalized email with a list of wellness resources and information on how to access them.

2. Medical staff outreach to physicians and APPs: Utilizing a smartphone application (PerfectServe) traditionally used for HIPAA-protected communications about hospitalized patients, Wellstar psychologists sent over 2,500 personalized messages to medical staff colleagues to offer support in the event that stress was becoming unmanageable or problematic.

Wellstar's approach to clinician resiliency is further informed by social identity theory, which appreciates the human psychological need to affiliate with a group perceived to be comparable to oneself. Recognizing the social psychology of group identification, our system's approach to clinician wellness aimed to remove barriers via the creation of distinct "lanes" for physicians and nurses, and through customization of resources that align with the cultural norms inherent within different clinical groups. Particular attention was paid to the language inherent in the culture of physicians, for example, and the socializing of "performance optimization" approaches in lieu of "mental health resources." The intent of this method was to offer resources in a manner that was more palatable to physicians and reduced the stigma some associate with mental health care. A concrete example of this method was Wellstar Psychology's leveraging of the PerfectServe app to provide 24/7 peer coaching support to physicians and APPs expressing symptoms of burnout or distress.

Future Directions for Wellstar's Wellness Program

Over the course of the past three years, Wellstar has taken tangible steps to infuse wellness into the culture of the organization. And while external stressors have represented unequivocal challenges, these crises can also serve as catalysts to accelerate meaningful offerings to our clinicians in need of resources.

Our leadership recognizes, however, that strategic planning requires intentionality and thoughtfulness, and that the provision of stress management resources is an insufficient proxy for a successful, sustainable, or comprehensive program. Burnout will never be mitigated effectively by managing the emotional symptoms downstream. We have significant work ahead to move upstream—leveraging the individual strengths and resilience of our workforce on the front end, and systematically resolving the contributing drivers that negatively affect our workforce. Continued evolution of our work necessitates a shift from symptom management to prevention, a focus on improving our processes, and a willingness to assess burnout at various altitudes. We recognize a need to attend appropriately to the macro-level and organizational contributors while also understanding burnout at more granular levels. We need to better understand the needs of our clinicians—what motivates them to provide excellent and quality care, and what could drive them away from a profession that once resonated with their core values. We will continue to put our people first.

Part Four

Tools for Battling Healthcare Burnout

Give us the tools and we will finish the job.

WINSTON CHURCHILL, BBC BROADCAST,
FEBRUARY 8, 1941[1]

Framework and Format for the Tools

Churchill's words came at a time during World War II when the British were fighting the Nazis alone, France having been quickly overrun in 1940. His appeal to US president Franklin Roosevelt and Congress was not for the US to declare war but rather for it to approve either the sale of munitions or the lend-lease program to give the British the naval bases and destroyers to do the job.[2] Similarly, all of us as leaders must have the tools to finish the job of battling burnout.[3] Part Four presents a format and details for using each of the 22 tools to battle healthcare burnout and create the leadership skills necessary to provide adaptive capacity or resiliency. The tools are listed by chapter (**Figure P4-1**):

- tools for personal passion and adaptive capacity: Chapter 17
- tools for shaping culture: Chapter 18
- tools for hardwiring flow and fulfillment: Chapter 19

(All of the slides for the tools are available for free in PowerPoint format by requesting them from the author.) The tools have specific targeted areas for the team, as summarized in the sections describing them. Like a surgeon's or a mechanic's tools, each has a specific function and is designed to deal with a specific issue.

The framework and format for the tools are the same and so are listed here, as opposed to repeating them in each chapter.

A Framework for Action: Getting Started

Every journey is best guided by a compass and a map. In this case, the compass is making the team's job easier through intrinsic motivation while making the

Tools for Personal Passion and Resiliency

1. Love, Hate, Tolerate
2. Deep Joy, Deep Need
3. Sing with All Your Voices
4. Stress Tolerance Level
5. Strategic Optimism/Creative Energy
6. Disconnect Your Hot Buttons
7. Leave a Legacy
8. Do the Best You Can
9. Keeping a Gratitude Journal
10. Who Do You Burn Out and Why?

Tools for Shaping Culture

1. Mutual Accountability Jumbotron
2. A-Team/B-Team
3. Leading from the Front
4. What Kind of Leader Are You?
5. Trust
6. Shadow Shifting

Tools for Hardwiring Flow and Fulfillment

1. Stop Doing Stupid Stuff, Start Doing Smart Stuff, Send a Signal of Hope
2. Taxi, Takeoff, Flight Plans, Landings
3. Making the Patient Part of the Team
4. Precision Patient Care
5. Clinical Huddles and Five Demand-Capacity Questions
6. The EHR Solutions

Figure P4-1: The 22 Tools of Battling Healthcare Burnout

1. Get started
   - Educate the C-suite and the board on the problem and ROI
   - Be committed to changing the system, not just yourselves
2. Takeoff, landing—tap into their passion, ideas, and purpose
3. Dedicate resources and infrastructure
   - Educational resources
   - Survey resources
   - Chief wellness, human experience, or talent officer and support
4. Decide on a survey—commit to action on survey results
5. Precision solutions to decrease job stressors and leverage organizational and personal resilience
6. Proceed across all three core elements (culture, systems and processes, and personal)
7. Apply the tools of battling healthcare burnout

Figure P4-2: A Framework for Moving Forward in Implementing Efforts to Battle Healthcare Burnout

patients' lives better without burning out the team. The map is the previous experience of others in using the three precepts emphasized throughout the book:

1. Everyone on the team is a leader. *Lead yourself, lead your team.*

2. All leaders are performance athletes who need the tools to make it possible. *Invest in yourself, invest in your team.*

3. *The work begins within.*

The framework for getting started is listed in **Figure P4-2**, but whatever format for launching your resilience/burnout initiative should be shared with your leadership team and infused with an understanding that lowering job stressors and building adaptive capacity or resilience requires a willingness and commitment to changing the culture and the system, without which progress simply will not occur.

1. *Get started:* Use a dyad or triad leadership[4-5] approach combining nursing, administrative, and physician leadership to ensure that leaders are on the same page, with the same passion, commitment, and willingness to advance the plan to battle burnout. If the plan is organization-wide, make sure the C-suite and the board are fully briefed and committed, and that they understand the return-on-investment calculus of investing in solutions.[6]

2. *If they are not with you on the takeoff, they won't be with you on the landing:* Make sure you get key members of your team with you before presenting it to the broader team. Ask them for their specific support, as well as a critique of how the message can be better communicated, what the critiques of the plan will be, and from whom they will come. Tap into their passion, ideas, and purpose. Then and only then roll out the plan to the entire team, asking for their input and their commitment.[7] Battling burnout can never be a one-person show—it takes a team.

3. *Dedicate resources and infrastructure:* On the organizational level, tie the battling-burnout message to the system's mission, vision, and values. At all levels, make sure there are sufficient educational, survey, and data analysis resources to make meaningful and responsive changes as data come in. If the organization has committed to a chief wellness or human experience officer, who does he or she report to, and are there adequate resources to support the work? At a unit level, "recruit" mentors from both the nursing and physician ranks to champion and help lead the work.[8]

4. *Decide on a survey and commit to action on the results:* Chapter 7 discusses selection of surveys to measure burnout symptoms, engagement, and fulfillment. Regardless of what survey is selected and how the surveys will be administered, make sure team members' feedback is sought outside the survey, for both inclusiveness and speed of input. Be clear that both the formal and the informal feedback will be used to deliver team-based action plans, the results of which will be measured.

5. *Develop and implement precision solutions to decrease job stressors and increase organizational and personal resilience or adaptive capacity:* Your team members are extremely pragmatic—make sure you develop and implement precision approaches designed tactically and strategically to address their problems.

6. *Proceed across all three core elements:* Make sure the solutions cut across all the aspects of culture, hardwiring flow and fulfillment, and personal resiliency. Use the Mutual Accountability Jumbotron to summarize and delineate graphically the combined solutions, timelines, and measures of success.

7. *Apply the tools of battling healthcare burnout:* Each of the tools has a specific purpose and should be used by leaders to stimulate thought and discussion on an ongoing basis. Battling burnout is *always* an iterative problem—show the same resiliency and ability to adapt that you are asking the team to show.

The Format for the Tools of Battling Burnout

Each tool follows a format designed to make implementation easier **(Figure P4-3)**.

START WITH "WHY" BEFORE "HOW"

Make a clear, terse statement of why the tool is important, helpful, and actionable in decreasing stressors and increasing organizational or personal resiliency. "Getting the 'Why' right before the 'How'" is a fundamental insight for any change, as Nietzsche noted[9] and, more recently, Simon Sinek showed in a different context.[10]

Each of the tools should be framed by, "This makes your job easier and the patients' lives better because . . ." The details of making the job easier should arise from the specific feedback from the team regarding what is burning them out and why.

MOVE TO "WHO"

What groups of people are likely to benefit from this tool? Is this for a general audience or a more focused group?

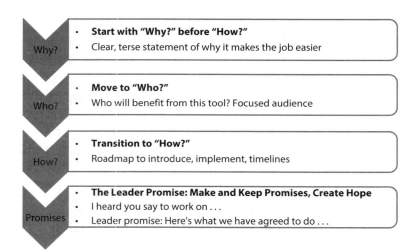

Figure P4-3: Battling Healthcare Burnout Toolkit Format

TRANSITION TO "HOW"

Give a roadmap to introduce, implement, and discuss the tool. What is the timing for breakout sessions, and how will summary reports work? Introduce the "ground rules" of transparency, confidentiality, inclusivity, and mutual accountability:

- What is said in here stays with us to make the team better.
- We want to hear all voices, but anyone can pass anytime they are called on.
- As the leader, if any team member has not been heard, ask him or her, "What are your thoughts?" If the team member passes, simply say, "OK, but do jump in whenever you want."
- If you don't understand an idea, ask clarifying questions, such as, "Help me understand that idea better."
- No personal attacks.
- Every idea is a good idea.
- "All lenses, all voices" should be seen and heard, as Steve Narang, CEO of Inova Fairfax Medical Campus, has said.[11]
- No interruptions while a team member is expressing their thoughts.
- When a team member tends to dominate a discussion, perhaps interrupting others to do so, simply say, "Thanks for that perspective, but let's hear from others who may have a different view."

Roadmaps also give an estimate of the amount of time needed to use the exercise in meetings.

THE LEADER PROMISE: MAKE PROMISES, KEEP PROMISES, CREATE HOPE

The leader promise means promising not to waste time with tools that don't make the job easier and patients' lives better and then keeping that promise, whether the work is on culture, hardwiring flow and fulfillment (systems and processes), or personal passion and resiliency. The promise is a clear symbol that you will *follow up and follow through*. This is the type of language that assists in the leader promise:

- "This is why this tool can make your job easier and the patients' lives better . . ."
- "This idea arose from what you collectively told us was causing burnout . . ."
- "Here's what I heard you say . . ."
- "Here's what I learned specifically . . ."

- "Here's my understanding of what we agree on . . ."
- "Here's my understanding of our differences and how we've agreed to work on coming to more common ground . . ."
- "I heard that we need to work on these three things in this category . . ."
- "Here's what we will do . . ."
- "Here's when we will reconvene to assess progress . . ."
- "But let's all continue to share thoughts before then . . ."

All the tools are designed to create hope that leadership is completely committed to finding team-based solutions and will follow up and follow through—with the help of the team members themselves. It is a mutual commitment to create a new path together. Now that we have a framework and format from which to work, let's move on to the tools themselves.

17

Tools for Personal Passion and Adaptive Capacity

There are 10 tools designed to help rediscover and reignite personal passion and build personal adaptive capacity or resilience.

Tool 1: Love, Hate, Tolerate

The "love, hate, tolerate" tool is the one that resonates the most with team members. Along with the "deep joy, deep need" tool, it targets the "why" of making the job easier, since everyone wants to spend as much of the day as possible doing what they love. Use **Figure 17-1** as the basis for the team's discussion.

- "Love" is why you came and why you stay, what wakes you up in the morning, what fires you up, your "deep joy" (see the next tool). Once this is listed, ask what can be done to maximize it.
- "Hate" is the job stressors burning you out, what keeps you up at night, what holds you down. What can be done to eliminate what we hate?
- "Tolerate" is the in-between, the things that neither drag you down nor lift you up, the necessities of the work. What can we do to minimize these more readily?

Once these areas are known, develop and implement strategies that correlate with them and make sure they are translated to specific actions reflected on the Mutual Accountability Jumbotron (Chapter 6). Recall the work done by Tait Shanafelt and colleagues that indicated, at least in an academic physician practice, that physicians who were able to spend about 20 percent of their time on their "love" or "deep joy" area were much better able to tolerate the things that otherwise burned them out.[1] Tap into this to help ensure that physicians, nurses, and other team members are able to pursue, to the best extent possible, what they love.

1. What do I love?   ➡   Maximize it

2. What do I hate?   ➡   Eliminate it

3. What do I tolerate?   ➡   Minimize it

Figure 17-1: The "Love, Hate, Tolerate" Tool

Revisit the "love, hate, tolerate" tool as often as necessary, but no less than quarterly.

Tool 2: Deep Joy, Deep Need

This is an important tool to use for all teams in the first phase of battling burnout since it is at the heart of the "why" that brought each of us to healthcare. It was referred to in the Introduction and Chapter 8. Start with "why" by accentuating the importance of making the job easier and patients' lives better.

Ask the team, "What is the deep joy that made you choose your career?"[2] "How did your deep joy sustain you through the hard work of school, training, testing, and continuing education?" When job stressors grow and your adaptive capacity is thinning, reach back and rediscover your deep joy.

WRITE A LETTER

Take a piece of paper (or open your computer) and write a deeply passionate note—to yourself. Subject? "I became a doctor/nurse/advanced practice provider/healthcare leader because . . ." If that doesn't help you reignite your passion and develop personal resilience, I'd be surprised.

FIND A PICTURE

Now find a picture from when you were in school or in residency. Take 15 minutes from your day and stare at that photograph—intently—and introduce yourself. Tell him or her who you have become. Don't focus on salary, positions, or accolades—focus on your deep joy and whether you have stayed true to it. Ask that person to help you find your way back to that joy.

Tool 3: Sing with All Your Voices—Use "Love" to Define Meaningful Work and Reinvent Yourself

This tool is closely related to the "love, hate, tolerate" tool and the "deep joy, deep need" tool and can be used in conjunction with them. Performing self-identified meaningful work as 20 percent or more of the total work done decreases burnout by 50 percent, at least in an academic setting. As the great Chuck Stokes notes, with artificial intelligence doubling knowledge every 18 months, those entering (or staying) in healthcare will need to reinvent themselves, since the work will be changing to keep pace with the knowledge.[3] Ask team members to use the "love" part of the "love, hate, tolerate" tool to help them identify what they consider to be the most meaningful work they do.

Ask them to consider what percentage of their time they spend on this meaningful work each day or week and write the percentage down. Ask how they increase that percentage. Ask whether that percentage has changed over the last year.

Use the "hate" and "tolerate" lists to identify the areas in which they may envision reinventing themselves. If you were not doing this job, what other job within healthcare would help you reinvent yourself to increase meaningful work ("loves")?

Tool 4: Stress Tolerance Level

While increasing stress causes us to increase performance, all of us have a point at which increasing stress causes our performance to peak—and then rapidly decline. That is known as the "Stress Tolerance Level." This exercise helps the team members recognize it.

1. Frame the issue by reminding team members that burnout is a ratio of job stressors to adaptive capacity or resiliency. As job stressors rise, we have to adapt.

2. Use **Figure 17-2** as an educational tool to show that stress can be positive, motivational stress, which is on the left side of the curve, where, as stress rises, performance also rises. But it can also be

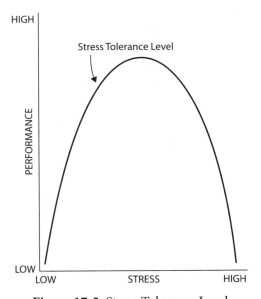

Figure 17-2: Stress Tolerance Level

negative stress or distress, where increased stress causes a dramatic fall-off in performance.

3. Make the point that we all have a stress tolerance level (STL), past which performance will plummet.

4. Ask these questions:
   - What do you look like as you approach your STL?
   - Do you recognize that in yourself?
   - If you don't, your fellow team members (and your family) can tell you *precisely* how you look and act when approaching your STL, if you have the courage to ask and they have the courage to tell you.
   - Can you think of a time you were approaching your STL?
   - Did you "tip over"? Why?
   - If not, how did you "slide back down" the curve?

Tool 5: Strategic Optimism/Creative Energy

Because energy and passion fuel our ability to lead, maximizing creative energy is a powerful "why" to reignite passion and increase personal resiliency. One factor determining workload demands and the capacity to deal with them is the amount of energy required to meet the demands (stressors) versus the energy available to you while at work (adaptive energy capacity). Similarly, the concept of strategic optimism is closely aligned with creative energy, and they can be used together or separately. The tool is designed to help team members understand the importance of leveraging their optimism strategically and closing their energy packets as a renewable source of energy.

1. Introduce the concept that energy drives all our efforts, mentally, physically, intellectually, and psychologically, and is paired with passion.

2. Define strategic optimism as the principle that life's greatest asset is our capacity for optimism, which is the ability to assess a situation and invest it with the most positive practical possibility. Since it is an asset, we are duty bound to maximize the return on investment to ensure we use it wisely and well and increase its "wealth," since none of us has unlimited optimism.

3. Joan Kyes used the term *creative energy* to describe how to best use energy creatively and strategically. While some people seem to have inexhaustible energy, Kyes believed that everyone has basically the same "energy reservoir" from which to draw. But people use that reservoir differently.

4. Each time an activity or project is started, a person removes an "energy packet" or optimism packet matched to the needs of the challenge, which depletes the reservoir but gives enough energy (presumably) for the task.

5. The more tasks you have "open" at one time, the less energy in the "tank" of your energy reservoir.

6. People with high energy levels don't actually have more energy; they simply use it more efficiently by completing the task and "redepositing" that energy back into the tank.

7. People who are constantly exhausted (a core symptom of burnout) probably have too many energy packets open at once, and thus have insufficient energy to do anything else.

8. Kyes's advice is to "close your energy packets quickly and efficiently— don't let them continue to drain you."

9. Once these concepts are developed, ask a series of questions:
   - What do you think is the fuel level of your energy tank or reservoir?
   - How many energy packets do you have open?
   - Why are they still open? Did you open the wrong package for the project?
   - Or are you "letting the perfect be the enemy of the good"?
   - What can you do *today* to close one to three of those packets? Write it down. Now do it.
   - Report back (to yourself) tomorrow—did you close those packets?
   - For the ones you can't close, make a plan to close them tomorrow, this week, this month . . . or let the project go.
   - Do you feel better now that the energy packets are back in the tank?
   - How much strategic optimism do you have right now?
   - Since it is not an infinite resource, how will you choose to invest your optimism to maximize your return on investment?
   - Since our last meeting, what have you invested your optimism and energy in and how has it gone?

Tool 6: Disconnect Your Hot Buttons

We can be massively distracted from the "why" of making our jobs easier when we allow our "hot buttons" to deflect energy, attention, and passion from our work. Hot buttons are ubiquitous, so we all need work on this "why" distraction.[4]

1. Introduce the concept of hot buttons, which are verbal or nonverbal situations in which our attention and energy are diverted from the task or work, causing us to involuntarily react in a negative way.

2. If possible, give an example of one of *your* hot buttons. Here is one of mine: When I am examining a patient and I ask them whether I can listen to their lungs, I put my stethoscope in my ears, place the chest piece on their chest, and . . . they start talking. I don't know why, but this is one of my hot buttons—it drives me to distraction.

3. Ask team members to go through the following process:
    - What are your hot buttons? Write them down.
    - How do you react? How do you think, feel, and act?
    - Recognize that they are not the patients' or team members' hot buttons—they are *yours*; you own them and only you can disconnect them.
    - Disconnect them by clearly identifying them, writing them down, and reflecting on why and where they arose.
    - Now use positive mental imaging to picture them happening and what you would do, say, and think to make them positive—or at least prevent yourself from reacting to them.
    - Use scripts for disconnecting them.
    - Continue to reinforce this over time.

Tool 7: Leave a Legacy

Making a difference in someone's life is what we all sought when we first answered our "deep joy" by choosing a healthcare career. Reconnect passion to purpose by making that difference more transparent. Nothing achieves the goals of "Lead yourself, lead your team" and "Invest in yourself, invest in your team" more powerfully than the legacy we leave.

1. Frame the discussion by briefly summarizing the "deep joy, deep need" concept and tying it to reigniting passion and personal resiliency.

2. Move to developing an understanding that one of the most fundamental human longings is to make a difference in others' lives. Given how hard it is to do the work of healthcare, we all deserve to reward ourselves while rewarding others.

3. "Leaving a legacy" means being able to connect the work to the passion by understanding our impact on others.

4. Our legacy is not the amount of money or property or life insurance we leave to our family. It is something much more profound and meaningful. The medieval Latin root of *legacy* means "an ambassador or envoy sent on a special, often sacred mission." We are all ambassadors on a mission for the benefit of our patients.

5. In healthcare we are fortunate since our legacy is measured by a simple yet stark metric: *our legacy is the difference we make for each patient for whom we care each day—one patient at a time.*

6. Ask the team to adopt a new habit—every time they leave to go home after work, ask them to pause a moment and reflect:
   - "What did I leave in there?"
   - "What legacy did I leave behind *today*?"
   - If you are not pleased with what you left behind *today*, what will you leave behind *tomorrow*?
   - What, specifically, will you do to make tomorrow's legacy better than today's?

An additional tool for "leave a legacy" is one I learned from my mentor, Chuck Stokes, who often quoted the question posed by George Washington Carver in **Figure 17-3**. Ask the team how they would complete that sentence. Then show them **Figure 17-4**, which finishes Carver's message.[5]

Close with this thought:

Every day, those of us on the healthcare team have the great honor and privilege of continuously being
- tender with the young
- compassionate with the aged
- sympathetic to the striving, and
- tolerant of the weak and strong, because
- every day you will serve *all* these people.

How far you go
in life depends
upon . . .

Figure 17-3: The Beginning of George Washington Carver's Important Message

How far you go in life depends upon your being . . .
Tender with the young
Compassionate with the aged
Sympathetic with the striving
And tolerant of the weak and strong
Because someday in your life
You will have been all of these things

Figure 17-4: George Washington Carver's Full Message

To be called to the great and noble work of healthcare, in which we not only can leave a legacy every day we work but can also measure that legacy, one patient at a time:
- what a challenge
- what a responsibility
- what an opportunity
- and ultimately what a joy

What better legacy can we in healthcare leave?

Tool 8: Do the Best You Can—Leave Your Guilt in the Trunk

This tool helps emphasize that we must forgive ourselves before forgiving others, in service of "leaving your guilt in the trunk." It makes the job easier because it helps us focus on doing the best we can and leaving behind idealized versions of ourselves as perfect nurses, doctors, and team members.

1. Simply write the phrase "Do the best you can" on a whiteboard or flip chart.

2. Then say, "I'm going to ask several of you to just read what I've written. Listen carefully to what you hear."

3. Ask someone to read the phrase out loud.

4. Listen to their response and then ask another and another.

5. After four to five people have read it, ask the audience what they heard.

6. Some will have emphasized "do," others "best," others "can." (Rarely does anyone emphasize "you.")

7. Discuss what they think the different emphasis means. (You can use **Figure 17-5** if you like.)

8. Ask, "What would it mean if we were a team that always celebrated our individual talents by saying, "Do the best *you* can"?

Tool 9: Keep a Gratitude Journal

One of the most powerful tools available is to keep a journal of your thoughts. The venerated Stoic philosopher Marcus Aurelius never wrote a book in his life. But he did keep a journal, known to us as his great work, *Meditations*.[6] It is still read today by many. A gratitude journal allows us to remember patients, who are the lifeblood of healthcare. There is no better way to reconnect to passion than to remind ourselves of the great patients whose care was entrusted to us—a powerful "why."

Emphasis	Meaning
• "Best"	• Focus on excellence, often extrinsic motivation
• "Do"	• Focus on action, do something even if wrong
• "Can"	• Focus on execution, what is possible, pragmatic
• "You"	• Focus on the individual: What can you do?

Figure 17-5: The "Do the Best You Can" Exercise

1. Frame the issue by making the point that the work we do is fundamentally heroic and in service to others.

2. Remind them of the three rules:[2]
   - *Rule 1:* Always do the right thing for the patient.
   - *Rule 2:* Always do the right thing for the people who take care of the patient.
   - *Rule 3:* Never confuse rule 1 and rule 2.

3. At its core, our work is an honor in that it allows us to enter people's lives to make them better in some small or large way.

4. There is a lot for which we should have gratitude in the course of the day—our patients, their families, and our teammates.

5. But we move so fast sometimes that it would be nice to have a way to capture those memories and thoughts.

6. A gratitude journal does just that—it is a discipline or habit of capturing positive moments so we can revisit and appreciate them later.

7. Make the point that journaling has a long and rich history of capturing the thoughts of great men and women. (Marcus Aurelius's *Meditations* was never intended to be published; it is his journals to himself, reflecting on the wisdom—or lack thereof—of the day.)

8. There are many ways to keep such a journal.
   - Keep three-by-five-inch cards in your lab coat or uniform so you can write down short notes about people for whom you are particularly grateful.
   - I prefer to use small notebooks because I can use them at work, in the car before going home, or at home. This also makes it easy to keep them. I have at least 100 of these notebooks that I have filled over the years. It is a real pleasure to revisit them, remembering (and in some cases, bringing back to life) patients, families, and teammates who enriched my life and for whom I will forever be grateful.

9. The Duke WISER program uses Three Good Things, Acts of Kindness, Relationship Resilience, Awe-Inspiring Things, and other concepts that can be a great start to get you thinking. No format is perfect for everyone, but here are a few others that you may want to experiment with:
   - Who and what made me laugh, smile, think, and perhaps cry today? (Remember Jim Valvano's ESPY Awards speech from Chapter 8.)
   - What went well today?
   - Whom did I thank today?
   - Whom should I have thanked today?
   - How can I be more thoughtful tomorrow?
   - I never want to forget . . .

10. I am often asked what to write in a note or say in a speech, and my answer is always the same: "Just open your heart and the words will come out." Do the same with your journal.

Tool 10: *Whom Do* You *Burn Out? Why?*

"Why" is often about making our jobs easier, but it also can be making our teammates' jobs easier. We are all leaders of ourselves and our teams. All great leaders have the integrity to ask, "What could I have done better?"

1. Once the team is familiar with the definitions of burnout and has worked to decrease job stressors and increase both organizational and personal adaptive capacity, return to the core concept, "The work begins within."

2. Pose a series of blunt questions to the team to work on, including the toughest, which is the first question:
   - Whom do *you* burn out?
   - Why?
   - How?
   - What could you do differently to reduce burnout in those with whom you work?
   - Are there trends by people, specialty, positions, and so on?
   - At some level, are you *proud* of burning others out?

3. For those who are courageous enough to offer examples, give some constructive alternatives on how things could be handled differently:
   - "What could I have done today to make your job easier?"
   - "What do you want to see more of from me?"
   - "What do you want to see less of from me?"
   - "What B-team attributes did I exhibit today?"
   - "How we can handle friction in the future so that we don't burn each other out?"

18

Tools for Changing Culture

As I have mentioned, culture is not just what we do but also what we say we do and how we think about the work and ourselves. We have to be careful that the "words on the walls" match the "happenings in the walls," or there will be a cultural disconnect. There are six tools to make sure they are aligned.

Tool 1: The Mutual Accountability Jumbotron

In Chapter 2, I stressed the importance of having a consensus-developed, evidence-based, metrics-supported, and transparent means of communicating the strategies and tools that will be used to battle healthcare burnout. The Mutual Accountability Jumbotron is the clearest way I have found to do so. It serves two important functions. First, it is a simple, clear graphic that shows the efforts that the team is undertaking and how each relates to all other efforts. Second, it allows a visual representation of mutual accountability for each of the team-developed strategies to increase fulfillment and attack burnout. It is an overall game plan the team generates and follows, even while adapting to iterative changes. **Figure 18-1** shows the context in which it should be developed, including the "three constant questions" regarding "data, delta, and decision."

The jumbotron is the single most important tool because it puts the change effort in perspective for the entire team, giving them the chance to "see the entire field," as we say in the NFL. It provides a pathway to the vision required to see how the efforts interrelate across culture, the hardwiring of flow and fulfillment, and personal passion and resiliency, as well as allowing updates to show progress. For those involved in collaborative, consortium, or benchmarking work, it also shows comparisons with the work from other organizations.

Tool 2: The A-Team/B-Team

One of the best ways of making the job easier can be demonstrated with this tool, which, like others in the toolkit, uses the Socratic method of posing questions to the team, whose answers illuminate knowledge they already implicitly

BURNOUT Organizational Personal	FOCUS	TOOLKIT
CULTURE •Passion •Fulfillment	PASSION	"Re-recruit" the A-team members
	PASSION FULFILLMENT	Servant leadership training, what kind of leader are you?
	PASSION	Appoint and fund wellness champions for each team
HARDWIRING FLOW + FULFILLMENT •Systems •Processes	EHR	Shadow shifting with A-team super users
	EHR	Unroof the "inbox abscess" champion
	FLOW	Stop doing stupid stuff, start doing smart stuff, send a signal of hope
	FULFILLMENT	Bounty hunt for unfairness, treasure hunt for fairness
	FLOW	Psychology of waiting tools and training
	FULFILLMENT	Develop and implement a "pain flight plan" champion
REIGNITING PERSONAL PASSION AND RESILIENCE	PASSION	"Love, hate, tolerate" tool
	RESILIENCE	ID stress tolerance level, disconnect hot buttons, don't let life be a surprise
	RESILIENCE	You are a performance athlete, do the things you tell your patients to do

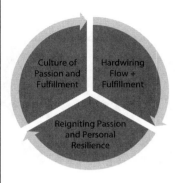

3 Constant Questions
What are the data?
What is the delta?
What is the decision?

Figure 18-1: The Mutual Accountability Jumbotron, the Three Core Elements, and the Three Constant Questions

had but had not explicitly expressed. It taps into fundamental insights regarding intrinsic versus extrinsic motivation and the necessity for personal as well as organizational change and resiliency. It was discussed in Chapter 5. It helps people understand that they were already doing what the change requires—just not consistently.

1. To set the stage, let them know this is an interactive exercise, the success of which depends on their honesty and willingness to participate.

2. Start by saying, "Let's talk a little bit about the teams with which we work, as well as what works for us and what doesn't work."

3. Pose this question: "Are there days when you go to work and you look around at the people you will be working with and say, 'Bring it on. This team is going to make things happen, no matter how busy it is'?"

4. When people nod their heads, ask them, "What do you call that 'can do' team?" They will all say, "The A-team."[1]

5. Then ask them, "What are the attributes or attitudes of the A-team?"

6. Capture the team's responses and build on them, possibly using a flip chart. Then ask, "These are the attributes you love, correct?"

7. Show them **Figure 18-2** and discuss it briefly, linking to the "why" of making the job easier.

- Positive
- Proactive
- Confident
- Competent
- Compassionate
- Communicative
- Works well on a team
- Trustworthy
- Is a good teacher
- Does whatever it takes
- Has a sense of humor
- Moves the meat

Figure 18-2: The Attributes and Attitudes of the A-Team Members

- Negative
- Reactive
- Confused
- Poor at communicating
- Lazy
- Late
- Constant complainer
- A member of the BMW club
- Can't do
- Always surprised
- Nurse Ratched
- Dr. Torquemada

Figure 18-3: The Attributes and Attitudes of the B-Team Members

8. Now ask them, "Are there also days when you come to work, see the people you will be working with, and think, 'Shoot me, shoot me, shoot me. I can't work with you—I worked with you yesterday. Who makes the schedule around here?"

9. After the laughter dies down, ask, "What do you call *that* team?"

10. After they say, "The B-team," ask them what the attributes and attitudes of the B-team members are. Briefly discuss and record them, then show them **Figure 18-3**, taking the time to read through the items listed.

11. When you come to "Nurse Ratched" and "Dr. Torquemada" (reminding them that Tomas Torquemada was the grand inquisitor of the Spanish Inquisition), ask, "Do you know who the Nurse Ratched and Dr. Torquemada are on your team?" After they say yes, make the point that *everyone knows who Nurse Ratched and Dr. Torquemada are, except Nurse Ratched and Dr. Torquemada.*

12. This helps make the point that the B-team members usually don't realize that they are B-team members, whose behavior is toxic to the people with whom they work.

13. For that reason, as leaders, we have to "hold the mirror up to them" to show them what their behaviors are doing to the team.

14. Finally, ask, "How many B-team members does it take to destroy an entire shift?" Be ready for them to literally shout the answer, "Just one."

15. This last piece is the wisdom they had all along, which is that B-team members and their behaviors are a major source of burnout among us all. (I like to say that B-team members are like "space-occupying lesions," since they are not neutral but in fact drain the energy of the team dramatically.)

Tool 3: Leading from the Front

The job is always easier when the leader is visible "on the front lines," particularly during times of change. Showing the way is an essential skill of all leaders at all levels.

1. Frame the discussion with the importance of leadership and the need to lead oneself and lead one's team.

2. Alexander the Great's wisdom is helpful: "An army of sheep who are led by a lion will always defeat an army of lions who are led by a sheep."

3. Discuss how all great leaders lead from the front, exposing themselves to the same dangers and threats as those they lead.

4. Use this background to pose several questions:
   - Who is the leader you have most admired in your career?
   - Why?
   - Did he or she lead from the front? Give an example.
   - Think of a leader who was not as effective. Why?
   - Did he or she lead from the rear?
   - How will you lead from the front next time?

Tool 4: What Kind of Leader Are You?

All team members are leaders, of themselves, their team, and their healthcare system. Every job is easier when leaders have a clear vision of their passion, as well as a mental model of what type of leader they aspire to be. Leading with purpose requires sufficient thought about the kind of leader you aspire to be. The type of leader you aspire to be will significantly shape your culture and that of the organization.

1. Frame the discussion by stressing the importance of leadership at all levels, from personal to organizational.

2. Discuss how great leaders have different styles and are influenced by many different ways of thinking.

3. Present team members with the following prompt: "Fill in the blank: 'I am a _____ leader.'" Here are some examples:
    - servant leader
    - influence leader
    - stoic leader
    - mindful leader
    - Zen leader (which has a certain paradoxical quality)
    - power leader
    - authoritarian leader
    - transformational leader

4. "What experiences or beliefs made you choose that particular word?"

5. "Did you have a mentor who was that type of leader?"

6. "If so, why were they a mentor to you?"

7. "If you can think of an example, please share it."

8. "If you have that mental model of leadership, what could you do to build those skills? What types of behavior would make you more of that type of leader?"

Tool 5: Trust—Leadership's Essential Tool

Trust is one of the most important and treasured facets of leadership. Without trust, there can be no teamwork, no courage to innovate, and no "glue" to hold the team together. Once trust is earned and cultivated, it makes all aspects of the job easier and thus provides a critical "why."

1. Frame the discussion simply:
    - A team is *not* a group of people who work together.
    - A team *is* a group of people who trust each other.

2. Leading ourselves and leading our teams require trust.

3. Trust takes time to build, but only a few seconds to destroy.

4. Pose these questions:
    - Whom do you trust?
    - Why?
    - How long did it take for that trust to develop?
    - Whom don't you trust?
    - Why?

- Was there a time that trust was present and lost?
- Why?
- How can we build trust in our team?

Tool 6: The Shadow-Shifting Tool

Change is difficult and requires changing old and often deeply ingrained habits. Part of the frustration arises from the "myths of impossibility and autonomy."[2] The myth of impossibility is, "It can't be done here—my patients are different." The myth of autonomy is, "That's not how I do things." Both are major obstacles to change and therefore progress.

Shadow-shifting is an excellent tool to break through these myths and make progress not just in metrics but also in making the job easier—the primary "why" of intrinsic motivation.

1. Frame the discussion by defining "shadow-shifting," which simply means that team members who have consistently attained metrics or a reputation for A-team behaviors and talents will share their experience with those who are struggling by rounding with them as a coach.

2. It is helpful to address the myths of impossibility and autonomy in this way:
   - "I appreciate your belief that 'it can't be done here,' but the fact is that it *is* being done here by others, which is supported by their scores. Perhaps it isn't being done consistently enough by all team members."
   - "We are a team, and great teams have coaches, who share the experience of their journey to excellence."
   - "As a team, we want to invest in you by giving you the best coaching your teammates can provide in a collegial, professional fashion. That's what shadow-shifting is all about."
   - "As to the myth of autonomy, we are a team, and teams share positive tools and techniques with each other. If your behavior is producing superior results, have the courage to share it. If not, have the courage to accept coaching and mentoring from your team."

3. In almost every instance, shadow-shifting is a change in culture and should be recognized as such.
   - B-team members will resist coaching. Respond by saying, "Staying the same isn't an option. We're offering help. Do you want that help?"
   - A-team members often resist coaching by saying, "Who am I to tell others what to do?" Respond by saying, "You've demonstrated sustained excellence. Don't you want to help your teammates, particularly those who are struggling?"

4. A-team members should round with B-team members. Here is a suggested format:
   - Two to four hours is plenty of time to get the necessary observational work done.
   - A-team members should observe, avoid interruptions, and generally take mental notes of what they see and how it compares with their habits.
   - Use evidence-based language to introduce yourself and your teammate to the patient: "I'm Dr. Mayer, and this is Dr. Schmitz, who is working with me today. You get two doctors at no extra charge. We will be comparing ideas to give you the best possible care."[3]

5. Broadly speaking, there are three formats to follow, but my experience is that the third works most effectively. If possible, allow the mentee to choose which format to use.
   - The coach can make comments after each patient encounter, giving gentle advice and suggestions each time. This has the advantage of giving immediate feedback and not having to recall previous patient encounters (which can be addressed by taking notes), but can have the disadvantage that the person being coached may feel he or she is constantly being criticized, no matter how gentle the coaching.
   - The coach can wait until the end of the shadow shift to summarize all the comments, which keeps from interrupting work flow, but can make the mentee feel as if he or she is "drinking from a fire hose" with all the coaching comments.
   - The coach and the mentee can pull up after either a certain number of patients or a specific period of time to share ideas.

6. Here are some suggestions for how the coaching can occur during shadow-shifting, always starting with the positives, and then moving to areas for improvement:
   - "First, you are clearly a very warm and caring physician, which all of us recognize. I noticed that you make a point to sit down when you talk to the patient, which works very well for me, too. Your clinical knowledge is without equal, as we all know."
   - "I noticed that you make a point of nodding your head and saying yes, which is something I want to develop as a habit. I like that."
   - "I noticed that when you don't sit, you have a tendency to cross your arms, which produces body language that says, unintentionally, 'I'm closed to your message.' I've found that using open body language is very effective for me."
   - "I'm sure you don't realize it, but you have a tendency to interrupt the patient before they have had a chance to fully answer your

question. It's always a rush around here, but I had to fight to make sure I let the patient give a full answer."

- "One of the things I've found helpful is to use active listening with the patient when I explain the treatment plan, testing, or discharge plan with the patient."
- "I noticed that several times you said, 'I'll take great care of you.' That's wonderful, but someone suggested using 'we' instead of 'I.' It helped me a lot. You might consider that."

19

Tools for Hardwiring Flow and Fulfillment

The six tools for hardwiring flow and fulfillment are designed to assist you and the team in your efforts to make the work easier and more fulfilling by adding value and eliminating waste from every system and process. For more detail on flow, see the "Additional Readings" section at the end of the chapter.

Tool 1: Stop Doing Stupid Stuff, Start Doing Smart Stuff—Send a Signal of Hope

This tool is excellent for the "why" of hardwiring flow and fulfillment, which is a part of organizational resiliency. "Stop doing stupid stuff, start doing smart stuff, and send a signal of hope" is the quintessential "why" of the systems and processes we devise and in which our teams work.[1]

For those whose healthcare systems have used lean methods, this is the type of "value-added, waste reduction" exercise with which you are familiar.

Everyone benefits, but everyone needs to actively participate in identifying what to stop, what to start, and how to send a signal of hope.

1. Frame the discussion by making clear that all ideas are equally valid until shown to be impossible, innovation is the key to creating "the new normal," and there are no "sacred cows" or processes that are off-limits.

2. Stress that no criticisms of "stupid stuff" should be personal in nature or perceived to be so. Transparency and confidentiality of attribution but not of ideas should frame all discussions.

3. Start with "stop doing stupid stuff":
   - What are we doing that we need to consider not doing, and why?
   - How can we do it a different way?

- Which groups of stakeholders on the teams could best work collaboratively to solve this problem, using creative and innovative ideas?
- When could they complete a draft plan for review?

4. Move quickly to "start doing smart stuff":
   - What smart stuff are we doing, and how can we accelerate and accentuate that?
   - What smart stuff can we use to replace the "stupid stuff"?
   - Which stakeholders can help devise and deliver these improved solutions?
   - How will we use the "three constant questions" of "What are the data? What's the delta? What's the decision?"?

5. Send a signal of hope by celebrating the change from "stupid" to "smart," thereby letting the team know that *their* innovative efforts are working.

Tool 2: Taxi, Takeoff, Flight Plans, Landings

This concept derives from evidence-based principles and makes the job easier by increasing consistency, predictability, reliability, and safety.[2] All work should be consensus based and should cut across the boundaries of the team. The concept applies to the entire team and should be presented at unit or department meetings so there is a shared mental model. Work groups should be developed across the most common clinical entities that the unit treats, which then report back to the larger group.

1. Introduce the idea with the analogy of naval aircraft carrier operations.
   - Taxi: moving into position safely and effectively, with the right information
   - Takeoff: the most thrilling launch possible when entering the room to meet the patient, with the most succinct but necessary information
   - Flight plan: evidence, experience, hardwiring flow, utilization of resources, safety, and so on
   - Landing: discharging the patient with attention to detail and Druckenbrod's queries **(Figure 19-1)**

2. Discuss the best practices of the "taxi."
   - What information is needed by each team member before greeting the patient?
   - Have you reviewed the information for accuracy and consistency?
   - Is there any other information needed? How will we get it?
   - Pause for a moment to prepare for the "takeoff," which is next.

- Summarize the journey
  (chief storyteller)
- "These tests/treatments
  showed…"
- Druckenbrod's queries
  - "Have I met your
    expectations?"
  - "What other questions do
    you have?"
  - "How did we do?"
- Discharge instructions with
  active listening
- Sign-out rounds at bedside

Figure 19-1: Landing: Discharging the Patient

3. Discuss the best practices of the "takeoff."
   - "You never get a second chance to make a first impression" should be a guiding principle.
   - What information does each team member want to communicate most effectively when you first greet the patient?
   - Think carefully about body language.
   - What can be done to "make the patient a part of the team"—moving from "What's the matter *with you*?" to "What matters *to you*?"
   - Use precision patient care: "What's the most important thing we can do to make this an excellent visit?"
   - Discuss common elements across team members.
   - Discuss using practice, filming, and so on to view "takeoffs" for critique.

4. Discuss the general principle of the "flight plan" without getting too far into the weeds on details.
   - Frame the metaphor with airlines and aircraft carriers—each has clearly delineated plans specific to the mission. In the case of health-care, plans should be developed for the most common clinical entities.
   - Discuss using demand-capacity questions to identify the most common clinical and patient experience presentations seen on the clinical unit.
   - Recruit cross-functional teams to develop "flight plans" for the most common clinical entities.

5. Discuss the concept of the "landing": the principle of completing the clinical encounter in the best possible way.
   - Summarize the journey—be the chief storyteller.
   - Make sense of the journey—be the chief sensemaker.

- Provide discharge instructions with active listening.
- Ask Druckenbrod's queries:
  ◦ "Have we met your expectations?"
  ◦ "What questions do you have?"
  ◦ "How did we do?"

Tool 3: Making the Patient a Part of the Team

Making the patient part of the team—and the center of the team—makes the job exponentially easier.[3] This transition is intuitive, but rarely executed as well as it needs to be, giving lots of room for improvement. This tool is an essential leadership tool for all team members at all levels.

1. Frame the discussion by emphasizing that patients are the only reason we have healthcare teams.

2. As logical and intuitive as "making the patient a part of the team" may be, it is not commonly enacted, in my experience. How do we make this a reality?

3. It starts with the following process:
   - Move away from "What's the matter *with you*?"
   - Move toward "What matters *to you*?"
   - Make clear that this does *not* mean that we are ignoring the clinical, technical aspects of care.
   - It *does* mean that we can't ignore what matters to the patient as we make them part of the team.
   - Have the team talk about one to three of the most common clinical entities and the differences between "with you" and "to you."

4. Discuss moving from perceiving patients as *recipients* of care to perceiving them as *participants* in their care:
   - "If that were your husband or wife/your dad or mom/your son or daughter, would you prefer them to be a recipient or a participant?"
   - Participants have input in the generation of care plans; recipients are passive receivers of care plans.

5. Introduce the motto that patients should have: "Nothing about me without me."
   - Are we committed to asking questions to assess the patients' input on their care so nothing is done to them without them?
   - Are we willing to hear what patients and families say to help guide our care?
   - Are we willing to act on addressing this input to incorporate patient and family choices and preferences?

- "Mrs. Jones, we have a team of dedicated people who are here to serve you. But you are the most important member of our team. We want to keep you fully informed of every aspect of your care, so please let us know if you have any questions at any time."
- "We want you, as the key team member, to participate in the diagnostic and treatment decisions and understand them."

- "Please let us know how the medication affects your pain/nausea/symptoms . . . "
- "I'd like to perform a physical exam. Would you be more comfortable if your family stepped out while we do that?"
- "Based on what we know so far, here's what we think our plan should be . . . Does that make sense? Do you agree?"

Figure 19-2: Scripts for Making the Patient Part of the Team

- – (In most cases, this does not dramatically change the actual evidence-based clinical diagnostic and therapeutic plan, but it does assure that the patient and family feel more a part of the process and decision-making.)

6. Discuss these questions:
   - – What actions are we taking to "make the patient part of the team"?
   - – What, specifically, are we doing differently?
   - – Is the entire team doing that?
   - – If we asked the team, would they agree?
   - – If we asked the patients, would they agree?

7. Begin to develop evidence-based language (scripts) to let patients know they are not only a part of the team but the most important part of the team **(Figure 19-2)**.

Tool 4: Precision Patient Care

What could make the job easier than knowing the patient's expectations, as well as the most important thing the team could do? Leading yourself and leading the team requires clarity about the patient's viewpoint.

1. Frame the discussion with the concept that every patient approaches the patient encounter carrying "baggage" that may not be visible but is nonetheless present.

2. That baggage is their expectations. Every patient has expectations for what the medical encounter will be like **(Figure 19-3)**.

3. How can we discover the complex calculus of patient expectations? Simply ask them, "What are your expectations?"

Figure 19-3: Understanding Patient Expectations

4. When expectations are not met, that creates dissatisfaction and patient complaints. But exceeding expectations is the key to patient loyalty.

5. The key to the ability to exceed expectations is precision patient care, which simply asks, "What is the *most important thing* we can do to make this an *excellent* experience?"

6. Ask the team members whether they are comfortable with this question.

7. If not, why not?

8. Ask, "Wouldn't it make our jobs easier if we knew what the most important thing was that we could do to make the experience excellent?"

Tool 5: Clinical Huddles and Demand-Capacity Management Tools

One of the most powerful ways to make the job easier is to be able to anticipate the work, deal with the rate-limiting steps and bottlenecks of the existing work, and be able to implement a plan for them. The combination of clinical huddles and demand-capacity tools can make this possible, since they are specifically focused on decreasing job stressors and increasing the team's resiliency.

1. Frame the discussion by defining the work done with the five demand-capacity questions **(Figure 19-4)** and clinical huddles **(Figure 19-5)**.

2. Focus on the intent of both to do the following:
   - Decrease job stressors by anticipating demands and sharing current workloads, bottlenecks, and so on.
   - Increase team resiliency to adapt to the circumstances.

1. Who's coming?
2. When are they coming?
3. What are they going to need?
4. Are we going to have it?
5. What will we do if we don't?

Figure 19-4: The Five Demand-Capacity Questions

- Create shared mental models
- Identify bottlenecks
- Assign clear accountability
- Identify safety issues
- Identify opportunities to leverage flow
- Use parallel vs. sequential processing
- Create hope

Figure 19-5: The Function of Clinical Huddles

- They fear something new (change vs. being changed)
- "It's just Kum-ba-yah!"
- "Forced intimacy"
- Exposes what you are (or aren't) thinking
- Who leads the huddle and why?

Figure 19-6: Sources of Resistance to Clinical Huddles

3. Open a discussion of, at a minimum, these points:
   - How are the huddles working?
   - What are the positives?
   - What are the negatives?
   - Are there discussions of bottlenecks or rate-limiting steps?
   - Are they effective in easing the problem?
   - How would you change the huddles to make them more effective?
   - Are the five demand-capacity questions being used?
   - What are the sources of resistance to clinical huddles (**Figure 19-6**)?

Tool 6: The EHR Solutions Summarized

The electronic health record (EHR) solutions are woven into all the other tools, so the time needed is variable. In most cases this will best be handled through assigned workgroups. Every team member who interfaces with the EHR is affected by its requirements and needs to be involved in devising solutions or work-arounds. Start with nurse- and physician-specific workgroups but integrate results early and often.

1. Make an early and visible commitment to "take on the EHR" and transition quickly to finding ways to work with the EHR.

2. Get a commitment from IT, preferably from the chief information officer and chief medical information officer, to work with your teams in a collegial fashion. If at all possible, have them come to the "kickoff" meeting where the work will be discussed.

3. Identify nursing and physician superusers and superstars to help guide the work. Working from within is always better than mandating solutions from outside.

4. The "love, hate, tolerate" tool is particularly helpful in finding EHR solutions.

5. Follow the principles delineated in Chapter 11 as templates for improvement.

6. Summarize successes early and often.

7. Identify obstacles and a plan to attack them.

Additional Readings

Mayer T, Jensen K. *Hardwiring Flow: Systems and Processes for Seamless Patient Care.* 2009; Gulf Breeze, FL: Fire Starter Press.

Mayer T, Jensen K. Hardwiring hospital-wide flow to drive sustainable competitive performance. *Management in Healthcare* 2019; 2: 27–35.

Jensen K, Mayer T. *The Patient Flow Advantage: How Hardwiring Hospital-Wide Flow Provides Sustained Competitive Advantage.* 2014; Pensacola, FL: Fire Starter Press.

Conclusion

Reconnecting Passion to Purpose

One more step in the journey of discovering where your deep joy meets the world's deep needs.

THOM MAYER[1]

Moving from "How" to "Yes": Your Deep Joy Is the Compass

Had enough with the "hows"? As conveyed in the title to Peter Block's intriguing and thought-provoking book, "The Answer to How Is Yes."[2] My experience in dealing with hospitals and healthcare systems beginning their journey to battle burnout is that they nearly always say, "Yes, but how?" Again, Block: "The question 'How' more than any other question looks for the answer outside of us. It is an indirect expression of our doubts."[2]

"Yes, but how?" is unintentionally a *deflection* from the necessity of action and a *diversion* from the certainty of continuing on the same path—the same path that generated the burnout epidemic. I understand this thinking, but choosing to battle healthcare burnout is a choice for change, for adventure. And adventure, exploring new territory, is always a choice for courage.

We have it within us to change the world for ourselves and others. (Lead ourselves, lead our teams.) We don't need a map, but we do need a compass. The compass is within us. (The work begins within.) What is the compass, the tool to keep track of "True North," as Stephen Covey called it?[3] Even the briefest of reflection will tell you, it is your "deep joy." Or more specifically, where your deep joy intersects the world's deep needs, as I discussed in Chapter 8. That is the compass for your courageous journey to make a difference through leadership. Pursue what is in your heart and you will be following True North. Without your deep joy, you have no fuel for the journey. With it, you cannot be stopped.

I have a secret to tell you—one I should have told you much sooner: *not everyone has the same deep joy as you do.* This is an important realization, since the deeper the joy, the deeper the passion it engenders, and the deeper we seek to have others bathe in those healing waters. Everyone must discover it for themselves, but you can help them in their journey to discovery. The Irish poet William Butler Yeats captured this in his wonderful line, "There is some One Myth for every man, which if we but knew it would make us understand all that he did and thought."[4] The difficulty is that many of us do not understand *our* One Myth, which makes it exponentially harder to uncover in others.

Trade the Certainty of Safety for the Uncertainty of Adventure

To change culture, hardwire flow and fulfillment, and reignite our passion, we must exchange what we know *how* to do for what *matters*—your deep joy, which is the exchange of certainty for adventure.

It may be disquieting to hear, but the answer is inside ourselves. In accepting this simple wisdom and acting on it, you will, in ways small and large, create a world that will solve for others what you have struggled with yourself. Do not let the struggle dissuade you—if it weren't a struggle, it wouldn't be fun, it wouldn't be change, and it wouldn't be worth the effort.

You already know—and care—a lot or you would never have picked up a book titled *Battling Healthcare Burnout*. If you did not have both a depth of knowledge and a considerable experiential base, "battling burnout" wouldn't even be understandable, much less intriguing. We want change, and a safe and predictable pathway to it. There is no such safe and predictable path, except that of following the deep joy within us. We are capable, we know our work as well as anyone, and we care for ourselves, our teams, and our patients with a fire unsurpassed by anyone—and matched by precious few. That must be enough . . . and it will be.

Finding the Fuel for Courage

If you need a dose of inspiration to fuel your courage as much as your passion fuels you, consider these words from former president Theodore Roosevelt, delivered at the Sorbonne on April 23, 1910, at precisely 3 p.m. It is known as "The Man in the Arena" speech, although the full address, which was several hours long, was titled "Citizenship in a Republic." Having read it many times, I can say with certainty that these are the *only* truly memorable lines in the entire essay:

> It is not the critic who counts; not the man who points out how the strong man stumbles, or where the doer of deeds could have done them better. The credit belongs to the man who is actually in the arena, whose face is marred by dust and sweat and blood; who strives valiantly; who errs, who comes short again and again, because there is no effort without error and shortcoming; but who does actually strive to do the deeds; who

knows great enthusiasms, the great devotions; who spends himself in a worthy cause; who at the best knows in the end the triumph of high achievement, and who at the worst, if he fails, at least fails while daring greatly, so that his place shall never be with those cold and timid souls who neither know victory nor defeat.[5]

While there will be some inevitable failures in battling healthcare burnout, count us among those who choose while "daring greatly" and spending ourselves in a worthy cause to never be "timid souls who know neither victory nor defeat."

From Courage to Crazy

In a way that can scarcely be understood in the internet age of information doubling every 12 months, it is difficult to imagine the 1950s and the explosion of theories in physics, the concepts of which were transforming the world.[6] The work of physicists in the 1940s had led to harnessing the power of the atom—and atomic bombs being exploded at Hiroshima and Nagasaki, ending World War II. The most exciting developments in science at the time were in physics.

In the summer of 1958, a conference was held at Columbia University where the best minds in theoretical physics presented their cutting-edge work. Wolfgang Pauli, fresh off developing a unified field theory, was invited to discuss his work. After he completed a presentation that was universally described as clear, succinct, and persuasive, multiple discussants took the stage. Finally, one of the greatest physicists of the time, Niels Bohr, was asked to give his closing comments. All eyes were on him, to hear his sage and gimlet-eyed wisdom. Bohr said, "We are all agreed that your theory is crazy. The question which divides us is whether it is crazy enough to have a chance of being correct?"[7]

My question is, "Are your ideas crazy enough, fueled by your courage and your deep joy, to finally change your culture, your system, and yourself?"

I certainly hope they are. If not, "go get crazy."

Are You Up to the Sisyphean Task?

In the lee of the storm of the coronavirus pandemic, many referred to the struggle as "Sisyphean," evoking the ancient myth of Sisyphus, condemned to endlessly roll a huge stone to the top of a hill, only to see it roll back to the bottom, where the effort began anew, throughout eternity.[8-9] Having read all these missives, and with the greatest respect for all of the authors who use this classic literary allusion, I ask, Isn't that the task to which we all attached our passion—to sublimate our efforts selflessly and happily for the good of others? All of us recall Hippocrates's wisdom, "First do no harm" (Primum non nocere). But fewer recall the next line: "Then do some good" (Deinde benefacere).[10] Be bold, be brave, then do some good. And it is wise to recall the last line of Camus's essay *The Myth of Sisyphus*: "One must imagine Sisyphus happy."[11]

Let us imagine ourselves equally happy, understanding as Camus did that "the struggle itself toward the heights is enough to fill a man's heart."[11]

The Star Thrower

You and your team are involved in one of the greatest endeavors one could hope for: caring for patients and families in need. It is an honored and honorable calling of which all of us should be proud. How can we communicate how much we honor each other? I have found this story to be highly effective. On the surface, it's a hokey story, yet it appeals to the passions and deep joys of your team. It was inspired by a short essay by the incomparable scientist and philosopher Loren Eiseley, "The Star Thrower of Costabel."[12] Here is how I tell it:

In the Nation's Capital Area, many people choose to take their summer vacations at the Outer Banks of North Carolina, the barrier islands off the coast, which extend well off the shore into the Atlantic Ocean and are connected by bridges and ferries. The story is told that a businessman took his family to the Outer Banks, where the houses are on the beach but are built on pylons, or "stilts," so that when the tides surge and the waves smash against them, the houses won't be torn down by nature's force. He checked in for the week on a Saturday afternoon, bright and sunny and perfect for a vacation. That night a massive storm howled in off the Atlantic, with driving rain and waves crashing against the pylons. But as you may have experienced, despite the violence of the storm, it had the odd effect of helping the businessman sleep very well.

The next morning, as usual, he awoke early, to find that the sky was crystal clear and the ocean was perfectly flat. But the tidal surge had the curious effect of washing what appeared to be every starfish in the sea onto the beaches of the Outer Banks. In fact, it appeared that starfish had rained down, covering the beach as far as he could see. As he walked down to the beach, he looked to the left and to the right and only saw one person on the beach, to his left, and he walked that way. As he did so, he became curious, as the person on the beach repeatedly, rhythmically bent over, paused, and then stood back up. As he walked farther in that direction, he became even more curious, because he realized it was a young girl, about nine years old, all alone. As he got closer, he realized she was picking up starfish, one by one, cleaning them off one by one, and throwing them back into the ocean.

As he reached the young girl, the businessman said, "Little girl, I couldn't help noticing what you are doing as I walked toward you. As noble as it is, I'm sorry to tell you this, but what you are doing can't possibly make a difference. I've been watching you for the last 15 minutes and you've only been able to clear this one small area about seven feet around." He continued, "There are thousands of starfish on this beach and many thou-

sands more we can't see," sweeping his arm to show her. "So, I am sorry to tell you this, but what you are doing can't possibly make any difference."

Looking down at the starfish in her hand, the little girl said, "It does to this one," as she threw the starfish back into the waves.

Well, as I said, it's a hokey story. But that's what *you* do, isn't it? Every time you take care of a patient, every time you come to work, every time you help out one of your team members, you make a difference in people's lives—you throw the starfish back into the sea.

If you have children, ask them what they want to do with their lives, and, regardless of their age, they will tell you, "I want to make a difference in people's lives." There is a word for those who work hard for others, who strive constantly, not for themselves but for others, often against seemingly impossible odds, all for the good of others. It is *hero.*

Here is my question to you: When you work at your hospital or in your healthcare system, regardless of your job description, *do you feel like a hero?*

You should, because if you are not a hero, who is? You take care of people who can't, won't, or don't take care of themselves. You take care of people who, through the ravages of time, disease, anguish, alcohol, drugs, and even, tragically, their own families, have lost their dignity—and you give it back to them. You do it with style, grace, dignity, and equanimity—and you do it person by person, day by day, week by week, year in, year out—and you don't do it for yourself; you do it for others.

If you are not a hero, who is?

The next time your head hits the pillow, take the time to smile and say to yourself, "I am a hero—I make a difference in people's lives."

Because you are—and I am very proud to be one of you.[1]

Begin the work within.

Be at peace.

Show courage.

You are a hero.

You make a difference.

And that is your deep joy.

References

Introduction: The Passion Disconnect of Burnout

1. Alighieri D. *The Comedy of Dante Alighieri*. Sayers D, Reynolds B, trans. 1949; New York: Penguin Books.

2. Foch F. *The Principles of War*. 1920; New York: Henry Holt and Company.

3. Mayer T. Getting back to the job you love: reconnecting with passion to battle burnout. *Healthcare Executive*. March–April 2020: 40–43.

4. Mayer T. Burnout: diagnosis, treatment, and prevention. In: Strauss RW, Mayer TA, eds. *Strauss and Mayer's Emergency Department Management*. 2nd ed. 2021; Dallas: American College of Emergency Physicians Press.

5. Dzau VJ, Kirch D, Nasca T. Preventing a parallel pandemic: a national strategy to protect clinicians' well-being. *N Engl J Med* 2020; 383: 513–515. doi: 10.1056/NEJMp2011027.

6. Hartzband P, Groopman J. Physician burnout, interrupted. *N Engl J Med* 2020; 382: 2485–2487. doi: 10.1056/NEJMp2003149. Accessed September 7, 2020.

7. Maslach C, Jackson SE. The measurement of experienced burnout. *J Organ Behav* 1981; 2: 99–113.

8. Batalden P. Like magic? ("every system is perfectly . . ."). Institute for Healthcare Improvement. August 21, 2015. http://www.ihi.org/communities/blogs/origin-of-every-system-is-perfectly-designed-quote. Accessed September 19, 2020.

9. Block P. *The Answer to How Is Yes: Acting on What Matters*. 2003; San Francisco: Berrett-Koehler.

10. Wachter R, Goldsmith J. To combat physician burnout and improve care, fix the electronic health record. *Harvard Business Review*. March 30, 2018. http://hbr.org/2018/03/to-combat-physician-burnout-and-improve-care-fix-the-electronic-health-record. Accessed April 18, 2020.

11. Gawande A. Why doctors hate their computers. *New Yorker*. November 5, 2018. http://www.newyorker.com/magazine/2018/11/12/why-doctors-hate-their-computers. Accessed April 20, 2020.

12. Truman H. Quoted in: McCullough D. *Truman*. 1992; New York: Simon and Schuster.

13. Mattis J, West B. *Call Sign Chaos: Learning to Lead*. 2019; New York: Random House.

Chapter 1: Why Burnout Matters

1. Confucius. *The Analects.* 1979; New York: Penguin Classics.

2. Mayer T. Getting back to the job you love: reconnecting with passion to battle burnout. *Healthcare Executive.* March–April 2020: 40–43.

3. Aiken LH, Sermeus W, Van Den Heede K, et al. Patient safety, satisfaction, and quality of hospital care: cross sectional surveys of nurses and patients in 12 countries in Europe and the United States. *BMJ* 2012; 344 (7851): e1717. doi: 10.1136/bmj.e1717.

4. Han S, Shanafelt TD, Sinsky C, et al. Estimating the attributed cost of physician burnout in the United States. *Ann Intern Med* 2019; 170 (11): 784–790. doi: 10.7326/M18 -1422. Accessed September 10, 2020.

5. West CP, Dyrbye LN, Shanafelt TD. Physician burnout: contributors, consequences, and solutions. *J Intern Med* 2018; 283 (6): 516–529. doi:10.1111/joim.12752. Accessed September 10, 2020.

6. Holden RJ, Scanlon MC, Patel R, et al. A human factors framework and study of the effect of nursing workload on patient safety and employee quality in working life. *BMJ Qual Saf* 2011; 20 (1): 15–24.

7. Wright TA, Bonett DG. The contribution of burnout to work performance. *J Organ Behav* 1997; 18 (5): 491–499.

8. Hartzband P, Groopman J. Physician burnout, interrupted. *N Engl J Med* 2020; 382: 2485–2487. doi: 10.1056/NEJMp2003149. Accessed February 4, 2021.

9. Maslach C. *Burnout: The Cost of Caring.* 1982; Englewood Cliffs, NJ: Prentice-Hall.

10. Sexton B. Personal conversation with the author, October 1, 2020.

11. National Academies of Sciences, Engineering, and Medicine. *Taking Action Against Clinician Burnout: A Systems Approach to Professional Well-Being.* 2019; Washington, DC: National Academies Press. https://doi.org/10.17226/25521. Accessed October 17, 2020.

12. Busis NA, Shanafelt TD, Keran CM, et al. Burnout, career satisfaction, and well-being among US neurologists. *Neurology* 2017; 88: 797–808.

13. Kane MA. *Medscape National Physician Burnout & Suicide Report.* 2020. https://www .medscape.com/slideshow/2020-lifestyle-burnout-6012460. Accessed September 10, 2020.

14. West CP, Dyrbye LN, Sinsky C, et al. Resilience and burnout among physicians and the general population. *JAMA Netw Open* 2020; 3 (7): e209385. doi: 10.1001/jamanetworkopen.2020.9385. Accessed September 7, 2020.

15. Mirrakhimov AE, Rimoin LP, Kwatra SG. Physician burnout: an urgent call for early intervention. *JAMA Intern Med* 2013; 173 (8): 710–711.

16. Reason J. Foreword. In: Croskerry P, Cosby KS, Schenkel SM, Wears RL, eds. *Patient Safety in Emergency Medicine.* 2009: Philadelphia: Lippincott, Williams, and Wilkins: p. xi.

17. Mayer T. Leadership, management, and motivation. In: Strauss RW, Mayer TA, eds. *Strauss and Mayer's Emergency Department Management.* 2nd ed. 2021; Dallas: American College of Emergency Physicians Press.

18. Shanafelt TD, Balch CM, Bechamps G, et al. Career fit and burnout among academic faculty. *Arch Intern Med* 2009; 251: 995–1000.

19. Dyrbye LN, Shanafelt TD, Balch CM, et al. Relationship between work-home conflicts and burnout among American surgeons: a comparison by sex. *Arch Surg* 2011; 146: 211–217.

20. Dyrbye LN, Varkey P, Boone SL, et al. Physician satisfaction and burnout at different career stages. *Mayo Clin Proc* 2013; 88 (12): 1358–1367.

21. Stokes C. Personal communication to the author, June 2, 2020.

22. Shanafelt TD, Boone S, Tan L, et al. Burnout and satisfaction with work-life balance among US physicians relative to the general population. *Arch Intern Med* 2012; 172: 1377–1385.

23. Shanafelt TD, Hasan O, Dyrbye LN, et al. Changes in burnout and satisfaction with work-life balance in physicians and the general US working population between 2011 and 2014. *Mayo Clin Proc* 2015; 90 (12): 1600–1613.

24. Shanafelt TD, West CP, Sinsky C, et al. Changes in burnout and satisfaction with work-life integration in physicians and the general US working population between 2001 and 2017. *Mayo Clin Proc* 2019; 94 (9): 1681–1694.

25. McHugh MD, Kutney-Lee A, Cimiotti JP, et al. Nurses' widespread job dissatisfaction, burnout, and frustration with health benefits signal problems for patient care. *Health Aff* 2011; 30 (2): 202–210.

26. Moss M, Good VS, Gozal D, et al. An Official Critical Care Societies collaborative statement: burnout syndrome in critical care healthcare professionals: a call for action. *Crit Care Med* 2016; 44 (7): 1414–1421.

27. Aiken LH, Clarke SP, Sloane M, et al. Hospital nurse staffing and patient mortality, nurse burnout, and job dissatisfaction. *JAMA* 2002; 288 (16): 1987–1993.

28. Flarity K, Gentry JE, Bebarta V, Dietz J. Compassion fatigue and resiliency. In: Strauss RW, Mayer TA, eds. *Strauss and Mayer's Emergency Department Management.* 2nd ed. 2021; Dallas: American College of Emergency Physicians Press.

29. Rushton CH, Batcheller J, Schroeder K, et al. Burnout and resilience among nurses practicing in high-intensity settings. *Am J Crit Care* 2015; 24 (5): 412–420.

30. Mayer T. Developing leadership and communication skills. Presented at the American College of Emergency Physicians Emergency Department Directors Academy, November 30, 2020, Dallas.

31. Ancillary. Merriam-Webster's Dictionary. https://www.merriam-webster.com/dictionary /ancillary#:~:text=of%20the%20Day-,ancillary,help%20or%20support%20%3A%20 auxiliary%2C%20supplementary. Accessed September 10, 2020.

32. Mayer T. Burnout in emergency departments: learning to love the job you have, while creating the job you love. In: Strauss RW, Mayer TA, eds. *Strauss and Mayer's Emergency Department Management.* 2nd ed. 2021; Dallas: American College of Emergency Physicians Press.

33. Coplan B, McCall TC, Smith N, et al. Burnout, job satisfaction, and stress levels in PAs. *JAAPA* 2018; 31 (9): 42–46.

34. Hoff TS, Carabetta S, Collinson GE. Satisfaction, burnout, and turnover among nurse practitioners and physician assistants: a review of the empirical literature. *Med Care Res Rev* 2019; 76 (1): 3–31.

35. Mayer T, Shanafelt TD, Trockel M, Athey L. *Burnout among Healthcare Leaders.* 2021; in press.

36. Templeton KC, Bernstein CA, Nora LM, et al. Gender-based differences in burnout: issues faced by women physicians. *NAM Perspectives* 2019; discussion paper, Washington, DC, National Academy of Medicine.

37. Peckham C. Medscape national physician and depression report 2018. 2017, Available at: www.medscape.com/slideshow/2018-lifestyle-burnoutdepression-6009235. Accessed February 4, 2021.

38. Robinson GE. Stresses on women physicians: consequences and coping techniques. *Depress Anxiety* 2003; 17 (3): 180–189.

39. McMurray JE, Linzer MR, Konrad J, et al. The work lives of women physicians: results from the Physician-Work-Life Study. *J Gen Intern Med* 2000; (6): 372–380.

40. Shanafelt TD, Gradishar WJ, Kosty M, et al. Burnout and career satisfaction among US oncologists. *J Clin Oncol* 2014; 32: 678–686.

41. Purvanova RK, Muros JP. Gender differences in burnout: a meta-analysis. *J Vocat Behav* 2010; 77 (2): 168–185.

42. Garcia LC, Shanafelt TD, West CP, et al. Burnout, depression, career satisfaction, and work-life integration by physician race/ethnicity. *JAMA Netw Open* 2020; 3 (8): e2012762. doi: 10.1001/jamanetworkopen.2020.12762. Accessed October 17, 2020.

43. Cantor JC, Mouzon DM. Are Hispanic, Black, and Asian physicians truly less burned out than White physicians? *JAMA Netw Open* 2020; 3 (8): e2013099. doi: 10.1001/jamanetworkopen.2020.13099. Accessed October 17, 2020.

44. Zafonte R, Pascual-Leone A, Baggish A, et al. The Football Players' Health Study at Harvard University: design and objectives. *Am J Ind Med* 2019; 62: 643–654.

45. Nguyen LH, Drew DA, Graham MS, et al. Risk of COVID-19 among front-line healthcare workers and the general community: a prospective cohort study. *Lancet* 2020; 5: e475–483. doi: 10.1016/S2468-2667(20)30164-X. Accessed October 17, 2020.

46. Shanafelt T, Goh J, Sinsky C. The business case for investing in physician well-being. *JAMA Intern Med* 2017; 177 (12): 1826–1832. doi: 10.1001/jamainternmed.2017.4340.

47. Patel RS, Bachu R, Adikey A. Factors related to physician burnout and its consequences. *Behav Sci* 2018; 8: 98–105.

48. Mayer T. Burnout in emergency medicine: diagnosis, treatment, and prevention. Presented to the American College of Emergency Physicians Emergency Department Directors Academy, February 6, 2020, Dallas.

49. Masters R, Anwar E, Collins B, et al. Return on investment of public health interventions: a systematic review. *J Epidemiol Community Health* 2017; 71: 827–834.

50. Toker S, Melamed S, Berliner E, et al. Burnout and risk of coronary heart disease: a prospective study of 8838 employees. *Psychosom Med* 2012; 74(8): 840–847.

51. Toppinen-Tanner S, Ahola K, Koskinen A, et al. Burnout predicts hospitalization for mental and cardiovascular disorders: 10 prospective results from the industrial sector. *Stress Health* 2009; 25: 287–296.

52. Appels A, Schouten E. Burnout as a risk factor for coronary disease. *Behav Med* 1991; 17: 53–59.

53. Salvagioni DAJ, Melanda AE, Mesas AE, et al. Physical, psychological, and occupational consequences of job burnout: a systematic review of prospective studies. *PLoS ONE* 2017; 12 (10): e0185781.

54. Rotenstein LS, Torre M, Ramos A, et al. Prevalence of burnout among physicians: a systematic review. *JAMA* 2018; 320: 1131–1150.

55. Langballe EM, Innstrand ST, Hagtvet KA, Falkum E, Aasland OG. The relationship between burnout and musculoskeletal pain in seven Norwegian occupational groups. *Work* 2009; 32 (2): 179–188. doi: 10.3233/WOR-2009-0804. Accessed September 10, 2020.

56. Potter P, Deshields T, Divanbeig J, et al. Compassion fatigue and burnout: prevalence among oncology nurses. *Clin J Oncol Nurs* 2010; 14: E56–E62.

57. Reith TP. Burnout in US healthcare professionals: a narrative review. *Cureus* 2018; 10 (12): e3681. doi: 10.7759/cureus.3681. Accessed September 10, 2020.

58. Gosseries O, Demertz A, Ledoux D. Burnout in healthcare workers managing chronic patients with disorders of consciousness. *Brain Inj* 2012; 1: 1–7.

59. Mayzell G. *The Resilient Healthcare Organization: How to Reduce Physician and Healthcare Worker Burnout.* 2020: New York: Taylor and Francis.

60. Shanafelt TD, Balch CM, Dyrbye L, et al. Special report: suicidal ideation among American surgeons. *Arch Surg* 2011; 146: 54–62.

61. Van der Heijden F, Dillingh G, Bakker A, Prins J. Suicidal thoughts among medical residents with burnout. *Arch Suicide Res* 2008; 12: 344–346.

62. Balayssac D, Periera B, Virot J, et al. Burnout associated comorbidities and coping strategies in French community pharmacies-BOP study: a nationwide cross-sectional study. *PLoS ONE* 2017; 12 (8): e0182956.

63. Jackson ER, Shanafelt TD, Hasan D, et al. Burnout and alcohol abuse/dependence among US medical students. *Acad Med* 2016; 91: 1251–1256.

64. Day AL, Sibley A, Scott N, et al. Workplace risks and stressors as predictors of burnout: the moderating impact of job control and team efficiency. *Can J Adm Sci* 2009; 26: 7–22.

65. Nietzsche F. *Beyond Good and Evil.* 2008; New York: SoHo.

66. Phillips D. The business of burnout: boosting physician resilience pays. September 26, 2017. Accessed at: www.medscape.com/viewarticle/886216. Accessed February 4, 2021.

67. Grumbach K, Bodenheimer T. Can healthcare teams improve primary care practice? *JAMA* 2004; 291: 1246–1251.

68. Smith CD, Balatbat C, Corbridge S, et al. Implementing optimal team-based care to reduce clinician burnout. *NAM Perspectives* 2018. Discussion paper, National

Academy of Medicine, Washington, DC. doi: 10.31478/201809c. Accessed September 10, 2020.

69. Welp A, Manser T. Integrating teamwork, clinician occupational well-being and patient safety—development of a conceptual framework based on a systematic review. *BMC Health Serv Res* 2016; 16 (1): 281.

70. Shanafelt T, Ripp J, Trockel M. Understanding and addressing sources of anxiety among healthcare professionals during the COVID-19 pandemic. *JAMA* 2020; 323: 2133–2134.

71. Dzau VJ, Kirch D, Nasca T. Preventing a parallel pandemic—a national strategy to protect clinicians' well-being. *N Engl J Med* 2020; 383: 513–515. doi: 10.1056/NEJMp2011027. Accessed September 7, 2020.

72. Hamidi MS, Bohman B, Sandborg C, et al. Estimating institutional physician turnover attributable to self-reported burnout and associated financial burden: a case study. *BMC Health Serv Res* 2018; 18: 851.

73. Windover AK, Martinez K, Mercer MB, et al. Correlates and outcomes of physician burnout in a large academic medical center. *JAMA Intern Med* 2018; 178: 491–499.

74. Shanafelt TD, Sloan J, Satele D, Balch C. Why do surgeons consider leaving practice? *J Am Coll Surg* 2010; 212: 421–422.

75. Dyrbye LN, Shanafelt TD, Sinsky CA, et al. Burnout among health care professionals: a call to explore and address this underrecognized threat to safe, high-quality care. *NAM Perspectives* 2017. Discussion paper, National Academy of Medicine, Washington, DC. doi: 10.31478/201707b. Accessed September 10, 2020.

76. Brennan J. Personal communication to the author, May 25, 2020.

77. Crandall W. The financial cost of physician burnout. *Healthcare IT Today.* January 7, 2019. https://www.healthcareittoday.com/2019/01/07/the-financial-cost-of-physician-burnout/. Accessed September 10, 2020.

78. Berg S. How physician burnout is costing your organization. American Medical Association website. October 11, 2018. https://www.ama-assn.org/practice-management/economics/how-much-physician-burnout-costing-your-organization. Accessed September 10, 2020.

79. Jones CB. The costs of nurse turnover, part 2: application of the nursing turnover cost calculation methodology. *J Nurs Adm* 2005; 35: 41–49.

80. Shanafelt TD, Mungo M, Schmitgen J, et al. Longitudinal study evaluating the association between physician burnout and changes in professional work effort. *Mayo Clin Proc* 2016; 91: 422–431. doi: 10.1016/j.mayocp.2016.02.001. Accessed September 10, 2020.

81. Shanafelt TD, Dyrbye LN, West CP, Sinsky C. Potential impact of burnout on the US physician workforce. *Mayo Clin Proc* 2016; 91: 1667–1668.

82. Pulcrano M, Evans SR, Sosin M. Quality of life and burnout rates across surgical specialties: a systematic review. *JAMA Surg* 2016; 151: 970–978.

83. Jones JW, Barge BN, Steffy BD, Fay LM, Kunz LK, Wuebker LJ. Stress and medical malpractice: organizational risk assessment and intervention. *J Appl Psychol* 1988; 73: 727–735. doi: 10.1037/0021-9010.73.4.727. Accessed September 10, 2020.

84. Parker PA, Kulik JA. Burnout, self- and supervisor-rated job performance and absenteeism in nurses. *J Behav Med* 1995; 18: 581–599.

85. Welp A, Meier LL, Manser T. Emotional exhaustion and workload predict clinician-rated and objective patient safety. *Front Psychol* 2015; 5: 1–13. doi: 10.3389/fpsyg.2014 .01573. Accessed September 10, 2020.

86. Welp A, Meier LL, Manser T. The interplay between teamwork, clinicians' emotional exhaustion, and clinician-rated patient safety: a longitudinal study. *Crit Care* 2016; 20: 110. doi: 10.1186/s13054-016-1282-9. Accessed September 10, 2020.

87. Cimiotti JP, Aiken LH, Sloane DM, Wu ES. Nurse staffing, burnout, and health care-associated infection. *Am J Infect Control* 2012; 40: 486. doi: 10.1016/j.ajic.2012.02.029. Accessed September 10, 2020.

88. West CP, Drybye LN, Erwin PJ, Shanafelt TD. Interventions to prevent and reduce physician burnout: a systematic review and meta-analysis. *Lancet* 2016, http://dx.doi .org/10.1016/50140-6736(16)31279-x. Accessed February 4, 2021.

89. Mayer T, Strauss R. Leadership medical director. In: Strauss RW, Mayer TA, eds. *Strauss and Mayer's Emergency Department Management.* 2014; New York: McGraw-Hill: 99–116.

90. Mayer T. Burnout, rustout, and resilience: learning to love the job you have, while creating the job you love. Presented at the American College of Healthcare Executives Congress, March 18, 2019.

91. Mayer T. Patient experience. Presented at the American College of Emergency Physicians Emergency Department Directors Academy, December 15, 2020, Dallas.

92. Delbanco T, Berwick DM, Boufford JI, et al. Healthcare in a land called PeoplePower: nothing about me without me. *Health Expect* 2001; 4: 144–150.

93. Snyderman R, Williams R. Prospective medicine: the next healthcare transformation. *Acad Med* 2003; 78: 1079–1084.

Chapter 2: Defining and Modeling Burnout

1. Frankl V. *Man's Search for Meaning.* 1992; Boston: Beacon Press.

2. Alighieri D. *The Inferno.* Ciardi J, trans. 2016; New York: New American Library.

3. Mayer T. Patient experience. Presented at the American College of Emergency Physicians Emergency Department Directors Academy, December 15, 2020, Dallas.

4. Bellow S. *Herzog.* 2003; New York: Penguin Classics.

5. Wilde O. *The Collected Works of Oscar Wilde.* 1987; London: Wordsworth.

6. Auden WH. Musée des beaux arts. *New Writing,* Spring 1939.

7. Deao C. *The E-Factor: How Engaged Patients, Leaders, Clinicians, and Employees Will Transform Healthcare.* 2016; Pensacola, FL: Fire Starter Press.

8. West CP, Dyrbye LN, Shanafelt TD. Physician burnout: contributors, consequences and solutions. *J Intern Med* 2018; 283 (6): 516–529. doi:10.1111/joim.12752.

9. Dzau VJ, Kirch D, Nasca T. Preventing a parallel pandemic—a national strategy to protect clinicians' well-being. *N Engl J Med* 2020; 383: 513–515. doi: 10.1056/NEJMp201 1027. Accessed September 7, 2020.

10. Wright W. Quoted in: Kelly FC. *The Wright Brothers: A Biography*. 1943; New York: Dover Publications.

11. Vaishnavi S, Connor K, Davidson JRT. An abbreviated version of the Connor-Davidson Resilience Scale (CD-RISC2), psychometric properties and applications in psychopharmacological trials. *Psychiatr Res* 2007; 152 (2–3): 292–297.

12. West CP, Dyrbye LN, Sinsky C, et al. Resilience and burnout among physicians and the general US working population. *JAMA Net Open* 2020; 3 (7): e209385. doi:10.1001/jamanetworkopen.2020.9385. Accessed September 7, 2020.

13. Roosevelt T. In Brands HW, ed. *The Selected Letters of Theodore Roosevelt*. 2002; Plymouth, UK: Rowman and Littlefield: 113.

14. Greene G. *A Burnt-Out Case*. 1960; London: Heineman.

15. Baudelaire C. *Les fleurs du mal*. 2016; London: Bishopstons Editions.

16. Selye H. *The Stress of Life*. 1956; New York: McGraw-Hill.

17. Kyes J. Quoted in: Mayer T, Cates R. *Leadership for Great Customer Service*. 2nd ed. 2014; Chicago: Health Administration Press.

18. Barkley C. *Who's Afraid of a Large Black Man?* 2005; London: Penguin.

19. Foxworth D. Personal communication to the author, February 6, 2018.

20. Hakenen JJ, Schaufeli WB. Do burnout and work engagement predict depressive symptoms and life satisfaction? A three-wave seven-year prospective study. *J Affect Disord* 2012; 141: 415–424.

21. Maslach C, Leiter MP. Understanding the burnout experience: recent research and its implications for psychiatry. *World Psychiatry* 2016; 15 (2): 103–111.

22. Swensen SJ, Shanafelt TD. *Mayo Clinic Strategies to Reduce Burnout*. 2020; Oxford, UK: Oxford University Press.

Chapter 3: The Six Maslach Domains

1. Palmer P. *Let Your Life Speak: Listening to the Voice of Vocation*. 2000; San Francisco: Jossey-Bass.

2. Freudenberger HJ. *Burnout: The High Cost of High Achievement*. 1980; Garden City, NY: Anchor Press.

3. Maslach C. *Burnout: The Cost of Caring*. 1982; Englewood Cliffs, NJ: Prentice-Hall.

4. Maslach C. Personal conversation with the author, August 12, 2018.

5. Adams H. *The Education of Henry Adams: An Autobiography*. 1999; New York: Modern Library.

6. Maslach C, Leiter MP. *The Truth about Burnout*. 1997; San Francisco: Jossey-Bass.

7. Mayer T. Presentations to the American College of Healthcare Executives Senior Executive and Executive Leadership program, Chicago, 2005–2017.

8. De Gaulle C. *The Complete War Memoirs of Charles de Gaulle*. 1955; New York: Simon and Schuster.

9. Junger S. *Tribe: On Homecoming and Belonging*. 2016; New York: Hachette Book Group.

10. Shakespeare W. *Henry V.* 1999; New York: Penguin Random House.

11. Berwick D. Tribute to the Medical School class of 2020. YouTube. May 20, 2020. https://www.youtube.com/watch?v=3vdCR6nKbOk. Accessed October 17, 2020.

12. Dzau VJ, Kirch D, Nasca T. Preventing a parallel pandemic—a national strategy to protect clinicians' well-being. *N Engl J Med* 2020; 383: 513–515. doi: 10.1056/NEJMp2011027. Accessed October 17, 2020.

13. Mayer T. Leadership in times of crisis: lessons from the NFL. Presented to "What's Right in HealthCare," Studer/Huron virtual conference, August 12, 2020.

14. Shanafelt TD, Gorringe G, Manaker R, et al. Impact of organizational leadership on physician burnout and satisfaction. *Mayo Clin Proc* 2015; 90: 432–440. doi: 10.1016/j.mayocp.2015.01.012. Accessed February 4, 2021.

15. Machiavelli N. *The Prince.* 2015; New York: Penguin Classics.

16. Strauss RW, Mayer TA, eds. *Strauss and Mayer's Emergency Department Management.* 2nd ed. 2020; Dallas: American College of Emergency Physicians Press.

17. Mayer T, Cates R. *Leadership for Great Customer Service: Satisfied Employees, Satisfied Patients.* 2nd ed. 2014; Chicago: Health Administration Press.

18. Kotter JP. *A Force for Change: How Leadership Differs from Management.* 1990; New York: Free Press.

19. Kotter JP. *Leading Change.* 2012; Boston: Harvard Business Press.

Chapter 4: Causes and Drivers of Burnout

1. Osler W. *Aequanimitus.* 1904; Philadelphia: HK Lewis Publishers.

2. Mayer T. Burnout in emergency departments: diagnosis, prevention, and treatment. In: Strauss RW, Mayer TA, eds. *Strauss and Mayer's Emergency Department Management.* 2nd ed. 2021; Dallas: American College of Emergency Physicians Press.

3. Dzau VJ, Kirch D, Nasca T. Preventing a parallel pandemic—a national strategy to protect clinicians' well-being. *N Engl J Med* 2020; 383: 513–515. doi: 10.1056/NEJMp2011027. Accessed October 17, 2020.

4. National Academies of Sciences, Engineering, and Medicine. *Taking Action against Clinical Burnout: A Systems Approach to Professional Well-Being.* 2019; Washington, DC: National Academies Press.

5. Shanafelt TD, Noseworthy JH. Executive leadership and physician well-being: nine organizational strategies to promote engagement and reduce burnout. *Mayo Clin Proc* 2017; 2: 129–146.

6. Mayer T. Getting back to the job you love: reconnecting with passion to battle burnout. *Healthcare Executive.* March–April 2020: 40–43.

7. Mayer T. Learning to love the job you have, while creating the job you love: the James Mills, Jr. MD Memorial Lecture. Presented to the American College of Emergency Physicians Scientific Assembly, 2016, Las Vegas.

8. Mayer T, Cates R. *Leadership for Great Customer Service: Satisfied Employees, Satisfied Patients.* 2nd ed. 2014; Chicago: Health Administration Press.

9. Shanafelt TD, Hasan O, Dyrbye LN, et al. Changes in burnout and satisfaction with work-life balance in physicians and the general US working population between 2011 and 2014. *Mayo Clin Proc* 2015; 90: 1600–1613.

10. Mayer T. The critical role of the medical director. 2021, presented to the American College of Emergency Physicians Emergency Department Directors Academy, February 2, 2021, Dallas.

11. Shanafelt T, Trockel M, Ripp J, et al. Building a program on well-being: key design considerations to meet the unique needs of each organization. *Acad Med* 2019; 94: 156–161.

12. Hartzband P, Groopman J. Physician burnout, interrupted. *N Engl J Med* 2020; 382: 2485–2487. doi: 10.1056/NEJMp2003149. Accessed September 7, 2020.

13. Sullivan MP. How boomer generational DNA will change healthcare. *Vital Speeches of the Day* 2004; 70: 443–445.

14. Maslach C, Leiter MP. *The Truth About Burnout.* 1997; San Francisco: Jossey-Bass.

15. *Going Lean in Health Care.* IHI Innovation Series white paper. 2005; Cambridge, MA: Institute for Healthcare Improvement. http://www.ihi.org/resources/Pages/IHIWhite Papers/GoingLeaninHealthCare.aspx. Accessed September 7, 2020.

16. Shanafelt TD, Dyrbye LN, Sinsky C, et al. Relationship between clerical burden and characteristics of the electronic environment with physician burnout and professional satisfaction. *Mayo Clin Proc* 2016; 91: 836–848.

17. Dyrbye LN, West CP, Satele D, et al. Burnout among US medical students, residents, and early career physicians relative to the general US population. *Acad Med* 2014; 89: 443–451.

18. Dyrbye LN, Shanafelt TD, Sinsky CA, et al. Burnout among health care professionals: a call to explore and address this underrecognized threat to safe, high-quality care. *NAM Perspectives* 2017. Discussion paper, National Academy of Medicine, Washington, DC. doi: 10.31478/201707b. Accessed September 11, 2020.

19. National Academies of Sciences, Engineering, and Medicine. *Taking Action against Clinician Burnout: A Systems Approach to Professional Well-Being.* 2019; Washington, DC: National Academies Press. doi: 10.17226/25521. Accessed October 17, 2020.

20. Barnett A. Using recovery modalities before training sessions in elite athletes. *Sports Med* 2006; 36: 781–796.

21. Conelly C. 20 performance tips that stand the test of time. Exos. N.d. https://blog .teamexos.com/exos-work-at-home-resources/top-health-tips. Accessed September 7, 2020.

22. Verstegen M. *Every Day Is Game Day.* 2014; New York: Penguin.

23. Mayer T. Leadership, management, and motivation. In: Strauss RW, Mayer TA, eds. *Strauss and Mayer's Emergency Department Management.* 2nd ed. 2020; Dallas: American College of Emergency Physicians Press.

24. Arendt H. *The Human Condition.* 1958; Chicago: University of Chicago Press.

25. Simpson KR, Lyndon A, Ruhl C. Consequences of inadequate staffing include missed care, potential failure to rescue, and job stress and dissatisfaction. *J Obstet Gynecol Neonatal Nurs* 2016; 45 (4): 481–490.

26. Garrett C. The effect of nurse staffing patterns on medical errors and nurse burnout. *AORN J* 2008; 87: 1191–1194.

27. Edwards ST, Helfrich CD, Grembowski D, et al. Task delegation and burnout trade-offs among primary care providers and nurses in Veterans Affairs patient-aligned care teams. *J Am Board Fam Med* 2018; 31: 83–93.

28. Rao SK, Kimball AB, Lehrhoff SR, et al. The impact of administrative burden on academic physicians: results of a hospital-wide physician survey. *Acad Med* 2017; 92: 237–243.

29. Anandarajah AP, Quill TE, Privitera MR. Adopting the quadruple aim: the University of Rochester experience: moving from physician burnout to resilience. *Am J Med* 2018; 131: 979–986.

30. Clay H. Quoted in: Unger HG. *Henry Clay: America's Greatest Statesman.* 2015; New York: Da Capo Press.

31. Shakespeare W. *The Life of Henry V.* 1995; New York: Washington Square Press.

32. Dudley JC. Advancing faculty wellbeing: targeted efforts to improve professional fulfillment and reduce burnout. Presented to the Brigham and Women's Hospital Medical Staff Executive Committee, October 4, 2019.

33. Mayer T, Jensen K. *Hardwiring Flow: Systems and Processes for Seamless Patient Care.* 2009; Gulf Breeze, FL: Fire Starter Press.

34. Mayer T, Jensen K. The patient flow advantage: how hardwiring hospital-wide flow drives competitive advantage. Presented at the American College of Healthcare Executives Congress, 2017, Chicago.

35. Argyris C. *Knowledge for Action: A Guide for Overcoming Barriers to Organizational Change.* 1993; San Francisco: Jossey-Bass.

36. Griffin BJ, Purcell N, Buskin K, et al. Moral injury: an integrated review. *J Trauma Stress* 2019; 32: 350–362.

37. Johnson-Coyle L, Opgenorth D, Bellows M, et al. Moral distress and burnout among cardiovascular surgery intensive care unit healthcare professionals: a prospective cross-sectional survey. *Can J Crit Care Nurs* 2016; 27: 27–36.

38. Hiler CA, Hickman RL, Reimer AP, et al. Predictors of moral distress in a sample of US critical care nurses. *Am J Crit Care* 2018; 27: 59–66.

39. Houston S, Casanova MA, Leveille M, et al. The intensity and frequency of moral distress among different healthcare disciplines. *J Clin Ethics* 2013; 24: 98–112.

40. Talbot SG, Dean W. Physicians aren't "burning out." They're suffering from moral injury. Stat. July 26, 2018. https://www.statnews.com/2018/07/26/physicians-not-burning-out-they-are-suffering-moral-injury/. Accessed September 11, 2020.

41. Epstein EG, Whitehead PB, Prompahakul C, et al. Enhancing understanding of moral distress: the measure of moral distress for health care professionals. *AJOB Empir Bioeth* 2019; 10: 113–124.

Chapter 5: The Calculus of Burnout and Leadership

1. Batalden P. Like magic? ("every system is perfectly . . ."). Institute for Healthcare Improvement. August 21, 2015. http://www.ihi.org/communities/blogs/origin-of-every-system-is-perfectly-designed-quote. Accessed April 12, 2020.

2. Mayer T. Getting back to the job you love: reconnecting with passion to battle burnout. *Healthcare Executive*. March–April 2020: 40–43.

3. Kierkegaard S. *Either/Or: A Fragment of Life*. 1992; London: Penguin.

4. Drucker PF. *Managing in the Next Society*. 2002; New York: St. Martin's Press.

5. Ensor P. The functional silo syndrome. *Target*, Spring 1988. http://www.ame.org/sites/default/files/target_articles/88q1a3.pdf. Accessed April 7, 2020.

6. Senge P. *The Fifth Discipline: The Art and Practice of the Learning Organization*. 1990; New York: Currency/Doubleday.

7. Kim D. Friday Night at the ER website. N.d. http://fridaynightattheer.com. Accessed April 9, 2020.

8. Mayer T. Developing leadership and communication skills. Presented at the American College of Emergency Physicians Emergency Department Directors Academy, Dallas, February 6, 2020.

9. Mayer T. Getting the "why" right before the "how." *Healthcare Executive*. May–June 2010: 66–68.

10. Mayer T, Cates R. *Leadership for Great Customer Service: Satisfied Employees, Satisfied Patients*. 2nd ed. 2014; Chicago: Health Administration Press.

11. Maslow A. *Motivation and Personality*. 1954; New York: Harper and Row.

12. Erikson E. *Childhood and Society*. 1993; New York: Norton.

13. Frankl V. *Man's Search for Meaning*. 1992; Boston: Beacon Press.

14. Block P. *The Answer to How Is Yes: Acting on What Matters*. 2003; San Francisco: Berrett-Koehler.

Chapter 6: A Model for Change and Mutual Accountability

1. Krzyzewski M. *Leading with the Heart: Successful Strategies for Basketball, Business, and Life*. 2005; New York: Warner Business.

2. Mayer T. Burnout, rustout, and resilience: learning to love the job you have, while creating the job you love. Presented at the American College of Healthcare Executives Congress, March 18, 2019.

3. Gerstner L Jr. *Who Says Elephants Can't Dance: Leading a Great Enterprise Through Dramatic Change*. 2002; New York: Harper Business.

4. Mayer T. Leadership, management, and motivation. In: Strauss RW, Mayer TA, eds. *Strauss and Mayer's Emergency Department Management*. 2nd ed. 2021; Dallas: American College of Emergency Physicians Press.

5. Argyris C. *Knowledge for Action: A Guide for Overcoming Business Barriers in Organizational Change*. 1996; San Francisco: Jossey-Bass.

6. Mayer TA, Strauss RW, Tavernero T, Jensen K. Improving performance through mutual accountability. In: Strauss RW, Mayer TA, eds. *Strauss and Mayer's Emergency Department Management.* 2nd ed. 2021; Dallas, American College of Emergency Physicians Press.

7. Emerson R. *Letters and Social Aims.* 2019; New York: Wentworth Press.

8. Mayer T, Jensen K. *Hardwiring Flow: Systems and Processes for Seamless Patient Care.* 2009; Gulf Breeze, FL: Fire Starter Press.

9. Badenowski R. Quoted in: Mayer T, Strauss RW. Defining patient experience: getting the "why" before the "how." In: Strauss RW, Mayer TA, eds. *Strauss and Mayer's Emergency Department Management.* 2nd ed. 2021; Dallas: American College of Emergency Physicians Press.

10. Cochrane A. *Effectiveness and Efficiency: Random Reflections on Health Service.* 1999; London: Royal Society of Medicine Press.

11. Wasson J. Quoted in: Berwick DM. What "patient-centered" should mean: confessions of an extremist. *Health Affairs.* May 19, 2009. https://www.healthaffairs.org/doi/pdf/10.1377/hlthaff.28.4.w555. Accessed September 10, 2020.

12. Maslach C, Leiter MP. *The Truth about Burnout.* 1997; San Francisco: Jossey-Bass.

13. Kaplan RS, Norton DP. *The Balanced Scorecard: Translating Strategy into Action.* 1996; Boston: Harvard Business Press.

14. Studer Q. *Hardwiring Excellence.* 2004; Gulf Breeze, FL: Fire Starter Press.

15. Kerfoot KM. What you permit you promote. *Nurs Econ* 2009; 27 (4): 245–246, 250.

Chapter 7: Meaningfully Measuring Burnout

1. Einstein A. In: Calaprice A, ed. *The Ultimate Quotable Einstein.* 2011; Princeton, NJ: Princeton University Press.

2. Kohn A. Why can't everyone get A's? Excellence is not a zero sum game. *New York Times.* June 15, 2019. https://www.nytimes.com/2019/06/15/opinion/sunday/schools-testing-ranking.html. Accessed September 11, 2020.

3. Mayer T. Leadership, management, and motivation. In: Strauss RW, Mayer TA, eds. *Strauss and Mayer's Emergency Department Management.* 2nd ed. 2021; Dallas: American College of Emergency Physicians Press.

4. Mayer T, Cates R. *Leadership for Great Customer Service: Satisfied Employees, Satisfied Patients.* 2nd ed. 2014; Chicago: Health Administration Press.

5. Mayer T. Burnout, resilience, and engagement: learning to love the job you have, while creating the job you love. Presented at the American College of Healthcare Executives Congress, March 19, 2019.

6. Mayer T. Learning to love the job you have, while creating the job you love: the James Mills, Jr. MD Memorial Lecture. Presented to the American College of Emergency Physicians Scientific Assembly, 2016, Las Vegas.

7. Kohn A. *Punished by Rewards: The Trouble with Gold Stars, Incentive Plans, A's, Praise, and Other Bribes.* 1999; New York: Houghton Mifflin.

8. Maslow A. *Motivation and Personality.* 1954; New York: Harper and Row.

9. Frankl V. *Man's Search for Meaning.* 1992; Boston: Beacon Press.

10. Peters T. *The Excellence Dividend: Meeting the Tech Tide with Work That Wows and Jobs That Last.* 2018; New York: Penguin Random House.

11. Berwick D. The toxicity of pay for performance. *Qual Manag Health Care* 1995; 4 (1): 27–33. doi: 10.1097/00019514-199504010-00003. Accessed September 7, 2020.

12. Block P. *The Answer to How Is Yes: Acting on What Matters.* 2001; San Francisco: Berrett-Koehler.

13. Muller JZ. *The Tyranny of Metrics.* 2018; Princeton, NJ: Princeton University Press.

14. Beamon N. Personal conversation with the author, May 19, 2020.

15. Block P. *Stewardship: Choosing Service over Self-Interest.* 1993; San Francisco: Berrett-Koehler.

16. Rhoads H. Personal conversation with the author, May 8, 2019.

17. Dyrbye LN, Meyers D, Ripp J, Dalal N, Bird SB, Sen S. A pragmatic approach for organizations to measure health care professional well-being. *NAM Perspectives* 2018. Discussion paper, National Academy of Medicine, Washington, DC. doi: 10.31478/201810b. Accessed September 11, 2020.

18. Maslach C, Jackson SE, Leiter MP. *Maslach Burnout Inventory Manual.* 3rd ed. 1996; Palo Alto, CA: Consulting Psychologists Press.

19. Shanafelt T, Goh J, Sinsky C. The business case for investing in physician well-being. *JAMA Intern Med* 2017; 177: 1826–1832.

20. Mayer T. Developing leadership and communication skills. Presented to the American College of Emergency Physicians Emergency Department Directors Academy, Dallas, November 30, 2020.

21. Kotter J. *Leading Change.* 2012; Boston: Harvard Business Review Press.

22. Mayer T. Leadership in times of crisis: lessons from the NFL COVID crisis. Presented at "What's Right in HealthCare," Studer/Huron conference, August 28, 2020.

23. National Academies of Sciences, Engineering, and Medicine. *Taking Action against Clinician Burnout: A Systems Approach to Professional Well-Being.* 2019; Washington, DC: National Academies Press. doi: 10.17226/25521. Accessed October 17, 2020.

24. Maslach C, Jackson SE, Leiter MP. *Maslach Burnout Inventory.* 4th ed. 2016; Palo Alto, CA: Mind Garden, Inc.

25. Trockel M, Bohman B, Lesure E, et al. A brief instrument to assess both burnout and professional fulfillment in physicians. *Acad Psychiatry* 2018; 42: 11–24.

26. Schaufeli WB, Leiter MP, Maslach C. Burnout: 35 years of research and practice. *Career Development International* 2009; 14: 204–220.

27. West CP, Dyrbye LN, Satele DV, Sloan JA, Shanafelt TD. Concurrent validity of single-item measures of emotional exhaustion and depersonalization in burnout assessment. *J Gen Intern Med* 2012; 27 (11): 1445–1452.

28. Sexton B. Personal communication with the author, October 1, 2020.

29. AMA Steps Forward website. N.d. https://edhub.ama-assn.org/steps-forward. Accessed September 7, 2020.

30. West CP, Dyrbye LN, Sloan JA, Shanafelt TD. Single item measures of emotional exhaustion and depersonalization are useful for assessing burnout in medical professionals. *J Gen Intern Med* 2009; 24 (12): 1318–1321.

31. Dyrbye LN, West CP, Shanafelt TD. Defining burnout as dichotomous variable. *J Gen Intern Med* 2009; 24: 440.

32. Kristensen TS, Borritz M, Villadsen E, Christensen KB. The Copenhagen Burnout Inventory: a new tool for the assessment of burnout. *Work Stress* 2005; 19 (3): 192–207.

33. Demerouti E, Bakker AB. The Oldenburg Burnout Inventory: a good alternative to measure burnout and engagement. In: Halbesleben JRB, ed. *Handbook of Stress Burnout in Healthcare*. 2008; Hauppauge, NY: Nova Science: 51–63.

34. Dyrbye LN, Satele D, Shanafelt T. Ability of a 9-item well-being index to identify distress and stratify quality of life in US workers. *J Occup Environ Med* 2016; 58: 810–817.

35. Dyrbye LN, Satele D, Sloan J, Shanafelt T. Utility of a brief screening tool to identify physicians in distress. *J Gen Intern Med* 2013; 28 (3): 421–427.

36. Trockel M, Bohman B, Lesure E., et al. A brief instrument to assess both burnout and professional fulfillment in physicians: reliability and validity, including correlation with self-reported medical errors, in a sample of resident and practicing physicians. *Acad Psychiatry* 2018; 42: 11–24. doi: 10.1007/s40596-017-0849-3. Accessed September 11, 2020.

37. Stanford WellMD Center website. N.d. https://wellmd.stanford.edu/center1.html. Accessed September 7, 2020.

38. Physician wellness research/surveys. Professional Wellness Academic Consortium, Stanford WellMD website. N.d. https://wellmd.stanford.edu/center1/survey.html. Accessed September 11, 2020.

39. Connor KM, Davidson JRT. Development of a new resilience scale: the Connor-Davidson Resilience Scale (CD-RISC). *Depress Anxiety* 2003; 18: 76–82.

40. Vaishnavi S, Connor K, Davidson JRT. An abbreviated version of the Connor-Davidson Resilience Scale (CD-RISC2), psychometric properties and applications in psychopharmacological trials. *Psychiatr Res* 2007; 152 (2–3): 292–297. doi: 10.1016/j.psychres.2007.01006. Accessed September 8, 2020.

Chapter 8: Sustaining Personal Passion and Resilience

1. Frankl V. *Man's Search for Meaning*. 1992; Boston: Beacon Press.

2. Hecato of Rhodes. Quoted in: Holiday R. *The Daily Stoic*. 2016; New York: Penguin Random House.

3. Peters T. The brand called you. *Fast Company*. August 31, 1997. https://www.fastcompany.com/28905/brand-called-you. Accessed September 7, 2020.

4. Singer M. *The Untethered Soul: The Journey beyond Yourself*. 2009; Oakland, CA: New Harbinger.

5. Maslach C, Leiter MP. Understanding the burnout experience: recent research and its implications for psychiatry. *World Psychiatry* 2016; 15 (2): 103–111.

6. Mayer T, Cates R. *Leadership for Great Customer Service: Satisfied Employees, Satisfied Patients.* 2nd ed. 2014; Chicago: Health Administration Press.

7. Waldinger R. Personal communication to the author, September 12, 2019.

8. Waldinger R. What makes a good life: lessons from the longest study on happiness. Presented to TedX Beacon Street, Boston, November 2015. https://www.ted.com/talks/robert_waldinger_what_makes_a_good_life_lessons_from_the_longest_study_on_happiness/discussion. Accessed September 21, 2020.

9. Cantor R. Personal communication to the author, May 7, 2020.

10. Simonds GR, Sotile W. *Thriving in Healthcare.* 2019; Pensacola, FL: Fire Starter Press.

11. Twain M. *Letters from the Earth: Uncensored Writings.* DeVoto B, ed. 1962; New York: Harper and Row.

12. Seneca L. *Letters from a Stoic.* 1969; New York: Penguin.

13. Jenike T. Personal communication to the author, September 17, 2020.

14. Mayer T. Burnout, rustout, and engagement: learning to love the job you have, while creating the job you love. Presented at the American College of Healthcare Executives Congress, March 20, 2019, Chicago.

15. Delbanco T, Berwick DM, Boufford JI, et al. Healthcare in a land called PeoplePower: nothing about me without me. *Health Expect* 2001; 4: 144–150.

16. Mayer T, Strauss R. Defining patient experience: getting the "why" right before the "how." In: Strauss RW, Mayer TA, eds. *Strauss and Mayer's Emergency Department Management.* 2nd ed. 2021; Dallas: American College of Emergency Physicians Press.

17. Mayer T. Leadership for great patient experience: the survival skills approach. In: Strauss RW, Mayer TA, eds. *Strauss and Mayer's Emergency Department Management.* 2nd ed. 2021; Dallas: American College of Emergency Physicians Press.

18. Mayer T. Burnout in emergency departments: diagnosis, treatment, and prevention. In: Strauss RW, Mayer TA, eds. *Strauss and Mayer's Emergency Department Management.* 2nd ed. 2021; Dallas: American College of Emergency Physicians Press.

19. Mayer T. The 5 habits of highly effective emergency physicians. Presented at American College of Emergency Physicians 2020 Unconventional, October 28, 2020, Dallas.

20. Korzybski A. *Selections from Science and Sanity.* 2nd ed. 2010; Fort Worth, TX: Institute of General Semantics.

21. Weick K. *Sensemaking in Organizations.* 1995; Thousand Oaks, CA: Sage Publishing.

22. Mayer T. Leadership in times of crisis: lessons from the NFL. Presented at "What's Right in Health Care," Studer/Huron conference, August 12, 2020, Chicago.

23. Stockdale J. *Thoughts of a Philosophical Fighter Pilot.* 1995; Palo Alto, CA: Hoover Institute Press.

24. John CC. The art of constructive worrying. *JAMA* 2018; 319: 2273–2274.

25. Stanos SP. "Do no harm, do some good": a call for members to attend the upcoming annual AAPM meeting in Vancouver, BC. *Pain Med* 2018; 19: 221–222.

26. Mayer T. Patient experience skills. Presented at the American College of Emergency Physicians Emergency Department Directors Academy, December 5, 2020, Dallas.

27. Mayer T. Getting back to the job you love: reconnecting with passion to battle burn-out. *Healthcare Executive*. March–April 2020: 40–43.

28. Mayer T. Leadership, management, and motivation. In: Strauss RW, Mayer TA, eds. *Strauss and Mayer's Emergency Department Management.* 2nd ed. 2021; Dallas: American College of Emergency Physicians Press.

29. Mayer T, Cates R. The A team toolkit: further disciplines of the "how" of patient experience. In: Strauss RW, Mayer TA, eds. *Strauss and Mayer's Emergency Department Management.* 2nd ed. 2021; Dallas: American College of Emergency Physicians Press.

30. Strauss R. Negotiation skills. In: Strauss RW, Mayer TA, eds. *Strauss and Mayer's Emergency Department Management.* 2nd ed. 2021; Dallas: American College of Emergency Physicians Press.

31. Armato C, Jenike T. Physician resiliency and wellness for transforming a health system. *NEJM* Catalyst 2018. https://catalyst.nejm.org/doi/full/10.1056/CAT.18.0188#:~:text =Reprints-,Physician%20Resiliency%20and%20Wellness%20for%20Transforming%20 a%20Health%20System,their%20personal%20and%20professional%20lives. Accessed September 7, 2020.

32. Peters TJ. *The Excellence Dividend: Meeting the Tech Tide with Work That Wows and Jobs That Last.* 2018; New York: Vintage Books.

33. LaPietra A, Motov S. A country in crisis: opioid sparing solutions to acute pain management. *Mo Med* 2019; 116 (2): 140–143.

34. Shanafelt T, Trockel M, Ripp J, et al. Building a program on well-being: key design considerations to meet the unique needs of each organization. *Acad Med* 2019; 94: 156–161.

35. Verstegen M. *Every Day Is Game Day.* 2014; New York: Penguin.

36. Barnett A. Using recovery modalities before training sessions in elite athletes. *Sports Med* 2006; 36: 781–796.

37. Conelly C. 20 performance tips that stand the test of time. Exos. N.d. https://blog .teamexos.com/exos-work-at-home-resources/top-health-tips. Accessed September 7, 2020.

38. Thoren P, Floras JS, Hoffman P, Seals DR. Endorphins and exercise: physiologic mechanisms and clinical implications. *Med Sci Sports Exerc* 1990; 22: 417–428.

39. Brees D. Personal communication to the author, September 3, 2019.

40. Verstegen M. Personal communication to the author, February 22, 2020.

41. Truesdale L. Yoga breathing—it's not just for yoga. Gaiam. N.d. https://www.gaiam.com /blogs/discover/yoga-breathing-it-s-not-just-for-yoga. Accessed September 7, 2020.

42. Rosen R. *The Yoga of Breath: A Step-by Step Guide to Pranayama.* 2002; London: Shamb-hala Press.

43. Brown RP, Gerbarg PL. Yoga breathing, meditation, and longevity. *Longevity, Regeneration, and Optimal Health* 2009; 1172: 54–62.

44. Harber VJ, Sutton JR. Endorphins and exercise. *Sports Med* 2012; 1: 154–171.

45. Verstegen M. *Core Performance: The Revolutionary Workout Program to Improve Your Body and Your Life.* 2004; New York: St. Martin's Press.

46. Brady T, Guerrero A. Personal conversation with the author. April 7, 2019.

47. Croteau K. Using pedometers to increase the non-workday steps of hospital nursing and support staff. *Workplace Health Saf* 2017; 65 (10): 452–456. doi: 10.1177/2165079916665399. Accessed September 7, 2020.

48. Shapiro CM, Bortz R, Mitchell D, Bartel P, Jooste P. Slow-wave sleep: a recovery period after exercise. *Science* 1981; 214: 1253–1254.

49. Vitale K, Owens R, Hopkins GR, Malhotra A. Sleep hygiene for optimizing recovery in athletes: review and recommendations. *Int J Sports Med* 2019; 40: 535–543.

50. Lombardi V Jr. *The Lombardi Rules.* 2003; New York: McGraw-Hill.

51. Mead MN. Benefits of sunlight: a bright spot for human health. *Environ Health Perspect* 2008; 116 (4): A160–A167.

52. Benefits of moderate sun exposure. Harvard Health Publishing. Updated January 20, 2017. https://www.health.harvard.edu/diseases-and-conditions/benefits-of-moderate -sun-exposure. Accessed September 7, 2020.

53. Singer M. *The Surrender Experiment: My Journey into Life's Perfection.* 2015; New York: Harmony Books.

54. Kabat-Zinn J. *Mindfulness for Beginners: Reclaiming the Present Moment—and Your Life.* 2012; Boulder, CO: Sounds True.

55. Siegel DJ. *Mindsight: The New Science of Personal Transformation.* 2010; New York: Bantam.

56. Dalai Lama. *The Art of Happiness: A Handbook for Living.* 1998; New York: Penguin Random House.

57. Nhat Hanh T. *You Are Here: Discovering the Magic of the Present Moment.* 2010; Boston: Shambhala.

58. Epictetus. *The Art of Living: The Classic Manual on Virtue, Happiness, and Effectiveness.* 1995; New York: HarperCollins.

59. Stockdale J. *Courage under Fire: Testing Epictetus' Doctrines in a Laboratory of Human Behavior.* 1993; Palo Alto, CA: Hoover Institution Press.

60. Davidson RJ, Kabat-Zinn J, Schumacher J, et al. Alterations in brain and immune function produced by mindfulness meditation. *Psychosom Med* 2003; 65 (4): 564–570.

61. Whyte D. *The Heart Aroused: Poetry and the Preservation of Soul in Corporate America.* 2002; New York: Currency-Doubleday.

62. Drucker P. *The Effective Executive: The Definitive Guide to Getting the Right Things Done.* 2006; New York: HarperCollins.

63. Harmon K. Motivated multitasking: how the brain keeps tabs on two tasks at once. *Scientific American.* April 15, 2010. https://www.scientificamerican.com/article/multitasking -two-tasks. Accessed September 7, 2020.

64. Skaugset LM, Farrell S, Carney M, et al. Can you multitask? evidence and limitations of task switching and multitasking in emergency medicine. *Ann Emerg Med* 2016; 68 (2): 189–195.

65. Mayer T. Rewarding the champions, corralling the stragglers. Presented at the American College of Emergency Physicians Emergency Department Directors Academy, December 17, 2020, Dallas.

66. Ensor P. The functional silo syndrome. *Target*, Spring 1988. http://www.ame.org/sites/default/files/target_articles/88q1a3.pdf. Accessed April 7, 2020.

67. Druckenbrod G. Personal communication to the author, September 7, 2010.

68. Covey S. *The 7 Habits of Highly Effective People: Powerful Lessons in Personal Change.* 2020; New York: Simon and Schuster.

69. Aurelius M. *Meditations.* 1997; Garden City, NY: Dover.

Chapter 9: Organizational Solutions for Improving Culture

1. Drucker PF. *Managing in the Next Society.* 2002; New York: St. Martin's Press.

2. Argyris C. *Knowledge for Action: A Guide to Overcoming Barriers to Organizational Change.* 1993; San Francisco: Jossey-Bass.

3. Mayer T. Burnout in emergency departments: diagnosis, prevention, and treatment. In: Strauss RW, Mayer TA, eds. *Strauss and Mayer's Emergency Department Management.* 2nd ed. 2021; Dallas: American College of Emergency Physicians Press.

4. Narang S. Personal communication with the author, September 1, 2020.

5. Schein E. *Humble Leadership: The Power of Relationships, Openness, and Trust.* 2018; San Francisco: Berrett-Koehler.

6. Mayer T, Strauss R. Leadership, medical director. In: Strauss RW, Mayer TA, eds. *Strauss and Mayer's Emergency Department Management.* 2nd ed. 2021; Dallas: American College of Emergency Physicians Press.

7. Peters T. *Re-imagine! Business Excellence in a Disruptive Age.* 1993; London: DK Press.

8. Peters T. *Everything You Need to Know about Strategy: A Baker's Dozen Eternal Verities.* 2001; West Tinmouth, VT: Tom Peters Company.

9. Mayer T. Burnout, resilience, and engagement: learning to love the job you have, while creating the job you love. Presented at the American College of Healthcare Executives Congress, March 19, 2019.

10. Mayer T, Jensen K. *Hardwiring Flow: Systems and Processes for Seamless Patient Care.* 2009; Gulf Breeze, FL: Fire Starter Press.

11. Deao C. *The E Factor: How Engaged Patients, Clinicians, Leaders, and Employees Will Transform Healthcare.* 2017; Gulf Breeze, FL: Fire Starter Press.

12. Branson R. *The Virgin Way: Everything I Know about Leadership.* 2013; New York: Penguin.

13. Wooden J, Jamison S. *Wooden on Leadership: How to Create a Winning Organization.* 2005; New York: McGraw-Hill.

14. Van Mol MMC, Kompanje EJO, Benoit DD, Bakker J, Nijkamp MD. The prevalence of compassion fatigue and burnout among healthcare professionals: a systematic review.

PLoS ONE 2015; 10 (8): e0136955. doi: 10.1371/journal.pone.0136955. Accessed September 1, 2020.

15. Brugha R, Varvasovsky Z. Stakeholder analysis: a review. *Health Policy Plan* 2000; 15: 239–246.

16. Hirschhorn L, Gilmore T. The new boundaries of the "boundaryless" company. *Harvard Business Review.* May–June 1992: 104–115.

17. Mayer T, Cates R. *Leadership for Great Customer Service: Satisfied Employees, Satisfied Patients.* 2nd ed. 2014; Chicago: Health Administration Press.

18. Mayer T. The disciplines of teams and teamwork. In: Strauss RW, Mayer TA, eds. *Strauss and Mayer's Emergency Department Management.* 2nd ed. 2021; Dallas: American College of Emergency Physicians Press.

19. Katzenbach JR, Smith DK. *The Wisdom of Teams: Creating the High Performance Organization.* 2003; New York: HarperCollins.

20. Mayer T. Getting back to the job you love: reconnecting with passion to battle burnout. *Healthcare Executive.* March–April 2020: 40–43.

21. Block P. *Stewardship: Choosing Service over Self-Interest.* 1993; San Francisco: Berrett-Koehler.

22. McManus P. *Coaching People.* 2009; Boston: Harvard Business Review Press.

23. Coutu D. What coaches can do for you. *Harvard Business Review.* January 2009: 91–97.

24. Block P. *The Answer to How Is Yes: Acting on What Matters.* 2003; San Francisco: Berrett-Koehler.

25. Peters T. *The Excellence Dividend: Meeting the Tech Tide with Work That Wows and Jobs That Last.* 2018; New York: Penguin Random House.

26. Drucker P. *The 5 Most Important Questions You Will Ever Ask Your Organization.* 2008; San Francisco: Jossey-Bass.

27. Mayer T, Narang S, Strauss R, et al. The emergency department-hospital leadership partnership: the view from the "C-suite." In: Strauss RW, Mayer TA, eds. *Strauss and Mayer's Emergency Department Management.* 2nd ed. 2021; Dallas: American College of Emergency Physicians Press.

28. Lewin K. *A Dynamic Theory of Personality: Selected Papers.* 2004; Durham, NC: Duke University Press.

29. Maslow A. *Toward a Psychology of Being.* 2014; Floyd, VA: Sublime Books.

30. Bridges W. *Managing Transitions: Making the Most of Change.* 2016; Boston: Perseus Books.

31. Kubler-Ross E. *On Death and Dying: What the Dying Have to Teach to Doctors, Nurses, Clergy, and Their Own Families.* 2014; New York: Scribner.

32. Kotter J. *Leading Change.* 1996; Boston: Harvard Business School Press.

33. Mattis J, West B. *Call Sign Chaos: Learning to Lead.* 2019; New York: Random House.

34. Gilbert M. *Winston Churchill's War Leadership.* 2004; New York: Random House.

35. Blumenson M. *Patton: The Man behind the Legend, 1885–1945.* 1985; New York: William Morrow.

36. Hamilton N. *Monty: The Making of a General.* 1981; New York: Harper.

37. Astor G. *Terrible Terry Allen: Combat Soldier of World War II—the Life of an American Soldier.* 2003; New York: Ballantine.

38. D'Este C. *Patton: A Genius for War.* 1995; New York: Harper Perennial.

39. Bryant J. *3:59.4: The Quest to Break the 4-Minute Mile.* 2004; New York: Penguin.

40. Taylor B. What breaking the 4-minute mile taught us about the limits of conventional thinking. *Harvard Business Review.* March 9, 2018. https://hbr.org/2018/03/what-breaking-the-4-minute-mile-taught-us-about-the-limits-of-conventional-thinking. Accessed September 1, 2020.

41. Mayer T. Leadership, management and motivation. In: Strauss RW, Mayer TA, eds. *Strauss and Mayer's Emergency Department Management.* 2nd ed. 2021; Dallas: American College of Emergency Physicians Press.

42. Greenleaf R. *Servant Leadership: A Journey into the Nature of Legitimate Power and Greatness.* 2002; New York: Paulist Press.

43. Hesselbein F. *My Life in Leadership: The Journey and Lessons Learned along the Way.* 2011; San Francisco: Jossey-Bass.

44. Spinoza B. *Ethics.* 1994; London: Penguin Classics.

45. Clay H. Quoted in: Unger HG. *Henry Clay: America's Greatest Statesman.* 2015; Boston: Perseus.

46. Dudley JC. Personal conversation with the author, September 1, 2020.

47. Battle C. Inova's mission, vision, and values. Inova website. N.d. https://www.inova.org/our-services/nursing-inova-fairfax-medical-campus. Accessed September 1, 2020.

48. Berry LL, Seltman K. *Management Lessons from Mayo Clinic: Inside One of the World's Most Admired Service Organizations.* 2008; New York: McGraw-Hill.

49. Kishore S, Ripp J, Shanafelt T, et al. Making the case for the chief wellness officer in America's health systems: a call to action. Health Affairs Blog. October 26, 2018. doi: 10.1377/hblog20181025.308059. Accessed September 1, 2020.

50. Chief Wellness Officer Course. Stanford WellMD website. N.d. https://wellmd.stanford.edu/center1/cwocourse.html. Accessed April 10, 2020.

51. Jha AK, Iliff AR, Chaoui AA, Defossez S, Bombaugh MC, Miller YR. *A Crisis in Health Care: A Call to Action on Physician Burnout.* 2019; Waltham, MA: Massachusetts Medical Society. http://www.massmed.org/news-and-publications/mms-news-releases/physician-burnout-report-2018. Accessed September 1, 2020.

52. Shanafelt T, Sinsky C. The business case for investing in physician well-being. *JAMA Intern Med* 2017; 177: 1826–1832.

53. Halbeselan JR, Wakefield B, Wakefield DS, Cooper LB. Nursing burnout and patient safety outcomes: nurse safety perception versus reported behavior. *West J Nurs Res* 2008; 30 (5): 560–577.

54. Cappelucci K, Zindel M, Knight HC, Busis N, Alexander C. Clinician well-being at the Ohio State University: a case study. *NAM Perspectives* 2019. Discussion paper, National Academy of Medicine, Washington, DC. doi: 10.31478/201908b.

55. Shanafelt TD, Noseworthy JH. Executive leadership and physician well-being: nine organizational strategies to promote engagement and reduce burnout. *Mayo Clin Proceed* 2017; 92: 129–146.

Chapter 10: Hardwiring Flow and Fulfillment

1. Aristotle. *Nicomachean Ethics.* 2019; New York: SDE Classics.

2. Mayer T, Jensen K. *Hardwiring Flow: Systems and Processes for Seamless Patient Care.* 2009; Gulf Stream, FL: Fire Starter Press.

3. Csikszentmihalyi M. Quoted in: Mayer T, Jensen K. *Hardwiring Flow: Systems and Processes for Seamless Patient Care.* 2009; Gulf Breeze, FL: Fire Starter Press.

4. Singer M. *The Surrender Experiment: My Journey into Life's Perfection.* 2015; New York: Harmony Books.

5. Brach T. *Radical Compassion.* 2019; New York: Penguin.

6. Junger S. *Tribe.* 2016; New York: Hachette Books.

7. Dzau V, Kirch D, Nasca T. Preventing a parallel epidemic: a national strategy to protect clinicians' well-being. *N Eng J Med* 2020; 383: 513–515. doi: 10.1056/NEJMp2011027. Accessed September 7, 2020.

8. Hartzband P, Groopman J. Physician burnout, interrupted. *N Engl J Med* 2020; 382: 2485–2487. doi: 10.1056/NEJMp2003149. Accessed September 7, 2020.

9. Maslach C, Leiter MP. Understanding the burnout experience: recent research and its implications for psychiatry. *World Psychiatry* 2016; 15 (2): 103–111.

10. Mayer T. Burnout, resilience, and engagement: learning to love the job you have, while creating the job you love. Presented at the American College of Healthcare Executives Congress, April 14, 2019, Chicago.

11. Csikszentmihalyi M. *Creativity: Flow and the Psychology of Discovery.* 1996; New York: Harper and Row.

12. Graban M. *Lean Hospitals: Improving Quality, Patient Safety, and Employee Engagement.* 3rd ed. 2016; New York: CRC Press.

13. Mayer T. Quality improvement and peer review. Presented at the American College of Emergency Physicians Emergency Department Directors Academy, February 5, 2020, Dallas.

14. Jung C. *Man and His Symbols.* 1964; New York: Random House.

15. Mayer T. Front-loading flow. In: Strauss RW, Mayer TA, eds. *Strauss and Mayer's Emergency Department Management.* 2nd ed. 2021; Dallas: American College of Emergency Physicians Press.

16. Jensen K, Mayer T. *The Patient Flow Advantage: How Hardwiring Flow Drives Competitive Performance.* 2015; Gulf Breeze, FL: Fire Starter Press.

17. Mayer T. Leadership: medical director. In: Strauss RW, Mayer TA, eds. *Strauss and Mayer's Emergency Department Management.* 2nd ed. 2021; Dallas: American College of Emergency Physicians Press.

18. Alexander WC, Geiger C. Scribes. In: Strauss RW, Mayer TA, eds. *Strauss and Mayer's Emergency Department Management.* 2nd ed. 2021; Dallas: American College of Emergency Physicians Press.

19. Shultz CG, Holmstrom HL. The use of medical scribes in healthcare settings: a systematic review and future directions. *Journ Am Board of Fam Med* 2015; 28: 371–381. doi: 10.3122/jabfm.2015.03.140224. Accessed September 1, 2020.

20. McNeilly L. Why we need to practice at the top of the license. ASHA Wire. February 1, 2018. https://leader.pubs.asha.org/doi/10.1044/leader.fmp.23022018.10. Accessed April 7, 2020.

21. Moawad H. Practicing at the top of your license. HCP Live. May 3, 2017. https://www.mdmag.com/physicians-money-digest/contributor/heidi-moawad-md/2017/05/practicing-at-the-top-of-your-license. Accessed April 7, 2020.

22. DePree M. *Leadership Is an Art.* 2004; New York: Doubleday.

23. Bush GHW. *All the Best: My Life in Letters and Other Writings.* 2013; New York: Scribner.

24. Brown B. *Daring to Lead: Brave Work, Tough Conversations, Whole Hearts.* 2018; New York: Penguin Random House.

25. Mayer T. Rewarding the champions, corralling the stragglers. In: Strauss RW, Mayer TA., eds. *Strauss and Mayer's Emergency Department Management.* 2nd ed. 2021; Dallas: American College of Emergency Physicians Press.

26. Studer Q. *Hardwiring Excellence: Purpose, Worthwhile Work, Making a Difference.* 2003: Gulf Breeze, FL: Fire Starter Press.

27. Mayer TA, Strauss RW, Tavernero T, et al. The discipline of teams and teamwork. In: Strauss RW, Mayer TA, eds. *Strauss and Mayer's Emergency Department Management.* 2nd ed. 2021; Dallas: American College of Emergency Physicians Press.

28. Osler W. *A Way of Life and Other Essays.* 2001; Durham, NC: Duke University Press.

29. Senge P. *The Fifth Discipline: The Art and Practice of the Learning Organization.* 1990; New York: Currency/Doubleday.

30. Peters TJ, Waterman RH. *In Search of Excellence: Lessons from America's Best-Run Companies.* 2009; New York: Harper Business.

31. Peters TJ. *The Excellence Dividend: Meeting the Tech Tide with Work That Wows and Jobs That Last.* 2018; New York: Vintage Books.

32. Mayer T, Cates R. *Leadership for Great Customer Service: Satisfied Employees, Satisfied Patients.* 2016; Chicago: Health Administration Press.

33. Ensor P. The functional silo syndrome. *Target,* Spring 1988. http://www.ame.org/sites/default/files/target_articles/88q1a3.pdf. Accessed April 7, 2020.

34. Maister D. The psychology of waiting lines. 1985. https://davidmaister.com/articles/the-psychology-of-waiting-lines. Accessed September 1, 2020.

35. Barry MJ, Edgman-Levitan S. Shared decision making—the pinnacle of patient-centered care. *N Engl J Med* 2012; 366 (9): 780–781.

Chapter 11: Burnout and the Electronic Health Record

1. Gawande A. Why doctors hate their computers. *New Yorker.* November 5, 2018. http://www.newyorker.com/magazine/2018/11/12/why-doctors-hate-their-computers. Accessed April 20, 2020.

2. Wachter R, Goldsmith J. To combat physician burnout and improve care, fix the electronic health record. *Harvard Business Review.* March 2018. http://hbr.org/2018/03/to-combat-physician-burnout-and-improve-care-fix-the-electronic-health-record. Accessed April 18, 2020.

3. Jha AK, Iliff AR, Chaoui AA, Defossez S, Bombaugh MC, Miller YR. *A Crisis in Health Care: A Call to Action on Physician Burnout.* 2019; Waltham, MA: Massachusetts Medical Society. http://www.massmed.org/news-and-publications/mms-news-releases/physician-burnout-report-2018. Accessed September 1, 2020.

4. Ambrose S. Personal conversation with the author, June 6, 2000.

5. Gold M, McLaughlin C. Assessing HITECH implementation and lessons: 5 years later. *Milbank Q* 2016; 94 (3): 654–687.

6. Kellerman AL, Jones SS. What it will take to achieve the as-yet unfulfilled promises of health information technology. *Health Aff* 2013; 32 (1): 63–68.

7. Taylor T. Personal communication to the author, April 15, 2020.

8. Ellsworth MA, Dziadzko M, O'Horo JC, Farrell AM, Zhang J, Herasevich V. An appraisal of published usability evaluations of electronic health records via systematic review. *J Am Med Inform Assoc* 2017; 24 (1): 218–226.

9. Khairat SG, Coleman GC, Russomagno S, Gotz D. Assessing the status quo of EHR accessibility, usability, and knowledge dissemination. *EGEMS* (Washington, DC) 2018; 6 (1): 9.

10. Ratwani RM, Savage E, Will A, et al. Identifying electronic health record usability and safety challenges in pediatric settings. *Health Aff* (Millwood) 2018; 37 (11): 1752–1759.

11. Roman LC, Ancker JS, Johnson SB, Senathirajah Y. Navigation in the electronic health record: a review of the safety and usability literature. *J Biomed Inform* 2017; 67: 69–79.

12. Sadoughi S. Quoted in: Gawande A. Why doctors hate their computers. *New Yorker.* November 5, 2018. http://www.newyorker.com/magazine/2018/11/12/why-dcotors-hate-their-computers. Accessed April 20, 2020.

13. Ratwani R, Reider MJ, Singh H. A decade of health information technology usability challenges and the path forward. *JAMA* 2019; 321 (8): 743–744.

14. Mayer T, Cates R. *Leadership for Great Customer Service: Satisfied Employees, Satisfied Patients.* 2nd ed. 2014; Chicago: Health Administration Press.

15. Committee on Systems Approaches to Improve Patient Care by Supporting Clinician Well-Being. Health information technology. In: National Academy of Sciences, Engineering, and Medicine. *Taking Action against Clinician Burnout: A Systems Approach to Professional Well-Being.* 2019; Washington, DC: National Academies Press. doi: 10.17226/25521.

16. Friedberg MW, Chen PG, van Busum KR, et al. *Factors Affecting Physician Professional Satisfaction and Their Implications for Patient Care.* 2013; Santa Monica, CA: RAND Corporation.

17. Gardner R, Cooper E, Haskell J, et al. Physician stress and burnout: the impact of health information technology. *J Am Med Inform Assoc* 2018; 26 (2): 106–114.

18. Merton RK. The unanticipated consequences of purposive social action. *Am Sociol Rev* 1936; 1: 894–904.

19. Sinsky CA, Willard-Grace R, Schutzbank AM, Sinsky TA, Margolius D, Bodenheimer T. In search of joy in practice: a report of 23 high-functioning primary care practices. *Ann Fam Med* 2013; 11 (3): 278–278.

20. Hill RG, Sears LM, Melanson SW. 4000 clicks: a productivity analysis of electronic medical records in a community hospital emergency department. *Am J Emerg Med* 2013; 31: 1591–1594.

21. Sinsky C, Colligan L, Li L, et al. Allocation of physician time in ambulatory practice: a time and motion study in 4 specialties. *Ann Intern Med* 2016; 165: 753–760.

22. Tipping MA, Forth VE, O'Leary KJ, et al. Where did the day go?—A time-motion study of hospitalists. *J Hosp Med* 2010; 5 (6): 323–328.

23. Tan M, Lipman S, Lee H, et al. Impact of the electronic medical record on nurse's time allocation during Cesarean delivery. *Obstet Gynecol* 2016; 127: 154S–159S.

24. Baron RJ. What's keeping us so busy in primary care? *N Engl J Med* 2010; 362: 1632–1636.

25. Shanafelt TD, Dyrbye LN, Sinsky C, et al. Relationship between clerical burden and characteristics of the electronic environment with physician burnout and professional satisfaction. *Mayo Clin Proc* 2016; 91: 836–848.

26. Shanafelt TD, Hasan O, Dyrbye LN, et al. Changes in burnout and satisfaction with work-life balance in physicians and the general US working population between 2011 and 2014. *Mayo Clin Proc* 2015; 90: 1600–1613.

27. Sinsky C. Date night with the computer. *NEJM Catalyst* 2017. https://catalyst.nejm.org/doi/full/10.1056/CAT.17.0304. Accessed September 11, 2020.

28. Mayer T. Leadership, management, and motivation. In: Strauss RW, Mayer TA, eds. *Strauss and Mayer's Emergency Department Management.* 2nd ed. 2021; Dallas: American College of Emergency Physicians Press.

29. Mayer T. Burnout, rustout, and resilience: learning to love the job you have, while creating the job you love. Presented at the American College of Healthcare Executives Congress, March 18, 2019.

30. Sinsky CA, Beasley JW, Simmons GE, Baron RJ. Electronic health records: design, implementation, and policy for higher-value primary care. *Ann Intern Med* 2014; 160: 727–729.

31. Shipman SA, Sinsky CA. Expanding primary care capacity by reducing waste and improving the efficiency of care. *Health Aff* (Millwood) 2013; 32: 1990–1997.

32. Emont S. *Measuring the Impact of Patient Portals: What the Literature Tells Us.* 2011; Oakland: California Healthcare Foundation. https://www.chcf.org/wp-content/uploads/2017/12/PDF-MeasuringImpactPatientPortals.pdf. Accessed April 19, 2020.

33. Tate C, Warburton P. *US Hospital EMR Market Share 2019: Significant Movement in Every Market Sector.* April 2019; Orem, UT: KLAS.

34. Taylor TB, McClay JC. Electronic health records. In: Strauss RW, Mayer TA, eds. *Strauss and Mayer's Emergency Department Management.* 2nd ed. 2021; Dallas: American College of Emergency Physicians Press.

35. Goss F, Meteer M, Bates D. NLP to improve accuracy and quality of dictated medical documents. Brigham and Women's Hospital, AHRQ-funded research, 2019. https://digital.ahrq.gov/ahrq-funded-projects/nlp-improve-accuracy-and-quality-dictated-medical-documents. Accessed November 24, 2020.

36. Berwick DM. Era 3 for medicine and health care. *JAMA* 2016; 315 (13): 1329–1330.

37. Adams J. Personal communication to the author, April 10, 2020.

38. Jiang F, Jiang Y, Zhi H, et al. Artificial intelligence in healthcare: past, present, and future. *Stroke Vasc Neurol* 2017; 2: e000101. doi: 10.1136/svn-2017-000101.

39. Woody SK, Burdick D, Lapp H, Huang ES. Application program interfaces for knowledge transfer and generation in the life sciences and healthcare. *NPJ Digit Med* 2020; 24: 1–5. doi: 10.1038/s41746-020-0235-5. Accessed September 11, 2020.

40. Campbell R. The five rights of clinical decision support: CDS tools helpful for meeting meaningful use. *Journal of AHIMA* 2013; 84 (10): 42–47. Web version updated February 2016. http://library.ahima.org/doc?oid=300027#.X1ooV2hKjZs. Accessed September 11, 2020.

Part Three: Other Voices

1. Block P. *The Answer to How Is Yes: Acting on What Matters.* 2003; San Francisco: Berrett-Koehler.

Chapter 16: Wellstar Health System

1. Maunder RG. The experience of the 2003 SARS outbreak as a traumatic stress among frontline healthcare workers in Toronto: lessons learned. *Philos Trans R Soc Lond B Biol Soc* 2004; 359 (1447): 1117–1125.

2. Maunder RG, Lancee WJ, Balderson KE, et al. Long-term psychological and occupational effects of providing hospital healthcare during SARS outbreak. *Emerg Infect Dis* 2006; 12 (12): 1924–1932.

3. Lai J, Ma S, Wang Y, et al. Factors associated with mental health outcomes among health care workers exposed to coronavirus disease 2019. *JAMA Netw Open* 2020; 3 (3): e203976. doi: 10.1001/jamanetworkopen.2020.3976.

4. Engel GL. The clinical application of the biopsychosocial model. *J Med Philos* 1981; 6: 101–123.

Part Four: Tools for Battling Healthcare Burnout

1. Churchill W. Give us the tools and we will finish the job. BBC Radio broadcast, February 8, 1941.

2. Larson E. *The Splendid and the Vile: A Saga of Churchill, Family, and Defiance during the Blitz.* 2020; New York: Crown.

3. Mayer T. Leadership, management, and motivation. In: Strauss RW, Mayer TA, eds. *Strauss and Mayer's Emergency Department Management.* 2nd ed. 2021; Dallas: American College of Emergency Physicians Press.

4. Sanford K, Moore D. *Dyad Leadership: When One Plus One Is Greater than Two.* 2015; Philadelphia: Wolters Kluwer.

5. Jones S. Personal communication with the author, October 17, 2020.

6. Mayer T, Narang S, Strauss R, et al. The emergency department-hospital leadership partnership: the view from the "C-Suite." In: Strauss RW, Mayer TA, eds. *Strauss and Mayer's Emergency Department Management.* 2nd ed. 2021; Dallas, American College of Emergency Physicians Press.

7. Brown B. *Daring to Lead: Brave Work, Tough Conversations, Whole Hearts.* 2018; New York: Penguin Random House.

8. Mayer T. Rewarding the champions, corralling the stragglers. In: Strauss RW, Mayer TA, eds. *Strauss and Mayer's Emergency Department Management.* 2nd ed. 2021; Dallas: American College of Emergency Physicians Press.

9. Nietzsche F. *Beyond Good and Evil.* 2008; New York: SoHo.

10. Sinek S. *Start with Why: How Great Leaders Inspire Everyone to Take Action.* 2009; New York: Penguin Group.

11. Narang S. Personal communication with the author, October 17, 2020.

Chapter 17: Tools for Personal Passion and Adaptive Capacity

1. Shanafelt TD, Dyrbye LN, West CP. Addressing physician burnout: the way forward. *JAMA* 2017; 317 (9): 901–902. doi: 10.1001/jama.2017.0076.

2. Mayer T, Cates R. *Leadership for Great Customer Service: Satisfied Employees, Satisfied Customers.* 2nd ed. 2014; Chicago: Health Administration Press.

3. Stokes C. Personal communication with the author, October 18, 2020.

4. Mayer T. Rewarding the champions, corralling the stragglers. In: Strauss RW, Mayer TA, eds. *Strauss and Mayer's Emergency Department Management.* 2nd ed. 2021; Dallas: American College of Emergency Physicians Press.

5. Carver GW. Quoted in Federer WJ. *George Washington Carver: His Life and Faith in His Own Words.* 2002; St. Louis: Amerisearch Publishers.

6. Aurelius M. *Meditations.* 1997; Garden City, NY: Dover.

Chapter 18: Tools for Changing Culture

1. Mayer T, Cates R. *Leadership for Great Customer Service: Satisfied Employees, Satisfied Patients.* 2nd ed. 2014; Chicago: Health Administration Press.

2. Mayer T. Leadership, management, and motivation. In: Strauss RW, Mayer TA, eds. *Strauss and Mayer's Emergency Department Management.* 2nd ed. 2021; Dallas: American College of Emergency Physicians Press.

3. Mayer T. Rewarding the champions, corralling the stragglers. In: Strauss RW, Mayer TA, eds. *Strauss and Mayer's Emergency Department Management*. 2nd ed. 2021; Dallas: American College of Emergency Physicians Press.

Chapter 19: Tools for Hardwiring Flow and Fulfillment

1. Mayer T, Jensen K. *Hardwiring Flow: Systems and Processes for Seamless Patient Care*. 2009; Gulf Breeze, FL: Fire Starter Press.

2. Mayer T, Narang S, Strauss R, et al. The emergency department-hospital leadership partnership: the view from the "C-Suite." In: Strauss RW, Mayer TA, eds. *Strauss and Mayer's Emergency Department Management*. 2nd ed. 2021; Dallas: American College of Emergency Physicians Press.

3. Mayer T, Cates R. *Leadership for Great Customer Service: Satisfied Employees, Satisfied Patients*. 2nd ed. 2014; Chicago: Health Administration Press.

Conclusion: Reconnecting Passion to Purpose

1. Mayer T, Cates R. *Leadership for Great Customer Service: Satisfied Employees, Satisfied Patients*. 2nd ed. 2014; Chicago: Health Administration Press.

2. Block P. *The Answer to How Is Yes: Acting on What Matters*. 2003; San Francisco: Berrett-Koehler.

3. Covey SR. *7 Habits of Highly Effective People: Powerful Lessons in Personal Change*. 2004; New York: Free Press.

4. Yeats WB. *Essays and Introductions*. 1961; New York: Macmillan.

5. Roosevelt T. *The Man in the Arena: Selected Writings of Theodore Roosevelt*. 2003; New York: Tom Dougherty Associates.

6. Kuhn T. *The Structure of Scientific Revolutions*. 50th anniversary ed. 2012; Chicago: University of Chicago Press.

7. Bohr N. Quoted in: Dyson FJ. Innovations in physics. *Scientific American* 1958; 199: 74–99.

8. Hartzband P, Groopman J. Physician burnout, interrupted. *N Engl J Med* 2020; 382: 2485–2487. doi: 10.1056/NEJMp2003149. Accessed September 7, 2020.

9. Mayer T. Leadership in times of crisis. In: Strauss RW, Mayer TA, eds. *Strauss and Mayer's Emergency Department Management*. 2nd ed. 2021; Dallas: American College of Emergency Physicians Press.

10. Stanos SP. "Do no harm, do some good": a call for members to attend the upcoming annual AAPM meeting in Vancouver, BC. *Pain Med* 2018; 19: 221–222.

11. Camus A. *The Myth of Sisyphus*. 2018; New York: Vintage Books.

12. Eiseley L. *The Star Thrower*. 1979; New York: Harvest Books.

Acknowledgments

Having had the honor of editing or writing 25 books, it is always humbling to think of the people whose influence has had a massive impact on a book's genesis, content, and production. In a single-author book, the responsibility of acknowledging those people is considerable. Henry Adams once wrote, "A teacher affects eternity. He can never tell where his influence ends." In writing this book, I have felt the influence of many teachers from many areas who materially contributed to the development of this book, even if they were not explicitly aware of it. To attempt to list all of them risks leaving some out, which I will try to avoid without becoming encyclopedic in length.

First, Lesley Iura, my editor at Berrett-Koehler, has been an absolute delight to work with, from the minute she approached me after giving a talk on burnout at the American College of Healthcare Executives (ACHE) Congress in Chicago in 2019. Her patience and grace are exceeded only by her incisive wisdom and laser-focused editing, which have greatly improved the book. It was a joy working with her throughout the process. She leads a team of people at a publisher whose entire work is dedicated to improving the lives of others, which shows in its every effort.

About Linda Sokhor-Cooper, my wonderful and wonderfully talented chief of staff, there are simply no words adequate to express not only how much easier she has made this process but also how much she has helped the clarity and concision of the manuscript. She is a uniquely multitalented person to whom Maureen and I are always grateful. Shakespeare's words about Hermia in *A Midsummer Night's Dream* apply to her: "Though she be but little, she is fierce."

Many of my fellow healthcare leaders have had a deep and lasting impact on my thinking about leadership generally and healthcare leadership specifically. I have shared the honor of working as co–chief editor of the "gold standard" textbook of emergency department management, *Strauss and Mayer's Emergency Department Management* (now in its second edition) with my friend Rob Strauss for over 25 years. The wisdom of his sharp mind is matched by his kindness and humor. He has offered many insights into my understanding of leadership and how it affects burnout, for which I will always be appreciative. Wisdom and humor, in equal measure, permeate all he does.

I have had the good fortune of having had Kirk Jensen as my coauthor on three highly successful books, one of which won the James Hamilton Award from the ACHE for the best book of the year on healthcare leadership. Together we created the concept of hardwiring flow, which is a key part of the burnout equation, focusing as it does on changing systems and processes that produce burnout to better ones that add value and fulfillment while eliminating waste and frustration. I was extremely fortunate to work with Kirk when we founded Best Practices, which became the most widely admired emergency physician practice in the nation. He has influenced my thinking and reasoning dramatically for the better in every area of leadership. He also graciously read and edited the entire manuscript, offering countless suggestions that improved the ideas and the presentation thereof. Working with him and Rob has made me both a better writer and a better man.

Several other healthcare leaders are trusted resources to whom I turned in developing the burnout solutions, including James Augustine, Greg Henry, Jay Kaplan, Doug Webster, and John Brennan.

Inova Health System, my clinical home as an emergency physician, is fortunate to have visionary leaders, all of whom are dedicated to creating a culture of increasing professional fulfillment while showing the courage to change systems and processes that create burnout among the team. Stephen Jones, the CEO of the system, is responsible for creating a vibrant and stimulating culture, as well as recruiting an incredible leadership team, including Steve Motew, chief of the clinical enterprise, who brought energy and fresh insights from his tenure at Novant Heath System. Steve Narang is the president of Inova Fairfax Medical Campus, which is where I practice. Steve's concept that the culture "comes straight from the airway of the organization" is one of the most penetrating insights I have heard. Toni Ardabell leads the hospital administration arm of Inova's "triad leadership team," and she has been a friend, colleague, and mentor to me for over 20 years. Together they have been inspirational, not just for me but also for countless others at Inova Health System.

While I could list every emergency physician and medical staff member at Inova whose lives have influenced this work, I will only mention a few, including Bob Cates, Glenn Druckenbrod, Tanveer Gaibi, Dan Hanfling, Mark Thiess, Alan Speir, Joanne Crantz, and Robin West.

Nicholas Beamon, founder of OneTeam Leadership, is a leadership coach without peer, and his deep wisdom concerning professional fulfillment made a lasting impression on me. He kindly introduced me to Tom Jenike, whose foundational work on leadership and burnout at Novant is profound. Both graciously spent hours with me discussing their work and their evolving perspective on this critically important subject.

I have had the good fortune to have Victor Dzau as my friend and mentor for over 20 years, first as the chancellor for health affairs at Duke University when I chaired the board of visitors, and now as the president of the National

Academy of Medicine, where he has led the efforts to define burnout and its solutions. He is a brilliant man with a kind and passionate spirit.

No one in the world has done more to advance our understanding of burnout in healthcare than my friend and colleague Tait Shanafelt, with whom I am working on a study to understand burnout in healthcare leaders through a project with the ACHE. His energy is inexhaustible, and his insights are legendary. I have learned a massive amount from him on burnout and fulfillment, for which I am deeply grateful. We share a similar, but independently developed, structure for considering the components of burnout.

Chuck Stokes is a giant in the field of hospital administration and leadership, having led not one but two organizations (North Mississippi Medical Center and Memorial Hermann Health System) to win the prestigious Malcolm Baldrige Award for Quality, as well as serving as president of the ACHE. I had the great honor of coteaching the ACHE's Executive and Senior Executive Leadership courses with Chuck, from whom I learned a great deal. His amazing insights and innovations are exceeded only by his even more considerable kindness. He epitomizes the values of servant leadership in his every action and word. No one has influenced my thoughts on leadership and burnout more than Chuck.

In some ways, my thoughts on burnout began to be galvanized into a system of action when I was invited to give a lecture named for one of the founders of the specialty of emergency medicine, James Mills Jr. When preparing the Mills Lecture, I reached out to the office of the originator of the term *burnout*, Christina Maslach. When I called for an appointment to discuss applying the term to physicians, I said that I was sure she was barraged with requests from physicians to discuss the topic. She shocked me by saying, "No, Thom, you are the first and only doctor who has ever reached out to discuss this." After I recovered from my surprise, we went on to have several conversations over a one-year period, in which she was generous with her time, her wisdom, and her insights. That the definition of burnout is still fundamentally bound to hers of 30 years ago is testament to her enduring wisdom, as is the fact that the Maslach Burnout Inventory remains the most widely used tool to assess burnout. She is justifiably a legend in this space and always will be.

Speaking of legends, I am proud to call Tom Peters a friend, and his insights are widely quoted in this book. We came to know each other from my work as one of the command physicians at the Pentagon on September 11, 2001, and his friendship has been a great joy to me. Tom kindly wrote the forewords for several of my books—I only hope that, someday, I will live up to the praise he bestowed on my work. His character and his humor have been a great source of inspiration to me over the years.

Peter Block has also been an inspiration for me and for many others, with his unique and incomparable lens into leadership as stewardship, as well as the many corollaries that derive from that fundamental insight. It is difficult to imagine a healthcare leader who would not be moved by his work.

Jean Ann Larsen is an extremely talented leader in the field of healthcare leadership development in the University of Alabama–Birmingham healthcare system. She kindly reviewed this book and offered countless insights and detailed improvements, all of which are deeply appreciated.

My friend and colleague at Huron Consulting, Craig Deao, has provided the best work on engagement in healthcare, as well as countless other ideas about evidence-based approaches to healthcare leadership. He also reviewed the entire book, and his suggestions vastly improved the clarity and brevity of the work.

Quint Studer served as a friend, colleague, mentor, and Yoda-like presence for me and many others in healthcare. He was always gracious in sharing ideas as well as the dais at the many meetings at which he invited me to speak. His contributions to my life and all of healthcare leadership are ongoing and enduring.

Many friends, teammates, and professors influenced my entire way of thinking along the way, including at Anderson High School (Rod Freeman, Mike Woodruff, Mike Armstrong, Kevin Lane, Phil Bledsoe, and Steve Voss), Hanover College (Enos Pray, Joseph Campbell, Keith White, Mike Paul, and Mark Levett), and Duke University (David Sabiston, Madison Spach, Robert Whalen, and May King). During residency and fellowship, Dale Johnson and John Holman were guiding forces.

Itzhak Shasha has been the closest of friends and the most incisive of mentors for over fifty years, and I have repeatedly relied on his sage and gimlet-eyed advice.

Many of the stories in the book derive from my work with the NFL Players Association (NFLPA). My debts to all those people are considerable, including permission to use the examples herein. Gene Upshaw, then executive director of the NFLPA, hired me on August 1, 2001, the day Korey Stringer, a tackle for the Vikings, died of heatstroke. The confidence and trust Gene showed in me will never be forgotten, and his untimely death was a blow to us all. He was succeeded by DeMaurice "De" Smith, who is simply one of the most astute, intelligent, and kind people I have ever met. Others with whom I work include Tom DePaso, George Atallah, Don Davis, Ernie Conwell, Mark Verstegen, Mark Cobb, and Tom Carter, each of whose wisdom is reflected in various ways in the book.

A special thanks to Sean Sansiveri at the NFLPA, my business associate and close friend, whose work with me and others in developing and implementing concussion, COVID-19, and other health and safety innovations took courage, intelligence, creativity, and tenacity, all of which he possesses to an uncommon degree. Geoff Ling, a founding member of the NFLPA's Mackey-White Player Health and Safety Committee and a legendary figure for years at the Department of Defense and Defense Advanced Research Projects Agency, is a sage and gimlet-eyed friend and mentor. When I ponder difficult issues, I wait until I see what Geoff says so I know what I should think.

Most important, as always, is my family. Their patience and kindness with my long preoccupation with this work and the long hours spent in writing and editing it know no bounds. Our sons, Greg, Kevin, and Josh, as well as Josh's wife, Val; their children, Eve, Audra, Clara, and Ryan; and Kevin's fiancée, Nicola, were constantly upbeat and supportive of it throughout.

As in all things good and great in my life, my beautiful, brilliant, and always inspiring wife, Maureen, has had an impact on my work in ways that defy full explanation. Whenever I was stalled or became frustrated with getting thoughts and experiences into words, she was ceaselessly positive about the need to do so—not for myself but for the reader. So often I heard, "You are writing this to help people—go ahead and help them." At every inflection point, her wisdom illuminated the pathway toward clarity and concision. I am forever grateful for all she has given me throughout our 42 years together. It is always wise to recall that the term *mentor* comes from Homer's *Odyssey*, but it was not Ulysses's friend Mentor who advised his son Telemachus but rather the goddess Pallas Athena who assumed Mentor's visage, meaning the first "mentor" was female. Maureen has been my Mentor throughout. This book, like everything good in my life, would never have been completed without her.

If I have failed to mention the many others whose influence was essential to completing this work, I apologize, but they all know who they are. Any insights or benefits arising from this book come from my friends and colleagues. Any failures are purely my own.

Index

About the Author

Thom Mayer is the medical director of the NFL Players Association and the founder of Best Practices, the nation's most respected emergency physician group, noted for innovations in burnout, patient experience, hardwiring flow, clinical best practices, and leadership and management. He is one of the most widely recognized speakers in healthcare and has won awards from the American College of Healthcare Executives, the American College of Emergency Physicians, the Robert Wood Johnson Foundation, the American Public Health Association, the United States Surgeon General, Huron/Studer Consulting, Press Ganey, and many other organizations. He has written over 150 peer-reviewed articles, over 250 book chapters, and 25 textbooks, including *Strauss and Mayer's Emergency Department Management* (2nd edition), *Leadership for Great Customer Service: Satisfied Employees, Satisfied Patients* (2nd edition), *Hardwiring Flow: Systems and Processes for Seamless Patient Care*, and *Leadership for Smooth Patient Flow*, which won the ACHE James Hamilton Award for the best leadership book of the year. Tom Peters has referred to his work as "gaspworthy."

Mayer has been at the forefront of crisis management throughout his career, serving as the command physician at the Pentagon on September 11, 2001, and the incident commander for the inhalational anthrax crisis in the nation's capital that same year. In addition, as the medical director for the NFL Players Association, he was responsible for guiding its highly successful program on risk mitigation of the coronavirus during the 2020–2021 NFL season. He was also the principal architect of the concussion protocols in the NFL, which have influenced the management of sports concussions worldwide.

He practices emergency medicine and sports medicine. He and his wife, Maureen, live in Wilson, Wyoming.

Dear reader,

Thank you for picking up this book and welcome to the worldwide BK community! You're joining a special group of people who have come together to create positive change in their lives, organizations, and communities.

What's BK all about?

Our mission is to connect people and ideas to create a world that works for all.

Why? Our communities, organizations, and lives get bogged down by old paradigms of self-interest, exclusion, hierarchy, and privilege. But we believe that can change. That's why we seek the leading experts on these challenges—and share their actionable ideas with you.

A welcome gift

To help you get started, we'd like to offer you a **free copy** of one of our bestselling ebooks:

www.bkconnection.com/welcome

When you claim your **free ebook**, you'll also be subscribed to our blog.

Our freshest insights

Access the best new tools and ideas for leaders at all levels on our blog at ideas.bkconnection.com.

Sincerely,

Your friends at Berrett-Koehler